최 상 위 권 을 위 한

능률고급 영문독해

Neungyule Education's
Advanced
English Reading...

최 상 위 권 을 위 한

능률고급영문독해

지은이	NE능률 영어교육연구소
선임 연구원	김지현
연구원	이은주 장민아 박연준 이하나
영문교열	Lewis Hugh Hosie MyAn Le Patrick Ferraro
표지 · 내지 디자인	민유화 오가영
맥편집	김재민
마케팅	박혜선 남경진 이지원 김여진
영업	한기영 이경구 박인규 정철교 김남준 이우현
Photo Credits	www.shutterstock.com

PREFACE

01

누구에게나 자신만의 소중한 꿈이 있습니다.
그 꿈을 처음으로 마음에 품을 때는 마치 저 하늘에 있는 별을 보는 것처럼 아득하고 닿을 수 없는 것처럼 느껴집니다. 하지만, 누구나 한 번쯤은 꿈을 이루기 위해 열심히 노력하여 그 꿈이 실현되는 것을 경험한 적이 있었을 것입니다. 영어를 잘하는 것도 여러분의 꿈이 될 수 있습니다. 좋은 독해 교재를 선정하여 영어 실력을 쌓는 것은 하늘에 있는 별에 다가가는 것보다 훨씬 쉽고, 실현하기도 쉬운 꿈이지요.

02

대입 전형이 날로 다양해지고 있습니다. 대부분 전형이 수준급의 영어 실력과 논리적 사고력, 비판력이 있다면 좋은 결과를 얻을 수 있습니다. 하지만, 수능 유형의 독해 문제나 교과서에 나온 지문만으로는 수준 높은 영어 실력을 갖추기 힘듭니다. 또한, 막상 대학에 입학하더라도 엄청난 분량의 원서 교재들을 제대로 소화해 낼 수 없겠지요. 이를 위해서는 미리 높은 수준의 영문 텍스트를 가지고 학습해야 합니다.

03

능률 고급영문독해가 이 모든 것을 원하는 여러분들을 위해 개정된 지문으로 새롭게 정비되었습니다. 최신 수능 유형 및 논술 기출 지문이 반영되었고 현 시류에 적합한 지문들로 구성되었습니다. 인문 · 사회과학 · 자연과학 · 시사를 아우르는 다양한 분야의 정보와 지식으로 가득 찬 지문들을 학습하다 보면, 영어 실력의 향상은 물론 논리적 사고력과 비판력 또한 길러지게 될 것입니다.

능률 고급영문독해가 여러분을 응원합니다!

STRUCTURE & FEATURES

능률 고급영문독해는,

어휘 · 구문 실력은 물론 사고력과 지성까지 높여 주는 대한민국 최고 수준의 독해 기본서입니다.
수능 수준을 뛰어넘어 최고가 되고 싶은 분들을 위한 완벽한 선택이 될 것입니다.

1

수능만점과 수시 논술 · 구술 면접 대비를 겨냥한 고난도 지문

진지한 '철학'에서부터 흥미로운 '시사 이슈'까지 사고의 폭을 넓혀주고 논리력을 길러주는 13개 분야별 62개 지문을 수록하였습니다.

2

고교 전 과정을 아우르는 엄선된 문제

수능과 내신 · 서술형 주관식 등 고교과정에서 꼭 필요한 다양한 유형의 문제들을 풀다보면 어떤 시험을 보더라도 자신감이 생길 것입니다.

3

친절하고 자세한 배경지식

지문 이해를 돕고 상식의 폭도 넓혀주는 지문 관련 배경 지식이 본문 곳곳에 수록되어 있습니다.

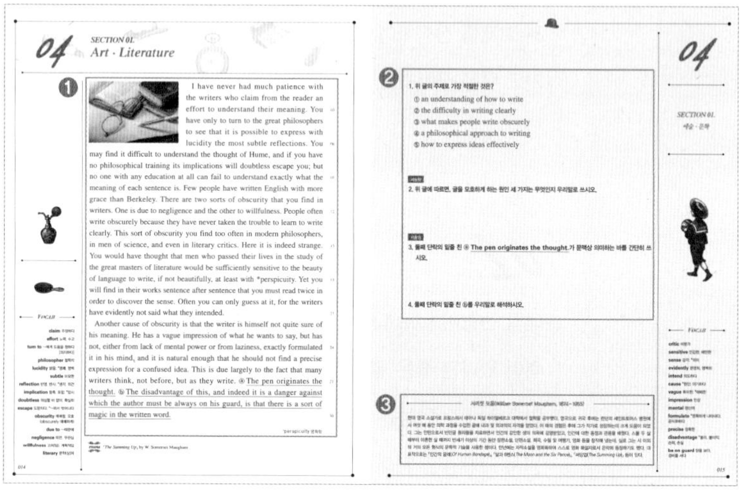

4

Word Test

고난도 지문인 만큼 어휘와 표현의 수준이 높습니다. 각 섹션 별로 해당 주제를 공부하고 난 후 관련 어휘와 표현 등을 꼼꼼히 정리하고 넘어가세요.

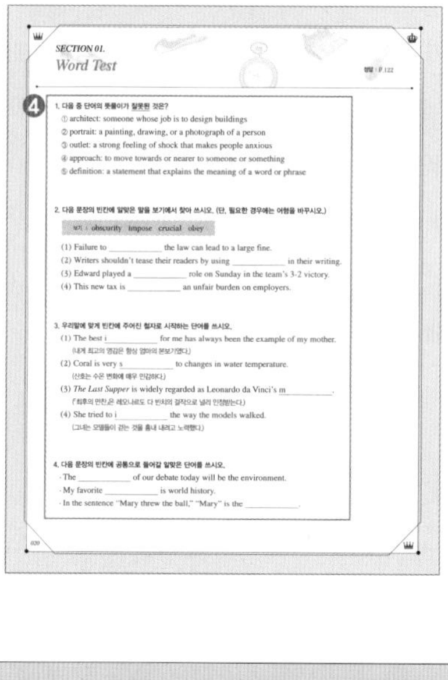

5

본문 필기노트

선생님의 설명을 들으며 직접 필기한 노트처럼 중요 구문과 독해 요령이 쉽고 자세하게 설명되어 있습니다. 각 단락별 요점 정리와 해석을 참고하여 난도 높은 영어 문장들을 혼자서 거뜬히 해결해가는 즐거움을 누려 보세요.

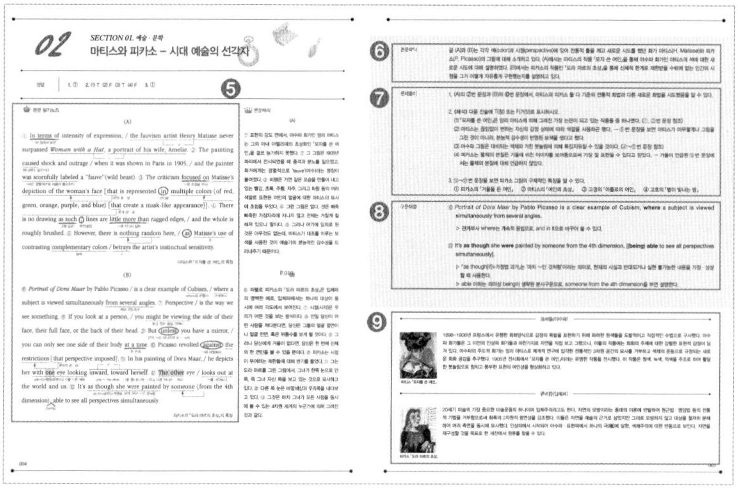
02 SECTION 01. 예술·문학
마티스와 피카소 – 시대 예술의 선각자

6

지문을 한눈에 보게 해주는 본문파악

7

자세하고 명쾌한 문제풀이

8

필기노트에서 못다한 추가 구문해설

9

상식을 넓히는 추가 배경지식

본문 배경지식에 이어 좀 더 심도 있는 지문관련 배경지식을 추가로 정리하였습니다. 62개 지문을 다 끝낸 후에는 정치 · 경제 · 사회 · 문화 · 과학 · 시사 등 다방면으로 상식이 풍부해진 것을 느끼게 될 것입니다.

10

쉬어가기 코너

수능과 논술에서 주요 소재로 쓰이는 미술 · 과학 · 철학 · 경제 · 정치 분야의 역사적 흐름 중 주요 이슈들을 사진과 함께 수록하였습니다. 그동안 각각의 텍스트들을 통해 이 분야와 관련된 정보를 습득했다면, 이 쉬어가기 코너를 통해 보다 시각적이고 일목요연하게 정리할 수 있습니다.

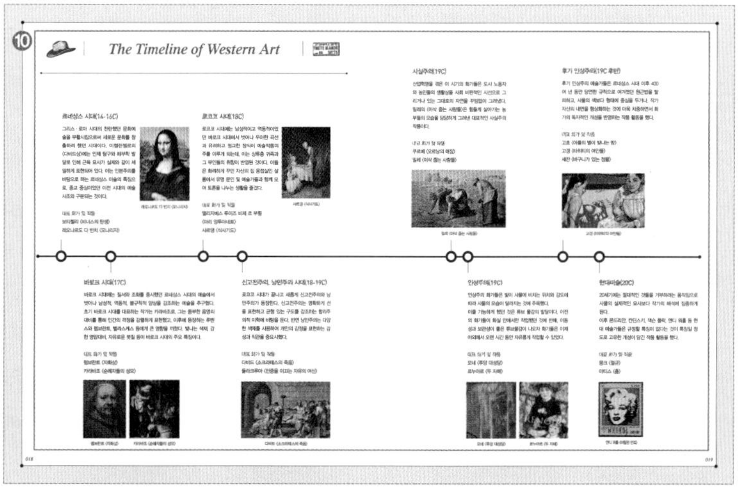
The Timeline of Western Art

CONTENTS

SECTION. 01

Art · Literature

예술 · 문학

SECTION 01.
Art · Literature

The traditional views of the artist are crucial to contemporary interpretations of creativity. In medieval Christianity, the artist was understood to be the vehicle through which God's creative inspiration found form. Through his disciplined training and craftsmanship, the medieval Christian artist brought God's vision to reality, recognizing that the inspiration and the artwork were gifts from God, and that the artist was merely the vehicle for God's inspiration. Therefore, the artist took no individual credit but rather identified himself as a craftsman, not as an originator or creator.

① With the Renaissance and its cultural shift toward the human, the artist became an individual who originated and created new visions. ② The human was the measure of all things and his potential was unlimited. ③ And people who were politically and financially powerful began to support famous painters and architects. ④ The ability to create works of art merely supported the Renaissance artist's sense of personal identity. ⑤ At the same time, the public definition of genius also shifted from one favored by God to one of extraordinary creativity and originality. The genius brought forth masterpieces, new paintings, and original styles.

In the 19th century, the Romantic Movement birthed a new and powerful definition of the artist as the rebel from society, the outcast who created out of a profound passion and sacrificed everything — social status, money, love, family — for this passion. As with the Renaissance genius, the Romantic artist was the source of originality, but unlike the Renaissance genius the Romantic artist was critical of society and sought a better world. The development of "modern," or 20th-century, schools of art, and their definition of the artist, were indebted to the Romantic myth of the artist.

FROM 「*Women, Creativity, and the Arts: Critical and Autobiographical Perspectives*」
by Diane Apostolos-Cappadona and Lucinda Ebersole

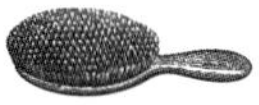

VOCAB

crucial 결정적인, 아주 중요한
contemporary 동시대의; *당대의
interpretation 해석
creativity 창조성
medieval 중세의
Christianity 기독교
vehicle *매개체, 전달 수단; 탈것
inspiration 영감
discipline 훈련[교육]하다
craftsmanship 솜씨
vision 시각; *비전, 미래상
recognize 인식하다; *인정하다
merely 단지
credit 신용; *칭찬, 찬사
identify 신분 증명을 하다; *인식하다
originator 창작자
creator 창조자
shift 변화(하다)
individual 개인(의)
originate 생기다; *시작하다
measure 척도

1. **What is the author mainly talking about?**

① modernism and its origin
② artists and their social activism
③ various artists and their originality
④ the development of artists' personal identity
⑤ changing views on the artist according to the times

2. **다음 중 위 글을 통해 알 수 있는 것이 아닌 것은?**

① 중세 시대의 예술가들은 예술의 중심을 신(神)에게 두었다.
② 문화적 변화는 예술가를 보는 시각에도 영향을 미친다.
③ 르네상스 시대의 예술가들은 개인의 창조성을 살릴 수 있었다.
④ 낭만주의 시대의 예술가들은 경제적인 부분을 중시하였다.
⑤ 20세기의 예술 학파들은 낭만주의 예술의 영향을 받았다.

3. **위 글의 둘째 단락에서 내용의 흐름과 관계없는 문장은?**

서술형

4. **위 글에 근거하여 르네상스 시대의 예술가와 낭만주의 시대의 예술가의 공통점과 차이점을 우리말로 간단히 쓰시오.**

(1) 공통점:
(2) 차이점:

VOCAB

potential 잠재력
unlimited 무제한의
financially 재정적으로
support 지지하다, 부양하다
architect 건축가
identity 정체(성)
definition 정의
extraordinary 비상한, 비범한
originality 독창성
bring forth ~을 낳다 (= give birth to)
masterpiece 걸작
original 독창적인
rebel 반역자
outcast 추방자, 방랑자
profound 심오한
passion 열정
sacrifice 희생하다
status *지위; 상태
school 학교; *학파
be indebted to ~에게 빚지다
myth 신화; *통념, 허구

02 SECTION 01. Art · Literature

(A)

In terms of intensity of expression, the Fauvism artist Henri Matisse never surpassed *Woman with a Hat*, a portrait of his wife, Amelie. The painting caused shock and outrage when it was shown in Paris in 1905, and the painter was scornfully labeled a "fauve"(wild beast). The criticism focused on Matisse's depiction of the woman's face that is represented in multiple colors of red, green, orange, purple, and blue that create a mask-like appearance. There is no drawing as such; lines are little more than ragged edges, and the whole is roughly brushed. However, there is nothing random here, as Matisse's use of contrasting complementary colors betrays the artist's instinctual sensitivity.

(B)

Portrait of Dora Maar by Pablo Picasso is a clear example of Cubism, where a subject is viewed simultaneously from several angles. Perspective is the way we see something. If you look at a person, you might be viewing the side of their face, their full face, or the back of their head. But unless you have a mirror, you can only see one side of their body at a time. Picasso revolted against the restrictions that perspective imposed. In his painting of Dora Maar, he depicts her with one eye looking inward, toward herself. The other eye looks out at the world and us. It's as though she were painted by someone from the 4th dimension, able to see all perspectives simultaneously.

VOCAB

(A)

in terms of *~의 점에서 보면, ~에 관하여
intensity 강도
Fauvism 야수파
surpass 능가하다
portrait 초상화
outrage 격분, 분개
scornfully 경멸적으로
label ~에 명칭[레테르]을 붙이다
fauve *야수; 야수파 화가
criticism 비평, 비판
focus on ~에 초점을 두다
depiction 묘사
represent 나타내다, 상징하다
multiple 복합의, 다수의
appearance 출현; *외관, 겉모양
ragged edge (벼랑 등의) 가장자리
roughly *거칠게; 대략

1. 위 글 (A)와 (B)를 통해 드러나는 마티스와 피카소의 공통된 특징은 무엇인가?

① 개척정신과 실험정신
② 다양한 색상의 사용
③ 전통 예술의 계승
④ 왜곡된 현실에 대한 비판
⑤ 사물에 대한 정교한 세부 묘사

2. **Mark T(True) or F(False) for the following statements.**

(1) *Woman with a Hat* was one of the most controversial works ever produced by Henri Matisse. □ T □ F

(2) Matisse used to use colors according to his constantly changing emotional state. □ T □ F

(3) Fauvism art could be characterized by contrasting colors and rough brushwork. □ T □ F

(4) Picasso believed that the essence of an object can best be expressed by showing its mirror image. □ T □ F

3. 위 글 (B)의 내용을 참고하여 다음 중 피카소의 그림을 고르시오.

①

②

③

④

VOCAB

random 임의의
contrasting 대조[대비]되는
complementary 보충의
betray 배반하다; *드러내다
instinctual 본능적인, 천성의
sensitivity 민감(성); *감수성
(B)
subject 주제; *대상, 제재
simultaneously 동시에, 일제히
angle 각, 각도
perspective 원근(법); *시점, 시각
full face 정면을 향한 얼굴
at a time 한 번에, 한꺼번에
revolt 반란을 일으키다, 반항하다
restriction 제한; *제약
impose (의무 등을) 지우다, 강요하다
depict 그리다, 묘사하다
inward *안으로; 마음속으로
dimension 치수, 용적; *차원

03 SECTION 01.
Art · Literature

Aristotle defined art as the realization of a true idea in an external form. He traced it back to human beings' inherent love of imitation and to the pleasure we feel in recognizing likenesses. Art, however, is not limited to simply copying. It idealizes nature and perfects its incompleteness; it seeks to identify the universal element in the individual experience. The distinction between poetry and history is therefore not that the one is written in rhyme, and the other is not. The distinction is that history documents only what has actually happened, while poetry depicts things in their universal character. Poetry is therefore more philosophical and more elevated than history. Such poetic representation may depict humans as being either better or worse than they generally are. Comedy, for example, imitates the worst examples of humanity because it takes what is low and shameful and makes it into something laughable and comic.

Tragedy, on the other hand, is the representation of serious or meaningful actions. It portrays events which create fear and pity in the minds of the audience. In the arousal of these feelings, the artist seeks to purify these emotions and draw out the sympathies of the audience. It is thus ______________ of the passions. Whereas art generally universalizes particular events, tragedy depicts passionate and critical situations to take the audience outside the selfish, individual standpoint, and connect it to the broader human experience. This is similar to Aristotle's explanation of the use of highly passionate music in the worship of the Greek gods: it provides an outlet for religious fervor and consequently steadies one's intense religious feelings.

VOCAB

define 정의하다
external 외부의
trace back to ~까지 거슬러 올라가다
inherent 본래부터 갖고 있는, 고유의
imitation 모방
recognize 인식하다
be limited to ~에 제한[국한]되다
idealize 이상화하다, ~의 이상을 그리다
perfect 완전한; *완전하게 하다
incompleteness 불완전함
identify 확인하다
element 요소
distinction 구별; *차이
rhyme 운율
document 문서, 기록; *문서에 기록하다
depict 그리다, 묘사하다
philosophical 철학적인
elevated 숭고한, 고결한
poetic 시적인

1. 예술에 대한 아리스토텔레스의 견해 중, 위 글의 내용과 일치하지 <u>않는</u> 것은?

① 외적인 형상을 통해 진리를 구현하는 것이 예술이다.
② 인간은 기본적으로 모방하는 것을 좋아한다.
③ 예술은 자연을 이상화하고 완전하게 하는 것이다.
④ 예술은 자연에서 경험할 수 없는 것을 보여준다.
⑤ 시에는 인간의 감정이 극대화되어 표현된다.

2. 다음 중 위 글 둘째 단락의 빈칸에 들어갈 말로 가장 적절한 것은?

① a renewal ② a parody ③ a curing
④ a denial ⑤ a development

3. 위 글 둘째 단락의 밑줄 친 <u>it</u>이 가리키는 바를 본문에서 찾아 쓰시오.

서술형

4. 아리스토텔레스의 견해에 따르면, 비극과 종교 음악이 가진 공통 기능은 무엇인지 20자 내외의 우리말로 쓰시오.

VOCAB

representation 표시, 표현
imitate 모방하다
shameful 부끄러운
tragedy 비극
portray 그리다, 묘사하다
pity 동정, 연민
audience 청중, 관객
arousal 각성
purify 정화하다
draw out ~을 꺼내다
sympathy 동정, 연민
passion 열정, 격정; *감정
universalize 보편화시키다
passionate 열정적인
critical 비판적인; *위험한; 중요한
standpoint 견지
broad 넓은
worship 숭배
outlet *배출구; 판로
fervor 열정
steady *안정시키다; 꾸준한
intense 강렬한

카타르시스(catharsis)

아리스토텔레스의 「시학(*Poetias*)」에서 처음으로 사용된 용어로, 예술 작품을 창작하거나 감상함으로써 내면에서 솟아나는 슬픔이나 공포의 기분을 토해내고 마음을 정화하는 것을 말한다. 카타르시스는 크게 두 가지로 해석되는데, 하나는 '정화(purification)'의 의미로서, 인간의 감정에서 불순한 부분을 씻어 없앤다는 뜻으로 해석된다. 또 다른 해석은 '배설(purgation)'로, 의학상의 배설의 의미가 '감정의 배설'이라는 은유로 해석된다. 카타르시스의 이러한 의미는 정신분석학에서 마음의 상처나 콤플렉스를 밖으로 발산시켜 치료하는 방법과도 일맥상통한다.

04 SECTION 01. Art · Literature

I have never had much patience with the writers who claim from the reader an effort to understand their meaning. You have only to turn to the great philosophers to see that it is possible to express with lucidity the most subtle reflections. You may find it difficult to understand the thought of Hume, and if you have no philosophical training its implications will doubtless escape you; but no one with any education at all can fail to understand exactly what the meaning of each sentence is. Few people have written English with more grace than Berkeley. There are two sorts of obscurity that you find in writers. One is due to negligence and the other to willfulness. People often write obscurely because they have never taken the trouble to learn to write clearly. This sort of obscurity you find too often in modern philosophers, in men of science, and even in literary critics. Here it is indeed strange. You would have thought that men who passed their lives in the study of the great masters of literature would be sufficiently sensitive to the beauty of language to write, if not beautifully, at least with *perspicuity. Yet you will find in their works sentence after sentence that you must read twice in order to discover the sense. Often you can only guess at it, for the writers have evidently not said what they intended.

Another cause of obscurity is that the writer is himself not quite sure of his meaning. He has a vague impression of what he wants to say, but has not, either from lack of mental power or from laziness, exactly formulated it in his mind, and it is natural enough that he should not find a precise expression for a confused idea. This is due largely to the fact that many writers think, not before, but as they write. ⓐ The pen originates the thought. ⓑ The disadvantage of this, and indeed it is a danger against which the author must be always on his guard, is that there is a sort of magic in the written word.

*perspicuity 명확함

FROM 「*The Summing Up*」 by W. Somerset Maugham

VOCAB

claim 주장하다
effort 노력, 수고
turn to ~에게 도움을 청하다[의지하다]
philosopher 철학자
lucidity 밝음; *명쾌, 명백
subtle 미묘한
reflection 반영, 반사; *생각, 의견
implication 함축, 포함; *암시
doubtless 의심할 바 없이, 확실히
escape 도망치다; *~에서 벗어나다
obscurity 애매함, 모호 (obscurely 애매하게)
due to ~때문에
negligence 태만, 무관심
willfulness 고의(임), 계획적임
literary 문학(상)의

1. 위 글의 주제로 가장 적절한 것은?

① an understanding of how to write
② the difficulty in writing clearly
③ what makes people write obscurely
④ a philosophical approach to writing
⑤ how to express ideas effectively

서술형

2. 위 글에 따르면, 글을 모호하게 하는 원인 세 가지는 무엇인지 우리말로 쓰시오.

서술형

3. 둘째 단락의 밑줄 친 ⓐ The pen originates the thought.가 문맥상 의미하는 바를 간단히 쓰시오.

4. 둘째 단락의 밑줄 친 ⓑ를 우리말로 해석하시오.

VOCAB

critic 비평가
sensitive 민감한, 예민한
sense 감각; *의미
evidently 분명히, 명백히
intend 의도하다
cause *원인; 야기하다
vague 희미한; *애매한
impression 인상
mental 정신의
formulate *명확하게 나타내다; 공식화하다
precise 정확한
disadvantage *불리, 불이익; 손해, 손실
be on guard 망을 보다, 경비를 서다

서머셋 모옴(William Somerset Maugham, 1874-1965)

현대 영국 소설가로 프랑스에서 태어나 독일 하이델베르크 대학에서 철학을 공부했다. 영국으로 귀국 후에는 런던의 세인트토머스 병원에서 여섯 해 동안 의학 과정을 수업한 끝에 내과 및 외과의의 자격을 얻었다. 이 때의 경험은 후에 그가 작가로 성장하는데 크게 도움이 되었다. 그는 인턴으로서 빈민굴 환자들을 치료하면서 인간의 강인한 생의 의욕에 감명받았고, 인간에 대한 동정과 관용을 배웠다. 스물 두 살 때부터 아흔한 살 때까지 반세기 이상의 기간 동안 장편소설, 단편소설, 희곡, 수필 및 여행기, 영화 등을 창작해 냈는데, 실로 그는 시 이외의 거의 모든 형식의 문학적 기술을 사용한 셈이다. 만년에는 자작소설을 영화화하여 스스로 영화 해설자로서 은막에 등장하기도 했다. 대표작으로는 「인간의 굴레(*Of Human Bondage*)」, 「달과 6펜스(*The Moon and the Six Pence*)」, 「써밍업(*The Summing Up*)」 등이 있다.

05

SECTION 01.
Art · Literature

William Golding published his famous novel *Lord of the Flies* in 1954. It tells the story of a group of English schoolboys stranded on a tropical island after their plane is shot down during a war. Although the novel is a work of fiction, its exploration of human evil is based on the real-life cruelty witnessed by Golding during World War II. Free from any rules, the boys on the island become like savages. They soon split up into groups, and whereas some work peacefully together, others violently rebel. The boys' behavior symbolizes the broader human struggle between the civilizing instinct to obey rules and behave morally and the savage instinct to attain power, ignore moral rules, and act violently.

Lord of the Flies is written in a very plain writing style, one which deliberately avoids highly poetic language, lengthy description, and philosophical passages. The novel is an allegory, meaning that the characters and objects all have a symbolic significance that is used to convey the novel's central themes and ideas. In his portrayal of the various ways in which the boys adapt to their new island surroundings and respond to their new freedom, Golding analyzes the broad range of ways in which human beings respond to change, fear, and tension.

Readers and critics have interpreted *Lord of the Flies* in a variety of ways since its publication. Some claim that the novel dramatizes the history of civilization, in particular the rise of the West. Some believe that it examines religious issues, such as original sin and the nature of good and evil. Others approach the novel through psychoanalytical theories. Ultimately, there is some validity to every interpretation; although Golding's story is confined to an isolated group of boys on a small island, it explores the universal conflict of humanity.

VOCAB

lord 주인; 군주
strand 오도가도 못하게 하다
tropical 열대의
exploration 탐험, 탐구
evil 나쁜; *악
cruelty 잔혹, 잔인성
witness 증인, 목격자; *목격하다
savage 야만인(의), 미개인(의)
split up into ~로 갈라지다
violently 폭력적으로
rebel 반항하다
symbolize 상징하다
struggle 싸움; 투쟁
civilize 문명화하다
instinct 본능
morally 도덕적으로
attain 이루다; *차지하다
ignore 무시하다
plain 명료한; 평이한
deliberately 일부러
lengthy 긴; 장황한
passage *한 구절; 통행, 통과

1. 위 글의 종류로 가장 적절한 것은?

① a journal ② a book review ③ an editorial
④ a letter ⑤ an advertisement

2. **Which of the following is NOT true about *Lord of the Flies*?**

① It's about a group of boys forced to live together on an island.
② The cruelty of life observed by the author himself is described.
③ It is written in a flowery style, using elaborate words and expressions.
④ Each character in it has important symbolic meaning.
⑤ It deals with the general conflict found in human nature.

서술형

3. 위 글에 따르면 인간 투쟁은 어떤 상황에서 일어나는지 30자 내외의 우리말로 쓰시오.

서술형

4. 위 글에서 소개된 소설 「파리대왕」의 작품 해설 두 가지를 우리말로 요약하시오.

VOCAB

allegory 비유담, 우화
symbolic 상징적인
convey 전하다, 전달하다
theme 주제, 테마
portrayal 묘사
adapt 적응하다
surrounding (*pl.*) 환경
analyze 분석하다
range 범위
tension 긴장
interpret 해석하다
publication 출판
dramatize 극화하다; 과장하다
original sin 원죄
psychoanalytical 정신분석학적인
validity 타당성
interpretation 해석
confine 제한하다
isolated 고립된
universal 일반적인; 보편적인
conflict 갈등

The Timeline of Western Art

르네상스 시대(14-16C)

그리스 · 로마 시대의 찬란했던 문화예술을 부활시킴으로써 새로운 문화를 창출하려 했던 시대이다. 미켈란젤로의 〈다비드상〉에는 인체 탐구와 해부학 발달로 인해 근육 묘사가 실제와 같이 세밀하게 표현되어 있다. 이는 인본주의를 바탕으로 하는 르네상스 미술의 특징으로, 종교 중심이었던 이전 시대의 예술 사조와 구분되는 것이다.

레오나르도 다 빈치 〈모나리자〉

대표 화가 및 작품
보티첼리 〈비너스의 탄생〉
레오나르도 다 빈치 〈모나리자〉

바로크 시대(17C)

바로크 시대에는 질서와 조화를 중시했던 르네상스 시대의 예술에서 벗어나 남성적, 역동적, 불규칙적 양상을 강조하는 예술을 추구했다. 초기 바로크 시대를 대표하는 작가는 카라바조로, 그는 풍부한 음영의 대비를 통해 인간의 격정을 강렬하게 표현했고, 이후에 등장하는 루벤스와 렘브란트, 벨라스케스 등에게 큰 영향을 끼쳤다. 빛나는 색채, 강한 명암대비, 자유로운 붓질 등이 바로크 시대의 주요 특징이다.

대표 화가 및 작품
렘브란트 〈자화상〉
카라바조 〈순례자들의 성모〉

렘브란트 〈자화상〉

카라바조 〈순례자들의 성모〉

로코코 시대(18C)

로코코 시대에는 남성적이고 역동적이었던 바로크 시대에서 벗어나 우아한 곡선과 유려하고 정교한 장식이 예술작품의 주를 이루게 되는데, 이는 상류층 귀족과 그 부인들의 취향이 반영된 것이다. 이들은 화려하게 꾸민 자신의 집 응접실인 살롱에서 유명 문인 및 예술가들과 함께 모여 토론을 나누는 생활을 즐겼다.

샤르댕 〈식사기도〉

대표 화가 및 작품
엘리자베스 루이즈 비제 르 부룅
〈마리 앙투아네트〉
샤르댕 〈식사기도〉

신고전주의, 낭만주의 시대(18-19C)

로코코 시대가 끝나고 새롭게 신고전주의와 낭만주의가 등장한다. 신고전주의는 명확하게 선을 표현하고 균형 있는 구도를 강조하는 합리주의적 미학에 바탕을 둔다. 반면 낭만주의는 다양한 색채를 사용하여 개인의 감정을 표현하는 감성과 직관을 중요시했다.

대표 화가 및 작품
다비드 〈소크라테스의 죽음〉
들라크루아 〈민중을 이끄는 자유의 여신〉

다비드 〈소크라테스의 죽음〉

사실주의(19C)

산업혁명을 겪은 이 시기의 화가들은 도시 노동자와 농민들의 생활상을 사회 비판적인 시선으로 그리거나 있는 그대로의 자연을 꾸밈없이 그려냈다. 밀레의 〈이삭 줍는 사람들〉은 힘들게 살아가는 농부들의 모습을 담담하게 그려낸 대표적인 사실주의 작품이다.

대표 화가 및 작품
쿠르베 〈오르낭의 매장〉
밀레 〈이삭 줍는 사람들〉

밀레 〈이삭 줍는 사람들〉

인상주의(19C)

인상주의 화가들은 빛이 사물에 비치는 위치와 강도에 따라 사물의 모습이 달라지는 것에 주목했다.
이를 가능하게 했던 것은 튜브 물감의 발달이다. 이전의 화가들이 화실 안에서만 작업했던 것에 반해, 이동성과 보관성이 좋은 튜브물감이 나오자 화가들은 이제 야외에서 오랜 시간 동안 자유롭게 작업할 수 있었다.

대표 화가 및 작품
모네 〈루앙 대성당〉
르누아르 〈두 자매〉

모네 〈루앙 대성당〉

르누아르 〈두 자매〉

후기 인상주의(19C 후반)

후기 인상주의 예술가들은 르네상스 시대 이후 400여 년 동안 당연한 규칙으로 여겨졌던 원근법을 탈피하고, 사물의 색보다 형태에 중심을 두거나, 작가 자신의 내면을 형상화하는 것에 더욱 치중하면서 화가의 독자적인 개성을 반영하는 작품 활동을 했다.

대표 화가 및 작품
고흐 〈아를의 별이 빛나는 밤〉
고갱 〈타히티의 여인들〉
세잔 〈바구니가 있는 정물〉

고갱 〈타히티의 여인들〉

현대미술(20C)

20세기에는 절대적인 것들을 거부하려는 움직임으로 사물의 실제적인 묘사보다 작가의 해석에 집중하게 된다.
이후 몬드리안, 칸딘스키, 잭슨 폴락, 앤디 워홀 등 현대 예술가들은 규정할 특징이 없다는 것이 특징일 정도로 고유한 개성이 담긴 작품 활동을 했다.

대표 화가 및 작품
뭉크 〈절규〉
마티스 〈춤〉

앤디 워홀 〈마릴린 먼로〉

SECTION 01.
Word Test

정답 | p.122

1. 다음 중 단어의 뜻풀이가 잘못된 것은?

① architect: someone whose job is to design buildings
② portrait: a painting, drawing, or a photograph of a person
③ outlet: a strong feeling of shock that makes people anxious
④ approach: to move towards or nearer to someone or something
⑤ definition: a statement that explains the meaning of a word or phrase

2. 다음 문장의 빈칸에 알맞은 말을 보기에서 찾아 쓰시오. (단, 필요한 경우에는 어형을 바꾸시오.)

보기 | obscurity impose crucial obey

(1) Failure to _____________ the law can lead to a large fine.
(2) Writers shouldn't tease their readers by using _____________ in their writing.
(3) Edward played a _____________ role on Sunday in the team's 3-2 victory.
(4) This new tax is _____________ an unfair burden on employers.

3. 우리말에 맞게 빈칸에 주어진 철자로 시작하는 단어를 쓰시오.

(1) The best i_____________ for me has always been the example of my mother.
(내게 최고의 영감은 항상 엄마의 본보기였다.)
(2) Coral is very s_____________ to changes in water temperature.
(산호는 수온 변화에 매우 민감하다.)
(3) *The Last Supper* is widely regarded as Leonardo da Vinci's m_____________.
(「최후의 만찬」은 레오나르도 다 빈치의 걸작으로 널리 인정받는다.)
(4) She tried to i_____________ the way the models walked.
(그녀는 모델들이 걷는 것을 흉내 내려고 노력했다.)

4. 다음 문장의 빈칸에 공통으로 들어갈 알맞은 단어를 쓰시오.

· The _____________ of our debate today will be the environment.
· My favorite _____________ is world history.
· In the sentence "Mary threw the ball," "Mary" is the _____________.

SECTION. 02

Science

과학

06 SECTION 02. Science

Pure science may seem useless in the usual sense, but over a long period of time it surely leads to economic and technological benefits. If we stop paying for pure science today, there will be no applied science tomorrow. Charles Darwin's work on evolution and Gregor Mendel's on the heredity of plants laid the foundations for the science of genetics, which eventually led to the discovery of DNA, which led to genetic engineering, which is now exploding with unimaginable applications. Michael Faraday's discovery of how a magnet can produce electricity made possible the first hydroelectric power plant fifty years later. Yet Darwin, Mendel and Faraday were not supported with any such profits in mind, nor could they have been. A nation cannot bet on pure scientists like betting on horses. It can, however, build stables.

Discoveries in pure science are not just about nature. They are about people as well. After Copernicus, we have taken a more humble view of our place in the cosmos. After Darwin, we have recognized new relatives hanging from the family tree.

FROM 「*In Defense of Pure Science*」 by Alan Lightman

서술형

1. 위 글의 밑줄 친 build stables의 의미를 우리말로 간단히 쓰시오.

VOCAB

lead to (~한 결과에) 이르게 하다
applied 응용의
evolution 진화; *진화론
heredity 유전
lay 놓다; *쌓다
foundation 기초, 토대
genetics 유전학
eventually 마침내, 결국
genetic engineering 유전 공학
explode 폭발하다; *폭발적으로 증가하다
application 응용
magnet 자석
electricity 전기
hydroelectric 수력의
power plant 발전소
profit 이득, 이익
bet *(돈)을 걸다; 내기하다
stable 마구간
humble 겸손한, 겸허한
cosmos 우주
recognize 인식하다
relative 친척, 일가; *동족, 동류
hang 매달리다, 늘어지다 (hung-hung)

If a scientist believes a certain hypothesis is true, but finds contradicting evidence, then in the scientific spirit, ① <u>the hypothesis</u> must be changed or abandoned. In that same scientific spirit, the idea must be changed or abandoned in spite of the reputation of the person advocating ② <u>it</u>.

As an example, the greatly respected Greek philosopher Aristotle claimed that falling objects fall at a speed proportional to their weight. This false idea was held to be true for more than 2,000 years because of Aristotle's compelling authority. In the scientific spirit, however, ③ <u>a single verifiable experiment</u> to the contrary outweighs any authority, regardless of reputation or the number of followers or advocates.

Scientists must strive to distinguish between what they see and ④ <u>what they wish to see</u>, for they, like most people, have a vast capacity for fooling themselves. People have always tended to adopt general rules, beliefs, creeds, ideas, and hypotheses without thoroughly questioning their validity and to retain them long after they have been shown to be meaningless, false or at least questionable. ⑤ <u>The most widespread assumptions</u> are often the least questioned.

서술형

1. 위 글에 따르면, 기존의 이론과 배치되는 확실한 이론을 발견했을 때 과학자는 어떻게 행동해야 하는지 우리말로 쓰시오.

2. 위 글의 ①~⑤ 중 내용상 나머지 넷과 상반되는 하나를 고르시오.

VOCAB

hypothesis 가설 (*pl.* hypotheses)
contradict 모순되다
evidence 증거
abandon 포기하다; *버리다
reputation 명성
advocate 옹호[주장]하다; 옹호자
claim 주장하다
proportional 비례하는
compelling 강제적인; *강력한
authority 권위
verifiable 입증할 수 있는
to the contrary 그와 반대의[로], 그렇지 않다는
outweigh ~보다 무겁다; *능가하다
strive 노력하다
distinguish 구별[구분]하다
vast 광대한; *대단한
capacity 수용량; *능력
adopt *채택하다; 입양하다
creed 신념
thoroughly 철저하게, 완전히
question 질문(하다); *의심하다
validity 정당성, 타당성
retain 유지하다, 보유하다
questionable 의심스러운
assumption 가정, 가설; *(증거도 없이) 사실이라고 생각함

08 SECTION 02. Science

A *paradigm is a general theory, like the Darwinian theory of evolution, which has achieved general acceptance in the scientific community. Paradigms help scientific communities to standardize their discipline in that they help the scientist to create avenues of inquiry, formulate questions, select methods with which to examine questions, define areas of relevance and establish or create meaning. A paradigm is essential to scientific inquiry — no natural history can be interpreted in the absence of at least some implicit body of theoretical and methodological beliefs that permit selection, evaluation, and criticism.

Then, how are paradigms created, and how do scientific revolutions take place? (A) In time, these descriptions and interpretations entirely disappear, and a pre-paradigmatic school appears. (B) During these early stages of inquiry, different researchers confronting the same phenomena describe and interpret them in different ways. (C) Inquiry begins with a random collection of "mere facts," although, often, a set of principles is already included in the collection. Such a school often emphasizes a special part of the collection of facts. Often, these schools compete for supremacy.

From the competition of these pre-paradigmatic schools, one paradigm emerges. To be accepted as a paradigm, a theory must seem better than its competitors, but it need not, and in fact never does, explain all the facts with which it can be confronted, thus making continued research necessary. As a paradigm grows in strength and in the number of advocates, the other pre-paradigmatic schools or the previous paradigm fade, bringing about a great change in science.

*paradigm 패러다임, 사고[이론]의 틀

VOCAB

theory 이론
evolution 진화
acceptance 인정, 받아들임
community (공통 특징을 가진) 집단, 사회
standardize 표준화하다
discipline 훈련; *학문 분야
in that ~라는 점에서
inquiry *연구, 탐구; 질문, 문의
formulate 정식[공식]화하다, 체계화하다
examine 조사하다
define 정의하다, 규정짓다
relevance 관련(성)
establish *정립하다; 설립하다
essential 필수적인
interpret 해석하다
in the absence of ~이 없이[없을 때는]
implicit 함축적인, 암시적인
a[some] body of 일련의[몇몇의] ~
theoretical 이론적인
methodological 방법론적인
evaluation 평가

08

SECTION 02.
과학

1. 위 글에서 둘째 단락의 (A) ~ (C)를 글의 흐름에 맞게 배열한 것으로 가장 적절한 것은?

① (A) - (C) - (B)
② (B) - (A) - (C)
③ (B) - (C) - (A)
④ (C) - (A) - (B)
⑤ (C) - (B) - (A)

2. **Which of the following is NOT mentioned in the passage?**

① the definition of a paradigm
② the role of a paradigm in scientific research
③ the importance of a paradigm in scientific inquiry
④ the process of a paradigm emerging
⑤ the difference between a paradigm and a theory

3. **Mark T(True) or F(False) for the following statements.**

(1) A paradigm can be compared to a frame which confines the limits of a line of research. □ T □ F
(2) To interpret natural history, we need some systematized beliefs. □ T □ F
(3) Scientific revolutions occur when previous paradigms disappear. □ T □ F
(4) A selected paradigm should satisfy all possible arguments. □ T □ F

VOCAB

criticism 비평, 비판
revolution 혁명
take place 일어나다, 발생하다
entirely 완전히, 아주
researcher 연구원
confront ~에 직면하다
phenomena 현상 (phenomenon의 복수형)
random 되는 대로의, 무작위의
mere 단순한
a set of 일련의
principle 원리, 원칙
emphasize 강조하다
compete 경쟁하다 (competition 경쟁) (competitor 경쟁자)
supremacy 최고(의 지위)
pre-paradigmatic 사전 패러다임의
school 학교; *학파
emerge 나오다, 나타나다
advocate 옹호하다; *옹호자
previous 이전의
fade 사라지다

패러다임(paradigm)의 유래

토머스 쿤이 저서 「과학혁명의 구조」에서 사용한 용어이다. 그에 의하면 과학사에는 과학 이전의 시기인 전(前)과학시대가 가장 먼저 있었다고 한다. 전과학시대에서 정상과학의 시대로 접어들게 되는데, 이 정상과학시대를 지배하는 논리 혹은 세계관을 쿤은 패러다임이라고 칭하였다. 한 패러다임이 지배하는 정상과학시대는 모든 과학적 문제점들이 패러다임에 도전하는 현상이 아니라 문제풀이과정으로 인식된다. 천동설을 하나의 패러다임이라 할 때 그에 어긋나는 별이 관측되었을 경우 그 별은 천동설을 부정하는 명확한 증거가 아니라 천동설을 더욱 정교하게 가다듬으면 해결될 수 있는 문제로 인식되는 것이다. 그런데 이러한 문제점들이 계속 축적되다 보면 정상과학은 유지되지 못하고 붕괴하게 된다. 그리고 혼란과정을 거쳐 새로운 패러다임에 입각한 새로운 정상과학이 탄생한다. 쿤은 과학사에 국한해 패러다임을 이야기했지만, 현재는 여러 분야에서 일반적인 용어로 사용되고 있다.

09

SECTION 02.
Science

Ptolemy's view of the solar system was accepted for fourteen hundred years until finally challenged by Copernicus, a mathematician and astronomer with a Polish father and a German mother, in 1530. Copernicus' view of the solar system had the sun at the center, with the earth revolving around it, along with all the other planets.

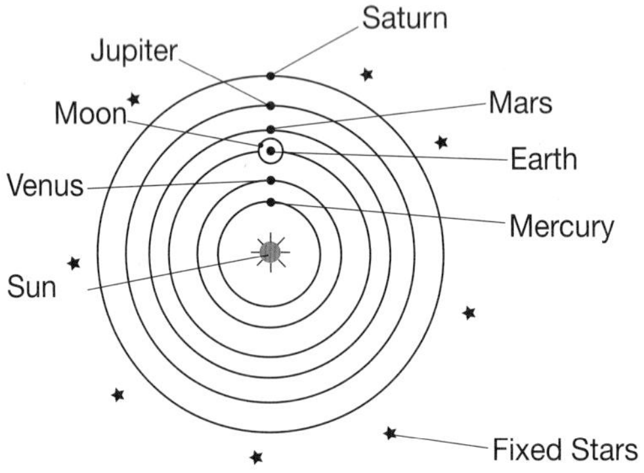

Shown here is the picture from his original publication. As can be seen, the only thing that doesn't go around the sun is the moon, which continues to go around the earth. One objection that people had to the picture was that if the earth was indeed just another planet, how come it was the only one with a moon? Other objections included why does it feel like the earth is standing still and why don't objects thrown into the air land far to the west? Also, if the universe had been created for mankind, then why wasn't mankind at the center?

Despite these problems, Pope Clement VII approved of Copernicus' work in 1530, and asked for a copy of the full work when it was available. This was not until 1543, the year that Copernicus died.

The real breakthrough that ultimately led to the general acceptance of Copernicus' theory was due to Galileo, but was actually a technological rather than a conceptual breakthrough. It was Galileo's improvement and use of the telescope that persuaded people that the moon was a lot like the earth, and in some ways so too were the planets.

VOCAB

solar system 태양계
mathematician 수학자
astronomer 천문학자
Polish 폴란드인의
revolve 회전하다; *공전하다
planet 행성
original 원래의
publication 출판(물)
moon 달; 위성
continue 계속되다
objection 이의, 반론
include 포함하다
stand still 가만히 서 있다
object 사물, 물체
throw 던지다
land 착륙하다; *떨어지다
universe 우주
mankind 인류
approve 승인하다, 찬성하다

1. **What is the best title for the passage?**

① A Big Revolution in the 1400s
② Courageous Choice for Science
③ How Copernicus Finally Won the Victory
④ False Views on the System of the Universe
⑤ The Long Argument Made by Copernicus

2. **Mark T(True) or F(False) for the following statements.**

(1) Ptolemy and Copernicus had opposing views on the planetary system. □ T □ F
(2) As was generally accepted at the time, Copernicus believed that the sun is in the center of the universe. □ T □ F
(3) Copernicus thought that the moon constantly revolves around both the sun and the earth. □ T □ F

3. **위 글에서 코페르니쿠스의 주장에 제기된 이의가 아닌 것을 고르시오.**

(1) 왜 지구 외에 위성을 가진 다른 행성은 없는가?
(2) 왜 지구는 멈춰 있는 것처럼 느껴지는 것인가?
(3) 공중으로 던져진 물체들은 왜 서쪽으로 떨어지지 않는가?
(4) 왜 우주는 인간을 위해 창조되었다고 생각하는가?

서술형

4. **From the 4th paragraph, it can be inferred that scientific beliefs are sometimes confirmed by ________________ development. (from the passage)**

09

SECTION 02.
과학

VOCAB

available 이용 가능한
breakthrough 돌파; *(과학 등의) 큰 발전
ultimately 궁극적으로, 결국
lead to ~에 이르다
acceptance 받아들임, 수용
due to ~ 때문에[덕분에]
technological (과학)기술의
conceptual 개념의, 개념적인
persuade 설득하다
〈그림〉
Venus 금성
Jupiter 목성
Saturn 토성
Mars 화성
Earth 지구
Mercury 수성
Fixed stars 항성(恒星)

10

SECTION 02.
Science

In 1978 NASA scientist Donald J. Kessler envisioned the possibility of a cascading chain reaction of space debris collisions taking place in low Earth orbit. This chilling potential scenario has since been dubbed the Kessler Syndrome. The underlying mechanism of the concept is that an impact between two manmade objects in space will generate further debris, ____, culminating in a situation in which a deadly swarm of shrapnel and space junk circles the planet devastating everything in its path, including functioning satellites and manned spacecraft.

Kessler made the pessimistic prediction that the density of space junk in orbit around the Earth would, by the year 2000, reach a level at which random collisions were inevitable. Although manmade objects in space were already being cataloged at that time in the interest of anticipating and avoiding collisions, the additional objects generated by such collisions were not being tracked and were often small enough to escape satellite detection.

Kessler proposed a reduction in the number of objects abandoned in orbit after they had ceased to function, hypothesizing that this would be the most prudent way of preventing future accidents. However, it wasn't until a 2009 collision between two communication satellites — one Russian, the other American — unleashed thousands of small pieces of debris into orbit and potentially set into motion Kessler's doomsday scenario, that international efforts to authoritatively address the situation were undertaken in earnest.

VOCAB

envision 상상하다
cascade 작은 폭포; *단계적으로 일어나다
space debris 우주 쓰레기
collision 충돌
orbit 궤도
chilling 냉랭한, 오싹한
dub ~라고 부르다
underlying 근본적인
mechanism 구조, 기제
manmade 사람이 만든, 인공의
culminate in ~로 끝이 나다
swarm 무리, 떼
shrapnel 파편
devastate 완전히 파괴하다
function 기능; *작동하다

10

SECTION 02.
과학

1. **What is the best title for the passage?**
   ① How to Deal with Unwanted Debris in Space
   ② The Global Competition to Put More Spacecraft in Orbit
   ③ Newly Discovered Weak Points in Kessler's Theory
   ④ The Hypothesis and Reality of a Threatening Space Junk Problem
   ⑤ The Scientific Effort among Scientists to Solve the Mystery of the Kessler Syndrome

2. **위 글 첫째 단락의 빈칸에 들어갈 말로 가장 적절한 것은?**
   ① resulting in an increase in spacecraft launches
   ② allowing spacecraft to capture images of the collisions
   ③ leading to an exponential number of subsequent collisions
   ④ collecting defunct manmade objects in orbit around Earth
   ⑤ calling for further research into collisions in low Earth orbit

3. **케슬러 신드롬에 대한 설명 중, 위 글의 내용과 일치하지 않는 것은?**
   ① NASA 과학자 케슬러가 제안한 가설이다.
   ② 우주에서 발생한 파편들의 충돌이 연쇄적으로 일어날 가능성을 제안한다.
   ③ 2000년쯤에는 충돌을 피할 수 없을 정도로 우주 쓰레기의 밀도가 높을 것이라 예상됐다.
   ④ 우주 물체 간 충돌을 막고자 충돌로 발생한 물체들도 목록화되었다.
   ⑤ 2009년이 되어서야 우주 쓰레기 대처에 대한 국제적인 노력이 본격화되었다.

서술형

4. **What did Kessler suggest as a way to stop further space debris collisions? (in Korean)**

우주 쓰레기와 파편(space junk and debris)

우주 쓰레기와 이로 인한 파편은 수명이 다한 인공위성부터 우주비행사가 사용하다 놓친 공구 등 다양한 크기로 구성되어 있으며, 전문가들은 약 350만 개가 우주에서 유영하는 것으로 예측한다. 우주 쓰레기와 파편은 고도 2,000Km 이하인 저궤도 상에 대략 70% 정도 있는 것으로 확인된다. 우주 쓰레기와 파편이 지상으로 떨어질 때는 대부분 대기권을 통과하는 도중 불타기 때문에 지구에 심각한 피해가 되진 않는다. 그러나 우주 안에선 초속 3~8㎞의 빠른 속도로 이동하면서 인공위성 간의 통신을 방해하거나, 또 다른 물체와 충돌해서 심각한 문제로 발전한다.

VOCAB

satellite 위성
pessimistic 비관적인
prediction 예측, 예언
density 밀도
inevitable 불가피한, 필연적인
catalog 목록; *목록을 작성하다
track 추적하다
detection 발견, 간파
abandon 버리다
cease 중단하다, 그만하다
hypothesize 가설을 세우다, 가정하다
prudent 신중한, 현명한
unleash 촉발시키다, 불러일으키다
doomsday 세상의 마지막 날
authoritatively 위압적으로
in earnest 본격적으로, 진지하게

The Timeline of Science

고대 과학: 자연 철학의 시대

과학은 고대 그리스의 자연 철학자들의 연구에서 시작되었다고 볼 수 있다. 자연 철학자들은 신화적 원리에 근거하지 않는 자연 변화를 설명하려 하였고 이를 바탕으로 합리적인 비판과 토론의 전통이 시작되었다.

이 시기의 대표적인 학자는 아리스토텔레스와 플라톤 등이 있으며, 특히 2세기 중엽의 프톨레마이오스는 지구가 우주의 중심이라는 천동설을 수학적으로 설명하였다. 이는 중세까지 유럽인들에게 진리로 통용됐다.

헬레니즘 시대와 이슬람 과학의 발전(334-30 BC)

헬레니즘 시대의 과학자들은 왕의 후원을 통해 많은 저작과 업적을 남겼다. 「기하학 원론」을 집필한 유클리드와 의학의 체계를 세운 갈레노스가 대표 학자이다. 마호메트가 아랍을 통일한 후 이들의 저서가 아랍어로 번역되면서 이슬람 과학이 발전하기 시작했다. 대수학, 아라비아 숫자 등은 모두 이슬람 과학에서 유래된 것이다. 천문학과 물리학 등 여러 과학 분야가 연구되기 시작되어, 이슬람 과학은 향후 서유럽 과학이 발전할 수 있는 토대를 제공했다.

중세 과학: 스콜라 학풍의 지배(9-15C)

중세 시대엔 신학을 학습하는 것이 주된 목표였던 스콜라 학풍이 지배했었다. 그리스 자연철학의 내용은 신학과 대립하는 면이 발견되면서 갈등이 시작되었고, 1277년에 교황은 신학과 대립하는 229개의 과학명제를 금지하기도 했다. 전 우주에는 '신'만이 유일한 진리라는 사상이 지배했던 과학의 암흑기를 보냈다.

과학 혁명기(15-16C)

15-16세기의 과학은 자연현상 자체를 분석하고 이론화하는 시도를 통해 과학이 독립적인 학문으로 발전할 수 있었다. 과학 학술단체와 과학 전문 학술지가 시작된 시기이기도 하다.

이 시기의 대표적인 과학자 코페르니쿠스는 1543년 「천구의 회전에 관하여」를 출간하여 지구의 자전과 공전을 설명했고 갈릴레오는 1609년에 망원경을 개발하여 달 표면과 금성 등의 위성변화를 측정했다.

아이작 뉴턴과 계몽사조(17-18C)

아이작 뉴턴의 위대한 업적은 역학(力學)에 있다. 뉴턴은 저서 「프린키피아」에서 수학적으로 설명할 수 있는 만유인력의 법칙을 확립해 새로운 천문학과 우주 구조를 설명했다. 화학과 물리학을 다룬 「광학」에서는 경험과 실험을 통한 탐구 방향을 제안했다. 뉴턴역학은 가설이나 독단이 아니라 수학적·합리적·경험적·실험적 방법만을 사용하여 성공하였다. 이에 영향을 받은 계몽주의자들은 합리적이고 수학적인 지식만을 추구하게 되었다. '과학적인' 면을 중시하는 이러한 경향은 향후 18세기 과학의 방향을 이끌었다.

20세기 과학: 실용과 격변의 세기

20세기는 과학 분야에서 비약적인 발전이 이루어진 시기였다. 기존의 과학 영역뿐만 아니라 IT와 항공 등의 발전으로 전 세계의 경제와 문화가 격변했다. 이러한 발전과 더불어 과학이 사회에 미치는 부정적 영향 또한 나타났다. 전쟁의 부산물인 화학무기 및 환경오염은 20세기 과학 발전의 대표적인 결점이다.

이에 토마스 쿤과 칼 포퍼 등의 철학자들은 과학의 본질에 대해 고찰하며 과학이 걸어온 길과 향후 나아갈 방향에 대한 시사점을 제기했다.

물리학의 발전, 그리고 아인슈타인(19-20C)

프랑스 혁명 이후, 기존 화학에 소속되어 있던 열 분야가 역학 분야와 함께 발전되며 물리학이 학문으로 구분되기 시작했다. 아인슈타인은 '기적의 해'라 불리는 1905년에 브라운운동 이론, 특수 상대성이론을 제시해 현대 물리학의 근간을 확립했다. 1916년에는 일반상대성이론을 발표해 세계적인 물리학자로 명성을 떨쳤다. 그는 여생을 전자기 현상과 중력 현상을 포괄하는 신규 이론인 통일장이론을 연구하는 데 보냈고, 이는 향후 전 세계 물리학자들의 중심 연구 주제로 자리 잡았다.

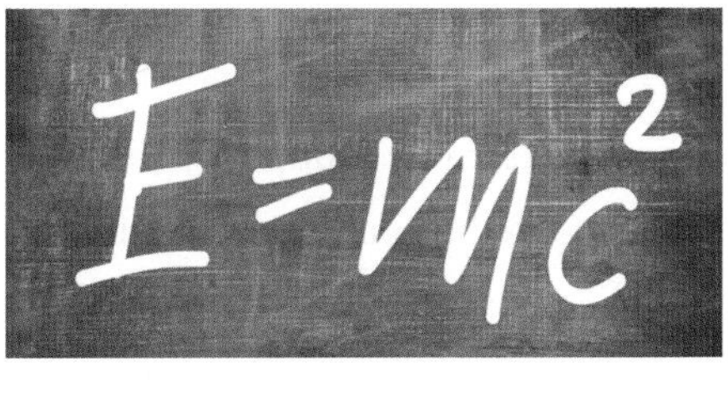

21세기 첨단과학: 융합의 시대

21세기 과학은 융합과학의 시대이다. 과학, 기술 그리고 인문학 등의 여러 학문이 결합되고 있다. 자연과학과 인문과학의 만남인 뇌과학, 생물학과 컴퓨터 공학의 융합인 생물정보학 등이 활발히 연구 중이다.

더불어 우주과학 역시 21세기 첨단과학의 지표이다. 위성을 통한 우주 관측을 넘어 행성 탐사, 태양계 밖의 우주에 관한 연구들이 진행 중이다.

SECTION 02.

Word Test

정답 | p.122

1. 다음 단어의 영영풀이로 알맞은 것을 찾아 선으로 연결하시오.

(1) collision · · ⓐ suggested or understood without being stated directly

(2) implicit · · ⓑ an accident in which two objects or people crash into one another

(3) hypothesis · · ⓒ happening or chosen without any definite plan or pattern

(4) random · · ⓓ an idea that attempts to explain something but has not yet been proved to be true

2. 다음 문장의 밑줄 친 부분과 바꿔 쓸 수 있는 단어를 고르시오.

(1) Many proverbs say that a humble attitude always leads to success.

① arrogant ② verifiable ③ cautious ④ critical ⑤ modest

(2) He is one of Linda's strongest supporters.

① rivals ② critics ③ advocates ④ opponents ⑤ counterparts

(3) Because their demands were met, the employees decided to cease the strike.

① halt ② devastate ③ standardize ④ recognize ⑤ claim

(4) The argument was inevitable since the two parties didn't try to negotiate.

① accepted ② undependable ③ unavoidable ④ unnecessary ⑤ questionable

3. 우리말에 맞게 빈칸에 공통으로 들어갈 알맞은 단어를 쓰시오.

· The couple were unable to have children of their own, but they hoped to ____________.

(그 부부는 아이를 가질 수가 없었지만, 입양하는 것을 바랬다.)

· The Senate unanimously ____________ed the committee's proposals.

(상원은 그 위원회의 제안을 만장일치로 채택했다.)

4. 다음 문장의 빈칸에 들어갈 가장 알맞은 단어를 고르시오.

(1) Human rights activists ____________ a society where we could all live free of poverty.

① outweigh ② prevent ③ persuade ④ refute ⑤ envision

(2) The witnesses' statements ____________ each other, so the facts remain unclear.

① approve ② verify ③ contradict ④ support ⑤ interpret

(3) Scientists are hoping for a(n) ____________ in the search for a cure for cancer.

① harm ② influence ③ evidence ④ breakthrough ⑤ objection

(4) We will continue the race, ____________ of the weather.

① ahead ② regardless ③ overall ④ despite ⑤ independent

SECTION. 03

Society · Culture

사회 · 문화

SECTION 03.

Society · Culture

Cultural relativism is a form of moral relativism that asserts all ethical truth is relative to a specific culture. According to cultural relativism, it is never true to say simply that a certain kind of behavior is right or wrong; rather, it can only ever be true that a certain kind of behavior is right or wrong within a specific society.

The strength of cultural relativism is that it allows us to value our moral intuitions without having to be judgmental about other societies that do not share those intuitions. If we (A) [reject / concede] cultural relativism then we face the difficulty of having to condemn past societies that did not conform to our modern moral code and present societies that do not already accept it. At a time when tolerance is seen as an important value, cultural relativism certainly seems to be a/an ________________.

This strength of cultural relativism, however, is also its weakness. Cultural relativism excuses us from judging the moral status of other cultures when doing so seems (B) [appropriate / inappropriate], but it also renders us powerless to judge the moral status of other cultures when doing so seems to be necessary. For example, faced with a culture that deems slavery morally acceptable, we need to judge that society to be morally (C) [inferior / superior] to our own, for the people who are suffering under the unjust system are in need of being rescued. In order to make such a judgment, we need a cross-cultural moral standard, which is precisely the kind of moral standard that cultural relativism claims does not exist.

VOCAB

relativism 상대주의 (relative 상대적인)
moral 도덕의, 도덕적인
assert 주장하다
ethical 윤리적인
specific 특수한, *특정의
rather 오히려, 차라리
strength 장점, 강점
value 평가하다; 가치
intuition 직관
judgmental 판단의; *비판적인, 주관적 판단의
share 공유하다
face *직면하다; 얼굴
condemn 규탄[비난]하다

1. **What is the author mainly talking about?**

① the necessity of establishing a moral standard
② how to overcome cultural relativism in our society
③ differences of moral standards among cultures
④ differences between the past and the present society
⑤ the advantage and limitation of cultural relativism

2. **위 글 둘째 단락의 빈칸에 들어갈 말로 가장 적절한 것은?**

① big challenge
② traditional obligation
③ attractive option
④ inappropriate path
⑤ difficult choice

3. **위 글의 (A), (B), (C) 각 네모 안에서 문맥에 맞는 어휘를 골라 짝지은 것으로 가장 적절한 것은?**

	(A)		(B)		(C)
①	reject	……	appropriate	……	inferior
②	concede	……	appropriate	……	inferior
③	reject	……	inappropriate	……	superior
④	reject	……	inappropriate	……	inferior
⑤	concede	……	inappropriate	……	inferior

서술형

4. **위 글에 따르면, 타문화가 도덕적으로 옳거나 혹은 그르다는 것을 판단하기 위해 필요한 것은 무엇인지 본문에서 찾아 쓰시오.**

인도의 사티(sati) 관습

사티는 인도의 순장 풍습으로, 남편이 죽으면 그를 화장할 때 아내도 함께 산 채로 화장하는 것이다. 사티를 실천한 여성은 그 순간부터 여신으로 추앙받게 된다. 인도를 지배했던 포르투갈과 네덜란드, 프랑스는 사티를 금지했으나 정식으로 '사티방지법(Sati Prevention Act)'이 실행된 것은 1987년이다. 하지만 여전히 시골 지역에서는 은밀하게 사티가 행해지고 있다고 한다. 홀어미를 부정한 존재로 취급하는 인도 문화의 영향과 남편 이외의 수입원이 전무한 촌락의 여성들에게 있어 사티는 어쩔 수 없는 선택이 되기도 한다.

VOCAB

conform (규칙 · 법 등에) 따르다[맞다]
moral code 도덕률
accept 받아들이다
tolerance 관용
excuse 용서하다; *면제해 주다
status 상태; *지위
render (~을 …하게) 만들다
deem (~을 …라고) 생각하다
slavery 노예제도
unjust 부당한
rescue 구조하다
cross-cultural 이(異)문화간의
precisely 정확히, 바로
claim 주장하다, 공언하다

12 SECTION 03. Society · Culture

One of the techniques/regulatory modes of power/knowledge cited by Michel Foucault, a French philosopher associated with the structuralist and post-structuralist movements, was the Panopticon, an architectural design put forth by Jeremy Bentham in the late 18th century for prisons, insane asylums, schools, hospitals, and factories. Instead of using violent methods, such as torture, the progressive and modern democratic state needed a different sort of system to regulate its citizens. The Panopticon offered a powerful and sophisticated form of internalized coercion, which was achieved through the constant observation of prisoners, each separated from the others, allowing no interaction or no communication. This modern structure would allow guards to continually see inside each cell from their vantage point in a high central tower, unseen by the prisoners. Constant observation would act as a control mechanism, a consciousness of constant surveillance that would be internalized.

The Panopticon was a metaphor that allowed Foucault to explore 1) the relationship between systems of social control and people in a disciplinary situation, and 2) the power-knowledge concept. In his view, power and knowledge come from observing others. It marked the transition to a disciplinary power, with every movement supervised and all events recorded. The result of this surveillance is acceptance of regulations and docility — a normalization of sorts, stemming from the threat of discipline. Suitable behavior is achieved not through total surveillance, but by panoptic discipline and inducing a population to conform by the internalization of <u>this reality</u>. The actions of the observer are based upon this monitoring and the behaviors he sees exhibited; the more one ____(A)____, the more ____(B)____ one becomes. The power comes from the knowledge the observer has accumulated from his observations of actions in a circular fashion, with knowledge and power reinforcing each other. Foucault says that "by being combined and generalized, they attained a level at which the formation of knowledge and the increase in power regularly reinforce one another in a circular process."

FROM 「*Foucault and His Panopticon*」 by Moya K. Mason (응용)

VOCAB

- **regulatory** 규제의
- **cite** 인용하다
- **structuralist** 구조주의자; *구조주의(의)
- **post- structuralist** 후기구조주의(의)
- **architectural** 건축의
- **put forth** 제안하다
- **insane asylum** 정신병원
- **progressive** 진보적인
- **regulate** 규제하다
- **sophisticated** 세련된, 정교한
- **internalize** 내면화하다
- **coercion** 강압, 억압
- **continually** 계속해서
- **vantage point** 유리한 위치
- **metaphor** 은유

1. 파놉티콘에 대한 설명 중, 위 글의 내용과 일치하지 않는 것은?

① 제러미 벤담이 설계한 건축 디자인을 일컫는다.
② 물리적인 힘을 가해 수감자들을 통제하는 시스템이다.
③ 수감자들은 서로 교류 없이 격리된 곳에 놓이게 된다.
④ 감시자들은 높은 중앙 탑에서 죄수들을 관찰한다.
⑤ 감시에 대한 자각이 수감자로 하여금 감시를 내재화하게 한다.

2. **According to the passage, which of the following is NOT a likely panoptic discipline?**

① transportation cards that record where users have been
② internet use that can be tracked through browser history
③ credit card details that can show what users have purchased
④ websites that allow users to upload and share videos they have made
⑤ electronic ID cards that have a chip containing personal information on them

서술형

3. 위 글의 밑줄 친 this reality가 가리키는 것을 우리말로 쓰시오.

4. 위 글의 빈칸 (A)와 (B)에 들어갈 말로 가장 적절한 것은?

	(A)		(B)
①	conforms	······	separated
②	observes	······	controlled
③	interacts	······	separated
④	observes	······	powerful
⑤	conforms	······	powerful

미셸 푸코(Michel Foucault, 1926–1984)

미셸 푸코는 후기구조주의를 대표하는 프랑스 출신의 철학자로, 인간의 지식이 형성되고 변하는 과정을 중점적으로 연구하였다. 그 과정에서 그는 각 시대의 지식[앎]은 무의식적 문화의 체계에 그 기저를 두고 있다는 결론을 내리게 된다. 그가 주목한 또 다른 연구 대상은 억압적인 권력의 구조이다. 이러한 그의 연구 성과를 나타내는 대표적 저서로는 「광기와 비이성」과 「감시와 처벌」이 있다. 「광기와 비이성」에서는 논리성을 대표하는 합리적 이성을 비판하고 소외된 비이성적 사고, 광기(狂氣)의 의미와 역사를 연구했다. 1970년대에 저술한 「감시와 처벌」에서는 지배계급이 체제 유지를 위해 법률과 억압적 통치구조를 어떻게 이용했는지 냉철히 분석하였다.

12

SECTION 03.
사회 · 문화

VOCAB

disciplinary 규율상의, 징계의 (discipline 규율, 통제)
transition 이행, 과도
supervise 감독하다, 통제하다
surveillance 감시
docility 온순, 순종
normalization 표준화
stem from ~에서 생겨나다
panoptic 모든 것이 한눈에 보이는
induce 유도하다
conform 순응하다
exhibit 전시하다; *드러내다
accumulate 축적하다
circular 원형의; *순회하는, 순환적인
reinforce 강화하다
generalize 일반화하다
regularly 정기적으로

13

SECTION 03.
Society · Culture

Ageism occurs across the human lifespan and is not limited to any particular age group. In fact, age is one of the first characteristics we notice about other people, whether they are young or old. ① From a person's perceived age, we make assumptions about their competencies, beliefs and abilities. For example, we may consider an older job applicant ② to be unsuitable because we imagine he or she will be forgetful, slow, or of poor health. We see young people in the street and associate them with antisocial behaviors. Ageism is the one p__________ that we all experience, regardless of our race, ethnicity, and gender.

The most widespread occurrence of ageism is that which is directed toward older adults: think of all the "over-the-hill" jokes ③ make as people approach middle age. It is this implicit nature of negative attitudes towards old age that makes ageism so insidious and difficult to counter. Furthermore, society tends to highlight exceptions to the commonly held stereotypes. Consider ④ how frequently the media reports on "exceptional" older adults, such as the astronaut John Glenn, or the woman who first climbed *Mt. Rainier at age 77.

Given that we are all aging, ageism encompasses the inner fear that many of us have of our own aging. Because humans tend to blend their personal and public attitudes, studying and understanding ageism is particularly complex and challenging. Accordingly, professionals need to become aware of their own ageism ⑤ when studying and working with older adults.

*Mt. Rainier 미국 워싱턴 주 Cascade 산맥의 최고봉

VOCAB

ageism 연령차별
occur 일어나다, 생기다 (occurrence 발생, 일어남)
lifespan 수명
particular 특정한
characteristic 특징
notice 알아채다, 감지하다
perceive 인식하다
assumption 가정, 추정
competency 능력, 역량
job applicant 취업 지원자, 구직자
unsuitable 부적당한
forgetful 잘 잊어버리는
associate A with B A와 B를 연관짓다
antisocial 반사회적인
regardless of ~에 관계없이
race 인종
ethnicity 민족성
gender 성(별)

1. 다음 중 위 글을 통해 알 수 있는 사실이 아닌 것은?

① Ageism is deeply rooted in our socio-cultural subconscious.
② Ageism makes it hard for senior citizens to find jobs.
③ Young people tend to be free from age discrimination.
④ Ageism comes from our inner fear of growing old.
⑤ One's attitude towards aging can affect their study of ageism.

서술형

2. 문맥을 고려하여 위 글 첫째 단락의 빈칸에 알맞은 한 단어를 쓰시오.

3. 위 글의 ①~⑤ 중에서 어법상 틀린 것을 찾아 바르게 고치시오.

4. 위 글 셋째 단락의 밑줄 친 문장을 우리말로 해석하시오.

13

SECTION 03.
사회 · 문화

VOCAB

widespread 널리 퍼진, 일반적인
over-the-hill 인생의 전성기가 지난
approach 접근하다
implicit 함축[암시]적인
insidious 교활한, 음흉한
counter 대항하다, 맞서다
highlight 강조하다
exception 예외 (exceptional 우수한; *예외적인)
stereotype 고정관념
frequently 자주, 빈번히
astronaut 우주비행사
encompass 포함하다
inner 내적인
blend 섞다
attitude 태도, 사고방식
challenging 도전적인; *힘든
professional 지적 직업의, 전문직인
become[be] aware of ~을 알아차리다[알다]

14

SECTION 03.

Society · Culture

(A)

The social state is at once so natural, so necessary, and so habitual to man, that, except in some unusual circumstances or by an effort of voluntary abstraction, he never conceives himself otherwise than as a member of a body. Now, society between human beings is manifestly impossible on any other footing than that the interests of all ① are to be consulted. In this way people grow up unable to conceive as possible to them a state of total disregard of other people's interests. They are also familiar with the fact of cooperating with others, and proposing to themselves a collective, not ____________, interest, as the aim (at least for the time being) of their actions. So long as they are cooperating, their ends are identified with ② that of others; there is at least a temporary feeling that the interests of others are their own interests.

(B)

The annual revenue of every society is always precisely equal to the exchangeable value of the whole annual produce of its industry, or rather is precisely the same thing with that exchangeable value. As every individual, therefore, endeavors as much as he can, both to employ his capital in the support of domestic industry, and so ③ to direct that industry that its produce may be of the greatest value, every individual necessarily labors to render the annual revenue of the society ④ as great as he can. He generally, indeed, neither intends to promote ____________ interest, nor knows how much he is promoting it. By preferring the support of domestic ⑤ to that of foreign industry, he intends only his own security; and by directing that industry in such a manner as its produce may be of the greatest value, he intends only his own gain; and he is in this, as in many other cases, led by an invisible hand to promote an end which was no part of his intention. By pursuing his own interest, he frequently promotes that of the society more effectually than when he really intends to promote it.

FROM 2013 서울시립대 수시 논술 (응용)

VOCAB

(A)

habitual 습관적인; *타고난
circumstance 환경, 상황
voluntary 자발적인; *고의의
abstraction 추상; *분리, 제거
conceive 상상하다, 생각하다
manifestly 명백히, 분명하게
footing 입장, 기반
consult 상담하다; *고려하다
disregard 무시
cooperate 협력[합동]하다
collective 집단적인
identify 동일시하다
temporary 일시적인

서술형

1. 위 글을 읽고, 각 개인이 사회적 이익을 증진시키게 되는 배경(이유)에 있어서의 차이점을 중심으로 (A)와 (B)의 내용을 비교하시오.

2. 위 글의 ①~⑤ 중에서 어법상 틀린 것을 찾아 바르게 고치시오.

3. 위 글 (A)와 (B)의 빈칸에 들어갈 말로 각각 알맞은 것은?

	(A)		(B)
①	a national	······	the individual
②	a domestic	······	the foreign
③	an individual	······	the public
④	a foreign	······	the domestic
⑤	a financial	······	the political

서술형

4. 위 글 (B)의 밑줄 친 it이 가리키는 것을 본문의 단어를 활용하여 쓰시오. (5단어)

공리주의(功利主義)

공리주의에서 바라본 인간은 쾌락을 추구하고 고통을 피하고자 하는 본성을 지닌 존재이다. 인간의 행동에 대한 윤리적 판단의 기준도 이러한 공리적 원리에 기초한다. 즉, 어떤 행동이 인간의 쾌락과 행복을 늘리는 데 기여한다면 그것은 선한 행위이지만, 고통과 불행을 야기한다면 그것은 악한 행위인 것이다. 나아가 '최대 다수의 최대 행복(the greatest happiness of the greatest number)'라는 공리주의의 기초원리를 실현하기 위해서는 가능한 한 많은 사람들이 최대한의 행복을 느낄 수 있도록 해야 하는데, 이를 위해서는 사회가 개인의 행위를 법적으로 규제할 필요가 있다. 여기서 민주적 의회제도의 필요성이 대두된다. 공리주의를 주창한 제러미 벤담과 존 스튜어트 밀 등의 철학적 급진파는 이후 다수결의 원리에 기반을 둔 민주주의 제도의 발달에 커다란 영향을 미쳤다.

VOCAB

(B)
annual 매년의, 연례의
revenue 수익
exchangeable value 교환 가치
industry 산업; (조직화된) 노동
endeavor 노력; *노력하다
employ 고용하다; *이용하다
capital 자본금, 자산
domestic *국내의; 가정의
direct 지휘하다, 안내하다
necessarily 반드시, 필연적으로
render (어떤 상태가 되게) 만들다
intend 의도하다 (intention 의도)
promote 촉진하다
prefer ~을 (더) 좋아하다
security 안전
invisible 보이지 않는
end 끝; *목적
pursue 추구하다
effectually 효과적으로

15

SECTION 03.
Society · Culture

The primarily Islamic tradition of females covering themselves from head to foot with a *burqa is an example of the intrinsic difficulty in evaluating the extent to which cultural practices promote individual autonomy. Critics of the burqa and similar *garments, especially critics from Western cultures, deem (A) them physically oppressive with the weight of the fabric; psychologically oppressive in that they seem to make women devoid of distinctiveness; and emotionally oppressive in that they are yet another manifestation of a male-dominated society in which women are subordinate. According to this view, the tradition of wearing such clothing is unjustified because it greatly restricts the autonomy of women.

Defenders of this practice, however, argue the opposite view. They insist that coverings like the burqa actually foster autonomy and liberate women for a number of reasons. For example, a burqa prevents women from being viewed as sexual objects; it encourages unity among female Muslims; and it promotes the appearance of holiness. Proponents of the burqa also ask questions of Western critics which force (B) them to examine their own clothing culture, such as, "Why is it considered oppressive to wear a head scarf but liberating to wear a miniskirt?" They insist the answer lies in the assumptions each culture makes about the women involved and their ability to make choices. They say that if the assumptions are wrong, and the wearing of the burqa and its variants is actually a matter of personal preference, then it is completely justified as a legitimate expression of individual autonomy.

*burqa 이슬람 여성들이 걸치는 장옷　*garments 옷, 의상

VOCAB

primarily 첫째로; *주로, 무엇보다 먼저
Islamic 이슬람교의
intrinsic 본질적인, 고유의
evaluate 평가하다
extent 정도
practice 연습; 실행; *관습
promote 승진시키다; *조장하다
autonomy 자율(성), 자치
critic 비평가, 비난자
deem (~을 …라고) 생각하다
physically 신체적으로
oppressive 억압하는, 압박하는
fabric 직물, 옷감
psychologically 심리적으로
in that ~라는 점에서
devoid of ~이 결여된
distinctiveness 독특함, 특색있음
emotionally 정서적으로
manifestation 명시, 표명
male-dominated 남성 지배의
subordinate 종속되는, 복종하는
unjustified 정당하지 않은
restrict 제한하다
defender 옹호자

서술형

1. 위 글의 밑줄 친 (A) them과 (B) them이 가리키는 바를 각각 우리말로 쓰시오.

2. 위 글에서 이슬람 국가의 여성들이 부르카를 입는 것을 비판하는 사람들의 주장을 요약하는 문장을 찾아 밑줄을 그으시오.

서술형

3. What does the underlined question in the 2nd paragraph suggest? (in Korean)

4. Which of the following is NOT a remark made by advocates of the burqa tradition?

① 부르카는 여성들이 성적 대상으로 보이는 것을 막아준다.
② 부르카는 이슬람 여성들 사이의 유대를 증진시킨다.
③ 부르카를 입는 여성들은 대체로 자긍심이 높다.
④ 부르카를 입는 여성들은 외적으로 경건해 보인다.
⑤ 부르카를 입는 것은 여성들의 선택의 문제일 수도 있다.

아프간 여성들과 부르카(burqa)

부르카는 원래 아프간 인구의 절반을 차지하는 파쉬툰족 여성들의 전통 복장이었다. 시골에서는 대부분 친족들이 모여 살기 때문에 머리 정도를 덮는 것이 관례였지만, 도심지역에서는 다른 종족 혹은 낯선 남성들로부터 여성을 보호한다는 명분으로 지금의 부르카를 착용하기 시작했다. 부르카는 남성과 여성의 불평등, 여성 인권의 경시 등의 의미가 숨어 있는, 이 나라의 오랜 전통적인 관습 중 하나로 볼 수 있다. 그러나 아프가니스탄의 치안 상태가 극도로 악화되었을 때 부르카는 실제로 여성을 보호해주는 역할을 하기도 했다. 탈레반 정권은 모든 여성들이 부르카를 강제로 착용하도록 법으로 정했는데, 그 이유는 치안의 부재로 인해 여성이 납치될 수 있다는 것이었다. 그 후 탈레반 정권이 붕괴되고 자유가 주어진 지금도 많은 여성들은 여전히 남편의 권유로 부르카를 착용하고 있다. 그러나 수도 카불을 중심으로 여성 탄압의 상징이었던 부르카 벗기가 진행되고 있는데, 다른 한편에서는 부르카를 여전히 이슬람 전통의상에 대한 자부심으로 여기며, 여성을 외모로만 보지 않겠다는 평등의식의 표현으로 생각하는 이들이 부르카 착용의 필요성을 외치고 있기도 하다.

VOCAB

opposite 반대의
covering 덮개
foster *조성하다; 양육하다
liberate 자유롭게 하다
prevent 방해하다, 막다
sexual 성의, 성적인
object 대상(물)
encourage 고무[조장]하다
unity 단결
Muslim 이슬람교도
appearance 외모
holiness 성스러움, 경건함
proponent 지지자
force 강요하다
examine 조사하다
lie in ~에 있다
assumption 가정, 가설
involve *관련시키다; 수반하다
variant 변형
preference 선호
completely 완전히
justify 정당화하다
legitimate *타당한; 합법적인

SECTION 03.
Word Test

정답 | P.123

1. 다음 밑줄 친 단어의 의미로 알맞은 것을 고르시오.

(1) A <u>legitimate</u> government can return once the army is overthrown.

① morally good ② allowed by law ③ very powerful
④ not changing ⑤ not controlled by something

(2) The company launched a <u>progressive</u> childcare policy for employees.

① recommending something ② saying logically ③ encouraged to do
④ unwilling to changes ⑤ supporting new methods

2. 다음 문장의 빈칸에 알맞은 단어를 보기에서 찾아 쓰시오.

보기 | collective intuition exceptional coercion

(1) Most students do not want to study under ______________.

(2) This is a(n) ______________ case; I've never seen anything like it before.

(3) The team admitted that there was ______________ responsibility for the failure of the previous project.

(4) I can't explain how I knew — My ______________ tells me there's been an accident.

3. 다음 문장의 밑줄 친 부분과 바꿔 쓸 수 있는 단어를 고르시오.

(1) The film's plot was so <u>complex</u> that I couldn't follow it.

① organic ② vague ③ complicated ④ habitual ⑤ implicit

(2) They were told to take whatever action they <u>deemed</u> necessary.

① excluded ② investigated ③ misunderstood ④ considered ⑤ highlighted

(3) I have never read a letter that was so <u>devoid</u> of emotion as this one.

① aware ② widespread ③ opposite ④ unjust ⑤ empty

4. 우리말에 맞게 빈칸에 공통으로 들어갈 알맞은 단어를 쓰시오.

· He is determined to put his thoughts into ______________.
(그는 자신의 생각을 실행에 옮기기로 단단히 결심했다.)

· You will become one of the faster sprinters on the team with ______________.
(너는 연습하면 팀의 빠른 단거리 주자 중 한 명이 될 수 있을 것이다.)

· Respecting the older generation is common ______________ in many Asian countries.
(노년층을 존중하는 것은 많은 아시아 국가의 일반적 관습이다.)

SECTION.04

Information Technology

정보 통신

16

SECTION 04.
Information Technology

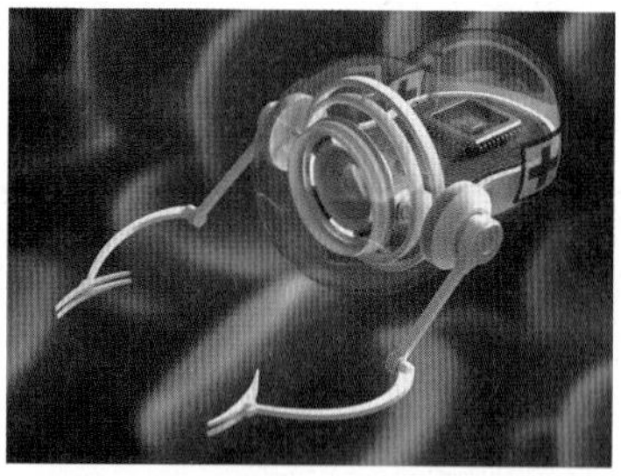

With technological innovations advancing at an exponential rate, interfacing physical reality with virtual reality is becoming more commonplace, with some experts predicting the widespread existence of virtual humans by as early as 2030. The development of nanobots, miniature robots as small as a human blood cell, and nonbiological intelligence affords opportunities for reshaping our interaction with the world.

Through the utilization of nanobots, experiencing a virtual world would not differ appreciably from experiencing the "real world," as external stimuli must be translated into signals in the brain. Nanobots strategically positioned in close proximity to sensory neurons could be programmed to modify the communication of interneuronal connections by either inhibiting or precipitating the firing of the neighboring neuron. The nanobots could remain present yet inactive in their position until the person wishes to enter the virtual environment, at which time ______________________________.

(A) The hybrid of human and computer thinking may seem like something out of a sci-fi film, but nonbiological cognition has already made its way into humans. (B) In addition to creating virtual worlds, the emerging technology gives rise to nonbiological thinking, and scientists are making inroads into incorporating machine intelligence into human intelligence. (C) Neural implants are currently being used in patients suffering from Parkinson's disease to act as a replacement for cells with impaired functioning. As the technology progresses, (humans' capacity, mental models of the world, from machines, to construct, be, sets us apart, a characteristic, that, will no longer).

VOCAB

innovation 혁신
exponential 기하급수적인, 급격한
interface 인터페이스; 접점; *연결하다
virtual 가상의
commonplace 아주 흔한
predict 예측[예견]하다
existence 존재, 실재
afford 여유가 되다; *제공하다
opportunity 기회
reshape 새 형태를 취하다
utilization 이용, 활용
appreciably 눈에 띄게
external 외부의
stimulus 자극 (*pl.* stimuli)
translate 번역하다; *(다른 형태로) 바꾸다
strategically 전략적으로
proximity 가까움, 근접
sensory 감각의
modify 수정하다, 바꾸다
inhibit 억제하다

1. 다음 중 위 글의 내용과 일치하지 않는 것은?

① 2030년쯤에는 가상 인간이 흔해질 거라고 예상된다.
② 나노봇을 통해 가상 세계를 현실 세계처럼 체험할 수 있다.
③ 나노봇은 전략적으로 감각 뉴런 가까이에 위치한다.
④ 나노봇은 근처 뉴런의 신호를 억제하는 기능만 있다.
⑤ 비생물학적 지능은 이미 일부 영역에서 사용되고 있다.

2. 위 글 둘째 단락의 빈칸에 들어갈 말로 가장 적절한 것은?

① the doctors could remove them and replace them with biological material
② the person would have to use an external computing system as an interface
③ there would be no need to alter the anticipated neural processes of the body
④ they would act in accordance with the brain to send out the proper messages
⑤ they could be activated to intercept sensory input and fire alternative signals

3. 위 글 셋째 단락의 (A)~(C)를 글의 흐름에 맞게 배열한 것으로 가장 적절한 것은?

① (A) - (C) - (B)
② (B) - (A) - (C)
③ (B) - (C) - (A)
④ (C) - (A) - (B)
⑤ (C) - (B) - (A)

4. 위 글의 셋째 단락의 괄호 안의 단어를 아래에 주어진 우리말의 뜻에 맞게 배열하시오.

인간의 세상에 대한 정신 모형을 구성하는 능력은 더 이상 우리를 기계와 구별하게 하는 특징이 아닐 것이다.

16

SECTION 04.
정보 통신

VOCAB

precipitate 촉발하다
neighboring 인접한
inactive 활동하지 않는; *사용되지 않는
hybrid 잡종; *혼성
cognition 인지
make one's way into ~안으로 들어가다
emerging 신생의, 신흥의
make inroads into ~을 잠식하다[침입하다]
incorporate 포함하다
neural 신경의
replacement 교체, 대체
impaired 손상된
capacity 용량; *능력
construct 건설하다; *구성하다
set A apart B A을 B와 다르게 만들다

17

SECTION 04. Information Technology

Advancements in quantum theory, a concept that defines how particles behave at the atomic and subatomic level, can be utilized in computer technology, a practice known as quantum computing. This field has the potential to enhance computer performance by a billion times or more, as the simultaneous processing of tasks could be accomplished at unprecedented speeds.

The capacity of high-performance quantum computers is facilitated by quantum *superposition, a phenomenon in which electrons hold two states, for example both 0 and 1, at the same time. As long as the electrons are not observed or measured, they continue to behave as if they were in both states. To control superposition, scientists use the process of *entanglement, in which a force is applied to two atoms to instantaneously create an interaction between them, no matter how distantly they're separated. If an atom is not disturbed, its spin state will be in multiple directions. However, if it is disrupted, it instantly begins spinning in a single direction. Meanwhile, the other atom it is entangled with will begin spinning in the opposite direction. Knowledge about one entangled atom, therefore, ______________________________. Using superposition and entanglement, undisturbed pairs of, qubits (quantum bits) can exhibit four states — 00, 01, 10 and 11 — at the same time, as compared to traditional computer bits, which can only exhibit one — 0 or 1. Adding qubits to the system allows the computing power to increase exponentially.

While there are numerous potential applications of quantum computing, these are limited by our current technology. Few algorithms have been devised for quantum technology, and scientists are still developing methods for keeping quantum computing devices at a low enough temperature for operation. Once these obstacles are overcome, we can fully reap the benefits of quantum computing.

*superposition 중첩 *entanglement 얽힘

VOCAB

advancement 발전, 진보
quantum 양자
define 정의하다, 규정하다
particle 입자
behave 처신[행동]하다; *행동[반응]을 보이다
atomic 원자의 (atom 원자)
subatomic 원자보다 작은, 아원자의
utilize 활용[이용]하다
potential 잠재력; 잠재적인
enhance 향상시키다
simultaneous 동시의
accomplish 완수하다, 성취하다
unprecedented 전례 없는
capacity 용량, 수용력; *생산 능력
facilitate 용이하게 하다
phenomenon 현상

1. **What is the best title for the passage?**

① A Newly Introduced Theory: Entanglement
② Quantum Computing: From Theory to Reality
③ Examples of the Successful Application of Quantum Computing
④ A New Possibility for Virtual Worlds through Quantum Computing
⑤ The Quantum Computers That Are Bringing the Economy up to Speed

서술형

2. **위 글을 읽고 'quantum superposition' 현상이 무엇인지 우리말로 쓰시오.**

3. **위 글의 둘째 단락의 빈칸에 들어갈 말로 가장 적절한 것은?**

① provides information about the other
② replaces the atom with multiple qubits
③ is unable to become involved with the other
④ makes the atom spin in multiple directions
⑤ undergoes increased force during entanglement

4. **According to the passage, which of the following is NOT true?**

① Quantum theory is concerned with the motion and interaction of subatomic particles.
② Computer technology will be able to benefit from improved quantum theory.
③ Entanglement affects the atoms whether they are close together or not.
④ Qubits can show four states simultaneously while superposition and entanglement take place.
⑤ Quantum technology uses algorithms that fix temperature to ensure optimum operation.

양자(quantum)와 양자역학(quantum mechanics)

'얼마나 많이'의 라틴어인 'quantus'에서 유래한 양자(quantum)는 상호작용과 관련된 모든 물리적 독립체의 최소단위를 뜻한다. 운동량, 에너지 등의 물리량이 연속값 없이 특정 최소단위로 표현이 가능할 때, 그 최소 단위의 양을 나타낸다. 이러한 양자를 기초로 해 원자, 분자 등의 미시적 대상에 적용되는 물리학을 양자역학이라고 한다. 1920년대 독일의 물리학자인 하이젠베르크가 만든 행렬역학과 오스트리아의 물리학자인 슈뢰딩거가 만든 파동역학이 정립되자 양자이론은 급속도로 발전하였다. 양자역학은 현대에도 지속해서 진보하고 있으며, 나노기술과 양자컴퓨터 모두 양자역학이 바탕이 된 것이다.

17

SECTION 04.
정보 통신

VOCAB

electron 전자
measure 측정하다
instantaneously 순간적으로, 즉석으로
distantly 멀리, 떨어져서
separate 분리되다; *분리하다
disturb 방해하다; *건드리다
disrupt 방해하다, 혼란시키다
instantly 즉각, 즉시
entangle 얽어매다
exhibit 전시하다; *드러내다, 보이다
exponentially 기하급수적으로
application 지원; *적용, 응용
algorithm 연산(법), 알고리즘
devise 창안[고안]하다
temperature 온도, 기온
obstacle 장애, 장애물
reap 거두다, 수확하다

18

SECTION 04.
Information Technology

VOCAB

(A)
dissemination 보급
increasingly 점점 더
rapid (속도가) 빠른
thanks to ~ 덕분에
advancement 발전, 진보
coexist 공존하다
threat 위협
privacy 사생활
confer 상의하다; *부여하다
safeguard (권익을) 보호하다
control over ~에 대한 통제
protection 보호
vulnerable ~에 취약한, 연약한
erosion 침식

(A)

The dissemination of information in the digital age has become increasingly rapid thanks to social networking services and cloud technology. (①) However, with these advancements coexists a threat to privacy, as information shared online is difficult, if not impossible, to remove. (②) The European Court of Justice has officially conferred "the right to be forgotten" on citizens, safeguarding individuals' control over their personal information. (③) Without such protections in place, individuals are highly vulnerable to the erosion of personal privacy. (④) By putting the right to be forgotten into place, we can expand the level of control people have over their personal privacy and protect individual rights. (⑤)

(B)

The amount of personal data available online and the technologically advanced methods of gathering such data have seen ⓐ <u>unprecedented</u> growth in recent years. Supporters of the right to be forgotten argue that citizens should be able to have certain data about them ⓑ <u>sustained</u> from the public sphere. However, this is in direct conflict with the right to freedom of speech, a central tenet of a free society. By ⓒ <u>upholding</u> the right to be forgotten, we are denying people the right to know and restricting the free flow of information. The right to be forgotten is also ⓓ <u>unfeasible</u> due to the considerable expenditure needed to develop and implement technology capable of carrying out the necessary "forgetting." Though there is a critical need for the responsible sharing of information, it should not be fulfilled to the ⓔ <u>detriment</u> of our essential freedoms.

1. **Which is the focus of (A) and (B)?**

① government policies that hinder the development of IT
② growing concerns about online privacy issues in Europe
③ whether or not the right to be forgotten should be respected
④ whether legally regulated copyrights are a benefit or a hindrance
⑤ the pros and cons of using social networking systems to share information reliably

2. **위 글 (A)의 ①~⑤ 중에서 다음 주어진 문장이 들어가기에 가장 적절한 곳은?**

The practical implication of this right is the requirement that search engines exclude or remove from their search results any data that is outdated or of a deeply personal nature.

3. **위 글 (B)의 ⓐ~ⓔ 중, 문맥상 낱말의 쓰임이 적절하지 <u>않은</u> 것은?**

서술형

4. **위 글을 읽고, '잊힐 권리'에 반대하는 이들이 내세우는 근거 두 가지를 우리말로 쓰시오.**

5. **위 글을 읽고 추론할 수 있는 것으로 가장 적절한 것은?**

① 언론의 자유를 지키는 데에는 많은 사회적 비용이 발생한다.
② 유럽 국가들이 타국가들보다 개인 권리 보호에 앞장서고 있다.
③ 양쪽 모두 정보를 공유하는 것의 중요성에 대해 동의하고 있다.
④ 디지털 기술의 발전은 잊힐 권리에 대한 이슈를 더욱 논쟁거리로 만들었다.
⑤ 새로운 정보가 넘치는 현대 사회에서 시대에 뒤처진 정보는 가치가 없다.

18

SECTION 04.
정보 통신

VOCAB

(B)
available 이용할 수 있는; *입수할 수 있는
unprecedented 유례없는
sphere 구; *영역
in conflict with ~와 충돌하는
tenet 주의, 신조
uphold 옹호하다
restrict 제한하다, 방해하다
unfeasible 실시하기 어려운
considerable 상당한, 많은
expenditure 지출, 비용
implement 시행하다
critical 비판적인; *중대한
responsible 책임감 있는
fulfill 실행하다, 완수하다
to the detriment of 결국 ~을 해치며
essential 본질적인, 없어서는 안 될

19

SECTION 04.
Information Technology

In the mid-1800s, a splendid accomplishment was attained in technology, which put an end to the modern natural sciences as represented by Newtonian mechanics. At the 1851 London Fair, so many novel and striking products were shown it seemed to prove Francis Bacon's projection that all things could be realized. Inasmuch as technology became highly developed and played an unprecedented role in social life over the next hundred years, many have called that period "the glorious beginning" of the technological era. However, while *homage was made to the technological progress, warnings were issued.

For example, in his novel *Brave New World*, Aldous L. Huxley described a future dominated by technology. In this society there would be great comfort, but at the cost of freedom, beauty, and privacy. In various science fiction novels, technology controlled humans. Robots reigning over the world indirectly reflected <u>this fear</u>. ① The formerly popular attitude that technology was a powerful tool for the betterment of humankind seemed to be one-sided at best. ② The view that technology was simply harmless did not accord with actuality. ③ In reality, the arrival of so many of the latest devices has made day-to-day living more convenient for everyone. ④ Slowly, the anti-technological tendency began to grow, primarily because the tremendous destructive power of technological progress made during wars constituted a grave danger to the planet and to the existence of humans themselves. ⑤ It was also due to such harmful outcomes caused by technological progress as traffic accidents, pollution of air and water, noise, and damage to the environment. These causes, and their negative effects, were immediately obvious. On a much deeper level, these negative effects were mainly due to the domination of humans by technology.

*homage 존경, 경의

VOCAB

splendid 화려한, 눈부신
accomplishment 업적
attain 달성하다
put an end to ~을 끝내다
represent 나타내다; *대표하다
mechanics 역학
fair 공정한; *박람회
novel *새로운; 진기한; 소설
striking 인상적인; 놀라운
projection 투사, 발사; *예상,전망
inasmuch as *~인 까닭에; ~하는 한
unprecedented 전례가 없는
era 시대
progress 진보, 발전
issue 문제; 발행; ~판; *나오다; 발행하다
dominate 지배하다
at the cost of ~을 희생하여
privacy 사생활

1. **What is the author mainly talking about?**

① how modern technology can progress further
② an introduction to famous science fiction novels
③ the advantages brought by the technological era
④ the negative aspects of technological development
⑤ the technological era and the responsibility of a novelist

2. **According to the passage, which of the following is true?**

① What Newton accomplished was criticized by modern scientists.
② Aldous Huxley was the first person to present a negative view of technology.
③ From the beginning, many people had serious doubts about the power of technology.
④ Technological development has resulted in formidable danger to mankind.
⑤ Environmental pollution has nothing to do with the development of technology.

서술형

3. **위 글 둘째 단락의 밑줄 친 this fear가 가리키는 바를 우리말로 설명하시오.**

4. **위 글 둘째 단락에서 내용의 흐름과 관계없는 문장은?**

올더스 헉슬리 「멋진 신세계(*Brave New World*)」

1932년에 출판된 풍자적 미래소설이다. 역설적 의미의 소설 제목은 셰익스피어의 희곡 「템페스트」에서 따온 것이다.
문명이 극도로 발달하여 모든 것을 지배하게 된 세계에서 사람들은 부모가 누구인지도 모른 채 인공수정으로 태어나 유리병 속에서 자란다. 지능의 우열만이 미래의 역할과 지위를 결정하는 요소가 된다. 고민이나 불안은 신경안정제 '소마(soma)'로 해결하며, 옛 문명을 보존하고 있는 나라에서 온 야만인은 이런 문명국에서 살 수 없어 자살하고 만다. '멋진 신세계'에서 사람들을 괴롭히는 것은 자신이 사고하지 않고 웃고 있다는 사실이 아니라 무엇에 대해 웃고 있는지, 왜 사고를 멈추는지를 모른다는 사실이다. '멋진 신세계'는 결국 모든 인간성과 개성이 상실되고 창조적 이성이 억압받고 말살되는 '끔찍한 신세계'이다.

VOCAB

reign 지배하다
reflect 반영하다
formerly 이전에
betterment 개량, 개선; *진보
one-sided 편파적인
at best 기껏해야
accord with ~와 일치하다
tendency 경향
primarily 첫째로; *주로
tremendous 엄청난
destructive 파괴적인
constitute 구성하다; *만들어 내다, 야기하다
grave 엄숙한; *심각한
the planet 지구
existence 존재
outcome *결과; 성과
immediately 곧, 즉시
obvious 명백한
domination 지배

20 SECTION 04.
Information Technology

Contemporary commuters who find themselves stuck in heavy traffic on the journey home may pass the time ① contemplating all the tasks that need to be accomplished once they reach their destination. In the near future, however, the Internet of Things (IoT) may allow them to do much more than that. While their smart cars navigate the roadways, the commuters will be able to remotely pre-heat their ovens, activate their washing machines, and ② impede their refrigerators to perform an inventory of their own contents and prepare a shopping list based on the results.

This may sound unrealistically futuristic, but many of the appliances and devices we already own ③ possess embedded computing systems of one degree of sophistication or another. What the IoT does is create a virtual network of these physical objects, allowing them to collect and exchange a wide range of data. In a sense, it serves as a bridge that allows for the direct integration of the physical realm into ______________. It is ④ estimated that by 2020 there will be nearly 50 billion individual objects wired into the IoT. This will lead to improvements in countless everyday tasks in terms of both efficiency and economy.

The manufacturing industry is currently at the vanguard of the IoT revolution, which is not surprising considering the benefits inherent in the adoption of such technology. The terms "Industry 4.0" and "the fourth industrial revolution" are currently being employed to refer to the next wave of manufacturing advances and innovations expected to ⑤ accompany the advent of the IoT. The factories of tomorrow will possess computer systems that continuously monitor and evaluate physical performance, using this information to make decentralized decisions, which is expected to boost efficiency.

VOCAB

contemporary 동시대의; *현대의
commuter 통근자
journey 여행; *(…으로의) 길
contemplate 고려하다, 생각하다
accomplish 성취하다, 완수하다
destination 목적지
smart car 자동 운전 승용차
navigate 길을 찾다
remotely 멀리서, 원격으로
activate 작동시키다
impede 방해하다
refrigerator 냉장고
inventory 재고 목록; *재고 조사
content *내용물; 내용
unrealistically 비현실적으로
futuristic 미래의, 시대를 앞서는
appliance 가전제품
device 장치, 기구
possess 소유하다; *(자질 · 특징을) 지니다
embed 끼워 넣다, 파묻다
sophistication 세련, 정교함

1. **What is the main idea of each paragraph? Choose the correct choice from the box below.**

(1) paragraph 1 _____ (2) paragraph 2 _____ (3) paragraph 3 _____

① what the IoT means for small businesses ② how the IoT functions and a forecast for its future ③ practical examples of how the IoT could affect people's lives ④ examples of successful business models in "Industry 4.0" ⑤ the definition of "Industry 4.0" and the way the IoT will transform the manufacturing industry

2. **위 글 둘째 단락의 빈칸에 들어갈 말로 가장 적절한 것은?**

① humanity ② data exchange ③ cyberspace
④ the mental realm ⑤ individual objects

3. **Mark T(True) or F(False) for the following statements.**

(1) Physically remote problems will not be easily circumvented obstacles in the IoT era. □ T □ F

(2) People already have many electronic devices, and these devices are expected to be networked to the IoT in the near future. □ T □ F

(3) The manufacturing industry is at the forefront of all industries in embracing the IoT. □ T □ F

(4) The fourth industrial revolution represents the development phase of manufacturing within the IoT era. □ T □ F

4. **위 글의 ①~⑤ 중, 문맥상 낱말의 쓰임이 적절하지 않은 것은?**

20

SECTION 04.

정보 통신

VOCAB

virtual (컴퓨터를 이용한) 가상의
integration 통합
estimate 추정하다
improvement 진보, 증진, 향상
efficiency 효율(성), 능률
manufacturing industry 제조업
vanguard 선봉, 선두
inherent 타고난, 고유의
industrial 산업의
employ 고용하다; *이용하다
innovation 혁신
accompany ~을 수반하다
advent 도래, 출현
continuously 끊임없이
decentralized 분산적
boost 신장시키다

SECTION 04.

Word Test

정답 | P.123

1. 다음 설명의 내용이 맞으면 T(True), 틀리면 F(False)를 괄호 안에 쓰시오.

(1) Sophistication is the quality of being more advanced than others. (　　)

(2) Stimuli are areas where there are many houses and buildings usually built at once. (　　)

(3) An accomplishment is something successful that is gained after much effort. (　　)

(4) An expenditure is a particular skill or knowledge in a certain subject by training. (　　)

2. 다음 문장의 밑줄 친 부분과 바꿔 쓸 수 있는 단어를 고르시오.

(1) The police will monitor the behavior of the crowd during the summit conference.

① reject　② prohibit　③ observe　④ interrupt　⑤ assist

(2) Recording meetings may inhibit people from expressing their ideas.

① reassure　② encourage　③ induce　④ accentuate　⑤ prevent

(3) The future eradication of diseases such as cancer is in the realm of possibility.

① construction　② area　③ space　④ capacity　⑤ particle

3. 다음 문장의 빈칸에 알맞은 말을 보기에서 찾아 쓰시오. (단, 필요한 경우에는 어형을 바꾸시오.)

보기 | uphold　considerable　represent　simultaneous

(1) Union leaders ____________ the teachers met with the government officials today.

(2) Judges should ____________ constitutional values whenever they hand down sentences.

(3) Leonardo da Vinci could draw with one hand, and write with the other ____________.

(4) The army has made ____________ military progress thanks to recent scientific developments.

4. 우리말에 맞게 빈칸에 공통으로 들어갈 알맞은 단어를 쓰시오.

· Scientists believe that the increase in smog have serious ____________s for the environment.
(과학자들은 스모그의 증가가 환경에 심각한 영향을 준다고 믿는다.)

· The ____________ in the article is the sales of organic cosmetics will greatly increase.
(그 기사가 암시하는 것은 유기농 화장품의 판매가 크게 증가할 것이라는 점이다.)

· The celebrity's ____________ in illegal wildlife trading has shocked everyone.
(그 유명인의 불법 야생동물 거래의 연루는 모든 사람들에게 충격을 주었다.)

SECTION. 05

Philosophy

철학

21 SECTION 05. Philosophy

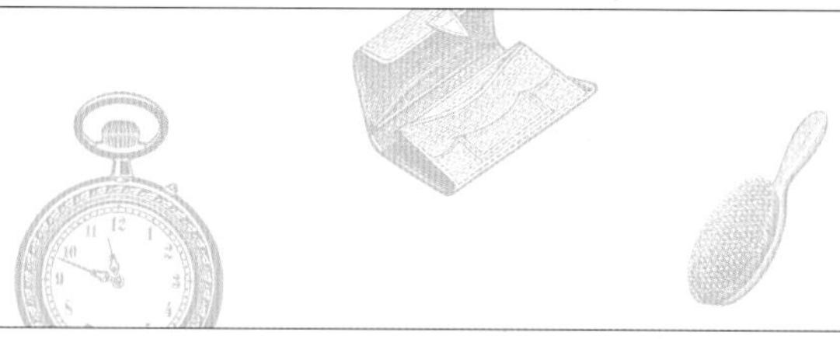

If philosophy is just "a residue" of unanswered questions or a pursuit of unanswerable questions, why should we keep doing it? One may say, why bother with problems we cannot solve? Because just dealing with the puzzle increases our understanding of the problem and the difficulties involved in it. Without philosophical curiosity displayed in this way, many important issues in the past (be) overlooked or forgotten. By continuing to raise questions and study their implications, we keep theoretical interest alive no matter whether it can yield positive results or not. Many questions that are now unanswered could turn one day into new areas of study. Those that are unanswerable in principle are still meaningful and important both intellectually and humanly. Thus, despite the fact that philosophy does not provide definitive answers, it is not a futile activity of the human mind. By studying philosophy we can achieve very profound and very significant insights into the world and the nature of the human condition.

VOCAB

residue 나머지
pursuit 추구
deal with ~을 다루다[처리하다]
puzzle 퀴즈; *어려운 문제
increase 증가시키다
be involved in ~에 관련되어 있다
philosophical 철학적인
curiosity 호기심
display 전시하다; *나타내다, 드러내다
overlook 간과하다
implication 내포, 암시
theoretical 이론상의, 이론적인
yield 산출하다; *가져오다, 내다
in principle 원칙적으로, 기본적으로
intellectually 지적으로
humanly 인간적으로
despite ~에도 불구하고
definitive 결정적인; *명확한
futile *쓸데없는, 무익한; 하찮은
achieve 성취하다; *획득하다
profound 심오한
significant 중요한
insight 통찰력

1. 위 글에서 주제문을 찾아 밑줄을 그으시오.

2. 위 글에서 괄호 안의 be동사를 문맥에 맞게 변형하여 쓰시오.

Pragmatism is a philosophical approach that was developed in America during the late nineteenth and early twentieth centuries. It is the only philosophical tradition to originate on American soil. So it reflects ideas implicitly accepted in the United States. Because pragmatism's highest ideal is action, it corresponds with the attitude of an *egalitarian nation built by immigrants who were eager to abandon the restrictive traditions of the old world. Pragmatism advocates only those ideas that can be practically applied, thus denying philosophy's reputation of being idealistic and abstract. Pragmatism states that the meaning of ideas lies in their consequences rather than in the ideas themselves. Accordingly, pragmatists believe in the importance of trying different methods and ways of life and then evaluating their effectiveness. Pragmatism finds fault with philosophy's insistence on truth and certainty. According to pragmatists, truth does not correspond to any ideals. Rather, truth exists in a theoretical relationship of meaning that is constantly changing according to the practical necessities of the present moment and at a particular age.

*egalitarian 평등주의의

1. 실용주의에 대한 설명 중, 위 글의 내용과 일치하지 않는 것은? (2개)

① 실용주의는 미국에서 발생한 유일한 철학 사조이다.
② 실용주의는 기존 철학이 제기한 의문점을 해결한다.
③ 실용주의는 기존 철학의 관념적인 태도를 부정한다.
④ 실용주의는 다양한 삶의 방식 추구를 중시한다.
⑤ 실용주의는 적용 가능한 불변의 진리를 추구한다.

실용주의(pragmatism)와 실용주의 철학자들

실용주의는 진화론의 등장과 함께 19세기에 발달한 생물학, 생리학, 심리학 등의 영향을 받아 19세기 후반 미국을 중심으로 일어난 새로운 철학 사조로, 철학의 기초를 구체적 경험에 둔다. 대표적인 실용주의자로 퍼스(C. S. Peirce), 제임스(W. James), 듀이(J. Dewey) 등이 있다. 퍼스는 실용주의의 창시자로, 행위와 관련이 있는 결과를 가져오지 못하는 관념은 무의미하다고 주장했다. 진리에 관한 그의 이론을 응용한 제임스는 진리가 성립하기 위해서는 목적에 도움이 되는 결과가 있어야만 하며, 인간 생활에서 유용성을 떠난 진리는 있을 수 없음을 강조하였다.
실용주의의 가장 대표적인 철학자인 듀이는 생활에 변화를 가져오지 못하고 그 자체로 추구되는 지식은 의미가 없다고 주장했다. 지식도 인간이 살아가기 위한 '도구'일 때만 가치가 있으며, 지식을 그 자체로 추구하지 않고 생활에 도움이 되는 하나의 수단으로 여겨, 그의 실용주의는 학자들 사이에서 도구주의(instrumentalism) 또는 도구적 실용주의라고 불린다. 그의 영향을 받아 콰인(W. O. Quine)과 화이트(M. White) 등이 1950년대 이후 언어철학 분야에서 '신실용주의'를 발전시켰다.

VOCAB

pragmatism 실용주의
approach 접근(법)
originate 일어나다, 시작되다
implicitly 암묵적으로
ideal 이상
correspond 일치하다, 부합하다
immigrant 이민자
eager 간절히 (~하고) 싶어하는
abandon 버리다, 포기하다
restrictive 제한적인
advocate 주장[옹호]하다
apply 적용하다
deny 부정[부인]하다, 거절하다
reputation 명성
abstract 추상적인
state 진술하다; *밝히다, 명시하다
lie in ~에 놓여 있다
consequence 결과
method 방법
evaluate 평가하다
effectiveness 효과
find fault with ~을 흠잡다[비난하다]
insistence 주장; 고집
correspond 일치하다, 부합하다
theoretical 이론상의, 이론적인
constantly 끊임없이

23 SECTION 05.
Philosophy

(A)

Descartes began his philosophical meditations from a position of absolute skepticism. In his search for a rational philosophical foundation, he attempted to eliminate anything that he could not know with 100% surety. He wanted to construct a foundation for knowledge that could not be doubted, just like the principles of mathematics. From this philosophical foundation Descartes thought he could deduce all other truths. The method he came up with was that of doubting the existence of all things until he arrived at the point where he could not doubt that he was doubting, and should therefore exist in order to doubt. This knowledge led to one of philosophy's most famous sayings: "cogito ergo sum" — "I think, therefore I am."

(B)

The ancient Greek philosopher Protagoras taught that "man is the measure of all things." This follows from the idea that all we know is our thoughts. If all I can know is what I think then I can never escape into reality. Thus, whatever I think is all there is for me to know. If all individuals are trapped in their own thought life then it is not possible to judge between alternative views — and there is no ultimate truth. Only if there is a neutral, objective measure that two individuals can look to, is there any way to know whether one's views are correct or not. Protagoras was so skeptical that he refused to believe that we could ever really know anything.

VOCAB

(A)

meditation 명상, 심사숙고
absolute 절대의, 절대적인
skepticism 회의(론)
rational 이성적인
foundation 기초, 근거
attempt 시도하다
eliminate 제거하다, 삭제하다
surety 보증, 담보; *확신함
construct 세우다, 고안하다
doubt 의심하다
principle 원리, 원칙
deduce 연역하다, 추론하다
method 방법
come up with (생각 등이) 떠오르다
existence 존재, 실재

23

서술형

1. **According to passages (A) and (B), both Descartes and Protagoras were ________________ of knowledge. The difference between them, however, was that while Descartes believed that he could come to understand ________________ knowledge, Protagoras doubted whether truth itself could ever exist. (each word from the passage)**

서술형

2. **위 글 (A)에서 밑줄 친 a foundation for knowledge에 해당하는 것을 본문에서 찾아 쓰시오.**

3. **위 글 (B)의 밑줄 친 문장을 우리말로 해석하시오.**

데카르트(Descartes, 1596–1650)

근대철학의 아버지라고 불리는 데카르트는 철학자이자 수학자, 물리학자로 잘 알려져 있다. 그의 형이상학적 사색은 그의 저서 「방법서설」에 소개된 방법적 회의에서 출발한다. 이를 통해 그는 '조금이라도 불확실한 것은 의심하다 보면 의심을 하고 있는 자신의 존재만이 유일하게 의심할 수 없다'라는 명제를 도출해 냈고, '나는 생각한다, 고로 나는 존재한다 (cogito ergo sum)'라는 유명한 말을 남겼다.

프로타고라스(Protagoras, 485–415 BC)

스스로 소피스트임을 자청한 최초의 인물로, 그의 유명한 '인간척도설'은 플라톤이 논한 '인간은 만물의 척도이다. 존재하는 것에 대하여는 존재하는 것의, 존재하지 않는 것에 대하여는 존재하지 않는 것의'라는 말에 의해 전해진다. 이는 진리의 기준을 개별 인간의 감각에서 찾으려는 것이며, 결국 절대 진리의 존재를 부인하고 상대주의를 지향하는 것으로 해석된다.

VOCAB

(B)
measure 측정, 측량 (기구)
escape 달아나다, 도피하다
trap 덫으로 잡다, 함정에 빠뜨리다
judge 판단하다
alternative 양자택일(의), 대안(의)
ultimate 궁극적인
neutral 중립적인
objective 객관적인
look to ~에 주의하다; ~에 의지하다; *~을 믿다
skeptical 회의적인
refuse 거절하다

24

SECTION 05.
Philosophy

In the West, there has always been a sharp distinction between philosophy and religion. Philosophy started out as a reaction against religion on the one hand, and against myth and magic on the other. Thales (c. 600 BC) was the first philosopher in ancient Greek times. A noted scientist as well, he was the first person to explain the nature of the universe in solely physical terms, saying that water was the substance out of (A) what / which the entire universe was made. Thales was famous for his questioning approach to the understanding of natural phenomena and for allowing his scientific observations and reasoning to govern his behavior instead of relying on myth and magic. In the West, philosophy has always tended to be a rational endeavor, (B) cut / cutting off from superstition, faith or godly intervention of any kind.

In Eastern philosophy, in contrast, there is no sharp distinction between philosophy and religion. From the beginning, there was never a conflict between them. Rather, Eastern philosophy actually heightened the meditative aspects of religion, while at the same time providing a theoretical framework and justification for the basic concepts of religion. It is even said that Eastern philosophy is to religion as Western theology is to religions like Christianity. Only it should also be noted that there are elements of Eastern philosophy that (C) represents / represent unique modes of perceiving reality, different from what religions generally teach. Furthermore, these modes are not based on such essentials of religion as ritual, belief or faith.

VOCAB

distinction 구분, 구별
religion 종교
reaction *반작용; 반응
myth 신화
noted 저명한, 유명한
solely 오직, 단지
physical 육체의; *물리적인
term *용어; 기간; 학기; 조건
substance 물질
entire 전체의, 전부의
questioning *의문을 나타내는; 탐구하는
approach 접근(법)
phenomena 현상 (phenomenon의 복수)
observation 관찰
reasoning 추론
govern 지배[통제]하다
rely on ~에 의존하다
rational 합리적인; *이성적인
endeavor 노력
superstition 미신

서술형

1. 위 글에 근거하여 동양철학과 서양철학의 차이를 우리말로 간략히 서술하시오.

2. 다음 중 위 글의 내용과 일치하지 않는 것은?

① 서양철학은 종교나 신화에 대한 반발로 시작되었다.
② 탈레스는 우주의 구성 물질을 물이라고 생각했다.
③ 탈레스는 과학적 법칙에 따라 행동하는 사람이었다.
④ 초기의 동양 철학은 종교와 갈등을 빚었다.
⑤ 동양철학은 종교의 명상적인 측면을 강화시켰다.

3. 위 글 둘째 단락의 밑줄 친 문장을 우리말로 해석하시오.

4. 위 글의 (A), (B), (C) 각 네모 안에서 어법에 맞는 낱말을 골라 짝지은 것으로 가장 적절한 것은?

	(A)		(B)		(C)
①	which	……	cutting	……	represents
②	which	……	cut	……	represent
③	which	……	cutting	……	represent
④	what	……	cut	……	represents
⑤	what	……	cutting	……	represents

탈레스(Thales, 624-546 BC)

고대그리스의 철학자이자 수학자이다. 아테네의 솔론 등과 함께 과학, 철학에 영향을 끼쳤던 정치가이기도 했으며, 그리스의 수학과 철학의 기초를 다졌다.
탈레스는 생명과 우주현상의 근본물질에 주목한 고대 그리스 최초의 철학자였다. 그는 만물의 근원을 '물'로 보았다. 지구를 무한한 대양 위에 떠있는 편평한 판이라고 생각했고(이집트인들의 사고에 영향을 받음), 만물 생존의 필수요소가 물이라는 것이 그 이유였다.
세상의 근원을 설명할 때 신화에 의존하지 않고 물질적 근원을 고찰한 것은 탈레스가 처음이었다. 물론 탈레스도 모든 물체에 신이 존재한다고 믿는 그리스인이었다. 하지만 그는 자연법칙의 해석을 초자연적인 설명에서 자연에 근거한 설명으로 바꾼 과학적 방법론의 시조라고 평가된다. 이런 이유로 탈레스는 최초의 '과학자'로 불리기도 한다.

VOCAB

faith 신뢰; 신념; *신앙
intervention 개입
in contrast 그와 대조적으로
conflict 갈등, 마찰
heighten 강화하다
meditative 명상적인
aspect (측)면
provide 제공하다
theoretical 이론적인
framework 틀, 골격
justification 정당성
concept 개념
theology 신학
Christianity 기독교
element 요소
represent 나타내다
unique 독특한
mode 방법, 양식
perceive 인식[인지]하다
essential 필수의 (것)
ritual 의식

25

SECTION 05.
Philosophy

Plato (c. 400 BC) was a famous Greek philosopher and prized student of Socrates. In 385 BC, he founded a school called the Academy, where rich young men, and even some women, studied philosophy and other subjects. Plato was both an idealist and a rationalist. He divided reality into two: On the one hand we have *idea* or *ideal*. This is ultimate reality, which is eternal and spiritual. On the other hand, there are *phenomena*, which are an imperfect manifestation of the ideal because they appear in the material, physical world, and are associated with matter, time, and space.

Whereas phenomena are illusions which decay and die, ideals are unchanging and perfect. Phenomena are inferior to ideals. For example, the idea of a triangle — the properties of its form — is eternal. Any individual triangle found in the everyday world is never quite perfect: they may be a little crooked, or the lines a little thick, or the angles not quite right. They are only ever an approximation of the ideal. Ideals are the basis of science: the law of gravity, $E=mc^2$, and so on — these are the unchanging laws of the universe. Ideals are available to us through thought, while phenomena are experienced through our senses. So, naturally, thought is a vastly superior means to get to the truth. This is what makes Plato a rationalist, as opposed to an empiricist. Senses can only give you information about the ever-changing and imperfect world of phenomena, and so can only provide you with implications about ultimate reality, not reality itself.

VOCAB

prized 중요한, 소중한
found 설립하다 (founded · founded)
subject 주제; 대상; *과목
idealist 이상주의자
rationalist 합리주의자
divide A into B A를 B로 나누다
reality 현실; *실재
ultimate 궁극적인
eternal 영원한
spiritual 영혼의; *정신적인
phenomena 현상 (phenomenon의 복수)
manifestation 표시, 표명
material 물질적인, 세속적인
be associated with ~와 관련되어 있다
matter 물질; *물체
illusion 환영, 환상

1. 다음 중 위 글의 주제로 가장 적절한 것은?

① Plato's world view: dualism
② the process of searching for the truth
③ various ways of understanding the world
④ the viewpoint of the ancient Greeks
⑤ Plato's outstanding achievements in philosophy

2. 다음은 플라톤이 말한 이데아와 현상의 속성을 정리해 놓은 것이다. 위 글의 내용과 일치하지 않는 것은?

	Ideal	Phenomenon
①	ultimate reality	imitation of ideal
②	eternal	ever-changing
③	spiritual	physical
④	truth	illusion
⑤	sense	thought

3. **Mark T(True) or F(False) for the following statements.**

(1) Both men and women could study philosophy in Plato's Academy. □ T □ F

(2) The ideal of a triangle can be realized under limited conditions in everyday life. □ T □ F

(3) Plato gave equal weight to both thought and senses as a means to reach the truth. □ T □ F

VOCAB

decay *쇠퇴하다; 부패하다
inferior 열등한 (↔ superior)
property 속성
crooked 굽은
approximation 비슷한 것
basis 기초
gravity 중력
available 이용 가능한
sense *감각; 의미
vastly 광대하게; *매우
means 수단
empiricist 경험주의자
ever-changing 변화무쌍한
imperfect 불완전한
provide A with B A에게 B를 제공하다
implication 포함; *암시

플라톤(Plato, 429–347 BC)의 철학

플라톤은 이원론적 이상주의자로 세상을 현상계와 이데아계로 나누어 보았다. 현상계는 감각적으로 경험되며, 생성, 소멸, 변화하는 불완전한 세계이다. 이데아계는 이성에 의해 파악되는 세계이며 영원불변의 완전한 세계이다. 플라톤에게 최고의 이데아는 선의 이데아로, 선의 이데아를 모방해서 사는 삶을 바람직하다고 보았다.
플라톤은 지혜, 용기, 절제가 조화된 상태를 정의로 규정하고 통치자 계급은 지혜, 수호자 계급은 용기, 생산자 계급은 절제가 필요하다고 보았다. 이상적인 인간은 이성에 의해 욕망과 기개를 잘 조절할 줄 아는 인간이며 지혜, 용기, 절제가 조화를 이룬 사람을 정의로운 사람이라고 보았다. 그에 따르면 이상 국가란 정의가 실현된 국가이며 곧 각 계급이 조화를 이룬 국가이다.

The Timeline of Philosophy

소크라테스(Socrates, 470-399 BC)

소크라테스는 '너 자신을 알라(gnothi seauton)'는 말을 근간으로 하여 인간의 무지와 독단적 지식을 지양하였다. 그는 사람들에게 끊임없이 질문을 함으로써 변증법을 통한 본질적인 답을 이끌어 내고자 했는데, 이러한 질문을 통해 누구나 근본적인 절대적 진리에 도달할 수 있다고 주장했다. 그의 절대주의적 사고방식은 이후 제자인 플라톤에게도 이어진다.

아리스토텔레스(Aristotle, 384-322 BC)

플라톤의 제자인 아리스토텔레스는 하나의 학문에 치중하지 않고 철학, 윤리학, 경제학, 정치학, 수학 등 다양한 학문의 전반적인 기초를 정립했다. 그 중에서도 제1철학은 현상을 너머 초월적인 근원을 탐구하는 학문으로, 후에 '형이상학'이라 불리게 된다. 플라톤이 철인 국가 통치를 주장한 것과는 반대로, 아리스토텔레스는 현실적 지혜를 가진 입법 전문가가 국가를 통치해야 함을 강조했다.

플라톤(Plato, 427-347 BC)

플라톤은 소크라테스의 절대주의를 확장하여 '이데아'를 제시했다. 이데아란 초월적인 진리의 세계로, 영원하고 불멸한 본질 세계이다. 이에 반해 현실 세계는 이데아의 그림자이다. 그의 대표적인 저서 「국가」에서 그는 철학자들이 육안이 아닌 지성의 눈으로 이데아를 인식해야 한다고 주장했으며, 이러한 지혜를 가진 철학자들이 국가를 다스려야 한다는 철인 국가 통치 이론을 내세웠다.

데카르트(Descartes, 1596-1650)

데카르트가 살았던 17세기는 종교와 교회의 권위가 약화하는 혼돈의 시대였다. 이에 신을 대체할 이성적, 합리적인 진리가 요구되었다. 데카르트는 진정으로 신뢰할 수 있는 절대적인 진리에 도달하기 위해서 가능한 한 모든 것을 의심하였다. 이러한 접근법은 '방법적 회의'라고 불린다. '나는 생각한다. 고로 존재한다(cogito ergo sum)'는 이러한 접근법을 대표하는 말이다.

칸트(Kant, 1724-1804)

칸트는 서양 철학의 양대 사상인 '합리주의'와 '경험주의'를 통합한 철학자이다. 합리주의란 인간은 태어날 때부터 지식을 가지고 있으며, 경험은 이 내재된 지식을 단지 일깨우는 역할만을 한다고 보는 사상이다. 이 사상은 인간의 지식이 경험으로부터 축적되는 것이라고 보는 경험주의와는 상반된다. 칸트는 이 두 사상을 조합하여, 인간은 내재된 인식 능력을 바탕으로 경험을 축적함으로써 보편적인 진리를 깨달을 수 있다고 강조하였다.

하이데거(Heidegger, 1889-1976)

하이데거의 철학 사상은 어렵고 생경한 용어로 표현되어 이해하기에 난해하기로 유명하다. 대표 저서 「존재와 시간」에서 그는 '존재한다'는 의미를 규정하였다. 그는 눈에 보이는 '존재자'에 대한 탐구에서 나아가 눈에 보이지 않는 '존재'의 내적인 의미를 파악하고자 했다. '인간의 존재'에 대한 탐구로 인해 그는 실존주의 철학자로 불리기도 하지만, 경험할 수 없는 절대적 '존재'에 대해 연구했다는 점에서 형이상학자로 분류되기도 한다.

니체(Nietzsche, 1844-1900)

니체는 기존의 합리적 철학, 기독교 윤리 등이 내세우는 진리를 전면으로 뒤집으려 했기 때문에 '망치를 든 철학가'라고 불린다. 니체는 '절대적인 진리는 존재하지 않는다'는 니힐리즘을 주장하였다. 니체는 당시의 종교적 가치 체계를 인간의 가치를 약화하는 수동적 니힐리즘으로 판단하고 배척했으며, 이에 '신은 죽었다'라고 주창하였다. 그는 인간 내부로부터 나오는 힘을 지향하여 적극적인 삶의 의의를 표방하는 능동적 니힐리즘을 제창하였다.

비트겐슈타인(Wittgenstein, 1889-1951)

비트겐슈타인은 언어를 연구한 철학자이다. 그에 따르면 언어는 세계를 묘사하는 것이다. 그런데 기존의 철학에서 말하는 종교, 윤리, 영혼, 도덕과 같은 관념들은 실제로 그것을 묘사할 수 있는 실재가 없다. 따라서 그에게는 거의 모든 철학적 명제들이 사실 아무런 의미가 없는 것들이었다. 그는 철학적 질문들은 참이나 거짓으로 분류되어 답을 할 수 없으며, 다만 그것들이 헛소리라는 것을 입증할 수 있을 뿐이라고 주장했다.

SECTION 05.

Word Test

정답 | p.124

1. 다음 단어의 영영풀이로 알맞은 것을 찾아 선으로 연결하시오.

(1) noted · · ⓐ the desire to know about something

(2) gravity · · ⓑ existing or continuing for ever

(3) eternal · · ⓒ the force that causes something to fall to the ground

(4) curiosity · · ⓓ well known or famous because of particular qualities

2. 다음 문장의 빈칸에 알맞은 말을 보기에서 찾아 쓰시오. (단, 필요한 경우에는 어형을 바꾸시오.)

보기 | substance overlook correspond superstition

(1) Accidents happen when safety checks are ____________.

(2) The melting point of a ____________ is also the freezing point.

(3) According to ____________, if you walk under a ladder it brings you bad luck.

(4) His story of what happened that night didn't ____________ with the witness's version.

3. 우리말에 맞게 빈칸에 주어진 철자로 시작하는 단어를 쓰시오.

(1) He a____________ed to escape through a window.
(그는 창문을 통해서 탈출을 시도했었다.)

(2) The sound quality is s____________ to that on a regular CD.
(소리의 질이 보통 CD에서보다 더 우수하다.)

(3) The project is designed to p____________ young people with work.
(그 계획은 젊은이들에게 일자리를 제공하기 위해 마련된 것이다.)

(4) In p____________ I agree with the idea, but in practice it's not always possible.
(원칙적으로 나는 그 생각에 동의하지만 실제로 그것이 항상 가능한 것은 아니다.)

4. 우리말에 맞게 빈칸에 공통으로 들어갈 알맞은 단어를 쓰시오.

· Please ____________ to traffic on the left.
(왼쪽 차량에게 양보해주세요.)

· Our research has only recently begun to ____________ important results.
(우리의 연구가 최근에 와서야 중요한 결과를 낳기 시작했다.)

· Management finally ____________ed to the demands of the workers.
(경영진은 마침내 근로자들의 요구에 굴복했다.)

SECTION. 06

Media

미디어

26 SECTION 06. Media

The modern industrialized world is saturated with the mass media. The television in the living room, the magazines on the coffee table, the radio in the car, and the billboards by the roadside are just a few of the outlets used by the mass media to deliver their constant stream of advertising, news, opinion, and other forms of mass communication.

Because the mass media are so firmly established in industrialized countries, they strongly influence how those populations view the world. In the United States, nearly all the news stations and newspapers are owned by one major news network. Thus the American public now experiences all major news events through the interpretative eyes of one powerful newsgroup.

Of course, not only do news media interpret the news, they also create the news by choosing what events to report. The "top story" of the day is selected from the millions of things that happen each particular day. After a news story is selected, managerial decisions are made on how much time or space to give it, whom to interview, and what pictures to use. All of these decisions create the audience's view of the world, putting those who influence the decision-making in an extremely powerful position.

The media, therefore, have enormous importance to conflict resolution because they are the primary source of information regarding conflicts in society. If a situation doesn't make the news, it simply does not exist for most people. When peaceful options such as negotiation and other collaborative problem-solving techniques are not covered, or their successes are not reported, they become invisible and are not likely to be considered or even understood as possible options in the management of a conflict.

VOCAB

industrialized 산업화된
be saturated with ~으로 가득 차다
billboard 광고[게시]판
outlet 배출구; *(표현의) 수단
deliver (의견 등을) 전달하다
constant 끊임없는
stream 시내; *흐름, 유출
advertising 광고
firmly 단단히; *확고하게
establish 세우다, 수립하다
influence ~에 영향을 미치다
population 인구; *모든 주민
view 바라보다
news station 방송국
major *주요한; 대형의
interpretative 해석의 (interpret 해석하다)

1. What is the main idea of each paragraph? Choose the correct choice from the box below.

(1) paragraph 1 ______ (2) paragraph 2 ______

(3) paragraph 3 ______ (4) paragraph 4 ______

① the critical role of mass media in solving conflicts in society
② the monopoly of the mass media by major newsgroups
③ the powerful influence of the people who make the news
④ the modern world which is flooded with mass media

2. Mark T(True) or F(False) for the following statements.

(1) In industrialized countries, the mass media play the role of a window through which everyone sees the world. □ T □ F

(2) News events are first selected by an influential newsgroup before being presented to an audience. □ T □ F

(3) The news enables us to see the real world in a fair and objective manner. □ T □ F

(4) The media presents direct solutions to social conflicts. □ T □ F

VOCAB

select 선택하다
particular 개개의
managerial 관리(자)의
decision 결정
decision-making 의사결정(의)
extremely 극도로, 대단히
enormous 거대한, 엄청난
conflict 갈등
resolution 결의; *해결
primary 주요한
regarding ~에 관한
option 선택(권)
negotiation 협상
collaborative 협조[협력]적인
cover 덮다; *보도하다
invisible 보이지 않는
management 관리, 경영; *처리

27

SECTION 06.
Media

There has been (A) [considerate / considerable] change in the nature of journalism and employment for journalists in recent years. Most notably, the growth of online media is encouraging newspapers and broadcasting companies to launch their own successful Internet ventures, creating more jobs for journalists. Despite some predictions that online technology would reduce journalists' employment by automating their jobs, the demand for reporters and editors has risen. Technological developments such as the Internet are in many respects helping journalists do their jobs better and more efficiently.

However, technological change does present some concerns and challenges. Freelancers are becoming increasingly concerned about electronic re-publication rights for their stories. Journalists have reason to be concerned that as new media and technology change the way news is gathered and distributed, ethics could be ignored in the rush, their independence could be threatened, and public trust in the news media could (B) [decline / incline] further.

The monopoly that newspapers and broadcasters once enjoyed has rapidly been eroded by online media, and now anybody with (C) [access / assess] to a computer can become a reporter. As a result, media institutions are having to answer more questions from their audiences in regard to accuracy. This loss of exclusivity with regard to information, and the weakening of the role of the media as news arbitrators, began in the 1990s, and continues to bring further changes to the professional and social functions of the journalist. Journalists need to embrace the technological changes in order to retain their professional standards and provide quality-oriented materials; otherwise, they may be severely challenged by the great influx of other news sources.

VOCAB

journalism 언론계
employment 고용
journalist 기자, 언론인
notably 현저하게, 주목할 만하게
encourage 격려하다; *장려하다
launch 출범시키다
venture 모험적 사업
create 창조하다, 만들어내다
prediction 예상
reduce 줄이다
automate 자동화하다
demand 수요
editor 편집자
respect 존경; *점, 사항
efficiently 효율적으로
freelancer 프리랜서, 자유 계약자
concerned about ~을 걱정하는
electronic 전자의
re-publication 재출판
gather 모으다
distribute 분배하다, 배급하다
ethics 윤리
ignore 무시하다, 모르는 체하다

27

SECTION 06.
미디어

1. **What is the best title for the passage?**

① New Media: What Does It Bring Us?
② Why We Must Adapt to New Media
③ Public Journalism in the Era of the Internet
④ New Media and the Role of the Journalist
⑤ Media Institutions and their Public Obligations

서술형

2. **According to the passage, with the widespread of the Internet, the ________________ that newspapers and broadcasting companies once held has been weakened, since ________________ is freely available now to anyone with a computer. (each word from the passage)**

서술형

3. **위 글에 따르면, 과학기술 발달에 의한 뉴미디어 시대에 기자들에게 요구되는 자질은 무엇인지 우리말로 쓰시오.**

4. **위 글의 (A), (B), (C) 각 네모 안에서 문맥에 맞는 어휘를 골라 짝지은 것으로 가장 적절한 것은?**

	(A)		(B)		(C)
①	considerate	……	decline	……	access
②	considerate	……	incline	……	access
③	considerable	……	decline	……	access
④	considerable	……	incline	……	assess
⑤	considerable	……	decline	……	assess

VOCAB

rush 돌진; *쇄도
independence 독립
threaten 위협하다
trust 신뢰
monopoly 독점
broadcaster 방송사, 방송업계
rapidly 급속히
erode 침식하다
institution 기관
in[with] regard to ~에 관하여
accuracy 정확성
loss 손실
exclusivity 독점성
arbitrator 중재자
function 기능, 역할
embrace 포옹하다; *받아들이다
retain 보유하다, 유지하다
quality-oriented 질 중심의
material 물질; 재료; *자료
otherwise 그렇지 않으면
severely 심하게
influx 유입
source 근원; *출처, 재료

28 SECTION 06.
Media

The mass media is responsible for creating cultural symbols, which greatly impact our society. As well as having overt primary meanings, these cultural symbols also have secondary, hidden meanings ① which are charged with psychological, emotional or ideological values. It is through the constant production of these symbols that cultural myths are produced.

These myths ② composed of stories, stereotypes, and images that symbolize the main aspects of culture. (A) Thus, women have been conditioned to spend their money on expensive clothes and cosmetic products. (B) For example, the mass media bombards us with images of female physical perfection. (C) Through these, the modern woman ③ has been taught the cultural myth that unless she is able to improve every feature of her face and body, she will never be considered successful as a woman.

Far from being a true representation of society, cultural myths are created by advertisers, journalists, television producers and movie directors. These myths influence consumers' thoughts and values, ④ working to create a society in which people consume products without thinking about the origins of the myths. Critics of mass culture consider it to be basic conditioning and manipulation. They think cultural producers use myths to make large profits. ⑤ When viewed this way, mass culture is nothing more than an illusion created by cultural industries.

VOCAB

create 창조하다
symbol 상징
impact ~에 영향을 미치다
overt 명백한, 공공연한
primary *제1의; 주요한
secondary 제2의; *부차적인
hidden 숨겨진
charge 부과하다; *가득 채우다
psychological 심리(학)적인
ideological 이데올로기적인
value 가치(관)
constant 끊임없는
myth 신화, (그릇된) 통념
stereotype 고정관념
symbolize 상징화하다
aspect 면, 측면
condition 조건; *(조건으로서) 규정하다
cosmetic product 화장품
bombard 폭격하다; *퍼붓다
physical 신체의

28

SECTION 06.
미디어

1. **What is the author mainly talking about?**

① the mass media and social values
② the mass media and mass production
③ cultural myths made by the mass media
④ various characteristics of mass culture
⑤ the effect of cultural myths on modern women

2. **위 글 둘째 단락의 (A)~(C)를 글의 흐름에 맞게 배열한 것으로 가장 적절한 것은?**

① (A) - (B) - (C)
② (B) - (A) - (C)
③ (B) - (C) - (A)
④ (C) - (A) - (B)
⑤ (C) - (B) - (A)

서술형

3. **위 글 셋째 단락의 밑줄 친 it이 의미하는 바를 우리말로 쓰시오.**

4. **위 글의 ①~⑤ 중에서 어법상 틀린 것을 찾아 바르게 고치시오.**

VOCAB

perfection 완벽성
improve 향상시키다
feature 특징
far from ~이기는 커녕, ~와는 거리가 먼
representation *표현; 대표
advertiser 광고주
journalist 기자
influence ~에 영향을 미치다
consumer 소비자 (consume 소비하다)
origin 기원
critic 비평가
manipulation 조작
profit 이익, 수익
view 보다; *~라고 생각하다
nothing more than ~에 지나지 않는
illusion 환영; *환상
industry 산업

대중문화의 폐해

대중문화는 대중매체를 통해 대중에게 전달된다. 여기서 문제가 되는 것은 소수가 창조한 문화가 다수에게 일방적으로 전달된다는 점이다. 또한 대중문화는 그 수량과 성격이 한정되어 있어 대중의 의식과 취향을 획일화시킨다. 대중문화는 사회의 부정적 가치를 전파할 위험성도 지니고 있다. 영화, 가요, TV 드라마 등 대중문화물 중 적지 않은 부분이 사회의 부정적 가치관을 비판 없이 담고 있는 경우가 많다. 또 대중문화는 주로 현실과 동떨어진 오락거리를 제공하기 때문에 결과적으로 대중의 의식을 탈정치화한다고 말할 수 있다. 한 국가의 구성원들이 사회문제나 정치문제 등에 관심을 두고 참여정신을 지닐 때 사회의 발전은 가능하다. 그런데 대중문화는 오락 기능에 치중함으로써 정치나 사회문제에 대한 사람들의 관심을 줄일 수 있다.

29

Media

Many different sports events take place in the Olympics, and each appeals to a different audience. For example, while track events appeal to some viewers, archery appeals to others. If both events are taking place simultaneously, then it is the job of gatekeepers to decide which event to televise. Gatekeepers estimate whether the demand for track events is greater than the demand for archery. If the demand to see both is equal, then gatekeepers consider broadcasting both events by continually switching between the two. However, if possible, gatekeepers try to avoid this option as it costs twice as much as covering just one event. ______(A)______, the majority of Olympics television coverage is of a single event at a time. Events such as table tennis are given a lot of coverage because they last for hours, and television companies only have to pay a lump sum to cover them. Shorter events such as pole-vaulting are avoided by smaller TV channels because they are relatively more expensive to cover.

Another way that gatekeepers make their decisions is according to nationality bias. For example, Chinese channels tend to give Chinese gymnasts considerable coverage. English-speaking channels tend to give a lot of coverage to athletes from the U.S.A. and Great Britain. All networks cover famous athletes in order to increase the audience. For example, in the 2000 Olympics, Hong Kong channels gave extensive coverage to the local 1996 gold-medalist windsurfer Lee San San. However, when it became evident that she was not going to win another medal, windsurfing coverage decreased considerably. In the end, gatekeepers have to try to decide who the events will appeal to and how many people will watch them. This sometimes results in two or three channels covering the same event in the hope of __________(B)__________.

VOCAB

take place 개최되다, 열리다
appeal to ~의 관심을 끌다, ~의 마음에 들다
audience 청중; 관중; *시청자
viewer 시청자
archery 양궁
simultaneously 동시에
gatekeeper 문지기, 수위; *게이트키퍼
televise 텔레비전으로 방송하다
estimate 어림하다, 견적하다
demand 수요
track event (달리기 · 허들 등) 트랙 경기
equal 동등한
broadcast 방송하다
continually 계속, 끊임없이
switch 바꾸다
avoid 피하다

서술형

1. 위 글에 따르면, 게이트키퍼는 어떤 일을 하는 사람인지 우리말로 간단히 쓰시오.

2. 위 글 첫째 단락의 빈칸 (A)에 들어갈 말로 가장 적절한 것은?

① For example ② Additionally ③ In fact
④ As a result ⑤ Nevertheless

3. 위 글 둘째 단락의 빈칸 (B)에 들어갈 말로 가장 적절한 것은?

① reducing costs ② attracting viewers
③ a better broadcast ④ maintaining consistency
⑤ winning a victory

서술형

4. 위 글에 따르면, 올림픽 경기 보도 시 게이트키퍼의 결정에 영향을 미치는 요인 세 가지는 무엇인지 우리말로 쓰시오.

VOCAB

option 선택(권)
cover 덮다; *보도하다
majority 대다수, 과반수
coverage 보도 (범위)
lump sum 일괄 지급(의 금액)
pole-vaulting 장대높이뛰기
relatively 상대적으로
nationality 국적; *국민임, 국민성
bias 편견; *성향, 경향
gymnast 체조선수
considerable 상당한
athlete 운동선수
network 방송망
extensive 광범위한
local 지역의, 현지의
evident 분명한
decrease 줄다
result in ~의 결과를 초래하다

SECTION 06.

Word Test

정답 | P.124

1. 다음 설명의 내용이 맞으면 T(True), 틀리면 F(False)를 괄호 안에 쓰시오.

(1) A billboard is a large sign for advertising. (　　)

(2) An arbitrator is someone whose job is to give their opinion about things such as books, films, or music. (　　)

(3) A myth is a fixed idea that people have about what someone or something is like. (　　)

(4) An audience is a group of people who watch, read, or listen to the same thing. (　　)

2. 다음 문장의 빈칸에 알맞은 단어를 보기에서 찾아 쓰시오.

보기 | demand　psychological　prediction　extensive

(1) Harry's problems are more ____________ than physical.

(2) Fire has caused ____________ damage to the island's forests.

(3) No one believed her ____________ that the world would end on November 12.

(4) 18,400 new houses will be needed by 2021 to cope with the ____________.

3. 우리말에 맞게 빈칸에 주어진 철자로 시작하는 단어를 알맞은 형태로 쓰시오.

(1) You have the o____________ of taking early retirement.
(당신은 조기 퇴직할 선택권이 있다.)

(2) The show's direct approach will a____________ to children.
(그 쇼의 직접적인 접근 방식이 아이들의 관심을 끌 것이다.)

(3) He doesn't fit the s____________ of the emotional Italian.
(그는 감정적인 이탈리아인이라는 고정관념에 맞지 않는 사람이다.)

(4) We're d____________ the product at a low price.
(우리는 그 제품을 싼 값에 배포하고 있다.)

4. 우리말에 맞게 빈칸에 공통으로 들어갈 알맞은 단어를 쓰시오.

· Give my ____________ to your parents.
(너희 부모님께 안부 전해줘.)

· I want you to ____________ this as your home.
(나는 네가 이곳을 너의 집으로 여겼으면 한다.)

· I am writing to you with ____________ to your letter of May 17.
(저는 당신의 5월 17일자 편지에 관해서 편지를 쓰고 있습니다.)

SECTION. 07

History

역사

30

SECTION 07. History

We historians have a responsibility to historical facts in general, and for criticizing the abuse of history in particular. I need say little about the first of these responsibilities. I would not have to say anything, but for two developments. One is the current fashion for novelists to base their plots on recorded reality rather than inventing them, thus *fudging the border between historical fact and fiction. The other is the rise of "postmodernist" intellectual fashions in universities, particularly in departments of literature and anthropology, which imply that all "facts" claiming objective existence are simply intellectual constructions — in short, that there is no clear difference between fact and fiction. But there is. And for historians, the ability to distinguish between the two is absolutely fundamental. We cannot invent our facts. Either Elvis Presley is dead or he isn't. The question can be answered unambiguously on the basis of evidence, in so far as reliable evidence is available.

*fudge 왜곡시키다

FROM 「*On History*」 by Eric Hobsbawm

서술형

1. 위 글에 제시된 'facts'에 대한 포스트모더니스트들의 입장과 필자의 입장을 간략히 비교하시오.

에릭 홉스봄(Eric John Ernest Hobsbawm, 1917–2012)

저명한 역사가인 홉스봄은 당시 대영제국의 식민지였던 이집트의 알렉산드리아에서 태어나, 독일의 베를린을 거쳐 1933년에 영국 런던에 정착하였다. 케임브리지의 킹스 칼리지에서 역사를 전공한 그는 역사가로서 그리고 마르크스주의자로서 활동하면서, 자본주의를 비판하면서도, 한편으로는 사회주의에 대한 비판과 더불어 역사 연구에 있어서의 이데올로기적인 시각보다는 객관적 사실에 충실할 것을 주장하였다. 이론과 현실의 통합을 추구하며 그는 나이가 들어서도 전세계를 순회하며 강의와 활발한 저술 활동을 했다.

VOCAB

abuse 남용, 악용, 오용
development 발달, 전개; *새로운 사태
fashion 유행; *일시적 풍습, 경향
base A on B A의 근거를 B에 두다
plot 줄거리
invent 발명하다; *창작하다
border 가장자리; *경계(선)
fiction 소설 (작품)
intellectual 지성의, 지적인
literature 문학
anthropology 인류학
imply 내포하다, 뜻하다
objective 객관적인
existence 존재, 실재
construction 구조
distinguish 구별하다, 식별하다
absolutely 정말로, 완전히
fundamental 근본적인; 중요한
unambiguously 분명하게
basis 기초, 토대
evidence 증거, 근거
in so far as ~하는 한
reliable 믿을 수 있는
available 쓸모 있는, 이용 가능한

SECTION 07.
History

31

In a speech delivered at the University of Oxford in 1957, British historian Hugh Trevor-Roper said there are two essential functions of human history: to be useful and to be controversial. According to him, history that cannot teach lessons to those in the present is nothing more than a diamond in the rough. And history that is not controversial is completely dead, for no subject is more open to interpretation than history.

By its very nature, human history is a subject that cannot be unbiased or factual. It is the study of man's past, specifically the past that is relevant to the present. But the past is mute, and so it doesn't tell us much at all. We can only try to analyze and reconstruct it on the basis of the records and evidence that have been preserved in one form or another. And this is where the controversial aspects of history arouse and provoke us. The analyses made by historians and the conclusions they come to are all based on their own personal interpretations, which are based on their own individual beliefs.

서술형

1. 위 글에서 필자가 역사를 논란의 여지가 많다고 보는 이유는 무엇인지 우리말로 쓰시오.

역사가에 대한 다양한 관점들

19세기 독일의 역사가 랑케(Reopold von Ranke)는 '역사가는 주관적인 판단을 배제하고 역사적 사실을 있는 그대로 기술해야 한다'고 주장했다. 그의 유명한 말인 "자신을 숨기고 사실로 하여금 말하게 하라"에서 알 수 있듯이, 랑케는 역사적 사실 그 자체에 비중을 두었다. 역사가는 주관을 배제하고 과거의 사실을 있는 그대로 복원해야 한다는 것이다.

이와는 달리 이탈리아의 크로체(Benedetto Croce)는 역사가를 현재의 눈을 통해 현재의 관점에서 과거를 보는 사람이라고 정의한다. 따라서 랑케가 주장한 것과 같이 역사를 객관적으로 서술하는 것은 불가능하며, 역사가의 시각에 따라 역사는 다르게 해석될 수 있다고 본다.

한편 20세기의 역사가 카(E. H. Carr)는 객관적 사실을 중시하는 랑케와 역사가의 주관적 해석을 강조하는 크로체를 모두 비판하면서 중립적인 견해를 펼쳤다. 그에 의하면, 역사는 '역사가와 사실의 부단한 상호작용 과정'이며, '현재와 과거의 끊임없는 대화'로서, 역사가는 과거의 역사를 사료를 통하여 객관적으로 탐구하고 그 결과를 자신의 사관을 바탕으로 하여 주관적으로 서술해야 한다.

VOCAB

deliver a speech 연설하다
essential 필수의
function 기능, 작용
controversial 논란의 여지가 있는
a diamond in the rough 미가공의 다이아몬드 (다듬어지지 않은 것)
interpretation 해석
unbiased 편견에 치우치지 않은
factual 사실의
specifically 구체적으로 (말하면)
relevant 관련된
mute 침묵한, 무언의
analyze 분석하다 (analysis 분석 (*pl.* analyses))
reconstruct 재구성하다
preserve 보존하다
aspect 면, 측면
arouse 생기다
provoke 도발하다, 선동하다
conclusion 결론
be based on ~을 토대로 하다

(A)

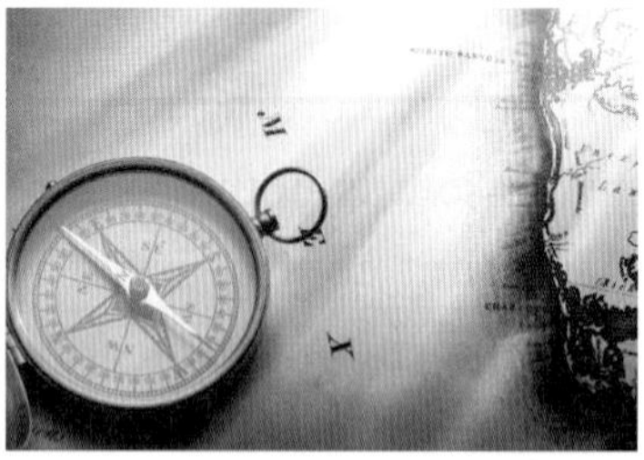

Some historians emphasize the necessity of constructing formulas in history. They insist that it is possible to ascertain historical laws and draw meaningful lessons from them, much the same as we do with scientific laws such as the laws of Kepler, the laws of wave theory, and so on. A historical law might specify that "whenever x happens, y is certain to follow" so that, ______________, "whenever a nation's resources are insufficient to maintain its population, that nation turns to war" is a historical law. For those who suppose that it is meaningful to talk of such laws, systematic historical investigation would be the way to validate ⓐ the claim.

(B)

Can anyone show that history develops according to historical laws? Karl Popper, one of the greatest social and political philosophers of 20th century, doubts it. According to him, the error lies in assuming that history is similar to science, when in fact, it differs greatly: scientific laws apply to closed systems, whereas history, which is composed of the actions of many individuals, is neither closed nor even a system at all. ______________, since the growth of scientific knowledge affects human behavior and hence history, the use of scientific laws to predict history is only possible if we can also predict the growth of the scientific knowledge. If we could do ⓑ that, however, we would already know it. As a result, there can be no historical laws.

VOCAB

(A)
emphasize 강조하다
construct 세우다, 건설하다
formula 공식
insist 주장하다
ascertain 확인하다, 알아내다
draw 그리다; 끌다; *끌어내다
specify *명시하다; 특수화하다
resource 자원
insufficient 불충분한
maintain 유지하다
population 인구
turn to ~에 의지하다
suppose 가정하다
systematic 체계적인

1. What is the best topic of passages (A) and (B)?

① the way we predict history
② the historical necessity of laws
③ human behavior and history
④ do historical laws exist or not?
⑤ the usefulness of scientific laws in history

서술형

2. 위 글 (A), (B)의 ⓐ the claim과 ⓑ that이 의미하는 바를 각각 우리말로 쓰시오.

서술형

3. According to passage (B), Karl Popper is skeptical about the existence of ________ ________, for he believes that, unlike science, history is concerned with ________ ________. (from the passage)

4. 위 글 (A), (B)의 각 빈칸에 들어갈 말로 가장 적절한 것은?

	(A)		(B)
①	as a result	……	Moreover
②	for instance	……	Moreover
③	however	……	Nonetheless
④	for instance	……	Naturally
⑤	as a result	……	Naturally

칼 포퍼(Sir Karl Raimund Popper, 1902–1994)

영국의 자연 · 사회 과학자이며 철학자로 논리 실증주의를 비판하고 비판적 합리주의를 주창하였다. 포퍼는 경험과학의 귀납적 방법을 반대하였고, 대담한 추측과 그에 대한 반증을 통해 과학이 발전한다고 보았다. 그에 따르면, 과학자는 자신이 가정한 규칙에 대해 예외적인 사례를 발견하려고 하고, 이때 반증이 성립하지 않으면 이론은 증명된다. 또한 그는 과학과 비과학을 구분하는 기준으로 반증가능성 원리를 제시하였고, 반증이 불가능한 점성학, 형이상학, 정신분석학, 마르크스주의 이론 등은 과학이 될 수 없다고 주장하였다. 주요 저서로는 「열린 사회와 그 적들」(1945), 「역사주의의 빈곤」(1957) 등이 있다.

VOCAB

investigation 조사, 연구
validate 정당성을 입증하다, 증명하다
claim (당연한 권리로서의) 주장

(B)
develop *발달하다; 발전시키다
doubt 의심하다
lie in ~에 (놓여) 있다
assume 추정[가정]하다
apply *적용되다; 신청하다
whereas ~에 반해서, 그런데
be composed of ~으로 구성되다
hence 따라서, 그러므로
predict 예측하다

33 SECTION 07. History

Have you ever heard that history is the story of the winners? If this is true, what should be considered is not just the accuracy of history textbooks, but the actual _______________ that goes along with being the ones who get their story heard. It is the history of the dominant group that gets to be told, and it is their story that is often the one that becomes normalized, while the stories of everyone else get 'othered' or ignored. Minority groups and outcasts in society don't get to tell their side of the story.

A classic example is the history of the *Stolen Generation in Australia. Until recently, the fact that 100,000 aboriginal children were taken from their families and raised in the homes of white families was not considered an important part of European history in Australia, and so there was no way for those to whom it happened to tell their story. Only with the increasing rise of *pluralism in Australia has it become possible for members of the Stolen Generation to speak out and be heard by the general public.

Because history is ultimately linked to power, it is extremely difficult to develop ways of using and managing resources when the historical stories make the owners of those resources invisible. (A) As long as these people go unrecognized, it is a legitimate activity to cut down their forests and sell their timber to First World nations. (B) It is also legitimate to ensure that the profits from such activity flow directly to the lumber companies without any recognition being given to the Penan for their prior ownership of the trees. (C) Consider the Penan people of the Borneo rain forest.

*Stolen Generation 도둑맞은 세대 (호주 원주민)
*pluralism 문화 다원주의

VOCAB

accuracy 정확성
actual 실제의
go along with ~와 동행하다; *~에 따르다[부수하다]
dominant 지배의, 지배적인
normalize *표준화하다; 정상화하다
ignore 무시하다
minority 소수
outcast 버림받은 사람들, 추방자
classic 고전의; *전형적인
aboriginal (호주) 원주민의
raise *기르다; 올리다
speak out 거리낌없이 이야기하다
ultimately 궁극적으로
link 연결하다
extremely 극히

33

SECTION 07.
역사

1. Which of the following can NOT be the title of the passage?

① Whose History is It?
② History as Reliable Witness
③ History and Real Power
④ History for Winners Only
⑤ History and Minorities

2. 위 글 첫째 단락의 빈칸에 들어갈 말로 가장 적절한 것은?

① influence
② reputation
③ damage
④ dignity
⑤ fact

3. 위 글 셋째 단락의 (A)~(C)를 글의 흐름에 맞게 배열한 것으로 가장 적절한 것은?

① (A) - (C) - (B)
② (B) - (A) - (C)
③ (B) - (C) - (A)
④ (C) - (A) - (B)
⑤ (C) - (B) - (A)

서술형

4. 위 글에 따르면, 호주의 도둑맞은 세대와 페낭인들의 공통점은 무엇인지 우리말로 쓰시오.

VOCAB

manage 관리하다, 운영하다
resource 자원
invisible 보이지 않는; *명시되지 않은
unrecognized 인정받지 못하는
legitimate 합법적인
timber 목재
First World 제1세계, (서방) 선진국
ensure 보장하다; 확보하다
profit 수익, 이익
flow 흐르다
lumber 재목, 제재
recognition 인정
Penan 페낭인의
prior 앞(서)의
ownership 소유권

도둑맞은 세대(stolen generation)

1770년 호주가 영국령으로 선포되고 나서 8년 뒤 1,500여명의 첫 이주민들이 호주 시드니에 도착했다. 이들 이주민 가운데 절반 이상이 범죄자들이었다. 이들이 이주한 뒤부터 호주 원주민 '애보리진'은 단지 원주민이라는 이유만으로 무자비하게 학살당했다. 이주민들은 애보리진을 노예로 부릴 가치도 없을 만큼 미개하다고 판단해 집단적이고 조직적으로 학살했다. 게다가 1910년부터 1970년대 말까지 전체 원주민 인구의 4분의 1에 해당하는 10만 명의 어린이들이 호주 정부의 격리 조치(문명화)에 따라 집에서 쫓겨나 강제 이주 당해야 했다. 이들은 국가에 의해 강제로 가족에게서 분리돼 정부 운영 기관에서 키워지거나 백인 가정에서 양육되었다. 그들은 원주민과 원주민 자녀들에게 '백인처럼' 생각하고 행동하는 법을 가르치고자 했다. 후에 이들은 '도둑맞은 세대'라고 불리게 되었다.

34

SECTION 07.
History

The early nineteenth century constituted a period of massive migration in the United States as white settlers moved westward in droves. The U.S. government enacted the forced relocation of Native American tribes to government-established reservations, but continued settlement further raised the demand for land. However, the Native American practice of communal use of land made it nearly impossible to acquire reservation land from tribes.

The avarice of settlers and the government for ever-increasing control of land ultimately led to the General Allotment Act of 1887, often referred to as the Dawes Act, as the legislation was sponsored by Senator Henry Dawes. Under the Dawes Act, land that had previously been held collectively by tribes was parceled out into allotments and then distributed to individual members of the tribe. The territory of the reservations was not fully distributed, however, and the remaining “surplus” — often the most well-positioned or mineral-rich land — was sold off to the highest bidder, who was usually a non-Indian settler or company.

(①) The division of communal lands forced Native Americans to assimilate into mainstream American culture, leading to the unwitting abdication of tribal sovereignty and the loss of cultural identity. (②) The dramatic shift in lifestyle for Native Americans, moving from working together as a closely tied community to individually cultivating small farms, was not only unwanted but also unfeasible. (③) The allotment system was abolished in 1934, but its far-reaching adverse effects are still felt today. (④) This is evidenced by the significant changes that the Indian way of life has undergone and the fact that some reservations still have more non-Indian than Indian residents. (⑤)

VOCAB

constitute *~이 되다; ~을 구성하다
settler 이주민
drove 무리
enact 제정하다, 규정하다
relocation 재배치, 이주
reservation 예약; *보호구역
communal 공동의
avarice 탐욕
allotment 할당
legislation 법률
sponsor 후원하다; *(법안 등을) 발의하다
senator 상원의원
collectively 집합적으로
parcel out 나누다
distribute 분배하다
territory 영토

34

SECTION 07.
역사

1. **What is the best title for the passage?**

① Henry Dawes: The First Native American Senator
② The Law that Destroyed Native American Culture
③ Native Americans' Contributions to U.S. Agriculture
④ The Beginning of Native American Communal Land Use
⑤ How Native Americans Used the Law to Protect Their Land

서술형

2. **What does the author suggest led to the Dawes Act? (Use the words from the passage.)**

3. **위 글의 ①~⑤ 중에서 다음 주어진 문장이 들어갈 곳으로 가장 적절한 것은?**

Many plots allotted to Native Americans were ill-suited for farming on a small scale, and those caring for the land lacked basic agricultural necessities.

4. **도스 법에 대한 설명 중, 위 글의 내용과 일치하지 않는 것은?**

① 법 시행 전, 원주민들은 토지를 부족 공용으로 썼다.
② 법을 발의한 상원의원의 이름을 따서 명명되었다.
③ 자원이 풍부한 토지는 대부분 원주민들 외의 정착자들에게 팔렸다.
④ 원주민들을 미국 주류 문화에 강제 동화시켰다.
⑤ 할당 제도가 폐지되자 원주민들의 삶의 방식 또한 원래대로 돌아갔다.

VOCAB

bidder 입찰자
assimilate 동화되다
unwitting 자신도 모르는
abdication 포기, 기권
sovereignty 통치권, 자주권
identity *정체성, 동일함
cultivate 경작하다
unfeasible 실행할 수 없는
abolish 폐지하다
far-reaching 멀리까지 미치는, 중요한
adverse effect 역효과, 부작용
evidence 증거; *입증하다
significant 중요한, 커다란
undergo (변화 등을) 겪다
resident 거주자[주민]

SECTION 07.

Word Test

정답 | P.124

1. 다음 밑줄 친 단어의 의미로 알맞은 것을 고르시오.

(1) The president has remained mute about the plans to reduce taxes.

① unable to hear ② not approving ③ unwilling to speak
④ impossible to see ⑤ showing agreement

(2) Her parents died when she was a baby, so she was raised by her aunt.

① lift highly ② collect money ③ mention something
④ save someone ⑤ take care of a person

2. 우리말에 맞게 빈칸에 공통으로 들어갈 단어를 알맞은 형태로 바꾸어 쓰시오.

· We advertised three jobs and over fifty people ____________.
(우리가 일자리 세 개를 광고로 내자 50명 이상의 사람들이 지원했다.)

· Do the same rules ____________ to part-time workers?
(똑같은 규칙이 시간제 직원에게도 적용되나요?)

· ____________ the suntan lotion evenly over the skin.
(선탠로션을 피부 위에 골고루 발라라.)

3. 다음 문장의 밑줄 친 부분과 바꿔 쓸 수 있는 단어를 고르시오.

(1) We aim to provide a service that is balanced and unbiased.

① unfair ② terrible ③ comfortable ④ impartial ⑤ reasonable

(2) I had to make a speech at my brother's wedding.

① support ② deliver ③ conclude ④ accept ⑤ spoil

(3) She refused to undergo medical treatment for religious reasons.

① distribute ② analyze ③ experience ④ imply ⑤ assume

(4) There's been a massive increase in the number of children victims of domestic violence looking for help.

① unfeasible ② dominant ③ factual ④ compatible ⑤ immense

4. 우리말에 맞게 빈칸에 주어진 철자로 시작하는 단어를 쓰시오.

(1) It's hard to give an o____________ opinion about your own children.
(당신 자녀들에 대해 객관적인 의견을 제시하기란 어렵다.)

(2) It was a good concert — I enjoyed the last song in p____________.
(그것은 훌륭한 콘서트였다. 특히 난 마지막 노래가 정말 좋았다.)

(3) Decisions are sometimes made on the b____________ of incorrect information.
(결정은 가끔 부정확한 정보를 근거로 하여 이루어진다.)

SECTION. 08

Environment · Ecology · Medicine

환경 · 생태 · 의학

35

SECTION 08.

Environment · Ecology · Medicine

Human activity has greatly affected the survival of Earth's plant and animal species. For millions of years, life evolved without significant impact from human beings. As early as the first settlements in Australia and North America, human beings caused the extinction of species through hunting or the use of fire. Since the nineteenth century, the role that human beings play in species survival has increased so much that many species survive only because ______________________.

Certain animal species survive in large numbers thanks to humans. For example, today there are about 10 billion chickens on Earth, or about fifteen times as many as there were a hundred years ago. This is because so many chickens are bred for human consumption. Similarly, we raise cattle, sheep, goats, and other domesticated animals in order to make use of them. In addition, modern civilizations have unintentionally ensured the survival of other species. Pests such as rats and cockroaches live on the food waste created by humans. Squirrels prosper in suburban landscapes where there are few predators.

Even as modern human beings intentionally or unintentionally promote the survival of a few species, we threaten many more. Thanks to technology, hunting has become vastly more efficient, pushing animals such as the blue whale and the North American bison to the brink of extinction. Many other animals, especially tropical forest species, suffer from destruction of their habitats through logging trees by humans.

VOCAB

affect ~에 영향을 미치다, 작용하다
survival 생존 (survive 생존하다)
species 종(種)
evolve 전개하다; *진화하다
significant 상당한
impact 영향, 충격
settlement 정착
extinction 멸종
billion 10억
breed 낳다; *사육하다 (bred · bred)
consumption 소비
raise *기르다; 들어올리다
domesticate 길들이다
make use of ~을 이용하다
civilization 문명
unintentionally 고의가 아니게, 부지불식간에 (↔ intentionally 의도적으로)

35

1. **What is the best title for the passage?**

① Wild Animals and Plant Life
② Changes in Animal Population
③ The Origin of Animal Domestication
④ Effects of Human-centered Evolution
⑤ Reasons for Environmental Destruction

2. **Which of the following is best fit for the blank in the 1st paragraph?**

① nature calls for it
② human beings allow it
③ they've changed their diet
④ they try to be like humans
⑤ they've been domesticated

3. **According to the passage, which of the following is NOT true?**

① Animals have been domesticated for many years.
② Modern civilization has allowed rats to thrive.
③ Surviving animals are all used for human consumption.
④ Modern technology threatens many animals and plants.
⑤ The North American bison is almost extinct.

4. **위 글 셋째 단락의 밑줄 친 문장을 우리말로 해석하시오.**

SECTION 08.
환경 · 생태 · 의학

VOCAB

ensure 확인하다; *보장하다
pest 해충, 골칫거리
cockroach 바퀴벌레
live on ~을 먹고 살다
prosper 번성하다, 번식하다
suburban 교외의
landscape 경치, 풍경
predator 육식동물
promote *조장하다, 증진시키다; 승진시키다
threaten 위협하다
vastly 광대하게; *매우
efficient 효율적인
blue whale 흰긴수염고래
bison 들소
brink 가장자리; *직전
tropical 열대의
destruction 파괴
habitat 서식지
log 벌채하다

36

SECTION 08.
Environment · Ecology · Medicine

(A)

So-called shallow environmentalism still dominates the mainstream. It encourages continuous economic growth and environmental protection through technological ideas, resources management such as replanting forests and recycling, and small changes in lifestyles. ______________, the Deep Ecology approach aims to achieve a major ecological change of our sociocultural systems, collective actions, and lifestyles. The Deep Ecology approach says that we must rethink our present culture and character, which threatens the earth. Deep Ecology does not separate humans from the natural environment. It sees the world as a network where all living things are connected. It calls for the protection of natural areas and areas of biodiversity in order to protect and sustain the environment and the value of everything in it.

(B)

The Sustainable Environmental System manages all of nature's problems at all levels. (These, socio-economic problems, concerns, include, usual, as well as, the, physical and scientific, environmental). The environment is complex and has many different dimensions to it. As such, any attempt to resolve environmental problems must also have many dimensions. ______________, air pollution is not just a problem of cars, but also of people using cars too much and too often. People drive for many reasons, ranging from commuting to work to grocery shopping. So a solution to this cause of air pollution must also include alternatives to driving. We could also provide economic incentive systems to discourage too much driving, or the location of services and employment could be changed so as to minimize the need to drive long distances. The Sustainable Environmental System is basically about trying to change all of the causes that lead to environmental problems.

VOCAB

(A)
so-called 소위, 이른바
shallow 얕은, 알팍한
environmentalism 환경보호주의
dominate 지배하다, 좌우하다
mainstream 주류, 대세
continuous 계속적인, 끊임없는
protection 보호
resource 자원
replant 이식하다
ecology 생태학
ecological 생태학적인
approach 접근(법)
threaten 위협하다
separate 분리하다
call for ~을 요구하다
biodiversity 생물의 다양성
sustain 떠받치다; *유지하다

1.위 글 (A)의 내용을 참고하여 다음 중 심층 생태학의 개념에 해당되는 도식을 고르시오.

①
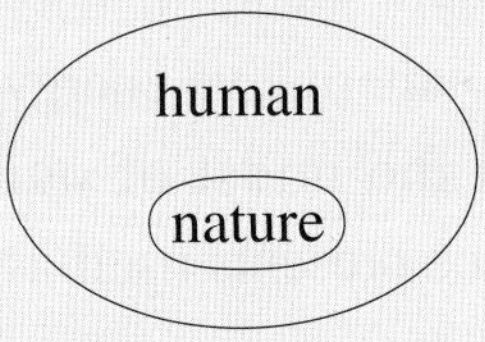

②
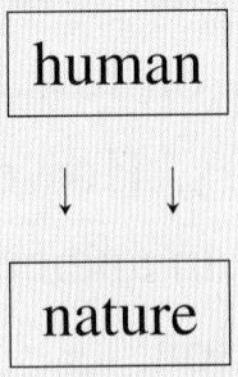

③
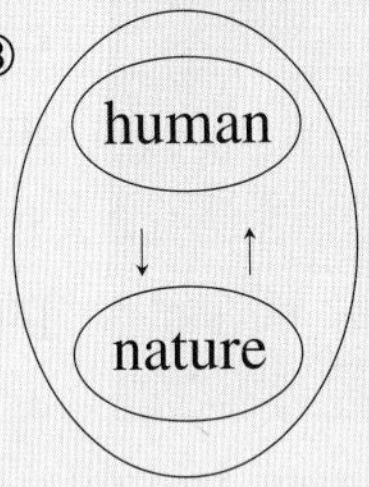

④
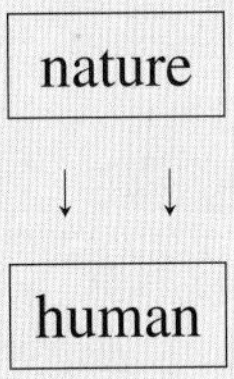

2. 위 글 (A)와 (B)의 각 빈칸에 들어갈 말로 가장 적절한 것은?

(A)		(B)
① However	……	Moreover
② In contrast	……	For instance
③ In contrast	……	That is to say
④ Meanwhile	……	As a result
⑤ Similarly	……	For instance

3. 위 글 (B)의 괄호 안의 단어를 아래에 주어진 우리말의 뜻에 맞게 배열하시오.

이것은 보통의 물리 · 과학적인 환경 문제뿐만 아니라 사회 경제적인 문제들도 포함한다.

VOCAB

(B)
sustainable 지속[유지]할 수 있는
concern *걱정, 염려; 관심사
complex 복잡한
dimension 규모; *범위; 차원
attempt 시도(하다)
resolve 해결하다
range from A to B 범위가 A에서 B에 이르다
commute 통근하다
cause *원인; 야기하다
alternative 대안(의)
incentive 유인, 동기; *보상금, 장려금
discourage 낙담시키다; *저지하다
location 위치
employment 고용
minimize 최소화하다
basically 근본적으로
lead to ~에 이르게 하다

37

SECTION 08.

Environment · Ecology · Medicine

The planet is approaching an energy crisis, and governments are spending more money on research into alternative energy sources. However, in the midst of our panic, an ancient practice presents itself as a solution: ______________________.

The meat and dairy industries use huge amounts of natural gas, electricity, and fossil fuels to house, heat, ventilate, water, feed, clean, transport and slaughter the billions of animals consumed by humans every year. In total, raising animals for food uses more than one-third of all materials and fossil fuels; a vegetarian diet would require only 2 percent of raw materials. So excessive is the amount of energy used by having a meat-based diet that if the world switched to a plant-based one, current petroleum reserves would easily last for another 360 years. The creation of a single hamburger patty uses enough fossil fuel to power a car 20 miles or heat water for seventeen showers.

In fact, if water used by the meat industry were not covered by taxpayers, ordinary hamburger meat would cost $35 a pound. Whereas it takes 25 gallons of water to produce a pound of wheat, it takes 2,500 gallons to generate a pound of meat.

______________ the energy costs of meat production, it is estimated that 60 percent of America's waterways have been polluted by livestock industries, which create three times more water pollution than other industrial sources combined. The places most animals are kept produce toxic methane and ammonia fumes so that poultry workers have to wear gas masks.

There are so many energy-wasting practices connected with eating animals. We can ease some of our own burden by adopting sensible eating habits.

VOCAB

the planet 지구
approach ~에 접근하다
crisis 위기
alternative 대체(의), 대안(의)
source 자료, 자원
panic 공포
ancient 고대의; *옛날의
practice 실행; *관행
dairy 낙농(업)의
electricity 전기
fossil fuel 화석연료
ventilate 통풍시키다
feed 먹이를 주다 (fed · fed)
transport 수송하다
slaughter 도살하다
consume 소비하다
in total 전부 합쳐
vegetarian 채식주의자의
raw 날것의; *가공하지 않은
excessive 지나친, 과도한
switch 전환하다

1. What is the author mainly talking about?

① environmental pollution due to animals
② the need to change our meat-based diet
③ health benefits of eating vegetables
④ the solution to reducing energy costs
⑤ ways to raise animals without wasting energy

2. 위 글 첫째 단락의 빈칸에 들어갈 말로 가장 적절한 것은?

① recycling
② saving on energy
③ vegetarianism
④ environment management
⑤ developing natural resources

3. 다음 중 위 글의 내용과 일치하지 않는 것은?

① 에너지 위기로 인한 대체 에너지 개발 비용이 증가하고 있다.
② 식용 동물을 사육하는 데는 화석연료의 1/3 이상이 사용된다.
③ 현재 지구의 석유 보유량은 360년 이상을 쓸 수 있는 양이다.
④ 축산업은 다른 산업에 비해 세 배 이상의 수질 오염을 야기한다.
⑤ 동물들이 사육되는 장소에서는 유독성 물질이 많이 배출된다.

4. 위 글 넷째 단락의 빈칸에 들어갈 말로 가장 적절한 것은?

① Because of
② Despite
③ Owing to
④ Contrary to
⑤ In addition to

37

SECTION 08.
환경 · 생태 · 의학

VOCAB

petroleum 석유
reserve 비축; *매장량
creation 창조
patty 고기 반죽
power 힘; *동력(을 공급하다)
cover 덮다; 포함하다; 보도하다; *(요금 등을) 메우다, 상쇄하다
taxpayer 납세자
ordinary 일반의, 평범한
gallon 갤런 (=3.7853ℓ)
generate 생성하다, 만들어 내다
estimate 추정하다
livestock 가축
combined 결합한
toxic 독성의, 유독한
methane 메탄가스
ammonia 암모니아
fume 연기, 가스
poultry 가금(家禽), 식용 사육 조류
adopt 채택하다
sensible 현명한

38

SECTION 08.

Environment · Ecology · Medicine

Noise has always been a chief environmental problem for humans. In ancient Rome, rules existed to limit the noise emitted from the ironed wheels of wagons which rattled over the stone roads, causing irritating sleep disturbance to citizens. In Medieval Europe, horse carriages and horseback riding were prohibited during nighttime in certain cities to ensure a peaceful sleep for the inhabitants. However, the noise problems of the past are incomparable with those of modern times. Day and night, an enormous number of cars, trucks and buses regularly pass through cities and the countryside. On top of this is the high level of noise created by aircraft, trains, and industrial machinery.

In comparison to other pollutants, the control of environmental noise has been ignored because of insufficient knowledge of its effects on humans, as well as a lack of defined criteria. While it has been suggested that noise pollution is simply a "luxury" problem for developed countries, one cannot ignore the fact that the exposure to noise is often higher in developing countries, where there are less regulations. Regardless of where it exists, noise pollution's effects are widespread and damaging. Accordingly, practical action to limit and control human exposure to environmental noise is essential.

Such action is now taking place in Europe, where it is estimated that 40 percent of residents, or 150 million people, are exposed to road traffic noise exceeding 55 *decibels, and over 30 percent suffer sleep-disturbing noise levels at night. Authorities are surveying areas to discover where noise levels are the highest, and producing computerized maps available on the Internet to warn people. The maps are color-coded according to decibel range, from green, the quietest, through to yellow, red and dark blue. These maps will be followed by E.U. legislation intend to reduce the noise levels in the worst, dark-blue areas.

*decibel 데시벨(음향 크기의 단위)

VOCAB

chief 주된, 주요한
ancient 고대의
emit 방사하다, 내뿜다
wagon 짐마차
rattle 덜컹덜컹 소리를 내다
irritating 짜증나게 하는
disturbance 방해; *장애 (disturb 방해하다)
citizen 시민
Medieval 중세의
carriage 마차, 탈것
prohibit 금지하다
ensure 보장하다
inhabitant 주민, 거주자
incomparable 비교가 되지 않는
enormous 엄청난
machinery 기계
in comparison to ~와 비교하여
pollutant 오염물질, 오염원
insufficient 불충분한
effect *영향; 효과

38

SECTION 08.

환경 · 생태 · 의학

1. 위 글에서 주제문을 찾아 밑줄을 그으시오.

2. 다음 중 위 글의 내용과 일치하지 않는 것은? (2개)

① 고대 로마와 중세 시대에도 소음에 대한 규제가 있었다.
② 산업화로 인한 기계의 발달이 소음 공해를 가중시켰다.
③ 개발도상국은 선진국에 비해 소음 공해가 적은 편이다.
④ 유럽에서는 절반 가량의 인구가 도로교통소음에 노출되어 있다.
⑤ 지도에서 소음이 가장 심한 지역은 빨간색으로 표시된다.

서술형

3. 위 글에 따르면, 소음 공해에 대한 규제가 상대적으로 등한시되었던 이유는 무엇인지 우리말로 쓰시오.

4. 위 글 셋째 단락의 밑줄 친 문장에서 어법상 틀린 부분을 찾아 바르게 고치시오.

VOCAB

define 정의하다; *규정짓다
criteria 기준, 척도 (criterion의 복수)
exposure 노출(된 상태), (위험 등에) 무방비 상태 (expose 노출시키다)
regulation 규제
regardless of ~와 관계없이
widespread 널리 퍼진; *광범위한
damaging 손해를 끼치는, 해로운
essential 필수적인
estimate 추정하다
resident 거주민
exceed 초과하다
authority (*pl.*) 당국
survey 조사하다
available 이용 가능한
color-coded 색으로 분류된
legislation 입법; *법률
reduce 줄이다

소음 측정 단위인 데시벨(dB)과 웨클(WECPNL)

데시벨은 소리의 크기를 나타내는 단위로, dB로 표기한다. 사람이 들을 수 있는 가장 작은 소리는 0dB이며, 일반적으로 도서관에서 속삭이는 정도는 30dB, 정상적인 대화는 60dB, 그리고 록 콘서트나 자동차 경적 소리는 115dB 정도로 측정된다. 85dB 이상의 소음을 지속적으로 듣게 되면 청각 장애가 일어날 수 있으며, 140dB의 소음에는 매우 짧은 시간 동안 노출되어도 청력에 손상을 입을 수 있다.
또 다른 소음 측정 단위인 웨클은 국제민간항공기구(ICAO)가 정한 항공기의 소음 단위이다. 하루 24시간 동안 항공기가 통과할 때마다 최고 소음의 데시벨을 측정하여 시간대별 가중치를 반영한 다음 평균치를 산정한다. 웨클 수치에서 13을 빼면 대략적인 데시벨 수치가 된다. 소음이 90웨클인 경우 전화 통화나 TV 수신이 어렵고 정상적인 대화가 불가능하다. 한국에서는 인천국제공항 주변의 일부 지역이 심각한 항공기 소음 공해 지역에 해당한다.

39 SECTION 08.
Environment · Ecology · Medicine

(A)

Hippocrates (c. 460-377 BC) believed in the dualistic nature of mind and body. (①) He radically proposed that disease occurred in the body and that this process was independent of the mind. (②) Hippocrates suggested that the body contained four specific fluids, called *humors. (③) According to Hippocrates, a person experienced health when these humors were balanced. (④) However, when the fluids were out of balance, disease occurred. (⑤) This approach to health and disease was radical for its time because disease had previously been thought to be the result of demons or spirits possessing the body. Hippocrates challenged this view and established a physical approach to health and disease. For this reason he is often described as the "father of medicine."

*humor 액, 체액

(B)

I hope that you can now understand that there is an extensive and significant relationship between mind and health. This relationship is controlled by our behavior together with the biological connections which exist between the brain and the immune system. These connections work in both directions, meaning that our physical health is able to influence our mental state, and vice-versa. In other words, all illnesses have psychological consequences as well as causes. Stress, depression and other psychological factors can affect our immunity to many diseases, including bacterial and viral infections, heart disease and cancer. Thus, our mental and emotional states are highly important in the maintenance of health. In that sense, our dualistic habit of contrasting mind and body, as though they were two separate entities, is deeply misleading.

VOCAB

(A)
dualistic 이원론적인
radically 급진적으로
propose 제안하다; *의견을 내다
occur 발생하다, 일어나다
independent of ~와 관계없는[별도인]
contain 포함하다
specific 특정의
fluid 액체
balance 균형(을 이루다) (out of balance 균형을 잃은)
approach 접근법
previously 이전에
demon 악마
possess 소유하다; *(악마 · 귀신이) ~에 들리다
establish 세우다, 정립하다
physical *신체의, 육체의; 물리의, 물리적인
(B)
extensive 광범위한
significant 중요한
biological 생물학적인

1. 위 글 (A)의 ①~⑤ 중에서 다음 주어진 문장이 들어갈 곳으로 가장 적절한 것은?

Treatment therefore involved an attempt to balance the four fluids.

2. **Hippocrates and the author of passage (B) have different viewpoints on ____.**

① the cause of viral diseases
② the definition of health and illness
③ the components of body structure
④ the connection between mind and body
⑤ the psychological factors causing illness

3. **Mark T(True) or F(False) for the following statements.**

(1) According to Hippocrates, diseases occur owing to the deficiency of body fluids. □ T □ F

(2) According to passage (B), anxiety, sadness or other negative emotions can cause illnesses. □ T □ F

(3) Someone who thinks like Hippocrates may insist that we should look after our mental and emotional states to keep our body healthy. □ T □ F

히포크라테스의 의술

히포크라테스는 인간의 질병을 혈액, 점액, 황담즙, 흑담즙 등 네 가지 체액 사이의 균형이 깨졌을 때 발생하는 것으로 보았다. 그리고 이 체액을 각각 사계절과, 공기, 물, 불, 흙 등의 네 가지 원소와 습하고 건조하며 뜨겁고 찬 네 가지 성질에 연결시켜 설명하였다. 당시 의사는 이곳저곳을 돌아다니며 의료 행위를 하였기 때문에 다양한 지역의 풍토에 대한 이해가 중요하였다. 히포크라테스가 인간의 체액을 자연의 원소와 성질에 연결한 것도 그 이유에서였다.
히포크라테스가 활동하던 시기의 의사들은 자신의 능력을 자랑하기 위해 능수능란한 언변을 중요하게 여겼으며 질병을 신들과 연결시켜 대중의 무지와 두려움을 이용하였다. 지금도 의사의 길을 걷고자 하는 이들이 '히포크라테스의 선서'를 하는 것은 히포크라테스가 바로 그러한 의사들의 행동을 비판하면서 신분을 초월하여 환자에 대해 최선을 다할 것과 경험적이고 체계적인 의학 연구를 강조하였기 때문이다.

VOCAB

connection 연관(성)
immune system 면역 체계
work 일하다; *작용하다
mental 정신의, 정신적인
state 주; 국가; *상태
vice-versa 역도 또한 같음
psychological 심리적인
consequence 결과
cause 원인
depression 우울증
factor 요소, 요인
affect ~에 영향을 미치다
immunity 면역성
bacterial 세균성의
viral 바이러스성의
infection 감염
cancer 암
maintenance 유지
contrast 대비시키다
separate 별개의
entity 존재(물)
misleading 잘못 인도하는, 오해하게 만드는

SECTION 08.
Word Test

정답 | P.125

1. 다음 중 단어의 뜻풀이가 잘못된 것은?

① vegetarian: someone who does not eat meat or fish
② commute: to regularly travel some distance to get to work
③ survival: something that makes it difficult to achieve something
④ extinction: the situation when a species of animal or plant no longer exists
⑤ immune: protected against a particular disease by particular substances in the body

2. 밑줄 친 단어의 동의어 또는 반의어를 보기에서 찾아 쓰시오. (단, 필요한 경우에는 어형을 바꾸시오.)

보기 | inhabitant influence deep have mental illness

(1) They swam in the shallow river. (↔ ____________)
(2) He is a child who has physical disabilities. (↔ ____________)
(3) Kate is a woman who possesses a rare intelligence. (= ____________)
(4) The divorce affected every aspect of her life. (= ____________)
(5) The local residents were angry at the lack of parking spaces. (= ____________)
(6) The first symptom of the disease is a very high temperature. (= ____________)

3. 우리말에 맞게 빈칸에 공통으로 들어갈 알맞은 단어를 쓰시오.

· I was born and ____________ed in Busan.
(나는 부산에서 태어나서 자랐다.)
· Please ____________ your hand if you know the right answer.
(정답을 알면 손을 들어 주세요.)
· We managed to ____________ $4,000 through donations and other events.
(우리는 기부와 다른 행사를 통해 그럭저럭 4천 달러를 모금했다.)

4. 다음 문장의 빈칸에 들어갈 가장 알맞은 단어를 고르시오.

(1) The new light bulbs ____________ less electricity.
① enhance ② submit ③ remove ④ consume ⑤ restore
(2) The pipeline acts to ____________ the fluid.
① rescue ② contain ③ involve ④ prevent ⑤ stop
(3) The sale of alcohol to adolescents is ____________ by law.
① revised ② advanced ③ prospered ④ prohibited ⑤ enforced
(4) 19% of those ____________ say they haven't decided who they'll vote for.
① implied ② produced ③ surveyed ④ emphasized ⑤ installed

SECTION.09

Economics · Business

경제 · 경영

40

SECTION 09.

Economics · Business

In the study of development and international trade, most controversies revolve around the question of who wins when trade is being conducted between countries with different national endowments. According to the conventional free-trade theory, countries fated by climate, geography, and history are to specialize in agricultural (bananas and coffee) or certain mineral (oil and gas) commodities, whereas countries rich in capital and technology are expected to produce capital-intensive, high-technology products and (A) [import / export] them in exchange for commodities and low-skill, labor-intensive products. The theory argues that free trade provides for optimal benefits for all parties while increasing world output overall. Taken to extremes, it holds that countries should specialize in a narrow bundle of products, or that agriculturally based economies ______________________________.

The specialization strategy under the assumption of comparative advantage, however, has had very little practical use for most mineral-specializing countries. Traditionally, abundant natural resources have been regarded as contributing to the successful development of Western countries, such as Australia, the US and Canada. However, during the past three decades, the star performers among developing countries, such as Korea and Taiwan, have been resource-poor, while the majority of the resource-rich countries, such as Argentina, Mexico, Peru, Saudi Arabia and Venezuela, have had (B) [higher / lower] than average annual growth rates overall.

What are the growth-retarding factors for a large number of resource-abundant countries? These countries are usually poor because the demand for their products is relatively inelastic: People consume about the same amounts of resources even as their prices fluctuate. In addition, the costs of making these products tend to rise as production (C) [increases / declines] because poorer natural resources have to be brought into production as the better ones are used up.

FROM 2011 한양대 수시 논술

VOCAB

controversy 논란
revolve 회전하다; *(토론 등이) ~에 초점을 맞추다
endowment (*pl.*) (타고난) 자질, 재능
conventional 전통적인, 종래의
fate 운명; *운명짓다
geography 지리
specialize in ~을 전문으로 하다
agricultural 농업의, 농사의 (agriculturally 농사와 관련하여, 농업적으로)
commodity 상품; *원자재, 미가공품
capital-intensive 자본 집약적인
labor-intensive 노동 집약적인

1. 위 글의 (A), (B), (C) 각 네모 안에서 문맥에 맞는 어휘를 골라 짝지은 것으로 가장 적절한 것은?

	(A)		(B)		(C)
①	import	……	higher	……	increases
②	import	……	lower	……	declines
③	export	……	higher	……	increases
④	export	……	lower	……	declines
⑤	export	……	lower	……	increases

2. Which of the following best fits the blank?

① should stick to agriculture rather than trying to industrialize
② should consider future forecasts about the growth of agriculture
③ should try to excel in both the agricultural and high-tech industries
④ should replace their agriculture system with an industrialized system
⑤ should not be satisfied with their agriculture advantage over other countries

3. Mark T(True) or F(False) for the following statements.

(1) According to the conventional free-trade theory, it is ideal to trade items which have a comparative advantage without assuring a profit for both sides. □ T □ F
(2) Historically, some Western countries experienced substantial economic growth because they were rich in natural resources. □ T □ F
(3) The comparative advantage theory hasn't worked recently regarding resource-rich countries. □ T □ F

서술형

4. According to the passage, how does inelastic demand for resource-abundant countries' products affect those countries? (in Korean)

VOCAB

optimal 최적의
output 생산량, 산출량
bundle (물건들의) 묶음, 일단
assumption 가정, 전제
comparative advantage 비교 우위
practical 실제적인
abundant 풍부한
contribute 기여하다
decade 십 년간
majority 대다수
annual 매년의, 연례의
retard 지연[지체]시키다
inelastic (경제) 비탄력적인
fluctuate 변동하다

41

SECTION 09.
Economics · Business

Thanksgiving is a time to gather with family and friends and eat a huge feast like *the Pilgrims did in 1623. We often forget, however, how extremely poor they once were.

Half the Pilgrims died or returned to England in their first year. Those who (A) [remained / reminded] went hungry. Despite religious convictions, the Pilgrims stole from one another. Finally, facing starvation for the fourth winter, Governor Bradford and others began to think of ways to grow corn more efficiently. One of the traditions the Pilgrims had brought with them from England was a practice known as "communal farming." Everything they produced was put into a common pool and rationed among them. This tradition, however, was challenged in light of the perilous conditions of the time. Young men, in particular, thought it an injustice to receive the same allotment of food as <u>those who didn't pull their weight</u>. Incentives were sorely needed. Thus, Bradford decided to experiment in the spring of 1623. He set aside a plot of land for each family so that they could grow their own crop and rely on themselves. The results were nothing short of miraculous. Those who previously claimed they were too old or ill to work (B) [opposed / accepted] the idea of private property and enjoyed the fruits of their labor. Given appropriate incentives, the Pilgrims produced and enjoyed a bountiful harvest in the fall of 1623 and set aside "a day of thanksgiving" to thank God for their good fortune.

However, according to 18th-century economist, Adam Smith, the Pilgrims merely responded to the "invisible hand" — a kind of enlightened self-interest which (C) [directs / liberates] people's actions and serves the interest of the whole society. It provided them with the incentive to produce a bountiful harvest, which they then celebrated in a feast, which we call Thanksgiving Day.

*the Pilgrims 1620년 메이플라워호를 타고 미국에 건너가 플리머스에 정착한 102명의 영국 청교도단

VOCAB

feast 향연, 축제; *진수성찬
extremely 극도로
religious 종교적인
conviction 신념
starvation 기아, 굶주림
governor 통치자, 총독
efficiently 효율적으로
tradition 전통
practice 실행; 연습; *관행, 풍습
communal 공동의
pool 웅덩이; *공동관리
ration 배급하다
challenge 도전하다; *문제 제기하다
in light of ~에 비추어 볼 때
perilous 위험한
in particular 특히
injustice 부정, 불법
allotment 할당
incentive 격려, 동기; *장려금, 보상물
sorely 대단히, 몹시
experiment 실험(하다)
set aside ~을 (따로) 챙겨 두다

1. **What does those who didn't pull their weight in the 2nd paragraph mean?**

① people who were strong enough to work
② people who didn't work as hard as they should
③ people who didn't receive an incentive
④ people who didn't follow the traditions of England
⑤ people who didn't know about communal farming

서술형

2. **위 글에서 초기 이주민들에게 '보이지 않는 손'으로 작용한 것이 무엇인지 본문에서 찾아 쓰시오.**

3. **다음 중 위 글에 언급되지 않은 내용은?**

① the origin of Thanksgiving Day
② the effect of incentives on the Pilgrims
③ the reason the Pilgrims left England
④ the policy that governor Bradford made
⑤ the needy environment the Pilgrims faced

4. **위 글의 (A), (B), (C) 각 네모 안에서 문맥에 맞는 어휘를 골라 짝지은 것으로 가장 적절한 것은?**

	(A)		(B)		(C)
①	remained	……	opposed	……	directs
②	reminded	……	accepted	……	liberates
③	remained	……	accepted	……	liberates
④	reminded	……	opposed	……	liberates
⑤	remained	……	accepted	……	directs

VOCAB

plot 소구획, 작은 지면
crop 농작물
rely on ~에게 의지하다
nothing short of 아주 ~한
miraculous 기적적인
previously 이전에
claim 주장하다
private 사적인, 개인의
property 재산
labor 노동
appropriate 적절한
bountiful 풍부한
harvest 수확
fortune 운, 행운
economist 경제학자
respond to ~에 반응하다
invisible 보이지 않는
enlightened 개화된, 진보한
self-interest 이기심, 이기주의
serve *~에 도움이 되다; ~의 역할을 하다
interest 관심; 이자; *이익
provide A with B A에게 B를 주다(=provide B for A)

42

SECTION 09.
Economics · Business

Economic agents base decisions about a trade on the information they possess. There may exist, however, an inequality in the amount of information held by various agents, ① providing an advantage to one or more sides, a situation referred to as asymmetric information. An illustration of this condition is when the buyer of a used vehicle utilizes market averages as a reference point while the seller has specific information regarding the quality and maintenance history, and therefore the true value, of the vehicle, thus creating an imbalance of power.

While the previous example highlights the presence of asymmetric information prior to completion of a transaction, the principle also applies to actions ② taken after a contract is in effect, a scenario known as a moral hazard. One framework for evaluating this premise is the principal-agent problem, ③ in which an agent is contracted by a principal to carry out a task. Following the contract's finalization, the agent may perform an action without the principal's knowledge or ④ gathering information unavailable to the principal. For instance, in the car insurance industry, the insurance provider, the principal, is unable to monitor the actions of the insured driver, the agent. Consequently, the hidden actions of the agent, such as careless or reckless driving, have an adverse monetary effect on the principal, who must cover the costs associated with accidents.

When asymmetric information causes a moral hazard, the principal must ______________________________. Instituting deductibles in insurance policies and increasing insurance premiums for drivers involved in repeated accidents ⑤ are some actions taken to encourage drivers to be careful.

VOCAB

agent 대리인; *주체, 동작주
inequality 불평등, 불균형
advantage 이익
asymmetric 비대칭의
illustration 삽화; *실례
utilize 이용하다
average 평균
reference point 기준
maintenance 유지, 정비
imbalance 불균형
previous 이전의
highlight 강조하다
presence 존재
completion 완료
transaction 거래
contract 계약; 계약하다
moral hazard 도덕적 위험
framework 틀

1. **According to the passage, which of the following are NOT moral hazards?**

(a) an employee investing in stocks during working hours without management finding out
(b) buffet restaurants usually having more customers who want to consume a lot of food than those who don't
(c) a distributor refurbishing smartphones that had malfunctions and sells them at a used phone market
(d) fund managers taking risks by investing customer money in an attempt to maximize their personal gain

① (a), (b) ② (a), (c) ③ (b), (c) ④ (b), (d) ⑤ (c), (d)

2. **위 글의 ①~⑤ 중에서 어법상 틀린 것을 찾아 바르게 고치시오.**

서술형

3. **According to the passage, why does an imbalance of power occur? (in Korean)**

4. **위 글의 셋째 단락의 빈칸에 들어갈 말로 가장 적절한 것은?**

① find some other agents that will guarantee maximum profits
② take more risks even though they understand the consequences
③ provide incentives and disincentives to counterbalance the effect
④ have better information about how much benefit they can extract
⑤ provide agents with information about all events that have occurred

레몬마켓(lemon market)과 피치마켓(peach market)

영어에서 레몬은 흔히 '불량품'을 의미한다. 이는 처음 레몬이 서양에 들어왔을 때, 오렌지와 비슷한 생김새와는 다르게 강한 신맛으로 인해 맛없는 과일이라 여겨진 데서 유래되었다. 경제학에서 '레몬마켓(lemon market)'은 소비자와 판매자 간의 정보의 불균형으로 인해 품질이 낮은 상품이 거래되는 시장을 일컫는다. 정보가 부족한 소비자는 손해 볼 것을 염려해 적은 비용만을 지불하려고 하고, 결과적으로 겉으로는 멀쩡해 보이지만 실제로는 품질이 낮은 상품을 구매할 가능성이 높다. 반면 상품에 대한 정보가 원활하게 공유되어 우수한 품질의 상품이 교류되는 시장을 '피치마켓(peach market)'이라고 부른다.

VOCAB

evaluate 평가하다
premise 전제
principal *주인; 주요한
carry out ~을 수행[이행]하다
finalization 체결
unavailable 이용할 수 없는
insurance 보험
reckless 무모한
adverse 불리한
monetary 금전적인
associated with ~와 관련된
institute 기관; *도입하다
deductible 공제 금액, 자기 부담금
insurance premium 보험료

43

SECTION 09.
Economics · Business

The term "crowdsourcing" is a blending of the words "crowd" and "outsourcing," and it refers to the business strategy of obtaining work, ideas or funding from a variety of collaborators. It is considered a type of open innovation, meaning it acts as a catalyst for innovative development by combining ideas, efforts and materials from both internal and external sources. The advent of this process has been facilitated by advances in networking technology, as a dedicated web platform — an Internet-accessible base upon which technologies and processes can be built — often serves as the focal point of crowdsourcing efforts.

Strategically speaking, the primary appeal of crowdsourcing can be found in the superior quality of the results it produces, the idea being that it allows businesses to selectively handpick the "cream of the crop" from a vast pool of proposals. This offers an inherent advantage over the traditional method of relying on a single provider of services or an internal research and development department. What's more, the external contributors in a crowdsourcing effort need not be limited to freelancers and professional partners — customers are also being included, and are, in fact, somewhat sought after for their unique perspective on the brands they favor and the products they purchase.

LEGO, for example, has launched a website onto which individuals can upload innovative ideas for future LEGO products; these ideas are then judged by the online LEGO community. If a proposal obtains 10,000 "likes," the product is slated for development and release, with the originator of the idea receiving one percent of the sales subsequently generated.

VOCAB

blending 혼합
outsourcing 외주, 외부 위탁
refer to ~을 나타내다
strategy 전략
obtain 얻다, 손에 넣다
collaborator 협력자
innovation 혁신, 쇄신 (innovative 획기적인)
catalyst 촉매
combine 결합하다
material (*pl.*) (특정 활동에 필요한) 자료
internal 내부의
external 외부의
advent 도래, 출현
facilitate 가능하게[용이하게] 하다
dedicated 헌신적인; *전용의
focal point 초점
strategically 전략적으로
selectively 선택적으로

1. What is the best title for the passage?

① Various Types of Crowdsourcing
② The Downside of Open Innovation
③ Unrestricted Sources, Improved Results
④ Crowdsourcing Raises Capital on Equity
⑤ Customer Surveys: An Indispensable Tool

2. Which of the following is NOT true about crowdsourcing?

① "crowd"와 "outsourcing"의 혼성어이다.
② 다양한 협력자로부터 일, 아이디어, 자금을 얻는 경영 전략을 일컫는다.
③ 오픈 이노베이션의 한 형태로 외부 자원만을 적극 활용해 혁신적 발전을 이끈다.
④ 네트워킹 기술의 발달이 크라우드 소싱을 용이하게 한다.
⑤ 단일 서비스 공급자가 아닌 수많은 공급자들과 함께 일한다는 점이 경쟁 우위 요소이다.

3. Why does the author mention "cream of the crop" in the 2nd paragraph?

① to explain why the term crowdsourcing is proper
② to provide an example of a downside of crowdsourcing
③ to stress that traditional methods are ineffective nowadays
④ to emphasize the exceptional quality of crowdsourcing-generated results
⑤ to show that businesses are able to gain popularity through quality, not quantity

서술형

4. LEGO is introduced as a company that has successfully used crowdsourcing based on the fact that it has made the best use of the invaluable brand insights of its ____________________. (from the passage)

VOCAB

handpick 손으로 따다; *주의해서 고르다
vast 방대한
proposal 제안, 제의
inherent 고유의, 타고난
contributor 기부자, 기여자
somewhat 어느 정도, 약간, 다소
sought after 수요가 많은, 인기 있는
perspective 관점
favor 호의를 보이다, 찬성하다
purchase 구입, 구매
future 미래의, 향후의
slate 추천하다, 선발하다
originator 창작자, 창시자
subsequently 다음에, 이어서
generate 일으키다, 초래하다

아웃소싱(outsourcing)

아웃소싱은 크게 두 가지로 분류된다. 첫째는 기업 내부의 프로젝트를 기업 외부의 제삼자에게 위임하여 진행하는 시스템이다. 해당 기업에 핵심적인 일은 내부에서 진행하고, 나머지 것들은 외부에 위탁하여 효율성을 극대화할 수 있다. 둘째는 외부의 정보 통신 전문 업체가 기업의 시스템 운영을 대행하거나, 서비스 수준 향상을 위해 기업 서비스의 전체 또는 일부를 외부 업체에 위탁해 고객에게 제공하는 시스템이다. 이를 통해 기업 조직이 유연해지고 고객 대응의 민첩성이 증가될 수 있다.

44

SECTION 09.

Economics · Business

Over the past few decades, consumers in wealthy nations have begun practicing ethical consumption, making informed purchasing decisions to support or avoid certain brands based on the company's record on human rights, fair labor practices, animal protection, and environmental sustainability.

While ethical consumption has its merits, critics argue that concentrating exclusively on consumer behavior at the individual level will only absolve governments and corporate entities of accountability. By emphasizing autonomy in consumer decision-making, the decrease in governmental oversight is reinforced, and consumers sacrifice the petitioning of the government to enact responsible economic policies.

____(A)____, the practice of ethical consumption is not solely determined by the individual's motivation to create a robust market for ethical goods and services. The ability to make such choices, such as buying organic food or expensive green products, is dependent upon a number of socio-economic factors, including household income and symbolic capital — that is, one's social status and reputation. As a result, many consumers with lower levels of economic and social status are excluded from participating in ethical consumption.

____(B)____, ethical consumption serves as a cultural force that initiates change in the market and, more importantly, raises important questions regarding the relationships among ethics, commerce, and politics, as well as the sustainability of these systems. This trend should not be dismissed as simply a passing fad or marketing tactic; instead, it should be treated as an opportunity to reshape consumer perspectives on the meaning of living "the ________ life."

VOCAB

consumer 소비자
wealthy 부유한, 부자인
practice 실행하다, 실천하다; 관행
ethical 윤리적인
consumption 소비
informed 정보에 근거한
right (*pl.*) 권리
fair 공정한, 공평한
protection 보호
sustainability 지속 가능성
merit 장점
critic 비평가; *비판하는 사람
argue 주장하다
concentrate 집중하다
exclusively 배타적으로, 독점적으로
absolve *(의무 등을) 면제하다; (죄를) 사하다
corporate entity 법인실체, 기업실체
accountability 책임
emphasize 강조하다
autonomy 자율성

44

1. **What is the author mainly talking about?**

① the characteristics of today's consumer behavior
② the reasons why ethical consumption is prevalent
③ the value and negative effects of ethical consumption
④ the relationship between consumption and quality of life
⑤ the importance of the government's role in boosting the economy

SECTION 09.
경제 · 경영

2. **위 글의 빈칸 (A), (B)에 들어갈 말로 가장 적절한 것은?**

	(A)		(B)
①	Furthermore	······	Similarly
②	For instance	······	Moreover
③	However	······	Nevertheless
④	Furthermore	······	Nevertheless
⑤	However	······	Moreover

서술형

3. **위 글에서 윤리적 소비가 가져오는 부정적 결과로 언급된 두 가지를 우리말로 간략히 쓰시오.**

4. **위 글 넷째 단락의 빈칸에 들어갈 말로 가장 적절한 것은?**

① unusual ② good ③ flexible
④ rebellious ⑤ materialistic

코즈 마케팅(cause marketing)

코즈 마케팅이란 사회적인 이슈에 대한 대의, 즉 '코즈(cause)'를 기업의 이익추구를 위해 활용하는 것을 말한다. 기업이 독자적인 이익만을 좇지 않고, 환경, 보건, 빈곤과 같이 사회적으로 대두되는 문제를 해결하려 할 때 소비자들은 그 기업에 호감을 가지게 되며, 자신도 사회적 활동에 동참하고자 그 기업의 제품을 구매하게 된다. 대표적인 코즈 마케팅의 성공사례로는 한 켤레의 운동화를 사면 빈민국 아이들에게 똑같은 한 켤레가 기부되는 TOMS나, 저체온증으로 인한 사망률이 높은 아프리카 신생아들을 위해 털모자를 떠서 보내는 캠페인에 모자 키트 제작과 판매 및 발송비를 후원하는 GS샵 등이 있다.

VOCAB

decision-making 의사 결정
oversight 간과; *감독, 관리
reinforce 강화하다
petition 탄원하다
enact 제정하다
responsible 책임감 있는
policy 정책, 방침
motivation 동기 부여
robust 튼튼한, 확고한
organic 유기농의
dependent 의존[의지]하는
socio-economic 사회 경제적인
household income 가계 소득
symbolic 상징적인
reputation 명성, 평판
exclude 제외하다
initiate 시작하다, 일으키다
commerce 무역, 상업
dismiss 묵살하다, 일축하다
tactic 전술
perspective 관점

The Timeline of Economic Systems

근대의 초기 자본주의(18C)

18세기 대표적인 고전 경제학자인 애덤 스미스는 「국부론」의 저술을 통해 근대의 초기 자본주의를 성립했다. 그는 자유방임주의 경제 체제를 주장했는데 이는 정부가 중앙에서 개입하지 않으며, 개인에게 이익을 추구할 완전한 자유가 주어지는 것을 말한다. 이때 생산자들은 다른 생산자들과의 경쟁에서 도태되지 않기 위해 소비자가 원하는 상품을 원하는 가격에 제공하게 된다. 이로 인해 자원이 효율적으로 배분된다. 스미스는 이러한 현상을 '보이지 않는 손'에 의한 것이라고 설명했다.

경제 대공황(1929)

경제 대공황은 전형적인 세계공황으로 1929년 10월 24일 뉴욕 주식거래소에서 주가가 대폭락한 데서 발단되었다. 이 공황은 발단 후 약 4년 동안 거의 모든 자본주의 국가들의 경제에 영향을 끼쳤다. 제1차 세계대전 후 미국은 표면적으로는 경제적 번영을 누리고 있는 것처럼 보였지만, 그 실상에는 과잉 생산과 실업자의 문제가 있었다. 이런 문제가 있는 상황에서 벌어진 주가 대폭락은 각 부문에 급속도로 영향을 끼쳐, 연쇄적인 기업 도산, 실업자 양산, 물가의 폭락 등 자본주의 각국의 경제활동을 마비시켰다.

제국주의(19C 말-20C 초)와 제1차 세계대전(1914-1918)

제국주의란 타국의 영토를 침략하여 자국의 정치 · 경제 세력을 키우는 국가 정책이다. 제국주의가 나타난 시대적 배경에는 과학 기술 발달과 산업혁명이 몰고 온 자본주의의 성장이 있다. 자본주의의 발달로 넘쳐나는 상품과 자본에 대한 새로운 수요 시장으로 서구 열강들은 식민지를 쟁탈하기 시작했다. 이러한 시대적 배경으로 영국 · 프랑스 · 러시아의 연합국과 독일 · 오스트리아의 동맹국 간의 제1차 세계대전이 발발하게 된다.

수정자본주의

수정자본주의란 자본주의의 발전으로 발생하는 독점의 횡포, 빈부 격차, 실업, 공황 등의 문제들을 국가가 개입하여 수정함으로써 자본주의 사회의 발전을 도모하려는 정책이다. 1929년 경제 대공황 이후 발생한 높은 실업률과 디플레이션을 극복하고자 미국 정부가 정책적으로 대규모의 토목공사를 일으켜 실업자 문제를 해결하려 한 뉴딜 정책이 대표적인 예이다. 또한 수정자본주의는 누진과세와 사회보장제도를 통해 사회 계층의 소득 불평등으로 발생하는 갖가지 문제들을 제거하고자 했는데, 영국의 '요람에서 무덤까지'를 표방하는 복지국가정책이 이에 해당한다.

공산주의

1929년 경제 대공황 이후 러시아는 자본주의를 버리고 공산주의를 채택했다. 공산주의 사상은 마르크스에 의해 확립되었는데 마르크스는 지배자와 피지배자의 계급 차이가 갈등을 일으키므로 계급의 폐지를 주도했다. 그는 인간에 의한 노동의 산물이 사유재산이 되면서, 오히려 이것으로 인해 피지배계급의 인간이 소외된다고 파악했다. 따라서 그는 이를 극복하고 인간의 본질을 회복하기 위해 개인의 소유가 제한되고 정부가 경제활동을 적극적으로 통제해야 한다고 주장했다.

사회주의

사회주의는 산업화가 진행되면서 생긴 자원의 낭비, 실업과 빈곤의 증대 등의 문제가 발생하면서 그 대안을 찾는 과정에서 나타난 이데올로기이다. 산업화의 결과로 나타난 여러 사회 문제들을 해결하기 위한 방법으로 생산수단을 국가가 소유하는 것, 그리고 사회 구성원이 노동을 통해 얻은 이익을 배분하는 것을 제기하였다. 공산주의와 사회주의는 종종 비슷한 의미로 잘못 사용되는데 이 두 사상은 혁명을 일으키는 주체가 누구냐에 따라 구분될 수 있다. 공산주의는 피지배계급인 프롤레타리아가 계급을 탈피하는 주체임에 반해, 사회주의는 엘리트 또는 부르주아가 스스로의 권리를 양보하고 피지배계급의 권리를 보장해주어야 한다고 여겼다.

제2차 세계대전(1939-1945)과 GATT(1948)

독일 · 이탈리아 · 일본을 중심으로 한 추축국과 영국 · 프랑스 · 미국 · 소련 등을 중심으로 한 연합국 사이에 벌어진 제2차 세계대전 이후, 국제경제협력 체제의 확립의 필요성이 대두되었다. 이에 1947년에 제네바에서 23개국의 서명을 얻어 GATT(관세 및 무역에 관한 일반협정)를 체결하여 1948년 1월부터 그 활동을 시작하였다. GATT 체제에서 자유 · 무차별 무역의 원칙을 실현하기 위해 각국은 협상을 진행하였고 이는 교섭을 통해 무역장벽을 제거하고자 하는 국제경제체제의 토대가 되었다.

신(新)자유주의(1991-오늘)

제2차 세계대전과 냉전시대 이후 공산주의는 쇠퇴했다. 또한 정부가 적극적으로 개입하며 시장의 자유를 축소했던 후기 자본주의 역시 한계가 있었다. 장기불황이 계속 되었고 이는 불황과 동시에 물가가 오르는 스태그플레이션으로 이어졌다. 이에 신자유주의가 등장하게 된다. 신자유주의는 정부의 강력한 개입으로 인한 조세 부담 등의 문제점을 비판한다. 따라서 정부의 간섭을 완전히 제외하지는 않지만 개입을 축소하고 시장과 개인에게 자유를 확대하는 체계, 즉 근대 초기의 자본주의로 회귀를 추구한다. 또한 공기업의 민영화를 통해 '작은 정부'를 지향하고 세계 무역 기구를 통한 자유 무역과 시장 경쟁의 확대를 실현하고자 한다.

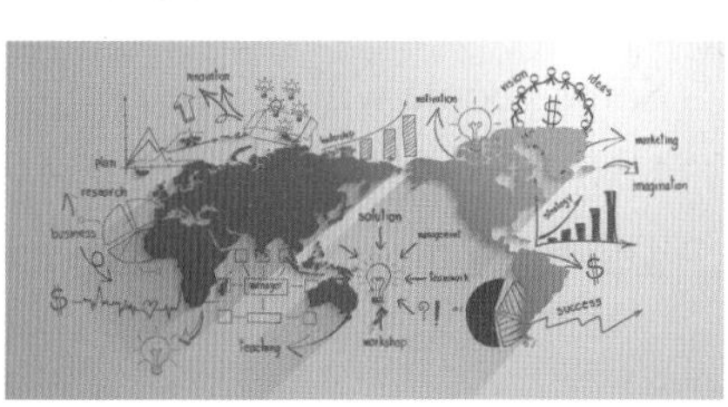

Word Test

정답 | P.125

1. 다음 중 단어의 뜻풀이가 잘못된 것은?

① hazard: a source of risk and danger
② external: placed on the outside or on a surface
③ exclude: to persuade someone to do something
④ tactic: a way that is planned to be used to achieve one's purpose
⑤ conventional: of a kind which has been considered typical for a long time

2. 다음 문장의 빈칸에 알맞은 말을 보기에서 찾아 쓰시오. (단, 필요한 경우에는 어형을 바꾸시오.)

보기 | commodity motivation initiate fluctuate

(1) Her poor grades for this semester are the result of a lack of ____________.
(2) The researchers have ____________ the first round of experiments on augmented reality.
(3) The water level in the lake ____________ each year depending on the previous winter's snowball.
(4) Corn and potatoes were the first farming ____________ brought to Europe from the New Continent.

3. 우리말에 맞게 빈칸에 주어진 철자로 시작하는 단어를 쓰시오.

(1) The c____________ form of 'wise' is 'wiser.'
('현명한'의 비교급은 '더 현명한'이다.)
(2) Apparently, in interviews she refuses to talk about her p____________ life.
(분명히, 그녀는 인터뷰에서 사생활에 대해 이야기하는 것을 거절한다.)
(3) The hotel is not responsible for any loss or damage to guests' personal p____________.
(호텔은 손님들의 개인 재산에 대한 분실이나 손해에 대한 책임이 없다.)
(4) These days, most a____________ products are being imported from many other countries.
(요즘에는 대부분의 농산물이 많은 다른 나라에서 수입되고 있다.)

4. 다음 문장의 빈칸에 공통으로 들어갈 알맞은 단어를 쓰시오.

· Some people will pay a ____________ to get the best seats at a show.
· I pay the ____________ for my health insurance via automatic withdrawal.
· The car company will launch its first ____________ sedan at the beginning of this year.

SECTION. 10

Ethics

윤리

45

SECTION 10.
Ethics

Before the explosion of the first atomic bomb, the scientist who created it must have been confused; the common understanding of a scientist's duties includes neither an obligation to consider the actual or prospective consequences of one's scientific findings nor a duty to warn the public. (①) But nevertheless, the scientist should not follow the same understanding as regards the development of nuclear power. (②) This reasoning is simple and straightforward, and I think it can be regarded as a basic pattern for deriving duties and responsibilities of the scientist. (③) The reasoning assumes a value judgment that we should try to avoid grave harm to mankind, and anyone should be able to agree on this. (④) And I wish to emphasize that the duties and responsibilities derived are closely connected with the scientist's role as a scientist, as a specialist of knowledge in a specific field. (⑤)

If we change the phrase "the scientist's role as a scientist" to other phrases such as "the carpenter's role as a building constructor" or "the physician's role as a medical specialist," the same reasoning can be applied; thus it should be used as a basis for professional ethics.

VOCAB

explosion 폭발
atomic bomb 원자 폭탄
confused 혼란스러운, 당황한
duty 의무
include 포함하다
obligation 의무
prospective 예기되는, 장래의
consequence 결과
finding *발견(물), 습득물; (조사 등의) 결과
warn 경고하다
as regards ~에 관한 한
nuclear power 원자력
reasoning 추론; *(추론의 결과로서) 논거, 논증
straightforward 간단한
regard A as B A를 B로 여기다
derive 끌어내다, 얻다
responsibility 책임감

45

SECTION 10.
윤리

서술형

1. What is the author mainly talking about? (2 words from the passage)

2. 위 글 첫째 단락의 ①~⑤ 중에서 다음 주어진 문장이 들어가기에 가장 적절한 곳은?

For there is no one other than him/her who can know the destructive consequences of it.

서술형

3. What is this in the 1st paragraph referring to? (in Korean)

서술형

4. 위 글 둘째 단락의 밑줄 친 the same reasoning이 의미하는 바를 우리말로 쓰시오.

과학자 오펜하이머(Robert Oppenheimer, 1904-1967)

1939년 미국 정부는 아인슈타인의 권유를 계기로 원자폭탄 개발 계획인 맨해튼 계획(Manhattan Project)을 세웠다. 이에 따라 물리학자 오펜하이머는 뉴멕시코에 세워진 연구소의 소장으로 임명되었고, 그는 '연구의 자유'라는 학자로서의 권리나 자신의 의지와는 상관없이 원자폭탄 개발에 참여하게 되었다. 우여곡절 끝에 마침내 1945년 원자폭탄 실험은 성공을 거두었고, 그해 8월에 일본의 히로시마와 나가사키에 원자폭탄이 투하되었다. 그 결과는 놀랄 만한 것이었고 반세기가 지난 지금까지 인류에게 엄청난 비극으로 남아있는데, 당시 오펜하이머는 과학자로서 양심의 가책과 고통을 느끼며 괴로워했다. 그는 1950년대에도 이와 유사한 고통을 다시 겪게 되는데, '수소폭탄의 아버지'라고 불리는 텔러(Edward Teller)가 수소폭탄 개발을 주장하는 것에 반대하다가 모함을 받고 모든 직책을 박탈당하기에 이른다. 이후 프린스턴 대학에서 이론물리학 교수로서 연구생활을 시작하게 된 그의 과학자로서의 유별난 이력은 우리로 하여금 과학의 사회적 책임, 국가와 과학의 관계, 그리고 과학의 발전에 대한 정치적 개입 등에 대해 생각해 보게끔 한다.

VOCAB

assume 추정[가정]하다; *(성질 등을) 나타내다
value judgment 가치 판단
grave 중대한, 심상치 않은
harm *해; 손해
mankind 인류
emphasize 강조하다
connect 연결하다, 잇다
specialist 전문가
specific 구체적인; *특정한
field 분야
carpenter 목수
constructor 건설자
physician (내과) 의사
apply 적용하다
basis 기본
professional 직업의
ethics 윤리

46 SECTION 10. Ethics

The purpose of ethics is to define a person's proper values and interests and the actions which he should take in regard to those interests. If an individual has no interests, no values with which to concern himself, then any discussion regarding ethics becomes as ______(A)______ as contemplation of how many angels will fit on the head of a pin. To begin this exploration, we first need to ask, "What are values?"

A value is something for which a person is willing to take some action in order to obtain and/or to keep that something — whether that something is a physical object such as a house or a nonphysical existent such as love. It is important to emphasize here that some "action" is involved. This serves conceptually to distinguish between values and desires (wants or wishes). I may want or desire a million-dollar home, but unless I am willing to take some action to try to obtain it, it is not a value. Values presuppose someone who values and acts.

But should this "acting person" be the one to benefit from what he does? And what are these values for? One popular answer to these questions comes from the proponents of *altruism. Altruism is the doctrine which states that only an action taken for others' benefit is the good, that is, constitutes proper behavior. According to altruism, anything done for one's self has no moral sanction. Any hint of selfish benefit received by the "acting person" is ______(B)______ by this credo.

*altruism 이타주의

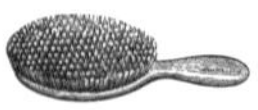

VOCAB

purpose 목적
ethics 윤리
define *정의하다; 규정짓다
proper 적당한, 적절한
value 가치
interest *흥미, 관심; 이득
in regard to ~에 관하여
individual 개인
concern *관계하다; 근심, 염려
regarding ~에 관하여[관한]
contemplation 숙고, 명상; *예상, 예기
fit 적합하다
exploration 탐구, 탐험
be willing to-v 기꺼이 ~하다
obtain 얻다, 획득하다
physical 육체의; *물질의
object 물체

46

SECTION 10.
윤리

1. 위 글의 빈칸 (A), (B)에 들어갈 말로 가장 적절한 것은?

(A)		(B)
① important	······	immoral
② careless	······	considerate
③ useless	······	immoral
④ stressful	······	considerate
⑤ complex	······	valuable

2. **According to the passage, which of the following is true?**

① Only physical objects can be said to have real value.
② There is a big difference between values and desires.
③ Values are best justified in pursuit of self-interest.
④ Acting is more important than desiring something.
⑤ Selfishness can be a value for altruists.

3. 위 글에 따르면, 다음 중 윤리적 가치를 실현한 사람은 누구인가? (2개)

① 지현: 늘 고생하시는 부모님께 감사한 마음을 갖고 있다.
② 현영: 아르바이트를 해서 갖고 싶던 MP3 플레이어를 구입했다.
③ 진수: 숙제를 대신해 달라는 친구의 부탁을 정중히 거절했다.
④ 현석: 몸이 불편하신 할머니를 부축해서 집까지 모셔다 드렸다.
⑤ 은아: 연말 자선 바자회에 평소 아끼던 책 몇 권을 내놓았다.

VOCAB

existent 존재물
emphasize 강조하다
involve 포함하다; *수반하다
serve to-v ~하는 데 도움이 되다
conceptually 개념상
distinguish 구분[구별]하다
desire 욕망(하다)
presuppose 전제하다
benefit 이익[이득](을 얻다)
proponent 발의자; *옹호자
doctrine *주의, 원칙; 교리
state 진술하다, 말하다; *명시하다
good 선(善)
constitute 구성하다, 만들어 내다
moral 도덕적인 (↔ immoral)
sanction 허가, 인가
a[any] hint of 약간의
credo 신조

윤리는 무엇인가?

윤리는 사회의 존속을 위해 지켜야 하는 사회규범이다. 따라서 윤리는 사회 내에 형성된 규범을 지킴으로써 사회 질서를 유지하는 것을 의미하며, 윤리에는 실천적 의미가 내포되어 있다. 윤리의 실천을 위해서는 '무엇이 올바른 것인지를 알고, 올바른 것을 소중히 여기며, 올바른 것을 행하는 것'이 매우 중요하다. 올바른 것을 안다는 것, 이것은 곧 의지와 확신이 뚜렷한 상태를 뜻하며, 이러한 마음가짐이 행동으로 이어진다는 의미가 된다. 실천하지 않는 윤리란 의미가 없고, 규범이나 질서와 같은 올바른 것을 실천하는 것, 이것이 바로 진정한 윤리인 것이다.

47 SECTION 10. Ethics

Imagine you are driving your car. You come to a *fork in the road and turn right. Next you come to a crossroads and turn left. There is no traffic to speak of, and there are no roadblocks. You seem to be completely free. This view of your situation might change dramatically, however, if we consider that the reason you turned right and then left is because you're addicted to (A) [smoke / smoking], and you're desperate to get to the nearest store to buy more cigarettes. Rather than driving, it's like you are (B) [driving / being driven], as your urge to smoke causes you uncontrollably to turn the wheel first in one direction and then the other. Moreover, you know that your turning left at the crossroads (C) [mean / means] you'll be late for an important appointment, but you do it anyway.

This story presents us with two contrasting ways of thinking about liberty. On the one hand, liberty is the absence of external restraints or obstacles. You are free if no one is stopping you from doing whatever it is you want to do. In the above story you appear, in this sense, to be free. On the other hand, one can think of liberty as the presence of control on the part of the person. To be free, you must be _______________, which is to say that you must be able to control your own destiny in your own interests. In the above story you appear, in this sense, to be unfree: you are not in control of your own destiny. That is to say, you are failing to control an addiction, which is preventing you from realizing your true interests. While in the first view liberty is simply about how many doors are open, in the second view it is more about going through the right doors for the right reasons.

*fork 갈림길

VOCAB

crossroad(s) 교차로
roadblock (도로의) 장애물
completely 완전히
view *견해; 광경, 조망
dramatically 극적으로
addicted 중독된
desperate 필사적인
urge 충동
uncontrollably 통제할 수 없을 정도로
(steering) wheel (자동차의) 핸들
present A with B A에게 B를 제공[제시]하다
contrast 대조하다; *대비를 이루다

47

SECTION 10.
윤리

서술형

1. 위 글에서 이야기하고 있는 자유의 두 가지 개념을 우리말로 간단히 쓰시오.

2. 위 글의 (A), (B), (C) 각 네모 안에서 어법에 맞는 표현을 골라 짝지은 것으로 가장 적절한 것은?

	(A)		(B)		(C)
①	smoking	……	driving	……	means
②	smoke	……	driving	……	mean
③	smoke	……	being driven	……	mean
④	smoking	……	being driven	……	mean
⑤	smoking	……	being driven	……	means

3. 위 글 둘째 단락의 빈칸에 들어갈 말로 가장 적절한 것은?

① self-destructive
② self-proclaimed
③ self-determined
④ self-abandoned
⑤ self-absorbed

소극적 자유와 적극적 자유의 의미

자유에는 두 가지 의미가 있다. 소극적 자유는 외부로부터 구속받지 않는 상태 또는 타인에 의한 강제에서 벗어나 있는 상태를 뜻하고, 적극적 자유는 자신이 바라는 대로 주체적으로 그리고 창조적으로 행동하는 것을 일컫는다. 이러한 자유의 개념은 개인의 차원에서뿐만 아니라, 개인과 국가의 관계를 살펴볼 때도 둘로 나뉘어진다. 소극적 자유주의자들은 국가의 간섭이 부재하거나 최소한에 그칠 것을 요구하는 데 반해, 적극적 자유주의자들은 개인의 자아실현에 장애가 되는 사회적인 요소나 사회 구조를 철폐하기 위한 국가의 적극적인 개입을 주장한다.

VOCAB

liberty 자유
absence 부재, 없음
external 외부의
restraint 제지, 억제; *구속, 속박
obstacle 장애(물)
appear 나타나다; *~인 듯하다
presence 존재 (상태)
destiny 운명
addiction 중독
prevent 막다, 방해하다
realize *깨닫다, 파악하다, 실현하다
interest 관심사; *이해 관계

48

SECTION 10.
Ethics

Suppose a daughter from a religious family deceives her dying father by promising him that she will not marry someone from a different religion. By lying to her father, has she done something good or bad?

Strict adherents of the *Kantian view would first examine the daughter's ______(A)______ for lying. They would find that she lied in order to reassure her dad and prevent him from suffering even more in his final hours on earth. She also lied to relieve herself of any guilt associated with the anger her father would have felt towards her had he known she was going to deny his final wish. Followers of Kant would be critical of the girl for lying. From their point of view, wanting to minimize suffering or guilt is not sufficient reason to lie. In other words, the daughter should tell the truth no matter what the consequences. It is a moral obligation to tell the truth and that is the standard we must all uphold.

The strict *utilitarian, on the other hand, would first look at the ______(B)______ of the daughter's deceitful action. By promising not to marry a man from another religion, she has made her father happy so that he can now die in peace. At the same time, by lying, she has kept herself free of any feelings of guilt for having caused her dad additional suffering in his final days. Utilitarians would find no fault with this action since it leads to preventing the pain and anguish the dying father would have experienced from knowing the truth. To them, the daughter has brought the greatest amount of happiness to everyone involved, and that is a good thing.

*Kantian 칸트주의자 *utilitarian 공리주의자

VOCAB

suppose 가정하다
religious 종교의; *독실한, 믿음이 깊은
deceive 속이다, 기만하다
religion 종교
strict 엄격한
adherent 지지자
reassure 안심시키다
prevent 막다, 방해하다
relieve A of B A에게서 B를 덜어 주다
guilt 유죄; *죄의식, 죄책감
associate A with B A를 B와 관련짓다

1. What is the author mainly talking about?

① Kant and his strict moral standards
② the role of moralists in modern society
③ the pros and cons of Kantian and utilitarian morality
④ the opposing viewpoints of followers of Kant and utilitarians
⑤ the importance of moral standards in our daily lives

2. 위 글의 빈칸 (A)와 (B)에 들어갈 말로 가장 적절한 것은?

	(A)		(B)
①	excuse	……	intentions
②	intention	……	causes
③	motive	……	causes
④	motive	……	results
⑤	excuse	……	objectives

3. Read the following cases and circle the correct words in the parentheses.

(1) According to the Kantian view, if someone steals a piece of bread to give it to the hungry, the person's behavior would be (desirable / undesirable).
(2) According to the utilitarian, if someone disobeys a red light to save a child from being hit by a car, he or she would be morally (right / wrong).

VOCAB

deny 부정[부인]하다
critical 비판적인
minimize 최소화하다
sufficient 충분한
consequence 결과
moral 도덕의, 도덕적인
obligation 의무
standard 표준
uphold 지지하다; *유지하다
deceitful 기만적인, 사기의
additional 부가의, 추가의
find fault with ~을 비난하다
anguish 고통; *고뇌
involved 연관된, 관련된

SECTION 10.

Word Test

정답 | P.126

1. 다음 단어의 영영풀이로 알맞은 것을 찾아 선으로 연결하시오.

(1) adherent ·　　　· ⓐ to get something that you want

(2) deceive ·　　　· ⓑ someone who supports a particular belief or plan

(3) physician ·　　　· ⓒ to make someone believe something that is not true

(4) obtain ·　　　· ⓓ a doctor who has general skill

2. 다음 문장의 빈칸에 알맞은 단어를 보기에서 찾아 쓰시오. (단, 필요한 경우에는 어형을 바꾸시오.)

보기 | **addict derive constitute emphasize**

(1) There are many kids ____________ to surfing the net these days.

(2) The English word "olive" is ____________ from the Latin word "olive."

(3) You can use italics to ____________ a word in a piece of writing.

(4) If several people or things ____________ something, they are the parts that together form it.

3. 다음 문장의 밑줄 친 부분과 바꿔 쓸 수 있는 단어를 고르시오.

(1) The situation is very <u>serious</u> and appears to be getting worse.

① positive　② grave　③ trivial　④ inspiring　⑤ perfect

(2) She always <u>finds fault with</u> the way he works.

① praises　② ignores　③ surpasses　④ criticizes　⑤ objects

(3) He read a newspaper article <u>regarding</u> the problems of overcrowded cities.

① blaming　② including　③ concerning　④ suggesting　⑤ except

(4) Parents are under a legal <u>obligation</u> to educate their children.

① measure　② duty　③ doctrine　④ penalty　⑤ dispute

4. 우리말에 맞게 빈칸에 공통으로 들어갈 알맞은 단어를 쓰시오.

· There are thousands of ____________s in the museum's collections.
(박물관의 소장품에는 수천 개의 물건들이 있다.)

· The ____________ of the game is to improve children's math skills.
(그 게임의 목적은 아이들의 수학 실력을 향상하는 것이다.)

· Would anyone ____________ if we started the meeting now?
(지금 회의를 시작하는 데 반대하시는 분 계십니까?)

SECTION. II

Politics

정치

49

SECTION 11.
Politics

Another example was the role of power distributed and issued within the state. Plato held the belief of the philosopher king. He believed that to ensure the ideal state "either philosophers become kings in their countries, or those who are now called kings and rulers come to be sufficiently inspired with a desire for wisdom." Plato believed only the wise could execute proper justice. A just city is an ideal city for Plato, one in which the philosopher was in total control. On the other hand, Aristotle's views greatly differ from Plato's. Aristotle believed that each individual made an important contribution to the *polis. He compares the polis to an extended and all-encompassing family, with each individual acting as a part of it. This describes individuals working as a whole to better the polis. By including all citizens Aristotle believed he had created the ideal city.

*polis 폴리스(고대 그리스의 도시 국가)

VOCAB

distribute 분배하다
issue 논쟁, 쟁점; *내다, 발하다
state *국가; 주(州); 진술하다
philosopher 철학자
ensure *보증하다; 확실히 하다
ruler 지배자, 통치자
sufficiently 충분히
inspire 고무시키다
execute 실행[수행]하다
proper 적절한, 올바른
justice 정의
contribution 기부; *공헌
compare A to B A를 B에 비유하다
extended 확대된
all-encompassing 포괄적인, 총망라한
better 더 좋은; *더 좋게 하다, 향상시키다
include 포함하다
citizen 시민

1. 위 글의 앞에 올 내용으로 가장 적절한 것은?

① 플라톤이 아리스토텔레스에게 미친 영향
② 플라톤과 아리스토텔레스 철학의 공통점
③ 플라톤과 아리스토텔레스 견해의 차이점
④ 민주 정치에서 통치자 역할의 중요성
⑤ 고대 그리스의 폴리스 발달 과정

서술형

2. 위 글에 나오는 이상 국가에 대한 플라톤의 견해와 아리스토텔레스의 견해를 각각 요약하시오.

SECTION 11.
Politics 50

In 1922, Walter Lippmann published an influential book entitled *Public Opinion*. In this book, Lippmann was very suspicious and critical of any model of democracy that placed excessive faith and power in the hands of the public.

People, he insisted, mostly know the world only indirectly, through "pictures they make up in their heads." And they receive these mental pictures largely through the media. The problem, Lippmann argued, is that the pictures people have in their heads are hopelessly distorted and incomplete, *marred by the irredeemable weakness of the press. Just as bad is the public's ability to comprehend the truth. Even if people happened to come across it, their understanding was undermined by human bias, stereotypes, inattentiveness, and ignorance. In the end, Lippmann thought citizens are like theatergoers who "arrive in the middle of the third act and leave before the last curtain, staying just long enough to decide who is the hero and who is the villain."

*mar 손상시키다

서술형

1. 위 글에 따르면, 리프먼이 대중을 부정적으로 보는 이유 두 가지는 무엇인지 우리말로 쓰시오.

VOCAB

publish 출간[출판]하다
influential 영향력 있는
entitle 부르다, 칭하다; *표제를 붙이다
public opinion 여론
suspicious 의심스러운; *의심하는
democracy 민주주의
excessive 과대한, 과도한
faith *신뢰; 신념
mental 정신의
distorted 비틀어진; *왜곡된
incomplete 불완전한
irredeemable 구제 불능의
the press 언론
comprehend 이해하다
happen to-v 우연히 ~하다
come across ~을 우연히 만나다; *이해하다
undermine 밑을 파다; *손상시키다
bias 편견
stereotype 고정 관념
inattentiveness 부주의
ignorance 무지
theatergoer 극장에 자주 가는 사람
act 행동, 행위; *(연극 등의) 막
villain 악당

리프먼(Walter Lippmann, 1889–1974)

20세기초 미국의 저명한 저널리스트였던 리프먼은 1962년 퓰리처상을 받은 그의 대표적 저서 「여론(*Public Opinion*)」에서 실재 세계와 우리가 인식하고 있는 세계와의 관계를 날카롭게 분석하고 있다. 그는 플라톤의 동굴 비유를 인용하면서 우리가 살고 있는 세계는 실재가 아닌 모조품, 즉 우리가 실재라고 지각하는 그림자인 '의사환경(pseudo-environment)'이며, 그 환경 가운데 미디어는 세상을 이해하는 데 필요한 상(像)을 머리 속에 그려주는 역할을 한다고 밝히고 있다. 이러한 실재 세계와 개인의 인식과의 관계, 그 과정에서 미디어의 역할은 여론 형성 과정에 대한 이론적 기초를 마련하였다.

51 SECTION 11. Politics

Usually voting is proposed as a reasonably democratic way of reaching a consensus. But voting is not a meeting process, it is simply a procedure. The goal of carrying out a vote is to record the preferences of a group of people and in some logical, fair, and equitable way (A) [come up with / coming up with] a good decision. Kenneth Arrow, a Nobel Prize winner in 1972, proved it was impossible to do this except under very simple circumstances; for example, situations when there are only two possible options. Furthermore, the act of voting necessarily ignores how strongly each individual feels about the matter (B) [voting on / being voted on] or the consequences that a final decision may impose. And even under the best of circumstances, voting necessarily means that some group of people will not get what they want and if severely beaten by the majority, may leave the group or retaliate.

Voting can therefore only produce satisfying decisions (C) [where / which] there is unanimity of opinion. Unanimity can sometimes be achieved if one person or group can persuade everyone else of the validity of their perspective and proposed solution. But if the problem has no clear solution, some people are personally devoted to a particular solution, or there is competition for power in the group, the process will quickly *bog down, factionalize, and/or revert to coercion.

*bog down 가라앉다

VOCAB

voting 투표
propose 제안하다
reasonably 합리적으로; *상당히
democratic 민주적인
consensus 일치, 합의
meet 만나다; *합의하다
process 과정, 처리, 방법
procedure 절차
preference 선호
logical 논리적인
fair 정당한, 올바른
equitable 공정한
come up with ~을 생각해 내다
circumstance (*pl.*) 상황
option *선택권; 선택할 수 있는 것
ignore 무시하다
individual 개인
vote on ~에 대해 표결하다

51

SECTION 11.
정치

1. **What is the author mainly talking about?**

① how to establish a fair voting procedure
② various responses to the result of voting
③ the fundamental limitations of a voting system
④ the necessity of respecting the minority opinion
⑤ voting systems as an essential component of democracy

2. **위 글의 (A), (B), (C) 각 네모 안에서 어법에 맞는 표현을 골라 짝지은 것으로 가장 적절한 것은?**

	(A)		(B)		(C)
①	come up with	……	voting on	……	where
②	come up with	……	being voted on	……	where
③	come up with	……	being voted on	……	which
④	coming up with	……	voting on	……	which
⑤	coming up with	……	being voted on	……	where

3. **아래는 어느 정당의 정책 결정 과정에서 행해진 투표 결과에 따른 의원들의 모습이다. 위 글에 언급된 내용과 다른 반응을 보인 의원을 고르시오.**

A의원: 투표 결과 내가 지지했던 의견이 채택되었으므로, 다른 의견들은 무시해야 한다. B의원: 정당 내의 다수 의원들과 의견이 맞지 않으므로 탈당을 결심했다. C의원: 나와 뜻을 같이 하는 동료 의원들을 당내에서 모아 집단투쟁을 벌일 것이다. D의원: 내가 반대했던 의견이지만 투표결과를 존중하고 따를 것이다.

투표

선거인이 누구를 당선인으로 할 것인지를 선택하는 의사 표시를 뜻한다. 어떤 사항에 대해 구성원(국민 또는 주민)의 찬성이나 반대의 의사 표시도 투표라고 하며, 국회와 같은 합의체의 의사 결정 시 구성원이 서면을 통해 의사 표시를 하는 것도 투표라고 한다. 그러나 일반적으로는 선거에서 선거인의 의사 표시를 말한다.

VOCAB

consequence 결과
impose 지우다, 부과하다
severely 심하게
beat 패배시키다
majority 대다수
retaliate 보복하다
unanimity 만장일치
persuade A of B A에게 B를 믿게 하다
validity 타당성
perspective 원근법; *견지, 견해
solution 해답, 해결책
devoted 헌신적인, 열심인
competition 경쟁
factionalize 파벌로 나뉘어지다
revert 복귀하다
coercion 강압, 압제

52 SECTION 11. Politics

A controversial issue in many countries around the globe, *affirmative action is essentially the policy of bestowing benefits upon groups that have traditionally faced discrimination. The specific policies vary from nation to nation, but their focal point tends to be the provision of impartial educational and employment opportunities.

① In France, for example, the constitution expressly forbids discrimination based on race, religion or gender. ② To ensure this, certain low-income neighborhoods with a high concentration of minority groups have been classified "Priority Education Zones," a designation which entitles them to supplemental government funding. ③ In addition, the French government makes educational support available to all citizens in a variety of forms, including grants, loans, and special scholarships earmarked for returning expatriates. ④ South Africa has also implemented affirmative action policies. ⑤ Since transitioning into a democracy in 1994, the nation has endeavored to rectify racial imbalances in employment through legislation compelling employers to hire non-white workers. There have also been government-backed efforts to enhance the employment opportunities of women and disabled people from all racial groups.

Advocates of affirmative action argue that it is imperative to offset economic disparities, capacitating students and workers from minority and underprivileged backgrounds, who tend to also be low-income, to properly compete with their more privileged peers. Opponents, however, charge that affirmative action unnecessarily harms people who happen to come from a privileged social group. Some go so far as to label affirmative action a form of ____________________, claiming that it simply replaces past injustices with new injustices, fostering resentment without actually ameliorating the living standard of those it seeks to aid.

*affirmative action 차별 철폐 조처

VOCAB

controversial 논란이 많은
essentially 기본적으로
bestow 부여하다
discrimination 차별
focal point 초점
provision 공급, 제공
impartial 공정한
constitution 헌법
expressly 명확히
concentration 집중, 밀집
classify 분류하다
designation 지정
entitle 자격[권리]을 주다
supplemental 보충의, 추가의
grant 승인하다; *보조금
earmark 배정하다
expatriate 국외 거주자
implement 시행하다

52

서술형

1. **According to the passage, affirmative action is the policy of favoring members of a group who have suffered from ____________ within a culture by providing unbiased ____________ and ____________ opportunities. (each word from the passage)**

2. 위 글의 둘째 단락에서 내용의 흐름과 관계없는 문장은?

서술형

3. 위 글에 제시된 'affirmative action'에 대해 찬성하는 입장의 주장을 우리말로 쓰시오.

4. 위 글 셋째 단락의 빈칸에 들어갈 말로 가장 적절한 것은?

① social welfare ② nonviolent protest ③ illegal legislation
④ national healing ⑤ reverse discrimination

VOCAB

transition 이행; *이행하다
endeavor 노력; *노력하다
rectify 바로잡다
legislation 입법, 법률
compel 강제하다
advocate 옹호자
imperative 반드시 해야 하는
offset 상쇄하다
disparity 차이
capacitate 가능하게 하다
underprivileged 혜택받지 못한
opponent 반대자
go so far as to-v ~하기까지 하다
injustice 불평등, 부당
resentment 분개, 분노
ameliorate 개선하다

셰릴 홉우드(Cheryl Hopwood)의 텍사스대학교 고소 사건

1992년 백인 여성인 셰릴 홉우드는 미국 텍사스대학교 로스쿨에 불합격 통보를 받았다. 그녀는 자신보다 낮은 성적을 받은 히스패닉과 흑인이 합격한 것에 대해 불합리하다고 생각했다. 셰릴은 자신과 비슷한 처지의 학생 세 명과 함께 1996년에 텍사스대학교를 소송했다. 소송은 7년간 계속되었고, 2003년 미국 연방 항소법원은 셰릴의 패소로 최종 판결을 내렸다. 흑인과 히스패닉은 텍사스 인구의 40%를 구성하고 있고 이에 따라 법조계에서 여러 인종이 필요하다는 다양성에 무게를 둔 것이다.

53

SECTION 11.
Politics

(A) ______________ by Edward W. Said

From at least the end of the eighteenth century until our own day, modern Occidental reactions to Islam have been dominated by a type of thinking that may still be called Orientalist. The general basis of Orientalist thought is an imaginative geography ① dividing the world into two unequal parts: the larger and *different* one called the Orient, the other, also known as *our* world, called the Occident or the West. Such divisions always take place when one society or culture thinks about another one, different from it, but it is interesting that even when the Orient has uniformly been considered an inferior part of the world, it has always been endowed both with far greater size and with a greater potential for power ② to the West. In so far as Islam has always been seen as belonging to the Orient, its particular fate within the general structure of Orientalism has been to be looked at with a very special hostility and fear. There are, of course, many obvious religious, psychological and political reasons for this, but all of these reasons ③ derive from a sense that so far as the West is concerned, Islam represents not only a formidable competitor but also a late-coming challenge to Christianity.

I have not been able to discover any period in European or American history since the Middle Ages ④ which Islam was generally discussed or thought about *outside* a framework created by passion, prejudice and political interests. This may not seem like a surprising discovery, but ⑤ included in the *indictment is the entire *gamut of scholarly and scientific disciplines which, since the early nineteenth century, have either called themselves Orientalism or tried systematically to deal with the Orient.

*indictment 비난 *gamut 전(全) 범위, 영역

VOCAB

Occidental 서양의
reaction 반응
dominate 지배하다
Orientalist 동양학의
imaginative 상상의, 가공의
geography 지리학
divide A into B A를 B로 분리하다[나누다]
Orient 동양
Occident 서양
division 분리
take place 생기다, 일어나다
uniformly 한결같이
inferior 열등한 (↔ superior)
endow A with B A에게 B를 주다[부여하다]
potential 잠재력, 가능성
(in) so far as ~하는 한
fate 운명
structure 구조
hostility 적대감

53

SECTION 11.
정치

1. 위 글의 빈칸 (A)에 들어갈 제목으로 가장 적절한 것은?

① Religion and Culture Shock
② Islam through Western Eyes
③ Western History and Christianity
④ Islamic Power in Western History
⑤ Islam and Oriental Civilization

2. **According to the passage, the attitude towards Islam by the West is ________.**

① favorable ② distorted ③ indifferent
④ neutral ⑤ dependent

서술형

3. 위 글의 첫째 단락의 밑줄 친 this가 가리키는 바를 우리말로 간단히 쓰시오.

4. 위 글의 ①~⑤ 중에서 어법상 틀린 것을 찾아 바르게 고치시오. (2개)

오리엔탈리즘(Orientalism)

오리엔탈리즘은 비동양인이 동양을 선입견을 가지고 바라보는 것을 말한다. 즉 서구인의 관점에서 왜곡된 동양의 모습을 일컫는다. 동양과 서양에 대한 일반적인 고정관념을 나누면 다음과 같다.

- 동양: 정절, 몰개성, 정적, 온순, 남성우월주의, 불결, 덜 진보됨, 흑백
- 서양: 자유, 개성, 동적, 활달, 남녀평등, 청결, 진보, 컬러

옥시덴탈리즘(Occidentalism)

동양인들이 서양을 동양보다 더욱 발전되어 있고, 살기 좋으며, 문명화되어 있고, 기술적이고, 진보되었다고 생각하는 것을 가리킨다. 즉 동양인의 관점에서 서양을 확인되지 않은 주관적 사실로 판단하는 것이 옥시덴탈리즘이다. 예를 들어 한방보다 양방을 더욱 선호하거나, 자국 제품이 훨씬 좋음에도 불구하고 서양 제품이 왠지 더 좋을 것 같다는 선입견 등이 옥시덴탈리즘에 속한다.

VOCAB

obvious 분명한, 명백한
religious 종교적인
psychological 심리적인
derive from ~에서 기인하다
sense 감각; *의식
represent 나타내다, 의미하다
formidable 무서운; *만만치 않은
competitor 경쟁자
Christianity 기독교
framework 틀
passion 열정, 격렬한 감정
prejudice 편견
interest 흥미, 관심; *이익
discovery 발견
entire 전체의
scholarly 학자적인
discipline 훈련; *학과, 학문 분야
systematically 조직적으로, 체계적으로
deal with ~을 다루다

The Timeline of Politics

민주정치의 뿌리: 고대 아테네(510 BC)

고대 아테네는 기원전 510년 민주정을 실현하게 된다. 이때, 독재 정치를 방지하기 위해 요주의 인물의 이름을 도자기 파편에 적어 6천 표를 넘으면 추방하는 도편추방제를 시행하는 등의 민주 정치가 전개되었다. 입법기관인 민회에서 18세 이상의 시민권을 가진 모든 시민이 참석해 중요 사안을 의결하기도 하였다.

여성과 외국인이 직접 민주주의에 참여할 수 없었다는 한계는 있지만, 기원전 338년 마케도니아에 의해 정복될 때까지 다양한 직접 민주 정치가 실현되어 향후 민주주의의 선례가 되었다.

근대국가의 탄생: 웨스트팔리아 조약(1648)

웨스트팔리아 조약(Peace of Westfalen)은 유럽에서 발생한 30년 전쟁(1618–1648)의 결과로 체결되었다. 이 조약 전에는 도시국가가 위주였고 국제관계의 규범 등이 존재하지 않았다.

웨스트팔리아 조약을 통해, 종교가 정치에 간섭하지 않게 되었고 대외적 독립성을 갖춘 국가가 탄생하게 되었다. 국가의 주권이 국제법적으로 확립되어 현대의 국제적 정치 체제의 기틀을 갖추게 되었다.

영국 헌법의 기틀: 대헌장 마그나카르타(1215)

마그나카르타(Magna Carta)는 영국의 존(John Lackland) 왕 시대에 개인의 권리를 문서로 만든 최초의 장전이다. 실정(失政)을 거듭하고 있는 존 왕에 대항해서 귀족들은 왕에게 요구 사항을 승인하게 하였다. 이처럼 본래는 귀족의 이해관계만을 주창하기 위한 문서였지만, 17세기에는 모든 국민이 권리를 주장할 수 있는 근거로 확장되었다. 마그나카르타는 모든 개인이 평등하게 자유와 권리를 행사할 수 있도록 발전시킨 헌장으로서, 영국 헌법의 토대가 되었다.

자유 · 평등 · 박애: 프랑스 혁명(1789-1794)

프랑스에서는 루이 14세의 신권정치(神權政治)에 이어 루이 16세의 미국독립혁명을 위한 군사비 지원으로 인해 재정 궁핍이 지속되면서 시민들의 불만이 참을 수 없는 수준까지 도달했다. 이에 시민계층은 불합리한 구제도인 앙시앵 레짐(Ancien Regime)을 개혁하고 개인의 자유와 평등을 확립하기 위해 합심하였다. 바스티유 감옥 습격을 포함하여 혁명은 걷잡을 수 없는 속도로 퍼져나갔으며, 루이 16세와 기존 성직자 및 귀족들이 숙청되는 결과를 맞이했다. 프랑스는 이후 국민이 투표를 통해 대표를 선출하는 공화국이 되었고 입헌적 자유주의를 바탕으로 계몽사상을 실천해 근대적 민주주의의 근간이 되었다.

전쟁의 막, 그리고 평화: 냉전시대(1947-1989)

미국과 소련은 연합국의 핵심 국가로 제2차 세계대전을 승리로 이끌었다. 하지만 1947년 그리스 · 터키 내전을 시작으로, 공산주의와 자유주의라는 이념의 차이로 인해 전투가 없는 갈등상태인 냉전(Cold War)체제에 돌입하게 됐다.

냉전으로 인해 안보 비용이 증가함에도 고조된 갈등이 더욱 불안을 느끼게 만드는 안보 딜레마 상황에 봉착하였고, 이는 소련의 급작스러운 붕괴를 초래하였다. 미국과 소련은 1989년 12월 몰타 회담(Malta Summit)을 통해 냉전이 종식됐음을 선언했다.

새로운 정치단위체의 등장: 국제기구와 비정부기구

현대에는 국가간 긴밀한 협력을 필요로 하는 사안들이 많아지면서 국제기구와 비정부기구(Non-Government Organization, NGO)들이 중요한 정치단위체로 등장했다. 국제기구는 세 국가 이상의 주권국가가 공식적인 조직과 규정을 갖춘 것을 뜻한다. 대표적인 국제기구로는 국제연합(United Nations, UN)이 있다. 이와 더불어 환경과 빈곤 문제 등 각 나라들이 적극적으로 해결하지 못하고 있는 사안을 해결하기 위한 비정부기구의 역할도 강화되고 있다. 대표적인 비정부기구로는 그린피스(Greenpeace)가 있다.

사라지고 있는 국경: 지역주의와 지역통합

냉전체제의 종식과 제3세계 국가의 민주화와 경제 개방이 시작되면서, 각 국가는 이념이 아니라 이익에 따라 협력하는 것이 화두가 되었다. 이에 따라 지역협력이 다양한 형태로 세계 각국에서 진행 중이다.

북미자유무역협정(NAFTA)과 환태평양경제동반자협정(TPP)처럼 관세 철폐 등의 경제적 측면의 지역통합부터, 정치 · 경제 · 군사까지 통합체로 발전한 유럽연합(European Union, EU)은 국경을 넘어 지역이 통합되고 있는 현대 정치체제의 모습을 보여준다.

시대의 변화: 여성의 정치 참여 확대

1893년 뉴질랜드 여성들은 탄원서 성명 등을 통해 최초로 여성참정권을 획득했고, 영국은 1928년 서프러제트(Suffragette)라고 불리는 여성 참정권 운동가들을 통해 21세 이상의 남녀가 평등하게 투표할 수 있는 참정권을 획득했다. 이와 같이, 여성들은 더 이상 정치적 약자가 아니다. 몇몇 국가에서는 여성 국회의원 할당량 등을 제정했으며, 우리나라를 포함하여 독일 · 칠레 등의 국가에서는 여성 정치인이 국가의 수장 역할을 해오고 있다. 미래 여성들의 정치 참여와 역할은 더욱 증대될 것으로 기대되고 있다.

SECTION 11.

Word Test

정답 | p.126

1. 다음의 설명에 해당하는 단어를 보기에서 찾아 쓰시오.

보기 | circumstance individual unanimity disparity

(1) a person considered separately from a group: ______________

(2) complete agreement among all the members of a group: ______________

(3) the conditions that affect a situation, action, event, etc.: ______________

(4) a dissimilarity between two or more things, especially an unfair one: ______________

2. 우리말에 맞게 빈칸에 주어진 철자로 시작하는 단어를 쓰시오.

(1) P____________ opinion is deeply divided on the issue.
(그 문제에 관해 여론이 크게 나뉘어졌다.)

(2) The amount of sugar you add will depend on personal p____________.
(첨가할 설탕의 양은 개인 선호에 따라 다를 것이다.)

(3) The f____________ theme of the play is how loneliness affects people's lives.
(그 연극의 중심 테마는 어떻게 외로움이 사람의 삶에 영향을 미치는가이다.)

(4) The president tried to r____________ the public's negative perception of the law.
(대통령은 그 법에 대한 대중의 부정적인 인식을 바로잡기 위해 노력했다.)

3. 다음 문장의 밑줄 친 부분과 바꿔 쓸 수 있는 단어를 고르시오.

(1) How could you possibly <u>comprehend</u> the difficulties of my situation?

① ignore ② understand ③ overcome ④ relieve ⑤ prevent

(2) That's not the <u>proper</u> way to do it!

① subtle ② false ③ pleasant ④ appropriate ⑤ particular

(3) The company is an affordable Internet provider. <u>In addition</u>, it makes shareware freely available.

① Namely ② However ③ Otherwise ④ Furthermore ⑤ Consequently

4. 우리말에 맞게 빈칸에 공통으로 들어갈 알맞은 단어를 쓰시오.

· The article appeared in the November ____________.
(그 기사는 11월호에 나왔다.)

· Public education was one of the biggest ____________s during the election campaign.
(공교육은 선거운동에서 가장 큰 쟁점거리 중의 하나였다.)

· The US Department of State ____________s millions of passports each year.
(미 국무부는 매년 수백만 개의 여권을 발행한다.)

SECTION. 12

Education · Psychology · Language

교육 · 심리 · 언어

54

SECTION 12.

Education · Psychology · Language

Considering the modern-day obsession with knowledge and so-called "decent" occupations, the original meaning of education and occupation should tell us something. Originally, the word "education" comes from two Latin terms *ek* and *ducere*. *Ek* means "out" and *ducere* means "to draw." Therefore, true education means to draw out knowledge from within. This is quite different from the established practice today of "stuffing in" knowledge, as somebody pointed out sarcastically: "The world is full of educated *derelicts."

And what does occupation mean? Literally, it implies something that "occupies" you. However, finding the appropriate occupation to suit a person's temperament is not an easy task. Often times we see that somebody who could have been a musician is a doctor and somebody who could have been a good doctor is a businessman. The importance of identifying the right job for the right person can only be gauged when you see the agony of <u>such square pegs in round holes</u>. Only an Albert Einstein could have the wisdom to reject an offer to become President of Israel because he argued that he did not have enough experience in working with human beings.

Therefore, it would be appropriate if the right knowledge came to the right individual with the active participation of the teacher at an early age. In addition, in determining one's occupation, one should above all focus on innate potential and interest. (education, clearly, calls for, one, a process-oriented, the situation, instead of, an input-oriented).

*derelict 낙오자, 버림받은 사람

VOCAB

obsession 강박관념
decent *좋은; 점잖은
occupation 직업
original 원래의
term 기간; *용어; 학기; 조건
draw *끌어내다, 얻다; 그리다
established 확립된, 기정의
practice 실행; *관행
stuff 채워[밀어] 넣다
point out ~을 지적하다
sarcastically 풍자적으로
literally 문자 그대로
imply 함축하다; *의미하다
occupy 점유하다
appropriate 적절한
suit ~에 적합하다
temperament 기질, 성질

1. According to the passage, which is the author's attitude toward the practice of education and finding jobs these days?

① neutral ② critical ③ indifferent
④ optimistic ⑤ satisfied

서술형

2. 위 글 둘째 단락의 밑줄 친 such square pegs in round holes의 문맥상 의미를 20자 이내의 우리말로 쓰시오.

3. Mark T(True) or F(False) for the following statements.

(1) Education today is more process-oriented than input-oriented. □ T □ F
(2) Today many people don't have jobs that suit them. □ T □ F
(3) Albert Einstein dreamed of becoming President of Israel for a short period. □ T □ F

4. 위 글 셋째 단락의 괄호 안에 있는 단어를 아래에 주어진 우리말의 뜻에 맞게 배열하시오.

상황은 확실히 주입 중심의 교육 대신에 과정 중심의 교육을 요구한다.

VOCAB

task 일, 임무
identify 확인하다, 인지하다
gauge 측정하다, 판단하다
agony 고민, 고통
square 사각, 정사각형
reject 거절하다
offer *제의; 제공
argue 주장하다
individual 개인
participation 참여
determine 결정하다
above all 무엇보다도
focus on ~에 초점을 두다
innate 타고난
potential 잠재력
process-oriented 과정 중심의
input-oriented 주입 중심의

55

SECTION 12.
Education · Psychology · Language

Logically we should learn about things before doing them and that is presumably why the *pundits enforce this in our educational system. But it is not the natural way nor, I venture to think, the best way. The adolescent wants to do things first, and only then ① does he appreciate the problems involved and want to learn more about them.

They do these things better in primitive life, for there at puberty the boy joins his father in making canoes, patching huts, going out fishing or hunting, and preparing weapons of war. He is serving his apprenticeship in the actual accomplishments of life. It is not surprising that anthropologists find that the adolescents of primitive communities do not suffer from the same neurotic 'difficulties' as ② that of civilized life. This is not, as some assume, because they are permitted more sexual freedom, but because they are given more natural outlets for their native interests and powers and are allowed to grow up freely into a full life of responsibility in the community.

In the last century this ③ was recognizing in the apprenticeship system, which allowed the boy to go out with the master carpenter, thatcher, or ploughman to engage in the actual work of carpentry, roof-mending, or ploughing, and so to learn his trade. It was the same in medicine, in which a budding young doctor of sixteen learnt his job by going round with the general practitioner and ④ helping with the blood-letting and other treatments. In our agricultural colleges at the present time young men have to do a year's work on a farm before their theoretical training at college. The great advantage of this system is that it lets the apprentice see the practical problems ⑤ before he sets to work learning how to solve them, and he can therefore take a more intelligent interest in his theoretical work.

*pundit 현인, 현자

FROM 「*Childhood and Adolescence*」 by James A. Hadfield

VOCAB

logically 논리적으로
presumably 아마도
enforce 실시[시행]하다
venture 위험을 무릅쓰고 ~하다; *과감히 ~하다
adolescent 청소년
appreciate *인지하다; 감상하다; 고맙게 여기다
involved 연루된, 관계있는
primitive 원시의
puberty 사춘기
canoe 카누
patch 헝겊 조각; *이어 맞추다
hut 오두막
weapon 무기
serve 봉사하다; *역할을 다하다
apprenticeship 도제 신분, 도제 제도
accomplishment 성취, 수행
anthropologist 인류학자
community 공동체; *사회
suffer *고통을 받다; 앓다
neurotic 신경의
civilized 문명화된

1. 다음 중 위 글의 요지로 가장 적절한 것은?

① 도제 제도는 현대의 교육 실정에 맞지 않는다.
② 원시시대 청소년들의 교육제도에 대한 연구가 필요하다.
③ 맡은 바 일에 책임감을 갖도록 교육하는 것이 중요하다.
④ 이론보다 실습을 먼저 경험해 보는 것이 중요하다.
⑤ 청소년들에게 좀더 많은 자유를 허용해야 한다.

서술형

2. 위 글에 따르면 도제 제도의 장점은 무엇인지 우리말로 쓰시오.

3. In the 3rd paragraph, the author mainly uses ______________ to express his idea clearly.

① metaphor ② contrast ③ comparison
④ example ⑤ time order

4. 위 글의 ①~⑤ 중에서 어법상 <u>틀린</u> 것을 모두 찾아 바르게 고치시오.

도제 제도

중세 시대에 수공업 분야에서 기능 후계자를 양성하던 방법으로, 제자가 스승 밑에서 수련하여 숙련공이 되면 독립을 하고, 그 역시 제자를 양성하여 기능을 전수해 주는 제도를 말한다. 수업 기간은 짧게는 2년에서 길게는 7~8년이었는데, 이 기간에 제자는 스승의 집에서 함께 생활하며 기술을 연수하였다. 도제가 되는 나이는 10~16세였으며, 도제 기간을 마친 후 다시 3년 정도의 장인 기간을 거치고, 일종의 기능 심사 시험을 거친 후에 한 사람의 도장인으로 독립할 수 있었다. 이후 공장제 수공업의 발전에 따라 도제 제도는 붕괴하였지만, 그들의 긍지와 전통은 오늘날까지 유럽 사회에 남아 있다.

VOCAB

assume 추정하다, 가정하다
permit 허락하다
outlet (배)출구
native 타고난
recognize 알아보다, 인식하다
master 대가, 거장
thatcher 지붕 이는 사람
ploughman 농부
engage in ~에 종사하다
carpentry 목수일
ploughing 경작
trade 무역; *직업, 생업
medicine 의학
budding 싹트는; *신참의
practitioner 개업의(醫), 개업자
blood-letting 방혈(放血)
treatment 치료(법)
agricultural 농업의
theoretical 이론의
advantage 장점, 이득
apprentice 도제, 견습생, 수습(공)
intelligent 머리가 좋은; *지성을 가진

56

SECTION 12.
Education · Psychology · Language

How you feel about yourself as a person is called self-esteem. People with high self-esteem believe they are capable, strong and worthy of a good life, while those with low self-esteem feel inadequate and worthless. Low self-esteem often develops in childhood and continues throughout adulthood, causing severe (A) [emotion / emotional] pain. Therefore, it is important to develop a healthy, positive sense of self from an early age.

Many people base their self-esteem on external factors such as how much money they earn, how much they weigh, and whether others like and appreciate them. If one of these external factors (B) [change / changes], their self-esteem can be greatly shaken. For example, if your self-esteem is based on the fact that someone else loves you, then you risk feeling vulnerable and worthless if that person's love ends. By the same token, building self-esteem is not an easy task if you have been hurt by others or have suffered years of personal, academic or professional failure.

To build up your self-esteem, you need to take an honest look at your strengths and weaknesses. Being at peace with yourself, with who you are and what you have to offer others, is a major part of having high self-esteem. This inner peace does not mean that you are ignorant of your weaknesses; rather, it means that you accept who you are and genuinely like the person you (C) [have become / will become].

VOCAB

self-esteem 자긍심, 자존감
capable 유능한, 능력 있는
be worthy of ~의 가치가 있다
inadequate 부적당한, 적격이 아닌
develop 발달하다
adulthood 성인(기)
severe 심한, 격심한
positive 긍정적인
base ~의 근거[논거]를 두다
external 외적인
factor 요인, 요소
appreciate 높이 평가하다; *가치를 인정하다; 감사하다

1. 자존감에 대한 설명 중, 위 글의 내용과 일치하지 않는 것은?

① 자존감은 자신에 대해 어떻게 느끼는지와 관련이 있다.
② 자존감이 높은 사람들은 강인하고 삶의 질도 높다.
③ 외적인 요소에 대한 신뢰는 자존감을 높여준다.
④ 부정적인 경험이 쌓이면, 올바른 자존감 형성이 어렵다.
⑤ 올바른 자존감을 위해서는 자신을 잘 아는 것이 중요하다.

2. **According to the passage, which of the following persons is NOT likely to have high self-esteem?**

① a person who is independent of others
② a person who accepts his or her faults
③ a person who gets over his or her failures
④ a person who expects credit from others
⑤ a person who believes in him or herself

서술형

3. 위 글에 따르면, 어릴 때 올바른 자아를 형성하는 것이 중요한 이유는 무엇인지 우리말로 쓰시오.

4. 위 글의 (A), (B), (C) 각 네모 안에서 어법상 알맞은 것끼리 짝지은 것으로 가장 적절한 것은?

	(A)		(B)		(C)
①	emotion	……	change	……	have become
②	emotion	……	change	……	will become
③	emotional	……	change	……	have become
④	emotional	……	changes	……	will become
⑤	emotional	……	changes	……	have become

56

SECTION 12.
교육 · 심리 · 언어

VOCAB

shake 흔들다
risk ~을 무릅쓰다[각오하다]
vulnerable 상처 입기 쉬운
worthless 무가치한
by the same token 마찬가지로
task 일
suffer (고통을) 겪다, 앓다
academic 학문적인
professional *직업적인; 전문적인
inner 내부의
ignorant 무지한, 모르는
genuinely 진정으로

57

SECTION 12.

Education · Psychology · Language

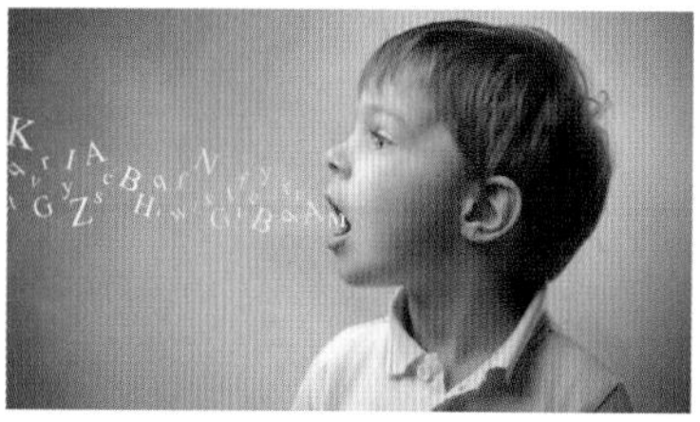

An important aspect of language systems is that they are ____________. That is, a language is not a finite set of messages from which the speaker must choose. Instead, any speaker can use the resources of the language — its vocabulary and grammatical patterns — to make up new messages, sentences that no one has ever said before. Because a language is a/an ____________ system, it can always be used to talk about new things. Bees have a remarkable system of communication, using a sort of "dance" in the air, in which the patterns of a bee's flight tell other members of the hive about food sources. However, all bees can communicate about is a nectar supply — its direction, distance, and abundance. As a consequence, a bee would make a very dull conversationalist, at least in human terms.

Another aspect of the communicative function of language is that it can be displaced. That is, we can talk about things not present — about rain when the weather is dry, about taxes even when they are not being collected, and about a *yeti even if no such creature exists. The characteristic of displacement means that human beings can abstract, can lie, and can talk about talk itself. It allows us to use language as a vehicle of memory and of imagination. A bee communicates with other bees about a nectar source only when it has just found such a source. Bees do not celebrate the delights of nectar by dancing for sheer pleasure. Human beings use language for many purposes quite unconnected with their immediate environment.

*yeti 설인(雪人)

FROM 「The Origins ans Development of the English Language」 by Thomas Pyles & John Algeo

VOCAB

aspect 면, 측면
a set of *일련의; 한 쌍의
finite 유한한
resource 자원, 원천
grammatical 문법(상)의, 문법적인
make up ~을 구성하다
remarkable 놀랄 만한
flight 날기, 비행
hive 벌집
source 근원, 출처
nectar *꽃의 꿀; 달콤한 음료
supply 공급(하다)
distance 거리
abundance 풍부함
as a consequence 결과적으로
dull 지루한

57

SECTION 12.
교육 · 심리 · 언어

1. **What is the best title for the passage?**

① How Can Humans Talk to a Yeti?
② Human Language vs. Animal Language
③ How was Human Language Developed?
④ Why Do Humans Communicate with Each Other?
⑤ Unique Features Present in Human Language

2. **위 글의 첫째 단락의 빈칸에 공통으로 들어갈 말로 가장 적절한 것은?**

① complicated ② open ③ interactive
④ limited ⑤ simple

서술형

3. **위 글에 따르면, 인간의 언어에서 어휘와 문법이 하는 역할은 무엇인지 우리말로 쓰시오.**

4. **Why does the author of the passage mention "bees"?**

① to show that bees are remarkable communicators
② to explain how bees discover new food sources
③ to show how bees communicate their emotions
④ to explain the characteristic of human language
⑤ to emphasize the superiority of humans over nature

꿀벌의 언어에 대한 언어학자 프리슈(Karl von Frisch)의 실험 결과

프리슈는 꿀벌들이 정보를 교환하는 것을 연구한 결과, 꿀벌의 의사소통은 간단한 원을 그리며 춤을 추거나, 8자 모양으로 선회하면서 춤을 추는 것이라는 것을 밝혀냈다. 또한, 꿀벌은 종족에 따라 서로 다른 언어, 일종의 사투리를 구사한다고 그는 주장했다. 예를 들면, 오스트리아의 카르니올라라는 종류의 꿀벌의 언어는 코카서스 종의 그것과 모든 점에서 동일하지만, 카르니올라 종이 코카서스 종보다 더 빠른 속도로 춤을 춘다는 것이다.

VOCAB

conversationalist 이야기하기 좋아하는 사람
term 용어; 기간; 조건; *기준
displace 옮기다; 치환하다; *전치하다 (displacement 전치)
tax 세금
collect 모으다; *징수하다
creature 생물, 동물
characteristic 특징
abstract 추상적인; *추상화하다
vehicle 탈것; *전달 수단, 매개체
sheer 비쳐 보이는; *완전한
purpose 목적
unconnected 연결되지 않은; *관련이 없는
immediate 즉각적인; *직접적인
environment 환경; *상황

58

SECTION 12.
Education · Psychology · Language

‘It’s a beautiful thing, the destruction of words. Of course the great wastage is in the verbs and adjectives, but there are hundreds of nouns that can be got rid of as well. It isn’t only the synonyms; there are also the antonyms. After all, what justification is there for a word which is simply the opposite of some other word? A word contains its opposite in itself. Take “good,” for instance. If you have a word like “good,” what need is there for a word like “bad”? ______(A)______ will do just as well — better, because it’s an exact opposite, which the other is not. Or again, if you want a ______(B)______ version of “good,” what sense is there in having a whole string of vague useless words like “excellent” and “splendid” and all the rest of them? “Plusgood” covers the meaning, or “doubleplusgood” if you want something ______(B)______ still. Of course we use those forms already. But in the final version of *Newspeak there’ll be nothing else. In the end the whole notion of goodness and badness will be covered by only six words — in reality, only one word. Don’t you see the beauty of that, Winston? It was B.B.’s idea originally, of course,’ he added as an afterthought.

*Newspeak 전체주의 국가의 신(新)언어

FROM 「1984」 by George Orwell

VOCAB

destruction 파괴
wastage 낭비, 소모
verb 동사
adjective 형용사
noun 명사
get rid of ~을 제거하다
synonym 동의어
antonym 반의어
justification 정당화, 변명의 사유
opposite 반대(의)
contain 포함하다
in itself 본래, 본질적으로
do 하다; *충분하다

1. **What is the speaker in the passage mainly talking about?**

① how to form new words
② the correct use of antonyms
③ the diverse nature of languages
④ the simplification of language
⑤ the importance of accuracy in speaking

2. **위 글의 빈칸 (A), (B)에 들어갈 말로 가장 적절한 것은?**

	(A)		(B)
①	Ungood	……	good
②	Ungood	……	stronger
③	Worse	……	stronger
④	Worse	……	better
⑤	Good	……	better

서술형

3. **위 글의 밑줄 친 that이 가리키는 바를 우리말로 쓰시오.**

소설 「1984」의 줄거리 및 작품 이해

사회학적 통찰과 풍자로 유명한 영국의 소설가 조지 오웰(George Orwell, 1903–1950)의 작품으로 원제는 「Eighty Four」이다. 소설 「1984」에서 조지 오웰은 인간의 의식과 정신이 언어 능력과 밀접한 관계에 있음을 말한다. 소설 속에 등장하는 빅브라더(B.B.)는 정보의 독점으로 사회를 통제하는 관리 권력, 혹은 이러한 사회체계를 지칭한다. 소설 속 전체주의의 화신으로 볼 수 있는 빅브라더의 언어통제는 인간의 정체성이 바로 언어와 그 상징성에 있음을 보여준다. 주인공 스미스는 자신의 상사인 오브라이언에게서 벗어나려고 하지만 그에 의해 휘둘리고 결국엔 사랑하는 여인 줄리아마저 허무하게 잃고 자신도 싫어하던 빅브라더를 진정 사랑한다고 믿으며 사형을 맞는다. 당국의 관리였던 주인공 윈스턴의 사랑과 의식마저도 통제하고 파멸시킬 수 있었던 것은 바로 언어에 대한 헤게모니를 쥐고 있었던 당국과 빅브라더이고, 언어 능력을 상실한다는 것은 인간 정신마저도 바꿀 수 있음을 말한다.

VOCAB

exact 정확한
version 번역; 변형; *~판
sense 감각; *의미
a string of 일련의
vague 모호한
splendid 멋진, 훌륭한
cover 덮다; *포함하다; 다루다, 보도하다
notion 개념
in reality 사실상
B.B.(Big Brother) 큰형; *수령님, 독재자
originally 원래
afterthought 재고; *보충부분, 추가분

SECTION 12.

Word Test

정답 | P.127

1. 다음 문장의 빈칸에 들어갈 가장 알맞은 단어를 고르시오.

(1) A(n) ____________ quality or ability is one that you were born with, not one that you have learned.

① decent ② innate ③ acquired ④ potential ⑤ individual

(2) Someone who is ____________ is weak or easy to hurt physically or mentally.

① diligent ② capable ③ positive ④ ignorant ⑤ vulnerable

2. 우리말에 맞게 빈칸에 주어진 철자로 시작하는 단어를 쓰시오.

(1) The earth's f____________ resources should be used with definite purpose.

(지구의 유한한 자원은 명백한 목적을 갖고 사용되어야 한다.)

(2) In the space marked "o____________" she wrote "police officer."

('직업'이라고 표시된 란에 그녀는 '경찰'이라고 썼다.)

(3) I said I felt like quitting, but I didn't mean it l____________.

(나는 그만두고 싶다고 말했지만, 문자 그대로 그런 의도는 아니었다.)

(4) An English-language v____________ of the book is planned for the autumn.

(그 책의 영어판은 가을에 출간될 계획이다.)

3. 다음 문장의 빈칸에 알맞은 단어를 보기에서 찾아 쓰시오. (단, 필요한 경우에는 어형을 바꾸시오.)

보기 | vague suffer opposite cover

(1) Exercise is a word which ____________ a vast range of activities.

(2) The car crashed into a truck coming from the ____________ direction.

(3) He has been ____________ from Alzheimer's disease for two years.

(4) Some aspects of the law were somewhat ____________ and ill-defined.

4. 우리말에 맞게 빈칸에 공통으로 들어갈 알맞은 단어를 쓰시오.

· What classes are you taking this ____________?

(이번 학기에 무슨 수업을 수강할 거니?)

· The Government's ____________ of office expires at the end of the year.

(정부의 임기는 올해 말에 끝난다.)

· Multimedia is the ____________ for any technique combining sounds and images.

(멀티미디어는 소리와 이미지를 결합한 기술을 일컫는 용어이다.)

SECTION. 13

Current Issues

시사 이슈

59

SECTION 13.
Current Issues

Recent studies have found that people who have grown up in the digital age differ significantly from the older generation in their ability to recall basic information without (A) [assistance / assistant] from an electronic device. Researchers believe that because it is easier to search for information, the skill of memorization has begun to atrophy due to a lack of regular practice.

Some neuroscientists argue that (B) [excessive / insufficient] interaction with digital technology has resulted in impairment resembling that of a person suffering from head trauma or a psychiatric disorder. This deficit in cognitive abilities, such as short-term memory and concentration, caused by the overuse of technology is known as digital dementia. Constant access to digital devices fosters an imbalance in the brain, with linear and information-searching skills being strengthened while intuitive thinking and emotional capabilities (C) [improve / deteriorate]. This results in not only impaired cognitive skills but also negative emotional conditions such as depression.

The good news is, however, that experts tentatively speculate that digital dementia can be reversed, based on the fact that this happens in some forms of dementia when the source of the problem is removed. The effects of digital dementia, therefore, may not be inevitable if users are willing to take measures to actively promote brain health.

VOCAB

significantly 크게, 상당히
recall 기억하다, 상기하다
atrophy 위축; *위축되다
neuroscientist 신경과학자
impairment 장애
resemble ~을 닮다
trauma 외상
psychiatric 정신 의학의
deficit 부족, 결손
cognitive 인식[인지]의

1. **What is the purpose of the passage?**

① to explain the process of brain development in youths
② to introduce new cures for digital dementia
③ to compare the positive and negative effects of using digital devices
④ to illustrate what causes digital dementia and outline its effect on the brain
⑤ to urge the government to introduce a policy that prevents digital dementia

2. **위 글의 (A), (B), (C) 각 네모 안에서 문맥에 맞는 어휘를 골라 짝지은 것으로 가장 적절한 것은?**

	(A)		(B)		(C)
①	assistance	……	excessive	……	improve
②	assistance	……	insufficient	……	improve
③	assistant	……	excessive	……	deteriorate
④	assistant	……	insufficient	……	deteriorate
⑤	assistance	……	excessive	……	deteriorate

서술형

3. **위 글에 따르면, 뇌의 불균형이 초래하는 결과가 무엇인지 우리말로 서술하시오.**

서술형

4. **The author of the passage has an o__________ attitude toward the possibility of curing digital dementia.**

VOCAB

concentration 집중
dementia 치매
linear 선의; *일차원적인
intuitive 직관적인
impaired 손상된
tentatively 시험적으로; *망설이며
speculate 추측[짐작]하다
reverse 반대의; *되돌리다
inevitable 불가피한
promote 촉진하다

팝콘브레인(popcorn brain)

통신기술과 디지털기술의 발전으로 즉각적인 반응을 확인할 수 있는 전자 기기에만 몰두하게 되어 현실에는 둔감한 반응을 보이도록 변형된 뇌 구조를 나타내는 용어이다. 팝콘처럼 바로 튀어 오르는 자극적이고 즉각적인 현상에만 반응하게 되고, 다른 사람의 감정이나 실제 현실의 변화에는 무감각하게 반응하게 되는 현상을 의미한다. 연구 결과에 따르면, 인터넷을 장기간 사용하는 사람의 뇌는 생각 중추를 담당하는 회백질의 크기가 실제로 줄어든 것을 확인할 수 있다. 전문가들은 이를 예방하기 위해 인터넷과 전자 기기의 사용 시간을 스스로 제한할 수 있는 절제 능력을 강화하는 것을 제안한다.

60

SECTION 13.
Current Issues

Across the world, social and political conflicts are frequently instigated by discord over immigration and the public policies (A) [formulate / formulated] in the interest of regulating it. While the issues related to immigration are often regionally specific, there are also underlying patterns that can be observed on a global scale and used to facilitate the legislation of effective immigration reform.

The economic benefits of immigration are often touted by advocates of open immigration policies, as an influx of new workers and consumers can boost local economic growth and raise tax revenues. What's more, immigrant workers — especially those of the low-skilled variety — have been shown ______________________________. In America, for example, (B) [which / where] the percentage of working-age adults without a high school education has plummeted from more than 80% in 1950 to about 10% currently, there are simply more low-skill positions available than potential employees willing to accept them. These advantages of immigration, however, do little to quell anti-immigrant sentiments, as these sentiments tend to possess social rather than economic roots. Social science research has shown that, despite the dire need for low-skilled workers, these types of immigrants are met with greater resistance from the native population than (C) [that / those] possessing professional skills, such as physicians and technicians. This may be because low-skilled migrants are likely to present a more alien image in terms of language, traditions and religion; such differences are commonly perceived as a social and cultural threat.

VOCAB

conflict 갈등
instigate 유발하다, 조장하다
discord 불화, 불일치
immigration 이주[이민]
regulate 규제하다
regionally 지역적으로
underlying 근본적인
facilitate 가능하게[용이하게] 하다
legislation 입법, 법률
effective 효과적인
reform 개혁[개선]
tout 장점을 내세우다, 선전하다
advocate 옹호자

1. 위 글 둘째 단락의 빈칸에 들어갈 말로 가장 적절한 것은?

① to adapt to new working environments quickly
② to conform to new social and cultural systems easily
③ to generally be more educated than native low-skilled workers
④ to be more competent when compared to native low-skilled workers
⑤ to largely complement the existing labor force rather than compete with it

서술형

2. 위 글에 따르면, 현지인들이 특히 저숙련 기술 이민자들에게 반이민 정서를 갖는 이유가 무엇인지 우리말로 쓰시오.

3. 위 글의 (A), (B), (C) 각 네모 안에서 어법에 맞는 표현을 골라 짝지은 것으로 가장 적절한 것은?

	(A)		(B)		(C)
①	formulate	......	which	......	that
②	formulated	......	which	......	those
③	formulated	......	where	......	those
④	formulate	......	where	......	those
⑤	formulated	......	where	......	that

세계시민주의(cosmopolitanism)

이민을 통한 인적 자원과 자본의 이동이 수월해진 현대사회에선 국가의 경계와 상관없이 적용될 수 있는 법과 제도의 중요성이 커지고 있다. 이에 적합한 개념 중 하나로 세계시민주의가 있다. 고전적인 세계시민주의는 전 세계 사람들을 자신의 동포로 생각하는 것으로 고대 그리스의 철학자인 디오게네스(Diogenēs)가 주창했다. 근대 이후부터는 자유주의적 세계시민주의와 민주적 세계시민주의의 논의가 활발하다. 자유주의적 세계시민주의는 평등한 전 세계의 시민들이 그들 스스로 이성적인 판단을 통해 초국가적 가치를 창출한다는 것이 핵심이며 존 롤스(John Rawls)의 「만민법」에서 볼 수 있다. 민주적 세계시민주의는 개별 국가에 대한 애국심을 기본으로 하여 전 지구 범위의 합의를 토대로 법과 제도를 통한 규제를 만들 수 있다는 것으로, 위르겐 하버마스(Jürgen Harvermas)의 헌정 국가 사상이 대표적이다.

VOCAB

influx 유입
boost 신장시키다, 북돋다
revenue 수익, 수입
plummet 곤두박질치다, 급락하다
do little to-v ~하는 데 거의 도움이 되지 않다
quell 진압하다; *가라앉히다
sentiment 정서, 감정
dire 심각한
resistance 저항
migrant 이주자
alien 이질적인
threat 위협

61

SECTION 13.

Current Issues

Renting a room from an overseas host with Airbnb or having someone else handle your grocery shopping with TaskRabbit — these are just two examples of the developing sharing economy, which has swelled to a staggering $26 billion globally and encompasses a diverse array of economic transactions. Sharing economy participants buy, rent, and sell unused or unwanted items collaboratively.

Sharing has been an integral component of human survival going back to hunter-gatherer societies and cooperative agriculture, but the modern-day obsession with private ownership in capitalist economies has resulted in excessive consumption and a surplus of personal belongings. However, in light of dwindling natural resources and a greater understanding of environmental issues, consumer behavior is shifting back toward more sustainable methods of consumption. Another contributing factor is the emergence of innovative technology, which has streamlined and simplified sharing-based transactions. The sharing economy allows consumers to reinvent the market by conducting transactions with each other directly. This approach to buying and selling, in contrast to the traditional market, has an impact on the culture itself, moving from a(n) ____(A)____ to a(n) ____(B)____.

As the number of participants in peer-to-peer transactions continues to grow, the success of the sharing economy will rely more heavily on its central principle — the establishment of trust between strangers. Inherent within all activities of a sharing nature, trust is the key to enabling these transactions to occur.

VOCAB

rent 빌리다
grocery 식료품
swell 부풀다
staggering 비틀거리는; *압도적인, 경이적인
encompass 포함하다, 아우르다
diverse 다양한
array 집합체
economic 경제의
transaction 거래
collaboratively 협력적으로, 합작으로
integral 필수적인
component 요소
agriculture 농업
obsession 강박, 집착
private 개인 소유의
ownership 소유권
capitalist 자본주의자; *자본주의적인

61

SECTION 13.
시사 이슈

1. What is the author mainly talking about?

① different types of collaborative consumption
② organizations supporting collaborative consumption
③ criticism and controversies related to the sharing economy
④ the development and cultural impact of the sharing economy
⑤ the rise of a new form of economy following the sharing economy

서술형

2. According to the author, there are several factors that have influenced the emergence of the sharing economy. First of all, consumer behavior has become more focused on sustainable methods of consumption because of decreasing __________ __________ and __________ __________. Secondly, the development of __________ __________ has accelerated the sharing economy by facilitating its processes. (each word from the passage)

3. 위 글의 빈칸 (A)와 (B)에 들어갈 말로 가장 적절한 것은?

	(A)		(B)
①	traditional industry	......	green economy
②	open perspective	......	closed perspective
③	hunter-gatherer society	......	an agricultural cooperative
④	an agricultural cooperative	......	industrialized economy
⑤	individualistic society	......	more collective perspective

4. Mark T(True) or F(False) for the following statements.

(1) The sharing economy has increased in size globally. □ T □ F
(2) The obsession with private ownership has helped the sharing economy develop. □ T □ F
(3) Trust is the key component to the success of the sharing economy. □ T □ F

노동력 중개 플랫폼, TaskRabbit

IBM의 소프트웨어 엔지니어였던 리 부스케(Leah Busque)는 강아지 사료를 사러 가는 것이 귀찮게 느껴진 나머지, 간단한 심부름을 대신해 줄 사람을 구할 방법을 모색하다 TaskRabbit이라는 이름의 사이트를 고안해냈다. TaskRabbit은 일종의 단기 아르바이트 제공 서비스로, 인력이 필요한 사람과 일거리가 필요한 사람을 연결해주는 중개 플랫폼이다. 인력이 필요한 사람이 일거리 내용과 금액을 기재하면, 자신이 적임자라고 생각하는 사람이 지원하는 방식이다. 일거리의 종류로는 장보기나 전자 제품 출시일에 맞춰 매장 앞에 줄서기 등 간단한 심부름이 주를 이룬다. 사용하지 않는 노동력을 공유하기 때문에 공유경제를 기반으로 하는 대표적인 사례로 꼽힌다.

VOCAB

result in (결과적으로) ~을 야기하다
excessive 지나친, 과도한
consumption 소비
surplus 과잉, 잉여
belonging (*pl.*) 소유물, 재산
in light of ~에 비추어, ~을 고려하여
dwindling 줄어드는
natural resource 천연자원
shift 움직이다, 변화하다
sustainable 지속 가능한
emergence 출현, 발생
streamline 능률화하다
simplify 간소화[단순화]하다
reinvent 재발명하다; *개혁하다
conduct (특정한 활동을) 하다
have an impact on ~에 영향을 주다
inherent 내재하는, 타고난

62

SECTION 13.
Current Issues

American universities and colleges have become a breeding ground for a new form of *political correctness. This movement is barely recognizable from its predecessor of the 1980s and '90s, whose dual aim was to place restrictions on hate speech while paving the way for minority voices and perspectives to be better represented in the presentation of literature and history.

The recurrence of politically correct speech in its present-day form focuses on the emotional welfare of the individual, operating on the assumption that the fragile psyche of university students must be shielded from offense, thereby preventing psychological damage. This predominantly student-driven movement has precipitated a shift in interpersonal communication, and the previously obscure terms "microaggression" and "trigger warning" have come to the forefront of modern language. A microaggression is an action or speech act that is classified as a form of violence despite a seeming lack of hostile or discriminatory intent. A trigger warning is a statement given to an audience signaling that the following content may contain potentially unsettling material. University professors are increasingly expected to issue such warnings so that students who have experienced trauma in the related area may opt to avoid exposure to the work altogether, thus forestalling the evocation of unpleasant memories or feelings.

Those who obstruct the campaign to erase uncomfortable ideas from university life, whether intentional or not, face harsh accusations of insensitivity, ignorance, hostility, and more. This culture of fierce protectiveness may be tightening the stranglehold on ____________________ ____________________.

*political correctness 도의적 공정성

VOCAB

breeding ground 번식지, 온상
recognizable 알아볼 수 있는
predecessor 전임자, 이전 것
dual 두 부분으로 된, 이중의
restriction 제한, 제약
hate speech 편파적 발언
pave the way for ~를 위해 길을 닦다[여건을 조성하다]
minority 소수
perspective 관점
represent 대표하다
recurrence 되풀이, 반복
welfare (개인 · 단체의) 안녕[행복]
assumption 상정, 추정, 전제
fragile 부서지기 쉬운; *허약한
psyche 마음, 정신
shield 방패; *보호하다
predominantly 대개, 대부분
precipitate 촉발하다

1. What is the best title for the passage?

① Is Politically Correct Speech Actually Effective?
② Words That Trigger Learning in the College Classroom
③ Speech Therapy: A New Form of Psychological Healing
④ Recipients of Verbal Assault Suffer from Mental Trauma
⑤ A Movement to Protect Students from Unintended Discrimination

서술형

2. 위 글에 근거하여 80~90년대의 도의적 공정성 운동과 오늘날 운동의 차이점을 우리말로 서술하시오.

3. Read the following cases and circle the correct one in the parentheses.

(1) Asking non-Caucasian students where they are from is a (microaggression / trigger warning), as it implies that their status as Americans is illegitimate.
(2) A professor gave a (microaggression / trigger warning) before giving a lecture about book that portrays domestic abuse, so that any students who had been victimized by such abuse could avoid the class.

4. 위 글 셋째 단락의 빈칸에 들어갈 말로 가장 적절한 것은?

① racial harmony and social cohesion
② traditional stereotypes and the use of slurs
③ bullying behavior and classroom intimidation
④ intellectual diversity and freedom of expression
⑤ affordable learning and equal-opportunity education

VOCAB

obscure 잘 알려져 있지 않은
forefront 맨 앞, 선두
classify 분류[구분]하다
violence 폭행, 폭력
hostile 적대적인 (hostility 적의, 적대감)
discriminatory 차별적인
intent 의도
unsettling 불안하게 하는, 동요하게 하는
opt to-v ~하기로 선택하다
exposure (유해한 환경 등에의) 노출
forestall 미리 방지하다
evocation 불러냄, 환기
obstruct 방해하다, 막다
accusation 비난
insensitivity 무감각, 둔감
ignorance 무지, 무식
stranglehold 목 조르기, 옥죄기

SECTION 13.
Word Test

정답 | P.127

1. 다음의 설명에 해당하는 단어를 보기에서 찾아 쓰시오.

보기 | cognitive innovative influx fragile

(1) easily broken, destroyed, or damaged: ______________
(2) bringing in new thoughts or systems: ______________
(3) the arrival of a considerable number of people: ______________
(4) referring to conscious mental activities like understanding or thinking: ______________

2. 다음 문장의 밑줄 친 부분과 바꿔 쓸 수 있는 단어를 고르시오.

(1) The police obstructed the demonstrators at the protest march.
① facilitated ② blocked ③ clustered ④ precipitated ⑤ defined
(2) The gifted singer has had a visual impairment since birth.
① issue ② dementia ③ operation ④ disposal ⑤ disorder
(3) The unknown donator gave a staggering sum of money to the orphanage.
① incredible ② mundane ③ contributing ④ enabling ⑤ total

3. 우리말에 맞게 빈칸에 주어진 철자로 시작하는 단어를 쓰시오.

(1) The country's marriage customs were completely a______________ to the traveler.
(그 나라의 결혼 관습은 그 여행자에게 완전히 생경한 것이었다.)
(2) You can check your banking t______________ records with your cell phone.
(당신은 휴대 전화를 통해서 은행 거래 기록을 확인할 수 있다.)
(3) The musical industry is struggling to attract a d______________ audience.
(뮤지컬 산업은 줄어드는 관객을 유치하기 위해 고투 중이다.)

4. 다음 문장의 빈칸에 들어갈 가장 알맞은 단어를 고르시오.

(1) Surprisingly, this best-selling book was written by an ______________ philosopher.
① expected ② unwanted ③ effective ④ available ⑤ obscure
(2) John detests animal abuse as he is an enthusiastic ______________ of animal rights.
① judge ② physician ③ advocate ④ conductor ⑤ resistance
(3) Tina has an ______________ with cleanliness, so she washes her hands every hour.
① impact ② obsession ③ accusation ④ evocation ⑤ establishment

MEMO

지은이

NE능률 영어교육연구소

NE능률 영어교육연구소는 혁신적이며 효율적인 영어 교재를 개발하고
영어 학습의 질을 한 단계 높이고자 노력하는 NE능률의 연구조직입니다.

능률고급영문독해

펴 낸 이 주민홍
펴 낸 곳 서울특별시 마포구 월드컵북로 396(상암동) 누리꿈스퀘어 비즈니스타워 10층
(주)NE능률 (우편번호 03925)
펴 낸 날 2016년 3월 30일 개정판 제1쇄 발행
2023년 12월 15일 제13쇄
전 화 02 2014 7114
팩 스 02 3142 0356
홈페이지 www.neungyule.com
등록번호 제 1-68호
I S B N 979-11-253-1163-8 53740
정 가 16,000원

NE 능률

고객센터

교재 내용 문의 : contact.nebooks.co.kr (별도의 가입 절차 없이 작성 가능)
제품 구매, 교환, 불량, 반품 문의 : 02-2014-7114
☎ 전화문의는 본사 업무시간 중에만 가능합니다.

NE능률 교재 MAP

독해

아래 교재 MAP을 참고하여 본인의 현재 혹은 목표 수준에 따라 교재를 선택하세요.
NE능률 교재들과 함께 영어실력을 쑥쑥~ 올려보세요!
MP3 등 교재 부가 학습 서비스 및 자세한 교재 정보는 www.nebooks.co.kr 에서 확인하세요.

초1-2
- 초등영어 리딩이 된다 Start 1
- 초등영어 리딩이 된다 Start 2
- 초등영어 리딩이 된다 Start 3
- 초등영어 리딩이 된다 Start 4

초3
- 리딩버디 1

초3-4
- 리딩버디 2
- 초등영어 리딩이 된다 Basic 1
- 초등영어 리딩이 된다 Basic 2
- 초등영어 리딩이 된다 Basic 3
- 초등영어 리딩이 된다 Basic 4

초4-5
- 리딩버디 3
- 주니어 리딩튜터 스타터 1

초5-6
- 초등영어 리딩이 된다 Jump 1
- 초등영어 리딩이 된다 Jump 2
- 초등영어 리딩이 된다 Jump 3
- 초등영어 리딩이 된다 Jump 4
- 주니어 리딩튜터 스타터 2

초6-예비중
- 주니어 리딩튜터 1
- Junior Reading Expert 1
- Reading Forward Basic 1

중1
- 1316 Reading 1
- 주니어 리딩튜터 2
- Junior Reading Expert 2
- Reading Forward Basic 2
- 열중 16강 독해+문법 1
- Reading Inside Starter

중1-2
- 1316 Reading 2
- 주니어 리딩튜터 3
- 정말 기특한 구문독해 입문
- Junior Reading Expert 3
- Reading Forward Intermediate 1
- 열중 16강 독해+문법 2
- Reading Inside 1

중2-3
- 1316 Reading 3
- 주니어 리딩튜터 4
- 정말 기특한 구문독해 기본
- Junior Reading Expert 4
- Reading Forward Intermediate 2
- Reading Inside 2

중3
- 리딩튜터 입문
- 정말 기특한 구문독해 완성
- Reading Forward Advanced 1
- 열중 16강 독해+문법 3
- Reading Inside 3

중3-예비고
- Reading Expert 1
- 리딩튜터 기본
- Reading Forward Advanced 2

고1
- 빠바 기초세우기
- 리딩튜터 실력
- Reading Expert 2
- TEPS BY STEP G+R Basic

고1-2
- 빠바 구문독해
- 리딩튜터 수능 PLUS
- Reading Expert 3

고2-3, 수능 실전
- 빠바 유형독해
- 빠바 종합실전편
- Reading Expert 4
- TEPS BY STEP G+R 1

고3 이상, 수능 고난도
- Reading Expert 5
- 능률 고급영문독해

수능 이상/ 토플 80-89 · 텝스 600-699점
- ADVANCED Reading Expert 1
- TEPS BY STEP G+R 2
- RADIX TOEFL Blue Label Reading 1,2

수능 이상/ 토플 90-99 · 텝스 700-799점
- ADVANCED Reading Expert 2
- RADIX TOEFL Black Label Reading 1

수능 이상/ 토플 100 · 텝스 800점 이상
- RADIX TOEFL Black Label Reading 2
- TEPS BY STEP G+R 3

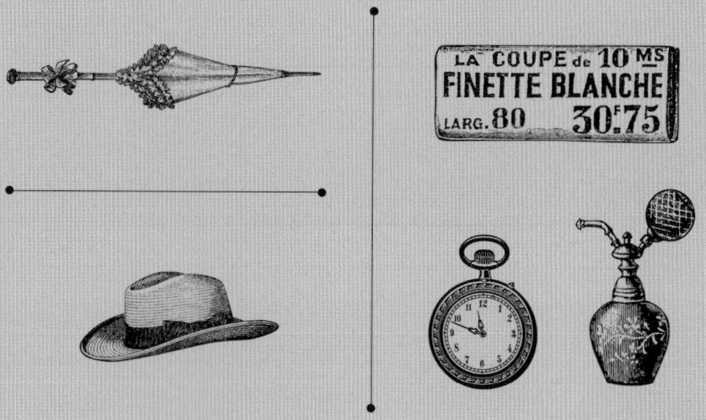

최 상 위 권 을 위 한

능률고급 영문독해

정답 및 해설

NE 능률

최 상 위 권 을 위 한

능률고급 영문독해

정답 및 해설

01

SECTION 01. 예술 · 문학

예술가에 대한 시대별 관점

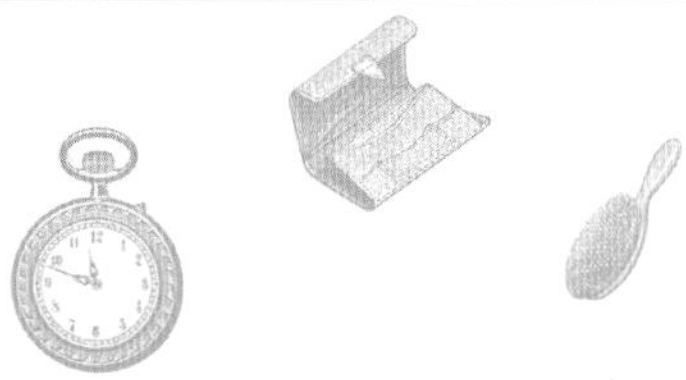

P.008

정답	1. ⑤ 2. ④ 3. ③ 4. (1) 공통점: 예술가가 독창성의 원천이 된다는 점(예술가의 독창성이 중시된 점) (2) 차이점: 르네상스 예술가와 달리 낭만주의 시대의 예술가들은 사회 비판적이고 사회 개혁 의지가 있었다는 점

본문 필기노트

① The traditional views of the artist / are crucial / (to) contemporary interpretations of creativity. ② In medieval Christianity, / the artist was understood to be the vehicle [through which God's creative inspiration found form]. ③ Through his disciplined training and craftsmanship, / the medieval Christian artist brought God's vision to reality, recognizing [(that) the inspiration and the artwork / were gifts from God, / and (that) the artist was merely the vehicle / for God's inspiration]. ④ Therefore, the artist took no individual credit / but rather identified himself as a craftsman, not as an originator or creator.

a view of: ~에 대한 견해[관점] / to: ~에 / ~인 것으로 이해되다 / 목적격 관 · 대 / that 이하는 목적어 / bring A to B: A를 B의 상태가 되게 하다 / =as[while] he recognized(분사구문) / (recognizing) / 단지 ~일 뿐인 / 칭찬, 찬사 / 오히려 / identify A as B: A를 B라고 인정하다

중세 시대의 예술가: 신의 영감을 전달하는 자

⑤ (With) the Renaissance and its cultural shift toward the human, / the artist became an individual [who originated and created new visions]. ⑥ The human was the measure of all things and his potential was unlimited. (⑦ And people [who were politically and financially powerful] began to support famous painters and architects.) ⑧ The ability [to create works of art] merely supported the Renaissance artist's sense of personal identity. ⑨ At the same time, the public definition (of) genius also shifted (from) one [favored by God] (to) one (of extraordinary creativity and originality). ⑩ The genius brought forth masterpieces, new paintings, and original styles.

~로 인해 (전치사) / 주격 관 · 대 / S / 주격 관 · 대 / V / 창조하는(형용사적 용법) / ~에 대한 / =a person / from A to B: A에서 B로 / bring forth: ~을 낳다

르네상스 시대의 예술가: 비범한 창조성을 지닌 개인

⑪ In the 19th century, / the Romantic Movement birthed a new and powerful definition (of) the artist (as) the rebel from society, the outcast [who created out of a profound passion and sacrificed everything (—) social status, money, love, family (—) for this passion]. ⑫ As with the Renaissance genius, / the Romantic artist was

S / V / O / ~에 대한 / ~로서(전치사) / = / 주격 관 · 대 / = from / 부연설명 / ~과 마찬가지로

본문해석

① 예술가에 대한 전통적 관점들은 창조성에 대한 당대의 해석에 아주 중요하다. ② 중세 기독교에서는, 예술가가 신의 창조적 영감이 형상화하는 수단으로 이해되었다. ③ 훈련된 교육과 솜씨를 통해서, 중세 기독교 예술가는 영감과 예술 활동은 신이 주신 재능이며 예술가란 단지 신의 영감을 전달하는 수단에 불과하다고 여기면서 신의 비전(이상)을 실재화했다. ④ 따라서 예술가는 개인적인 찬사를 전혀 받지 않고, 오히려 자신을 창시자나 창조자가 아닌 기능인으로 여겼다.

⑤ 르네상스와 그것으로 인한 인간에 대한 문화적 변화로 인해, 예술가는 새로운 비전을 일으키고 창조해 내는 개인이 되었다. ⑥ 인간이 모든 것들의 척도였고 인간의 잠재력은 무한했다. (⑦ 그리고 정치적 · 경제적으로 세력이 강한 사람들이 유명한 화가와 건축가를 지원하기 시작했다.) ⑧ 예술 작품을 창조하는 능력은 단지 르네상스 예술가의 개인적 정체성을 뒷받침할 뿐이었다. ⑨ 동시에, 천재에 대한 대중의 정의 또한 신에 의해 은혜를 받은 사람에서 비범한 창조성과 독창성을 갖춘 사람으로 바뀌었다. ⑩ 천재는 걸작, 새로운 그림, 그리고 독창적인 스타일을 탄생시켰다.

⑪ 19세기에, 낭만주의 운동은 예술가를 사회의 반항아, 즉 심오한 열정에서 창조하고 이러한 열정 때문에 사회적 지위, 돈, 사랑, 가족 등 모든 것을 희생한 방랑자라고 보는 새롭고 강력한 정의를 탄생시켰다. ⑫ 르네상스 시대의 천재와 마찬가지로, 낭만주의 예술가는 독창성의 원천이었지만, 르네상

the source of originality, but unlike the Renaissance genius / the Romantic artist was critical of society and sought a better world. ⑬ The development of "modern," or 20th-century, schools of art, and their definition of the artist, / were indebted to the Romantic myth of the artist.

~와 달리 / 즉, 다시 말해 / =the schools' / ~의 덕택이다

19세기 및 20세기의 예술가: 사회를 비판하고 개혁하려는 세력

스 시대의 천재와 달리 낭만주의 예술가는 사회에 대해 비판적이었고 보다 나은 세상을 추구했다. ⑬ '현대의,' 즉 20세기의, 예술 학파들의 발달과 예술가에 대한 그들의 정의는 예술가에 대한 낭만주의의 통념 덕택이었다.

본문파악

예술가를 보는 시대별 관점의 흐름에 대해 설명하고 있다. 첫째 단락은 예술가를 신의 영감의 전달자로 보았던 중세 시대의 예술가에 대한 관점이고, 둘째 단락은 예술가를 독창성이 뛰어난 개인으로 보았던 르네상스 시대의 예술가에 대한 관점이다. 셋째 단락은 예술가를 사회 비평 내지 개혁을 선도하는 사회적 반항아로 본 19세기 및 20세기의 예술가에 대한 관점이다.

문제풀이

1. 《해석》 위 글의 주제는 무엇인가?
   이 글은 예술가를 보는 관점의 시대별 변화상을 서술하고 있으므로, 주제로는 '⑤ 시대에 따라 변하는 예술가들에 대한 관점'이 가장 적절하다.
   ① 모더니즘과 그 기원 ② 예술가들과 그들의 사회적 행동주의
   ③ 다양한 예술가들과 그들의 독창성 ④ 예술가들의 개인 정체성의 발달

2. ④ → 낭만주의 시대의 예술가에 대한 설명은 셋째 단락에 나오는데, 이 내용은 언급된 바 없다.
   ① (첫째 단락 참조) ② (⑤, ⑪번 문장 참조) ③ (⑤번 문장 참조) ⑤ (⑬번 문장 참조)

3. 둘째 단락은 르네상스 시대의 예술가에 대한 관점을 설명하고 있다. '③ 그리고 정치적 · 경제적으로 세력이 강한 사람들이 유명한 화가와 건축가를 지원하기 시작했다.'는 단락의 주제에서 벗어난 문장이다.

4. ⑫번 문장 참조

르네상스와 르네상스 미술

'부활' 또는 '재생'을 뜻하는 르네상스는 유럽 문화의 뿌리가 되는 고대 그리스와 로마의 문화를 부활 또는 재생한다는 의미를 담고 있다. 르네상스에서는 단순한 복고 정신뿐 아니라 인간성의 부활에 큰 의미를 두었다. 중세의 암흑기 동안 교회는 인간성을 배제한 채 신의 권위만을 강조해 왔고, 이에 반기를 든 르네상스를 인간 중심의 문화 또는 인본주의라고 일컫는다.
르네상스 시기를 분명히 구분하는 것은 매우 어렵다. 유럽 내에서도 각 지역마다 그 시기가 서로 다르며 고딕 시대에도 르네상스의 기운이 일부에서 싹트고 있었기 때문이다. 그러나 일반적으로 14세기를 전기 르네상스, 15세기를 초기 르네상스, 16세기를 전성기 르네상스로 구분한다.
교회 중심의 미술뿐 아니라 건축, 문학, 과학 등 문화 예술의 전반에 걸쳐 눈부신 발전을 이룩한 르네상스 문화는 이탈리아를 중심으로 발전하여 전 유럽으로 퍼져 나갔다. 다양한 분야들 중에서도 특히 르네상스 미술 양식은 단순히 서양 미술사 한 시대의 미술 양식 이상의 의의를 지니고 있다. 르네상스 미술은 교회 건축을 포함하여 일반 공공건물도 포함하는데, 교회 건축에서 시작된 조각과 회화는 주로 종교적인 내용을 담고 있기는 하지만 중세와는 달리 인간적인 모습을 띠고 있다. 이제 예수나 마리아의 모습은 인간과 동일하게 묘사되었고, 자애롭고 온화한, 지극히 인간적인 모습으로 표현되었다. 또한 고딕식의 첨탑이 사라지고, 안정감과 균형미를 지닌 고대 그리스나 로마의 건축 양식을 지향하였다.

02 SECTION 01. 예술 · 문학

마티스와 피카소 – 시대 예술의 선각자

P.010

정답	1. ① 2. (1) T (2) F (3) T (4) F 3. ①

본문 필기노트

(A)

① In terms of intensity of expression, / the fauvism artist Henry Matisse never
~의 점에서 보면 =
surpassed *Woman with a Hat*, a portrait of his wife, Amelie. ② The painting
=
caused shock and outrage / when it was shown in Paris in 1905, / and the painter
야기하다, 일으키다
was scornfully labeled a "fauve"(wild beast). ③ The criticism focused on Matisse's
~라고 경멸적으로 이름이 붙여지다 ~에 초점을 두다
depiction of the woman's face [that is represented in multiple colors (of red,
주격 관 · 대 ~(으)로
green, orange, purple, and blue) [that create a mask-like appearance]]. ④ There
주격 관 · 대
is no drawing as such ; lines are little more than ragged edges, / and the whole is
그와 같은 부연설명 ~에 지나지 않는
roughly brushed. ⑤ However, there is nothing random here, / as Matisse's use of
S
contrasting complementary colors / betrays the artist's instinctual sensitivity.
보색 V

마티스의 「모자를 쓴 여인」의 특징

(B)

⑥ *Portrait of Dora Maar* by Pablo Picasso / is a clear example of Cubism, / where a
where의 선행사 관계부사
subject is viewed simultaneously from several angles. ⑦ Perspective / is the way we
여러 각도에서
see something. ⑧ If you look at a person, / you might be viewing the side of their
보고 있는 중일 것이다
face, their full face, or the back of their head. ⑨ But unless you have a mirror, /
만약 ~이 아니라면 (if ~ not)
you can only see one side of their body at a time. ⑩ Picasso revolted against the
한 번에 ~에 대항하여
restrictions [that perspective imposed]. ⑪ In his painting of Dora Maar, / he depicts
목적격 관 · 대 =
her with one eye looking inward, toward herself. ⑫ The other eye / looks out at
with+O+형용사[분사]: O를 ~한 채로 one ~ the other ...: (둘 중) 하나는 ~이고 다른 하나는 …이다 ~를 내다보다
the world and us. ⑬ It's as though she were painted by someone (from the 4th
as though[if]+가정법 과거: 마치 ~인 것처럼
dimension), able to see all perspectives simultaneously.
(being)

피카소의 「도라 마르의 초상」의 특징

본문해석

(A)

① 표현의 강도 면에서, 야수파 화가인 앙리 마티스는 그의 아내 아멜리에의 초상화인 「모자를 쓴 여인」을 결코 능가하지 못했다. ② 그 그림은 1905년 파리에서 전시되었을 때 충격과 분노를 일으켰고, 화가에게는 경멸적으로 'fauve'(야수)라는 명칭이 붙여졌다. ③ 비평은 가면 같은 모습을 만들어 내고 있는 빨강, 초록, 주황, 자주, 그리고 파랑 등의 여러 색깔로 표현된 여인의 얼굴에 대한 마티스의 묘사에 초점을 두었다. ④ 그런 그림은 없다. 선은 삐죽삐죽한 가장자리에 지나지 않고 전체는 거칠게 칠해져 있으니 말이다. ⑤ 그러나 여기에 임의로 된 것은 아무것도 없는데, 마티스가 대조를 이루는 보색을 사용한 것이 예술가의 본능적인 감수성을 드러내주기 때문이다.

(B)

⑥ 파블로 피카소의 「도라 마르의 초상」은 입체파의 명백한 예로, 입체파에서는 하나의 대상이 동시에 여러 각도에서 보여진다. ⑦ 시점(시각)은 우리가 어떤 것을 보는 방식이다. ⑧ 만일 당신이 어떤 사람을 쳐다본다면, 당신은 그들의 얼굴 옆면이나 얼굴 전면, 혹은 뒤통수를 보게 될 것이다. ⑨ 그러나 당신에게 거울이 없다면, 당신은 한 번에 신체의 한 면만을 볼 수 있을 뿐이다. ⑩ 피카소는 시점이 부여하는 제한들에 대해 반기를 들었다. ⑪ 그는 도라 마르를 그린 그림에서, 그녀가 한쪽 눈으로 안쪽, 즉 그녀 자신 쪽을 보고 있는 것으로 묘사하고 있다. ⑫ 다른 쪽 눈은 바깥세상과 우리쪽을 내다보고 있다. ⑬ 그것은 마치 그녀가 모든 시점을 동시에 볼 수 있는 4차원 세계의 누군가에 의해 그려진 것과 같다.

본문파악

글 (A)와 (B)는 각각 색(color)과 시점(perspective)에 있어 전통적 틀을 깨고 새로운 시도를 했던 화가 마티스(H. Matisse)와 피카소(P. Picasso)의 그림에 대해 소개하고 있다. (A)에서는 마티스의 작품 「모자 쓴 여인」을 통해 야수파 화가인 마티스의 색에 대한 새로운 시도에 대해 설명하였다. (B)에서는 피카소의 작품인 「도라 마르의 초상」을 통해 신체적 한계로 제한받을 수밖에 없는 인간의 시점을 그가 어떻게 자유롭게 구현했는지를 설명하고 있다.

문제풀이

1. (A)의 ②번 문장과 (B)의 ⑩번 문장에서, 마티스와 피카소 둘 다 기존의 전통적 화법과 다른 새로운 화법을 시도했음을 알 수 있다.

2. 《해석》 다음 진술에 T(참) 또는 F(거짓)로 표시하시오.
(1) 「모자를 쓴 여인」은 앙리 마티스에 의해 그려진 가장 논란이 되고 있는 작품들 중 하나였다. (①, ②번 문장 참조)
(2) 마티스는 끊임없이 변하는 자신의 감정 상태에 따라 색깔을 사용하곤 했다. → ⑤번 문장을 보면 마티스가 아무렇게나 그림을 그린 것이 아니라, 본능적 감수성이 반영된 보색을 썼다고 했다.
(3) 야수파 그림은 대비되는 색채와 거친 붓놀림에 의해 특징지어질 수 있을 것이다. (④~⑤번 문장 참조)
(4) 피카소는 물체의 본질은 거울에 비친 이미지를 보여줌으로써 가장 잘 표현될 수 있다고 믿었다. → 거울이 언급된 ⑨번 문장에서는 물체의 본질에 대해 언급하지 않았다.

3. ⑪~⑬번 문장을 보면 피카소 그림의 구체적인 특징을 알 수 있다.
① 피카소의 「거울을 든 여인」 ② 마티스의 「여인의 초상」 ③ 고갱의 「아를르의 여인」 ④ 고흐의 「별이 빛나는 밤」

구문해설

⑥ *Portrait of Dora Maar* by Pablo Picasso is a clear example of Cubism, **where** a subject is viewed simultaneously from several angles.

▷ 관계부사 where는 계속적 용법으로, and in it으로 바꾸어 쓸 수 있다.

⑬ It's **as though** she **were** painted by someone from the 4th dimension, [(**being**) **able** to see all perspectives simultaneously].

▷ 「as though[if]+가정법 과거」는 '마치 ~인 것처럼'이라는 의미로, 현재의 사실과 반대되거나 실현 불가능한 내용을 가정 · 상상할 때 사용한다.
▷ able 이하는 의미상 being이 생략된 분사구문으로, someone from the 4th dimension을 부연 설명한다.

포비즘(야수파)

마티스 「모자를 쓴 여인」

1898-1908년 프랑스에서 유행한 회화양식으로 감정의 폭발을 표현하기 위해 화려한 원색들을 도발적이고 직접적인 수법으로 구사했다. 야수파 화가들은 그 이전의 인상파 화가들과 마찬가지로 자연을 직접 보고 그렸으나, 이들의 작품에는 회화의 주제에 대한 강렬한 표현적 감정이 담겨 있다. 야수파의 주도적 화가는 앙리 마티스로 체계적 연구에 입각한 전통적인 3차원 공간의 묘사를 거부하고 색채의 운동으로 규정되는 새로운 회화 공감을 추구했다. 1905년 전시회에서 「모자를 쓴 여인」이라는 유명한 작품을 전시했다. 이 작품은 청색, 녹색, 적색을 주조로 하여 활달한 붓놀림으로 힘차고 풍부한 표현의 여인상을 형상화하고 있다.

큐비즘(입체파)

피카소 「도라 마르의 초상」

20세기 미술의 가장 중요한 미술운동의 하나이며 입체주의라고도 한다. 자연의 모방이라는 종래의 이론에 반발하여 원근법 · 명암법 등의 전통적 기법을 거부함으로써 화폭의 2차원적 평면성을 강조했다. 이들은 자연을 예술의 근거로 삼았지만 그대로 모방하지 않고 대상을 철저히 분해하여 여러 측면을 동시에 묘사했다. 인상파에서 시작되어 야수파 · 표현파에서 하나의 극(極)에 달한, 색채주의에 대한 반동으로 보인다. 자연을 재구성할 것을 목표로 한 세잔에서 원류를 찾을 수 있다.

03

SECTION 01. 예술 · 문학

아리스토텔레스의 「시학」

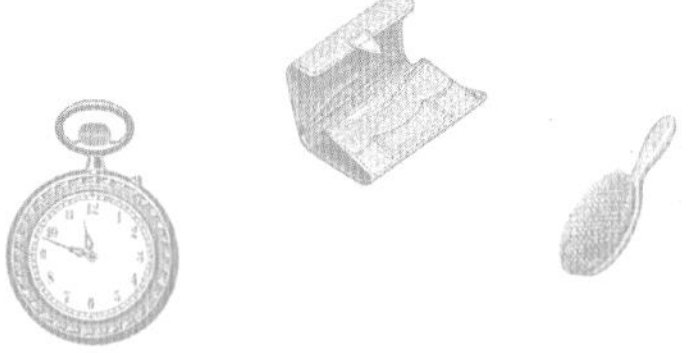

P.012

정답	1. ④	2. ③	3. the audience	4. 인간의 격렬한 감정을 배출시켜 평정을 찾게 해준다.

본문 필기노트

① Aristotle defined art as the realization of a true idea / in an external form. ② He traced it back to human beings' inherent love of imitation and to the pleasure [we feel in recognizing likenesses]. ③ Art, however, is not limited to simply copying. ④ It idealizes nature and perfects its incompleteness ; it seeks to identify the universal element / in the individual experience. ⑤ The distinction between poetry and history / is therefore not [that the one is written in rhyme, / and the other is not]. ⑥ The distinction is [that history documents only [what has actually happened], while poetry depicts things / in their universal character]. ⑦ Poetry is therefore more philosophical and more elevated than history. ⑧ Such poetic representation / may depict humans as being either better or worse than they generally are. ⑨ Comedy, for example, imitates the worst examples of humanity / because it takes what is low and shameful / and makes it into something (laughable and comic).

- defined ~ as: define A as B: A를 B라고 정의하다
- the pleasure [we: (which/that)
- is not limited to: ~에 국한되다
- its: =nature's
- ; : 부연설명
- seeks to identify: seek to-v: ~하는 것을 추구하다
- that: that 이하는 보어
- between ~ and: between A and B: A와 B 사이의
- is: V
- the one: =poetry
- the other: =history
- that: that 이하는 보어
- documents: V
- what: ~한 것(=the thing which)
- while: ~인 반면에
- more ~ than: A is more ~ than B: A는 B보다 더 ~하다
- as: ~로서
- either ~ or: either A or B: A이거나 B이거나
- it: =comedy

예술과 시(희극)에 대한 아리스토텔레스의 견해

⑩ Tragedy, on the other hand, is the representation of serious or meaningful actions. ⑪ It portrays events [which create fear and pity / in the minds of the audience]. ⑫ In the arousal of these feelings, / the artist seeks to purify these emotions and draw out the sympathies of the audience. ⑬ It is thus a curing of the passions. ⑭ Whereas art generally universalizes particular events, / tragedy depicts passionate and critical situations [to take the audience / outside the selfish, individual standpoint, / and connect it to the broader human experience]. ⑮ This is similar to Aristotle's explanation of the use of highly passionate music / in the worship of the Greek gods : it provides an outlet for religious fervor and consequently steadies one's intense religious feelings.

- on the other hand: 반면에
- which: 주격 관 · 대
- and draw: (to)
- Whereas: ~인 반면에
- to take: 데려가기 위해서(부사적 용법)
- and connect: (to)
- it: =the audience
- to: ~에, ~로
- is similar to: ~와 비슷하다
- explanation of: 부연설명
- the use of: ~에 대한
- of highly: ~의
- it: S
- provides: V_1
- steadies: V_2

비극의 특징 및 비극과 음악의 공통점

본문해석

① 아리스토텔레스는 예술을 진리(진정한 개념)가 외적인 형상으로 실현된 것이라고 정의했다. ② 그는 예술의 출처를 찾아 인간이 본래부터 갖고 있는 모방에 대한 사랑과 우리가 비슷함을 깨닫는 데서 느끼는 즐거움까지 거슬러 올라갔다. ③ 그러나 예술은 그저 모방하는 것에만 국한되지 않는다. ④ 그것은 자연을 이상화하고 자연의 불완전함을 완성하는 것으로, 개인의 경험에서 보편적 요소를 확인하고자 한다. ⑤ 그러므로 시와 역사의 차이는 하나는 운율에 맞게 쓰여지고, 다른 하나는 그렇지 않다는 것이 아니다. ⑥ 차이점은 역사는 실제로 일어난 일만을 기록하는 반면에, 시는 사물을 그것들의 보편적인 특징으로 묘사한다는 것이다. ⑦ 그러므로 시는 역사보다 더 철학적이고 더 숭고하다. ⑧ 그러한 시적 표현은 인간을 일반적인 인간보다 더 좋거나 나쁜 것으로 묘사할지도 모른다. ⑨ 예를 들어, 희극은 인간성의 가장 나쁜 예를 모방하는데 왜냐하면 그것은 저속하고 우스꽝스러운 것을 택해서 우습고 희극적인 무언가로 만들어내기 때문이다.

⑩ 반면에 비극은 진지하거나 의미 있는 행동들에 대한 표현이다. ⑪ 그것은 청중의 마음에 두려움과 연민을 자아내는 사건들을 그린다. ⑫ 이러한 감정들을 일깨움으로써, 예술가는 감정들을 정화하고 청중의 동정심을 끌어내고자 한다. ⑬ 그러므로 비극은 감정의 한 치료책이다. ⑭ 일반적으로 예술이 특정 사건들을 보편화시키는 데 반해, 비극은 청중을 자기중심적이고 개인적인 견지에서 벗어나 보다 넓은 인간 경험으로 연결하기 위해 강렬하고 위험한 상황을 묘사한다. ⑮ 이것은 그리스 신들의 숭배에 아주 강렬한 음악을 사용하는 것에 대한 아리스토텔레스의 설명과 유사하다. 그것은 종교적 열정의 배출구를 제공하며, 그 결과 인간의 격렬한 종교적 감정을 안정시켜 준다.

본문파악 이 글은 예술, 특히 시(희극과 비극)에 대한 아리스토텔레스의 견해를 설명하고 있다. 첫째 단락에서는 예술에 대한 정의와 함께 시와 희극의 특성에 대해 논하고 있고, 둘째 단락에서는 비극의 특성 및 비극과 음악의 예술적 기능을 설명하고 있다.

문제풀이

1. ④ → ③~④번 문장에서 예술은 자연을 모방하고, 이상화하며, 그것의 불완전함을 완성한다고 했다. 자연에서 경험할 수 없는 것을 보여준다는 말은 언급되지 않았다.
① (①번 문장 참조) ② (②번 문장 참조) ③ (④번 문장 참조) ⑤ (⑧~⑨번 문장 참조)

2. 빈칸이 포함된 문장은 비극이 두려움이나 연민과 같은 감정들을 정화시키고 동정심을 갖게 해준다는 앞 문장 내용에 대한 필자의 판단이다. 또한, ⑮번 문장에서 비극과 마찬가지로 종교음악도 인간의 격렬한 종교적 감정을 완화시켜 준다고 언급한 것으로 보아, 비극은 인간의 감정을 치료해 주는 역할을 한다는 것을 추론할 수 있으므로 빈칸에는 '③ a curing'이 들어가는 것이 알맞다.
① 갱신 ② 패러디 ④ 부정 ⑤ 발전

3. 문맥상 '비극은 청중(the audience)을 자기중심적이고 개인적인 견지에서 벗어나 보다 넓은 인간 경험으로 연결한다'는 내용이 되어야 자연스럽다.

4. ⑭~⑮번 문장을 통해 비극과 음악 모두 인간의 격한 감정을 배출시켜 마음의 평정을 찾게 해 주는 기능을 하는 것을 알 수 있다.

구문해설

⑤ The distinction between poetry and history is therefore not [**that the one** is written in rhyme, and **the other** is not].

▷ [ ]는 be동사의 보어 역할을 하는 명사절로 '~이라는 것'의 의미이다.
▷ 「the one ~ the other ...」는 '전자는 ~, 후자는 …'의 의미로, the one은 poetry를 the other는 history를 가리킨다. 참고로 one 앞에 the가 없는 '(둘 중) 하나는 ~ 다른 하나는 …'란 뜻의 「one ~ the other ...」 구문과 혼동하지 않도록 유의한다.

⑥ The distinction is [that history documents only **what has actually happened**, while poetry depicts things in their universal character].

▷ 이 문장은 앞 문장의 not that 이하와 대구를 이루어 '(시와 역사의 차이는) ~라는 것이 아니라 …라는 것이다'로 이해하면 좋다.
▷ what ... happened는 선행사를 포함하는 관계대명사절로, 여기서 what은 '~한 것(=the thing which)'이라는 의미이며 what ... happened는 동사 documents의 목적어이다.

아리스토텔레스의 비극론

아리스토텔레스는 이성적 동물인 인간에게 있어서 모방은 본능적인 것이며, 모방을 인지하는 것은 즐거운 일이라고 했다. 모방은 일종의 학습이며, 학습 효과를 창출하기 때문에 즐겁다. 따라서 보편적인 인간의 행위를 모방한 비극(tragedy)은 인간에게 즐거움을 준다.
그의 비극론에 따르면, 훌륭한 비극을 만들기 위해서, 즉 보편적인 인간 행위를 모방하기 위해서는 우선 구성(plot)이 개연적이면서도 필연적이어야 한다. 잘 짜여진 구성 내에서 사건의 기복과 급전은 공포와 연민을 불러일으키는 데 강력한 요소가 되기 때문이다. 또한 비극의 주인공은 운명에 의해서가 아니라, 실수로 보편적 행운에서 불행에 이르러야 한다. 우연한 실수에 의해 주인공이 불행해지는 것을 보고, 사람들은 자신에게도 그런 불행이 일어날 수 있다는 생각에 두려워하게 된다. 이 주인공은 특별히 악하거나 선하지 않은 보통의 사람이어야 한다. 그래야만 사람들이 선한 사람은 왜 불행에 빠지는가, 악한 사람은 왜 주인공이 되는가 등의 의문을 품지 않고 주인공의 불행에 감정이입을 하고 연민을 느끼게 되기 때문이다.
이러한 공포와 연민을 통하여 감정의 적절한 정화와 배설을 자연스럽게 경험하는 것이 바로 카타르시스를 느끼는 것이며, 아리스토텔레스의 비극론의 요지에 해당한다.

04

SECTION 01. 예술 · 문학

왜 명료한 글을 쓸 수 없는가?

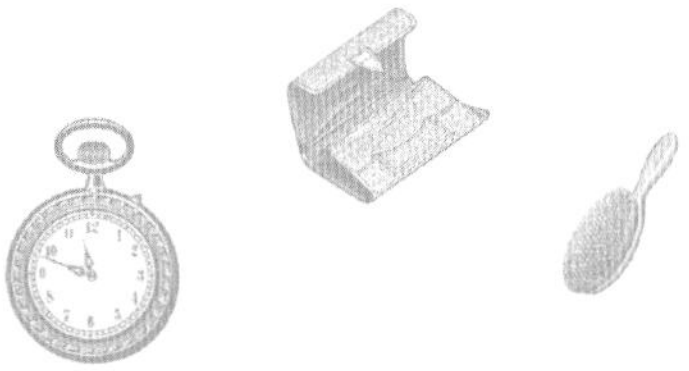

P.014

정답

1. ③ 2. 태만, 고의성, 필자가 자신이 말하고 싶은 것을 정확히 알지 못함 3. 쓰기 전에 미리 생각하는 것이 아니라 쓰면서 생각한다.
4. 이것의 불리한 점은 이는 실로 작가가 항상 경계해야 하는 위험인데, 글에는 일종의 마력이 있다는 것이다.

본문 필기노트

① I have never had much patience with the writers [who claim from the reader an effort to understand their meaning]. ② You have only to turn to the great philosophers to see [that it is possible to express (with lucidity) the most subtle reflections]. ③ You may find it difficult to understand the thought of Hume, / and if you have no philosophical training / its implications will doubtless escape you; but no one with any education at all / can fail to understand exactly what the meaning of each sentence is. ④ Few people have written English with more grace than Berkeley. ⑤ There are two sorts of obscurity [that you find in writers]. ⑥ One is due to negligence and the other to willfulness. ⑦ People often write obscurely / because they have never taken the trouble to learn to write clearly. ⑧ This sort of obscurity you find too often / in modern philosophers, in men of science, and even in literary critics. ⑨ Here it is indeed strange. ⑩ You would have thought [that men [who passed their lives / in the study of the great masters of literature] would be sufficiently sensitive to the beauty of language to write, / if not beautifully, at least with perspicuity]. ⑪ Yet you will find in their works sentence after sentence [that you must read twice in order to discover the sense]. ⑫ Often you can only guess at it, for the writers have evidently not said what they intended.

글을 모호하게 쓰는 이유: 태만과 고의성

⑬ Another cause of obscurity is [that the writer is himself not quite sure of his meaning]. ⑭ He has a vague impression of what he wants to say, but has not, (either from lack of mental power or from laziness), exactly formulated it in his mind, / and it is natural enough [that he should not find a precise expression for a confused idea]. ⑮ This is due largely to the fact [that many writers think, not before, but as they write]. ⑯ The pen originates the thought. ⑰ The disadvantage

본문해석

① 나는 독자들에게서 자신들의 의도를 이해하기 위한 노력을 요구하는 작가들에 대해서는 결코 참을 수가 없었다. ② 가장 난해한 생각들을 명료하게 표현하는 것이 가능하다는 것을 알기 위해서 당신은 위대한 철학자에게 의지하기만 하면 된다. ③ 당신은 흄의 사상을 이해한다는 것이 어렵다는 것을 알지도 모르고, 만약 철학적 훈련이 전혀 되어 있지 않다면 그것의 깊은 의미는 틀림없이 생각나지 않을 것이다. 그러나 조금이라도 교육을 받은 사람은 각 문장의 의미가 무엇인지 정확하게 이해할 수 있다. ④ 버클리보다 더 세련되게 영어로 글 쓴 사람은 거의 없다. ⑤ 당신이 작가들에게서 발견하는 모호성에는 두 가지 종류가 있다. ⑥ 하나는 태만 때문이고, 다른 하나는 고의성 때문이다. ⑦ 사람들은 흔히 명료하게 글 쓰는 법을 배우려는 수고를 결코 한 적이 없기 때문에 모호하게 글을 쓴다. ⑧ 이런 종류의 모호성을 당신은 현대의 철학자, 과학자, 그리고 심지어 문학 비평가들에게서도 너무 자주 발견한다. ⑨ 그러나 이것은 정말 이상한 일이다. ⑩ 당신은 위대한 문호들의 연구에 평생을 보낸 사람들이 언어의 아름다움에 대해 충분히 민감하여, 아름답게 쓰지는 못하지만 적어도 명료하게 글을 쓸 것이라고 생각했을 것이다. ⑪ 그러나 당신은 그들의 글에서 문장마다 의미를 깨닫기 위해 두 번씩 읽어야 한다는 것을 발견할 것이다. ⑫ 흔히 당신은 그것(의미)을 추측할 수밖에 없는데, 왜냐하면 작가들은 그들이 의도하는 바를 분명히 말하지 않았기 때문이다.

⑬ 모호성의 또 다른 원인은 작자 자신이 자기가 의미하는 바를 전적으로 확신하지 못하는 데에 있다. ⑭ 그는 자신이 말하고 싶은 것에 대해 막연한 인상을 가지고 있지만, 정신력의 부족이나 나태함 때문에 머릿속에서 그것을 명확하게 만들지 못했으니, 그가 혼란스러운 개념에 대한 정확한 표현을 찾지 못하는 것은 너무나 당연하다. ⑮ 이것은 주로 많은 작가들이 쓰기 전이 아니라, 쓰면서 생각한다는 사실에 기인한다. ⑯ 펜이 사고를 만들어내는 것이다.

of this, (and indeed it is a danger [against which the author must be always on his guard]), is [(that) there is a sort of magic / in the written word].

목적격 관 · 대

V　that 이하는 보어

⑰ 이것의 불리한 점은 이는 실로 작가가 항상 경계해야 하는 위험인데, 글에는 일종의 마력이 있다는 것이다.

글을 모호하게 쓰는 이유: 자신이 말하고 싶은 것을 정확히 알지 못함

본문파악

이 글은 서머셋 모옴(W. Somerset Maugham)의 「써밍업(*The Summing Up*)」의 일부로, 여기서 모옴은 글의 모호함이 생기는 원인을 분석하고 명료하게 글을 쓰지 않는 당대의 작가들을 비판하고 있다. 모옴은 작가가 명료하게 글을 쓰지 않는 이유로 세 가지를 제시하고 있는데, 첫째가 작가의 태만, 둘째가 고의성, 셋째가 작가가 자신이 말하고 싶은 것을 정확히 알지 못하는 것이다.

문제풀이

1. 이 글은 작가들이 글을 모호하게 쓰는 이유를 다루고 있으므로, 주제로는 '③ 사람들이 애매하게 글을 쓰는 이유'가 적절하다.
   ① 글을 쓰는 방법에 대한 이해　② 명확하게 글을 쓰는 것의 어려움
   ④ 글쓰기에 대한 철학적 접근　⑤ 생각을 효과적으로 표현하는 방법

2. ⑥, ⑬번 문장 참조

3. 이 문장은 작가들이 생각을 한 후에 쓰는 것이 아니라 쓰면서 생각하는 태도를 비유적으로 표현한 것이다. (⑮번 문장 참조)

4. ⑰번 문장의 해석 참조

구문해설

③ You may find it difficult to understand the thought of Hume, and if you have no philosophical training its implications will doubtless escape you; but **no one** with any education **at all** can **fail** to understand exactly **what** the meaning of each sentence is.

▷ 부정의 뜻을 나타내는 동사 fail 앞에 부정어 no one ... at all이 쓰여서 강한 긍정을 나타내는 이중부정이 되었다. 결국 '조금이라도 교육을 받은 사람이면 이해할 수 있다'는 의미가 된다.
▷ what 이하는 간접의문문으로 동사 understand의 목적어이다. 간접의문문의 어순은 〈의문사+주어+동사〉이다.

⑧ This sort of obscurity (O) you (S) find (V) too often in modern philosophers, in men of science, and even in literary critics.

▷ 강조를 위해 목적어인 This sort of obscurity가 문두로 나간 경우로, 목적어를 강조하는 경우 주어와 동사는 도치되지 않는 것에 유의한다.

⑩ You **would have thought** [that men who passed their lives in the study of the great masters of literature would be sufficiently sensitive to the beauty of language to write, **if** (**they did**) not (**write**) beautifully, (they would write) at least with perspicuity].

▷ 「would have v-ed」는 '~이었을 것이다'라는 의미로, 과거에 대한 추측을 나타낸다.
▷ if 절은 삽입절로 쓰여 '~이지만, ~이긴 하지만'의 의미이다.

05

SECTION 01. 예술 · 문학

윌리엄 골딩의 「파리대왕」

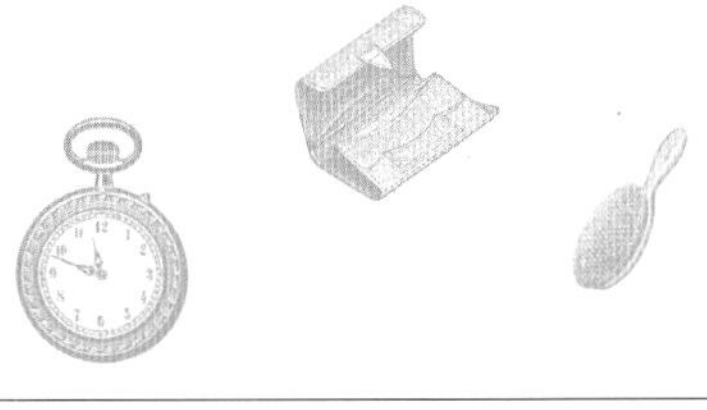

P.016

정답	1. ② 2. ③ 3. 문명화하려는 본능과 야만적인 본능이 충돌할 때 4. 서양의 부흥과 같은 문명의 역사를 극화한 것이라는 해석과 원죄나 선악의 본질과 같은 종교적인 문제를 탐구한 것이라는 해석

본문 필기노트

① William Golding published his famous novel *Lord of the Flies* in 1954. ② It tells the story of a group of English schoolboys [stranded on a tropical island / after their plane is shot down during a war]. ③ Although the novel is a work of fiction, / its exploration of human evil is based on the real-life cruelty [witnessed by Golding during World War II]. ④ Free from any rules, / the boys on the island become like savages. ⑤ They soon split up into groups, / and whereas some work peacefully together, others violently rebel. ⑥ The boys' behavior symbolizes the broader human struggle between the civilizing instinct [to obey rules and behave morally] and the savage instinct [to attain power, ignore moral rules, and act violently].

~에 관한 / 격추되다 / 허구 작품 / ~을 토대로 하다 / (Being) / ~처럼 되다 / ~로 갈라지다 / some ~, others ...: 몇몇은 ~, 다른 나머지는 … / between A and B: A와 B 사이의 / 복종하는(형용사적 용법) / 얻으려는 / 무시하려는 / 행동하는

「파리대왕」의 줄거리 및 주제

⑦ *Lord of the Flies* is written in a very plain writing style, / one [which deliberately avoids highly poetic language, / lengthy description, / and philosophical passages]. ⑧ The novel is an allegory, meaning [that the characters and objects all / have a symbolic significance [that is used to convey the novel's central themes and ideas]. ⑨ In his portrayal of the various ways [in which the boys adapt to their new island surroundings and respond to their new freedom], / Golding analyzes the broad range of ways [in which human beings respond to change, fear, and tension].

~로 / 주격 관 · 대 / V' / that 이하는 목적어 / =and it means(분사구문) / 주격 관 · 대 / 전달하기 위해(부사적 용법) / 목적격 관 · 대 / V'_1 / ~에 / V'_2 / S / V / O / 목적격 관 · 대

「파리대왕」의 문체상의 특징과 상징성

⑩ Readers and critics have interpreted *Lord of the Flies* in a variety of ways / since its publication. ⑪ Some claim [that the novel dramatizes the history of civilization, in particular the rise of the West]. ⑫ Some believe [that it examines religious issues, such as original sin and the nature of good and evil]. ⑬ Others approach the novel through psychoanalytical theories. ⑭ Ultimately, there is some validity to every interpretation ; although Golding's story is confined to an isolated

해석해 왔다(현재완료 계속) / ~으로 / 다양한 / ~이래로(전치사) / that 이하는 목적어 / 특히 / that 이하는 목적어 / A such as B: B와 같은 A / ~을 통해, ~으로 / =for(왜냐하면) / ~에 국한되다

본문해석

① 윌리엄 골딩은 그의 유명한 소설인 「파리대왕」을 1954년에 출판했다. ② 그것은 전쟁 중 비행기가 격추된 후에 한 열대 지방의 섬에 갇힌 한 무리의 영국 남학생들에 관한 이야기를 다루고 있다. ③ 비록 이 소설이 허구 작품이기는 하지만, 인간 악(惡)에 대한 탐구는 2차 세계대전 중 골딩에 의해 목격된 실재의 잔인함을 토대로 하고 있다. ④ 어떤 규칙도 없으므로, 섬에 있는 소년들은 야만인처럼 된다. ⑤ 그들은 얼마 지나지 않아 무리들로 분열하고, 몇몇은 평화롭게 함께 일하는 반면, 다른 이들은 폭력적으로 반항한다. ⑥ 소년들의 행동은 규칙을 따르고 도덕적으로 행동하는 문명화하려는 본능과, 권력을 얻고 도덕 규칙을 무시하며 폭력적으로 행동하는 야만적인 본능 사이의 보다 광범위한 인간 투쟁을 상징한다.

⑦ 「파리대왕」은 매우 평이한 문체, 즉 고도로 시적인 언어, 장황한 묘사, 그리고 철학적인 구절들을 일부러 회피한 문체로 쓰여 있다. ⑧ 이 소설은 비유담으로서, 이는 등장인물과 사물 모두가 소설의 중심 주제와 사상을 전달하기 위해 사용된 상징적인 의미를 지니고 있음을 뜻한다. ⑨ 소년들이 새로운 섬 환경에 적응하고 새로운 자유에 반응하는 다양한 방법들에 대한 묘사에서, 골딩은 인간이 변화, 공포, 그리고 긴장에 반응하는 폭넓은 범위의 방법을 분석한다.

⑩ 독자들과 비평가들은 「파리대왕」이 출간된 후 이것을 다양한 방법으로 해석해 왔다. ⑪ 어떤 이들은 이 소설이 문명, 특히 서구의 부흥에 관한 역사를 극화하고 있다고 주장한다. ⑫ 또 어떤 이들은 그것이 원죄와 선악의 본질과 같은 종교적인 문제를 탐구하고 있다고 생각한다. ⑬ 또 다른 이들은 정신분석학 이론을 통해 소설에 접근한다. ⑭ 결국, 모든 해석에는 어느 정도의 타당성이 있다. 비록 골딩의 이야기가 작은 섬에 고립된 한 무리의 소년들에게

group of boys on a small island, / it explores the universal conflict of humanity.

국한되기는 하지만, 그것이 인간의 보편적인 갈등을 탐구하기 때문이다.

「파리대왕」에 대한 다양한 작품해설과 그 공통점

본문파악

이 글은 윌리엄 골딩의 소설 「파리대왕(*Lord of the Flies*)」에 관한 서평이다. 첫째 단락은 이 소설의 개략적 줄거리와 주제를 언급하고 있고, 둘째 단락은 이 소설의 문체상의 특징과 상징성에 대해 다루고 있다. 셋째 단락은 소설 「파리대왕」에 대한 작품해석 두 가지를 소개하고, 이에 대한 필자 자신의 견해를 밝히는 것으로 결론을 맺고 있다.

문제풀이

1. 이 글은 윌리엄 골딩의 소설, 「파리대왕」의 줄거리, 주제, 문체, 작품 해석 등을 소개하고 있으므로, 글의 종류로는 '② 서평'이 적절하다.
   ① 일기 ③ 사설 ④ 편지 ⑤ 광고

2. 《해석》 다음 중 「파리대왕」에 대해 참이 아닌 것은?
   ① 어느 섬에서 함께 살도록 강요된 한 무리의 소년들에 대한 것이다. (②번 문장 참조)
   ② 저자 자신이 목격한 삶의 잔인성이 묘사되어 있다. (③번 문장 참조)
   ③ 화려한 문체로 쓰여져 있고, 정교한 어휘와 표현을 사용하고 있다. → 평이한 문체로 쓰여져 있고, 고도로 시적인 언어나 장황한 묘사 및 철학적 문구는 피했다고 했다. (⑦번 문장 참조)
   ④ 소설 속의 각 인물들은 중요한 상징적 의미를 지니고 있다. (⑧번 문장 참조)
   ⑤ 인간 본성에서 발견되는 보편적인 갈등을 다루고 있다. (⑭번 문장 참조)

3. ⑥번 문장이 단서이므로 이를 간략히 요약한다.

4. ⑪~⑫번 문장을 참조하여 요약한다. 참고로 ⑬번 문장에서 언급된 '정신분석학 이론'은 작품 해설을 위한 접근법이지, 작품 해설의 내용은 아니다.

구문해설

④ [(**Being**) **Free from** any rules], the boys on the island become like savages.

▷ [ ]는 이유를 나타내는 분사구문으로, 앞에 Being이 생략되어 있다. 「free from ~」은 '~이 없는'의 의미이다.

⑨ In his portrayal of the various ways [**in which** the boys adapt to their new island surroundings and respond to their new freedom], Golding analyzes the broad range of ways [**in which** human beings respond to change, fear, and tension].

▷ the way(s)가 선행사인 경우 how가 관계부사로 와야 하나, the way(s)와 how는 함께 쓰지 않으므로 in which를 쓴 것이다.

「파리대왕(*Lord of the Flies*)」

영국 작가 윌리엄 골딩(William Golding, 1911-1993)의 장편소설로, 1993년 노벨 문학상을 받으면서 전 세계 독자들의 주목을 받았다. 1963년 첫 영화화된 이래 몇 차례 영화로 제작되기도 했다. 이 소설의 제목은 히브리어의 '베엘제버브'를 번역한 것으로, 베엘제버브는 '곤충의 왕'이라는 뜻이다. 이 말은 악마를 가리키는 것으로 오역되었다고 밝혀진 바도 있으나, 소설의 내용으로 미루어 보아 '파리대왕'은 악(惡)을 가리키는 듯하다. 그러나 골딩이 종교적으로 악마가 존재한다고 믿었던 것은 아니다.
줄거리는 다음과 같다. 핵전쟁의 위험을 느낀 영국은 25명의 소년들을 핵전쟁으로부터 안전한 장소로 옮기려 했으나, 그들을 태운 비행기가 바다에 추락하여 소년들은 무인도에 상륙한다. 구조를 기다리는 동안 소년들 사이에서는 갈등이 일어나게 되고, 문명 세계의 사회 관습 대신 인간 본성에 잠재한 권력욕과 야만성이 드러나면서 섬은 지옥으로 변하게 된다. 몇 차례 죽을 고비를 넘긴 소년들은 결국 영국 순양함에 의해 구조된다.
소설에 등장하는 각 소년은 각기 다른 상징적 의미를 지니고 있으나, 특히 소년들 사이에서 지도자적인 역할을 하는 랄프와 잭을 살펴볼 필요가 있다. 랄프는 보통 인간들처럼 오류를 범하지만, 그래도 이성과 상식을 잃지 않으려고 노력하는 인간의 상징이다. 이에 맞서는 잭은 폭력을 집단화하고, 갖은 수단을 동원해 소년들을 수치심과 죄의식으로부터 해방시키려 한다. 랄프가 좌절된 이성의 세계를 상징하는 인간의 보호자라면, 잭은 전쟁 및 잔인성을 상징하는 인간의 파괴자이다.

06 SECTION 02. 과학

순수과학이 필요한 이유

P.022

정답	1. 순수과학을 연구할 수 있는 환경을 조성해 주는 것

본문 필기노트

① Pure science may seem (~처럼 보일지도 모른다) useless in the usual sense, but over (~동안, ~에 걸쳐) a long period of time / it surely leads to (~한 결과에 이르게 하다) economic and technological benefits. ② If we stop paying for (pay for: ~에 대한 비용을 지불하다) pure science today, / there will be no applied science (응용과학) tomorrow. ③ Charles Darwin's work (연구, 과제) on (~에 대한) evolution and Gregor Mendel's (work) on the heredity of plants / laid (V) the foundations for (~에 대한) the science of genetics (which의 선행사), which (주격 관 · 대(계속적 용법)) eventually led to the discovery of DNA (which의 선행사), which (주격 관 · 대(계속적 용법)) led to genetic engineering, which is now exploding with (폭발적으로 증가하다) unimaginable applications. ④ Michael Faraday's discovery of (~에 대한) how a magnet can produce electricity / made possible (가능하게 하다) / the first hydroelectric power plant / fifty years later. ⑤ Yet (그러나(접속사)) Darwin, Mendel and Faraday were not supported with any such profits in mind, nor (~ 역시 아니다) could (V) they (S) have been. ⑥ A nation cannot bet on (~에 (돈을) 걸다) pure scientists / like (~처럼) betting on horses. ⑦ It can, however, build stables.

순수 과학이 필요한 이유

⑧ Discoveries in pure science / are not just about nature. ⑨ They are about people as well (또한, 마찬가지로). ⑩ After Copernicus, we have taken a more humble view of (take a view of: ~을 관찰하다) our place in the cosmos. ⑪ After Darwin, we have recognized new relatives [hanging from the family tree].

순수 과학과 인간

본문해석

① 순수과학은 일반적인 의미에서 쓸모없이 보일지도 모르지만, 장기적으로 확실히 경제적, 기술적 이익에 이르게 한다. ② 만약 오늘 우리가 순수과학에 투자하는 것을 멈춘다면, 내일은 어떤 응용과학도 없을 것이다. ③ 진화에 대한 찰스 다윈의 연구와 식물의 유전에 대한 그레고르 멘델의 연구는 유전과학에 대한 기초를 쌓았으며, 유전과학은 결국 DNA의 발견으로 이어졌고, DNA의 발견은 유전공학으로 이어졌으며, 유전공학은 오늘날 상상할 수 없을 만큼 폭발적으로 응용되고 있다. ④ 자석이 전기를 발생시키는 법에 대한 마이클 패러데이의 발견은 50년 후에 최초의 수력발전소를 가능하게 했다. ⑤ 그러나 다윈, 멘델, 그리고 패러데이는 그러한 이익을 염두에 두고 지원받지 않았으며, 그렇게 될 수도 없었다. ⑥ 국가는 마치 경마에 돈을 거는 것처럼 순수과학자들에게 돈을 걸 수는 없다. ⑦ 그러나 그것은 마구간은 지을 수는 있다.

⑧ 순수과학에서의 발견들은 자연에 관한 것만이 아니다. ⑨ 그것들은 또한 인간에 관한 것이다. ⑩ 코페르니쿠스 이후, 우리는 우주에서의 우리의 위치에 대하여 더욱 겸허하게 관찰해 왔다. ⑪ 다윈 이후, 우리는 같은 계보에 속하는 새로운 종족들을 알게 되었다.

본문파악

이 글은 앨런 라이트맨(A. Lightman)의 「순수과학을 옹호하며(*In Defense of Pure Science*)」의 일부분으로, 순수과학의 중요성에 대한 글이다. 오랜 기간에 걸쳐 얻어낸 순수과학의 발견들이 결국 오늘날의 응용과학을 발전시키는 계기가 되었다는 내용으로, 예시를 통해 다양한 근거를 제시하고 있다.

- 단락 1: 순수과학의 발견 → 응용과학의 발전 – 다윈 · 멘델 · 패러데이의 예
  - 다윈의 진화론 · 멘델의 유전학 → DNA의 발견 → 유전공학
  - 패러데이의 자석 내 전기의 발견 → 수력발전
- 단락 2: 순수과학의 발견은 자연뿐 아니라 인간에 관한 발견으로도 이어짐.
  - 코페르니쿠스와 다윈의 예

문제풀이

1. '마구간을 짓는(build stables)' 것은 경마에 돈을 거는 것처럼 당장의 이익을 위한 것이 아니라, 말이 경마에서 우승할 수 있도록 편히 쉴 수 있는 환경을 조성해 주기 위한 것이다. 문맥상 '말(horses)'은 '순수 과학자들(pure scientists)'에 해당하고, '마구간을 짓는(build stables)' 것은 이들이 연구에 매진할 수 있는 환경을 조성해주는 것을 뜻한다.

구문해설

② If we **stop paying** for pure science today, there will be no applied science tomorrow.

▷ stop v-ing: '~하는 것을 멈추다[그만두다]' *cf.* stop to-v: '~하기 위해 멈추다'

④ Michael Faraday's discovery of [**how** a magnet can produce electricity] made(V) possible(OC) the first hydroelectric power plant(O) fifty years later.

▷ how 이하는 전치사 of의 목적어에 해당한다. 관계부사 how는 '~하는 (방)법'이라고 해석되며, 선행사 the way와 함께 쓸 수 없다.

▷ make+O+OC(형용사): 'O를 ~하게 하다'의 의미로, 여기서는 O가 길어 OC 뒤로 도치시켰다.

⑤ Yet Darwin, Mendel and Faraday were not supported with any such profits in mind, **nor**(부정어) could(V) they(S) have been (supported with any such profits in mind).

▷ 부정을 나타내는 어구가 문두에 오면 반드시 도치가 일어나는데, 여기서는 부정어 nor가 문두로 와서 주어와 동사가 도치되었다. nor는 앞에 언급된 내용에 대해 '~ 역시 아니다'의 의미를 나타낼 때 사용한다.

기초과학(basic science)과 응용과학(applied science)의 차이점

기초과학 또는 순수과학은 특정한 대상의 현상을 탐구하는 과학에 대하여 일반적인 개념 또는 방법론을 제공하는 과학이다. 예를 들어, 천문학, 지질학, 해양학 등에 대한 기초과학은 물리학, 화학을 들 수 있고, 동식물을 연구하는 동물생리학과 식물생리학에 대해서는 생화학을 들 수 있다. 응용과학이라는 말은 이와는 상대적인 의미로 사용되는데, 다른 학문을 응용하여 실용적인 목적으로 이용하는 것을 의미하며, 공학, 의학, 약학, 가정학, 농학 등이 여기에 해당한다. 그러나 일반적으로 기초과학이라는 용어는 응용과학의 기초가 되는 과학을 가리키므로, 기초과학과 순수과학은 같은 의미로 둘 다 응용과학의 반의어로 사용되는 경우가 일반적이다.

07 SECTION 02. 과학

과학자와 객관성

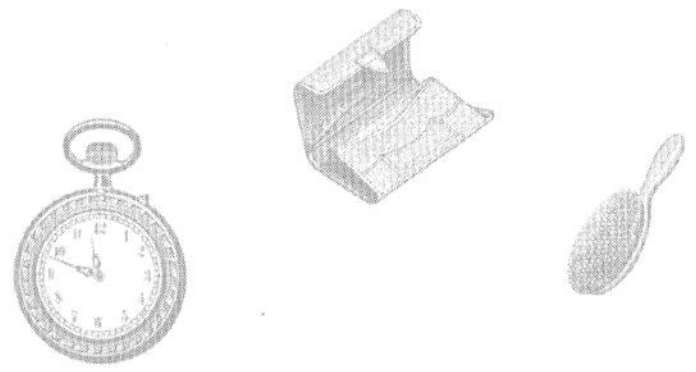

P.023

정답 | 1. 그 이론에 대한 일반적 믿음이나 그 이론을 세운 과학자의 명성과 상관없이 자신의 신념을 밀고 나가야 한다. 2. ③

본문 필기노트

① If a scientist believes a certain hypothesis is true, but finds contradicting evidence, / then in the scientific spirit, / the hypothesis must be changed or abandoned. ② In that same scientific spirit, / the idea must be changed or abandoned / in spite of the reputation of the person [advocating it].

V'1 (that) V'2 / S V / (who are) / ~에도 불구하고

과학자의 바람직한 태도

③ As an example, the greatly respected Greek philosopher Aristotle / claimed [that falling objects / fall at a speed [proportional to their weight]]. ④ This false idea was held to be true / for more than 2,000 years / because of Aristotle's compelling authority. ⑤ In the scientific spirit, however, a single verifiable experiment to the contrary / outweighs any authority, / regardless of reputation or the number of followers or advocates.

~로(써) / = / S V / that 이하는 목적어 / (which/that is) / ~ 동안(전치사) / ~ 이상 / 그와 반대의 / ~에 관계없이

잘못된 과학적 이론이 과학자의 명성으로 인해 지속된 예

⑥ Scientists must strive to distinguish between what they see and what they wish to see, / for they, (like most people,) have a vast capacity for fooling themselves. ⑦ People have always tended to adopt general rules, beliefs, creeds, ideas, and hypotheses / without thoroughly questioning their validity / and to retain them / long after they have been shown to be meaningless, false or at least questionable. ⑧ The most widespread assumptions / are often the least questioned.

distinguish between A and B: A와 B를 구별하다 / 왜냐하면(접속사) S / 삽입절 / V / O / ~에 대한(전치사) / tend to-v: ~하는 경향이 있다 / without v-ing: ~하지 않고 / (have always tended) / =general rules, beliefs ... and hypotheses / 가장 적게 의심받는

과학자가 객관적인 태도를 가져야 하는 것의 중요성

본문해석

① 만일 어느 과학자가 특정 가설이 사실이라고 믿었으나 모순되는 증거를 발견한다면, 과학의 정신에서 그 가설은 변경되거나 폐기되어야 한다. ② 그 같은 과학의 정신에서, 그 견해는 그것을 주장하는 사람의 명성에도 불구하고 수정되거나 폐기되어야 한다.

③ 하나의 예로, 매우 존경받는 그리스 철학자 아리스토텔레스는 낙하하는 물체는 그 무게에 비례하는 속도로 떨어진다고 주장했다. ④ 이 그릇된 견해는 아리스토텔레스의 강력한 권위 때문에 2,000년 이상 사실로 간주되었다. ⑤ 그러나, 과학의 정신에서 그 반대를 확인할 수 있는 하나의 실험은 추종자나 옹호자의 명성이나 그 수와 관계없이 어떤 권위도 능가한다.

⑥ 과학자들은 그들이 보는 것과 그들이 보고 싶은 것을 구별하려고 노력해야 하는데, 왜냐하면 대부분의 사람처럼 그들도 자기 자신을 속이는 것에 대한 대단한 능력을 지니고 있기 때문이다. ⑦ 사람들은 항상 일반적인 규칙, 신념, 신조, 견해, 그리고 가설을 그 타당성을 전혀 의심하지 않고 채택하며, 그것들이 의미 없고 거짓이거나 적어도 의심스럽다고 드러난 지 오랜 후에도 그것들을 유지하는 경향이 있어 왔다. ⑧ 가장 널리 알려진 주장은 흔히 가장 적게 의심받는다.

본문파악

이 글은 과학자의 객관적 태도의 중요성을 강조한 글이다. 첫째 단락은 과학적 가설이나 이론은 그에 모순되는 증거가 발견되면 그것을 세운 과학자의 명성과 관계없이 수정되거나 폐기되어야 한다는 내용이다. 둘째 단락에서는 이에 대한 예증으로 아리스토텔레스의 낙하 법칙을 들고 있다. 셋째 단락에서는 과학자들이 객관적인 태도를 유지해야 할 것을 강조하고 있다.

문제풀이

1. 첫째 단락 참조

2. ③은 기존의 과학적 가설이나 주장과 상반되는 것을 가리키는 반면, 나머지는 모두 기존의 잘못된 가설이나 이론을 가리킨다.

구문해설

④ This false idea **was held to be true** for more than 2,000 years because of Aristotle's compelling authority.

▷ hold+O+(to be) ~: 'O를 ~하다고 생각하다'의 의미로, 여기서는 'O+is held+(to be) ~'의 수동태로 쓰였다.

⑥ Scientists must **strive to distinguish** between [**what** they see] and [**what** they wish to see], for they, like most people, have a vast capacity for fooling themselves.

▷ strive to-v: '~하려고 노력하다'
▷ 두 개의 [ ] 부분은 선행사를 포함하는 관계대명사 what이 이끄는 명사절이고, 여기서 what은 '~하는 것(=the thing which)'의 의미이다.

과학혁명(scientific revolution)

과학혁명이란 과학의 한 분야 또는 여러 분야에 걸쳐 일어난 급격한 변화를 말한다. 예를 들어 코페르니쿠스의 지동설, 다윈의 진화론, 라부아지에의 새로운 화학 체계, 아인슈타인의 상대성 이론 등이 과학혁명을 일으켰다고 볼 수 있다. 좁은 의미의 과학혁명은 역사상 유럽에서 16~17세기에 걸쳐 일어난 현상을 가리키며, 약 2,000년 동안 서양의 과학관과 세계관을 지배해온 아리스토텔레스의 이론을 뒤집은 사건을 의미한다.
아리스토텔레스는 모든 물질은 물, 불, 흙, 공기 등 네 가지 원소로 이루어져 있고, 이들의 비율에 따라 물질의 성질이 달라진다고 보았다. 또한 운동은 이들 원소가 본래의 자리를 찾아가려는 성질에서 비롯되는 것이며, 우주는 이 네 가지 원소와 더불어 에테르를 포함한 다섯 가지 원소로 이루어진 것으로 생각했다. 그의 이론은 13세기 이탈리아의 철학자이자 신학자였던 토마스 아퀴나스에 의해 종교적인 사상과 합쳐져 오랫동안 추앙받았다.
이러한 아리스토텔레스의 이론을 부정하고 나선 대표적인 과학자들이 코페르니쿠스, 케플러, 갈릴레오, 뉴턴 등이었다. 이들에 의해 일어난 과학혁명은 아리스토텔레스의 이론과 대치되었으며, 16세기 중반부터 17세기 후반에 이르기까지 급격한 과학의 진보를 이루었다. 과학혁명 시기의 과학자들은 그들이 이룩한 업적 자체뿐만 아니라, 당시 절대적으로 받아들여지고 있던 아리스토텔레스의 이론을 반박한 용기로 인해 높이 평가될 만하다. 수많은 노력과 끈기 있는 관찰, 그리고 검증의 과정을 거쳐 그들은 확실한 이론을 수립했으며, 이들에 의한 과학혁명은 과학에만 국한된 것이 아니라 과학의 방법론, 목적, 그리고 과학의 사회적 위치에도 변화를 일으키며 많은 사상적, 사회적 변화를 초래했다. 과학혁명은 유럽 문화 전반에 걸쳐 영향을 끼친 것이다.

08 SECTION 02. 과학
패러다임(paradigm)

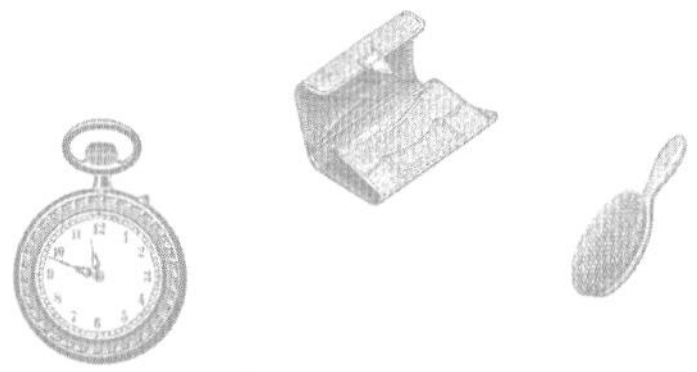

P.024

정답 | 1. ⑤ 2. ⑤ 3. (1) T (2) T (3) T (4) F

본문 필기노트

① A paradigm is a general theory, (like the Darwinian theory of evolution), [which has achieved general acceptance / in the scientific community]. ② Paradigms help scientific communities to standardize their discipline in that they help the scientist to create avenues of inquiry, formulate questions, select methods [with which to examine questions], define areas of relevance and establish or create meaning. ③ A paradigm is essential to scientific inquiry — no natural history can be interpreted in the absence of at least some implicit body of theoretical and methodological beliefs [that permit selection, evaluation, and criticism].

패러다임의 정의와 기능

④ Then, how are paradigms created, / and how do scientific revolutions take place? ⑤ (C) Inquiry begins with a random collection of "mere facts," / although, often, a set of principles is already included in the collection. ⑥ (B) During these early stages of inquiry, / different researchers [confronting the same phenomena] describe and interpret them in different ways. ⑦ (A) In time, these descriptions and interpretations entirely disappear, and a pre-paradigmatic school appears. ⑧ Such a school often emphasizes a special part (of the collection of facts). ⑨ Often, these schools compete for supremacy.

사전 패러다임이 나타나기까지의 과정

⑩ From the competition of these pre-paradigmatic schools, / one paradigm emerges. ⑪ To be accepted as a paradigm, / a theory must seem better than its competitors, / but it need not, (and in fact never does,) explain all the facts [with which it can be confronted], [thus making continued research necessary]. ⑫ As a paradigm grows in strength and in the number of advocates, / the other pre-paradigmatic schools or the previous paradigm fade, [bringing about a great change in science].

하나의 패러다임이 정해지는 과정

본문해석

① 패러다임이란 다윈의 진화론처럼 과학계에서 보편적인 인정을 받은 일반적인 이론이다. ② 패러다임은 과학자가 연구 방법을 만들어 내고 의문을 체계화하고 의문에 대해 조사해야 하는 방법을 선택하고 관련 분야를 규정하고 의미를 만들거나 정하도록 도움을 준다는 점에서 과학계가 그들의 학문 분야를 표준화하도록 도와준다. ③ 패러다임은 과학 연구에 필수적인데, 어떤 자연의 역사도 선택, 평가, 그리고 비평을 허락하는 최소한의 일련의 암묵적인 이론적 및 방법적 신념들 없이 해석될 수 없기 때문이다.

④ 그렇다면, 패러다임은 어떻게 만들어지고, 과학 혁명은 어떻게 일어나는가? ⑤ (C) 연구는 '단순한 사실들'을 임의로 모아둔 것으로 시작되는데, 비록 종종 일련의 원리들이 그 모아둔 것에 이미 있을지라도 말이다. ⑥ (B) 이러한 연구의 초기 단계 동안에는, 동일한 현상을 접하는 연구원들마다 그것들을 서로 다른 방법으로 묘사하고 해석한다. ⑦ (A) 조만간 이러한 묘사와 해석은 완전히 사라지고, 사전 패러다임 학파가 나타난다. ⑧ 그런 학파는 종종 사실들을 모아놓은 것의 특정 부분을 강조한다. ⑨ 종종 이 학파들은 최고의 자리를 놓고 경쟁한다.

⑩ 이러한 사전 패러다임 학파들의 경쟁에서, 하나의 패러다임이 나타난다. ⑪ 패러다임으로 인정받기 위해서 이론은 경쟁 대상들보다 더 나아 보여야 하지만, 직면하게 될 모든 사실을 설명할 필요도 없고 사실 결코 그렇게 하지도 못하는데, 그렇기 때문에 지속적인 연구가 필요한 것이다. ⑫ 한 패러다임의 힘과 옹호자들의 수가 증가함에 따라, 다른 사전 패러다임 학파들이나 이전의 패러다임은 사라지고, 과학에서는 큰 변화가 일어난다.

본문파악

이 글은 패러다임에 대해 설명한 것이다.
- 단락 1: 패러다임의 정의와 기능
- 단락 2: 패러다임이 만들어지는 과정 – 사전 패러다임의 형성
- 단락 3: 패러다임이 만들어지는 과정 – 하나의 패러다임의 확정

문제풀이

1. (A)의 these descriptions and interpretations는 (B)에서 언급된 '연구자마다 동일한 현상을 다른 방식으로 묘사하고 해석한다'는 내용을 가리키는 것이므로, (A)는 (B) 뒤에 와야 하고, (B)의 these early stages of inquiry는 (C)에서 나온 'Inquiry'를 가리키는 것이므로, (B)는 (C) 뒤에 와야 한다.

2. 《해석》 다음 중 위 글에서 언급되지 않은 것은?
① 패러다임의 정의 (①번 문장 참조)
② 과학연구에 있어서 패러다임의 역할 (②번 문장 참조)
③ 과학 연구에서 패러다임의 중요성 (③번 문장 참조)
④ 패러다임이 나타나는 과정 (둘째, 셋째 단락 참조)
⑤ 패러다임과 이론의 차이 → 본문에서 언급된 바 없다.

3. 《해석》 다음 진술에 대해 T(참) 혹은 F(거짓)로 표시하시오.
(1) 패러다임은 연구 방향의 한계를 정하는 하나의 틀에 비유될 수 있다. (②번 문장 참조)
(2) 자연의 역사를 해석하기 위해서 우리는 조직화된 신념이 필요하다. (③번 문장 참조)
(3) 사전 패러다임이 사라질 때 과학혁명이 일어난다. (④, ⑫번 문장 참조)
(4) 선택된 패러다임은 모든 가능한 논쟁들을 만족시켜야 한다. → ⑪번 문장에서 한 이론이 패러다임으로 선택되더라도 그 이론이 직면하게 될 모든 사실을 다 설명할 필요는 없으며, 설명할 수도 없다고 했다.

구문해설

② Paradigms **help** scientific communities **to standardize** their discipline [**in that** they **help** the scientist **to create** avenues of inquiry, (to) **formulate** questions, (to) **select** methods [**with which to examine** questions], (to) **define** areas of relevance and (to) **establish** or **create** meaning].

▷ help+O+to-v: 'O가 ~하도록 돕다'의 의미로 주절과 in that이 이끄는 종속절 모두에 쓰였으며, 종속절에서는 동사 자리에 create, formulate, select, define, establish, create가 모두 접속사 or로 병렬연결되었다.
▷ [ ] 부분의 with which to examine questions는 with which they should examine questions를 to부정사를 이용해 간단히 표현한 어구로 methods를 수식하며, 이때의 with는 '~으로'란 뜻의 수단을 나타낸다.

⑪ To be accepted as a paradigm, a theory must seem better than its competitors, but it **need not**, and in fact **never does**, **explain** all the facts [**with which** it can be confronted], thus making continued research necessary.

▷ need not은 explain에 걸리는 조동사이고, and in fact never does는 삽입구로 여기서 does는 동사 explain을 대신하는 대(代)동사이다.
▷ [ ] 부분은 all the facts를 수식하는 〈전치사+관계대명사〉절로, be confronted with는 '~에 직면하다'라는 뜻이다.

09

SECTION 02. 과학
지동설과 망원경

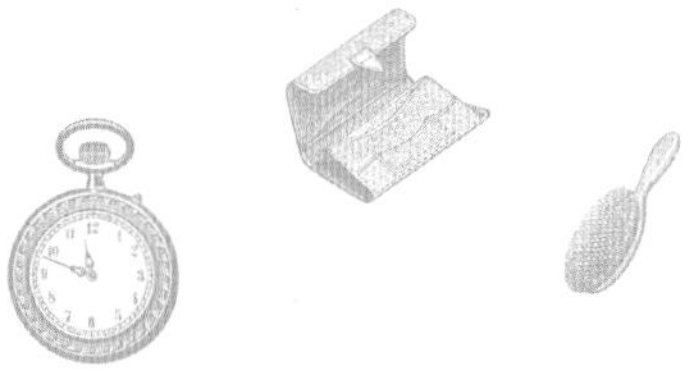

P.026

정답 | 1. ③ 2. (1) T (2) F (3) F 3. (4) 4. technological

본문 필기노트

① Ptolemy's view of the solar system / was accepted for fourteen hundred years / until finally challenged by Copernicus, a mathematician and astronomer (with a Polish father and a German mother), in 1530. ② Copernicus' view of the solar system had the sun at the center, with the earth revolving around it, along with all the other planets.

~에 대한 / 인정받았다 / ~ 동안 / ~까지 (it was) / = / ~에 / with+O+분사[형용사]: O가 ~하는 채로, O를 ~하면서 / ~와 함께

코페르니쿠스의 지동설

③ Shown here is the picture (from his original publication). ④ As can be seen, / the only thing [that doesn't go around the sun] is the moon, which continues to go around the earth. ⑤ One objection [that people had to the picture] was [that / if the earth was indeed just another planet, / how come it was the only one with a moon]? ⑥ Other objections included [why does it feel like the earth is standing still / and why don't objects [thrown into the air] land far to the west]? ⑦ Also, / if the universe had been created for mankind, / then why wasn't mankind at the center?

보어 / V(도치) / S / (그림에서) 알 수 있듯이 / 주격 관 · 대 / V / that 이하는 보어 / 목적격 관 · 대 / ~에 대해서 / V / =why / =planet / S / V / ~인 것처럼 느껴지다 / 떨어지다

코페르니쿠스의 지동설에 제기된 여러 가지 이의들

⑧ Despite these problems, / Pope Clement VII approved of Copernicus' work in 1530, and asked for a copy of the full work / when it was available. ⑨ This was not until 1543, the year [that Copernicus died].

~에도 불구하고 / V_1(~을 승인하다) / V_2(~을 요구하다) / 그것이 사용 가능했을 때 / = / (=when)

교황 클레멘트 7세의 지동설 인정

⑩ The real breakthrough [that ultimately led to the general acceptance of Copernicus' theory] was due to Galileo, but was actually a technological rather than a conceptual breakthrough. ⑪ It was Galileo's improvement and use of the telescope that persuaded people [that the moon was a lot like the earth, and in some ways so too were the planets].

S / 주격 관 · 대 / ~에 이르게 하다 / V_1 / ~ 때문에 / V_2 / A rather than B: B라기보다는 오히려 A / It is ~ that ... 강조구문 / ~의 / persuade+O+that ~ : O에게 ~을 설득시키다 / 어떤 면에서는 / so (too)+V+S: ~도 역시 그렇다

갈릴레오의 망원경으로 인한 지동설의 보편화

본문해석

① 태양계에 대한 프톨레마이오스의 견해는 1530년에 폴란드인 아버지와 독일인 어머니를 둔 수학자이자 천문학자인 코페르니쿠스에 의해 마침내 도전받기까지 1,400년간 인정받았다. ② 태양계에 대한 코페르니쿠스의 견해는 태양이 중심에 있고 지구가 다른 모든 행성들과 함께 태양의 둘레를 공전하는 것이었다.

③ 여기 그의 최초의 출판물에서 나온 그림이 제시되어 있다. ④ 그림에서 알 수 있듯이, 태양의 둘레를 공전하지 않는 유일한 것은 달로서, 그것은 지구 둘레를 계속해서 돌고 있다. ⑤ 사람들이 그 그림에 대해 가졌던 이의는, 만일 지구가 정말로 단지 또 하나의 행성일 뿐이라면, 왜 그것만이 위성을 갖고 있는 것이냐 하는 것이었다. ⑥ 다른 반론들은 왜 지구가 여전히 정지해 있는 것처럼 느껴지는지와, 왜 공중으로 던져진 물체가 서쪽으로 멀리 떨어지지 않는 것인지를 포함하고 있었다. ⑦ 또한, 만일 우주가 인류를 위해 창조되었다면, 왜 인류가 중심에 있지 않았을까?

⑧ 이러한 문제점들에도 불구하고, 교황 클레멘트 7세는 1530년에 코페르니쿠스의 업적을 인정했고, 완성작이 이루어졌을 때 그것의 사본을 요청했다. ⑨ 이는 코페르니쿠스가 사망한 해인 1543년에야 이루어졌다.

⑩ 마침내 코페르니쿠스의 이론이 보편적으로 수용되게 한 실질적인 발전은 갈릴레오 덕분이었지만, 개념적인 발전이라기보다는 사실 과학기술적인 발전이었다. ⑪ 달은 지구와 매우 흡사하며 어떤 면에서 행성들도 그렇다고 사람들을 설득한 것은 바로 갈릴레오의 망원경의 개량과 사용이었다.

본문파악

이 글은 코페르니쿠스의 지동설이 보편적으로 받아들여지기까지의 과정을 설명한 글이다. 이 글에서는 지동설이 보편화될 수 있었던 것은 결국 갈릴레오가 망원경을 개량해 사용했기 때문이라고 말한다. 첫째 단락과 둘째 단락에서는 코페르니쿠스의 지동설을 소개하고 그것에 대해 일반인들이 제기한 의문점들을 다루었다. 셋째 단락에는 지동설이 교황에 의해 부분적으로 인정되었다는 내용이 나오고, 마지막 단락에는 갈릴레오의 망원경의 도움으로 마침내 지동설이 보편적 이론으로 받아들여졌다는 내용이 나온다.

문제풀이

1. 《해석》 위 글의 제목으로 가장 적절한 것은?
이 글은 코페르니쿠스의 지동설이 보편적으로 인정받기까지의 과정을 개괄적으로 설명하고 있다. 제목으로는 '③ 코페르니쿠스가 마침내 어떻게 승리를 거두었는가'가 가장 적절하다.
① 1400년대에 일어난 대혁명 ② 과학을 위한 용기 있는 선택
④ 우주 체계에 대한 잘못된 견해들 ⑤ 코페르니쿠스에 의해 주창된 오랜 논쟁

2. 《해석》 다음 진술에 대해 T(참) 또는 F(거짓)로 표시하시오.
(1) 프톨레마이오스와 코페르니쿠스는 태양계에 대해 반대되는 견해를 가지고 있었다. (①번 문장 참조)
(2) 당시에 일반적으로 인정되던 바와 같이 코페르니쿠스도 태양이 우주의 중심에 있다고 믿었다. → ①번 문장을 보면 태양이 우주의 중심이라는 주장은 당시 코페르니쿠스에 의해 처음 제기된 것이다.
(3) 코르페니쿠스는 달이 항상 태양과 지구 둘레를 공전한다고 생각했다. → ④번 문장에서 코르페니쿠스는 달이 태양이 아닌 지구 둘레를 공전한다고 믿었던 것을 알 수 있다.

3. (4) → 우주가 인류를 위해 창조되었다면, 왜 인류가 행성들의 중심에 있지 않느냐고 반문한 것이지, 우주 창조에 대한 의문을 제기한 것은 아니다. (⑦번 문장 참조)

4. 《해석》 넷째 단락에서 과학적 신념은 때때로 과학기술의 발전으로 인해 확인된다는 것을 유추할 수 있다. (본문에서)
⑩번 문장에서 코페르니쿠스의 주장이 갈릴레오의 망원경 덕에 보편적으로 인정받게 되었다는 것으로 보아, 새로운 과학적 발견이 보편적으로 인정받기 위해서는 '과학기술의(technological)' 발전도 한몫한다는 것을 알 수 있다.

구문해설

① Ptolemy's view of the solar system was accepted for fourteen hundred years **until** (**it was**) finally challenged ... .

▷ '~(할 때) 까지'란 뜻의 접속사 until 뒤에는 it was가 생략되어 있으며, 이때의 it은 주절의 주어인 Ptolemy's view of the solar system을 가리킨다.

⑥ Other objections (S) **included** (V) **why** does it feel like the earth is standing still (O_1) and **why** don't objects thrown into the air land far to the west? (O_2)

▷ 동사 include는 and로 연결되는 두 개의 목적어를 취하고 있다.
▷ 두 개의 why 절의 동사를 현재형으로 쓴 것은 일반적인 사실이기 때문이다.

⑨ This was **not until** 1543, the year that Copernicus died.

▷ A is not until B: 'B에서야 비로소 A이다'

10 SECTION 02. 과학

케슬러 증후군(Kessler syndrome)

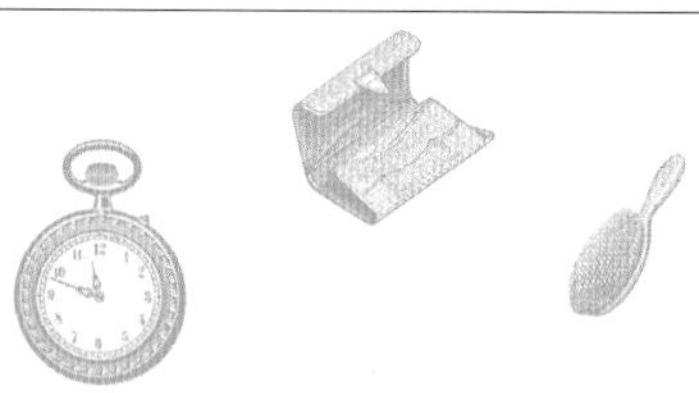

P.028

정답 | 1. ④ 2. ③ 3. ④ 4. 기능이 중단된 후에 궤도에 버려지는 물체의 수를 줄이는 것

본문 필기노트

① In 1978 NASA scientist Donald J. Kessler envisioned the possibility of a cascading chain reaction of space debris collisions [taking place in low Earth orbit].
(동격 / 동명사구의 의미상 주어 / 동명사구)

② This chilling potential scenario has since been dubbed the Kessler Syndrome.

③ The underlying mechanism (of the concept) is [that an impact (between two manmade objects in space) will generate further debris, [leading to an exponential number of subsequent collisions, [culminating in a situation [in which a deadly swarm of shrapnel and space junk circles the planet [devastating everything in its path, including functioning satellites and manned spacecraft]]]]].
(S / V / that 이하는 be동사의 보어 / 부대상황의 분사구문 / 결과의 분사구문 / 목적격 관 · 대 / 부대상황의 분사구문 / ~을 포함하여(전치사))

케슬러 증후군의 개념

④ Kessler made the pessimistic prediction [that the density of space junk in orbit around the Earth would, by the year 2000, reach a level [at which random collisions were inevitable]]. ⑤ Although manmade objects in space were already being cataloged at that time in the interest of anticipating and avoiding collisions, the additional objects [generated by such collisions] were not being tracked and were often small enough to escape satellite detection.
(동격의 that / ~쯤에 / ~주위에, 둘레에 / ~일 것이다(추측) / 목적격 관 · 대 / 비록 ~일지라도 / ~을 (도모하기) 위하여 / S / V_1 / V_2 / 형용사+enough to-v: ~하기에 충분히 …한)

케슬러의 비관적 예측

⑥ Kessler proposed a reduction / in the number of objects [abandoned in orbit / after they had ceased to function, [hypothesizing [that this would be the most prudent way of preventing future accidents]]. ⑦ However, it wasn't until a 2009 collision between two communication satellites — one Russian, the other American — unleashed thousands of small pieces of debris into orbit and potentially set into motion Kessler's doomsday scenario, that international efforts [to authoritatively address the situation] were undertaken in earnest.
(과거완료 / (=while he hypothesized) / that 이하는 목적어 / it is not until ~ that ...: ~가 되어서야 비로소 …하다 / 부연설명 / one ~ the other ...: (둘 중) 하나는 ~이고 다른 하나는 …이다 / ~(속으)로 / 해결하는(형용사적 용법) / 본격적으로, 진지하게)

우주 쓰레기의 현황과 그에 대한 대응

본문해석

① 1978년 NASA 과학자 도널드 J. 케슬러는 지구 저궤도에서 우주 쓰레기 충돌의 순차적인 연쇄 반응이 일어나는 가능성을 상상했다. ② 이 오싹한 잠재적 시나리오는 그 후로 케슬러 증후군이라고 불렸다. ③ 그 개념의 근본적인 기제는 우주에서의 인공 물체 두 개의 충돌이 추가적인 쓰레기를 생성하여, 기하급수적인 수의 연쇄 충돌로 이어져서, 치명적인 파편과 우주 쓰레기더미가 지구를 떠돌며 작동하는 위성과 인공 우주선을 포함하여 경로에 있는 모든 것을 파괴하는 상황으로 끝이 난다는 것이다.

④ 케슬러는 지구 궤도를 도는 우주 쓰레기의 밀도가 2000년에는 무작위의 충돌이 불가피한 수준에 도달할 것이라는 비관적인 예측을 했다. ⑤ 당시에 충돌을 예측하고 피하기 위해 이미 우주의 인공 물체들이 목록화되고 있었지만, 그러한 충돌로 생성된 새로운 물체들은 추적되고 있지 않았으며 보통 위성 탐지를 피할 정도로 작았다.

⑥ 케슬러는 기능을 중단한 후에 궤도에 버려지는 물체의 수를 줄일 것을 제안하며, 이것이 미래의 사고를 방지하는 가장 현명한 방식이라고 가정하였다. ⑦ 그러나, 2009년에 두 개의 통신 위성 — 러시아 위성과 미국 위성 — 의 충돌이 수천 개의 작은 쓰레기 조각을 궤도로 보내 케슬러의 멸망 시나리오를 잠재적으로 발동시키고 나서야, 비로소 위압적으로 그 상황을 해결하려는 국제적인 노력이 본격적으로 이루어졌다.

본문파악

이 글은 과학자 케슬러가 제기한 우주 쓰레기 간 충돌에 관한 내용이다. 첫째 단락은 도입부로 케슬러 증후군의 개념을 소개하고 있다. 둘째 단락에서는 케슬러가 구체적으로 예측한 시나리오를 설명하고 있다. 셋째 단락은 2009년에 발생한 미국과 러시아의 통신 위성 충돌 이후 우주 쓰레기와 관련한 국제적인 노력이 본격화되었다는 내용이다.

문제풀이

1. 《해석》 위 글의 제목으로 가장 적절한 것은?
우주 쓰레기 문제를 제기한 케슬러 증후군을 설명한 후 실제 현황을 언급하고 있으므로, '④ 위협적인 우주 쓰레기 문제에 대한 가설과 현실'이 글의 제목으로 가장 적절하다.
① 우주의 불필요한 쓰레기를 처리하는 방법
② 더 많은 우주선을 궤도에 올리기 위한 세계 경쟁
③ 새로 발견된 케슬러 이론의 약점
⑤ 케슬러 증후군의 불가사의를 풀기 위한 과학자들의 과학적 노력

2. 인공 물체 두 개의 충돌로 추가적인 쓰레기가 생기는 빈칸 앞부분과, 결과적으로 대규모의 파편과 쓰레기가 지구를 돌며 모든 것을 파괴하는 빈칸 뒷부분 사이의 단계를 설명하는 부분이므로, 빈칸에는 '③ 기하급수적인 수의 연쇄 충돌로 이어져서'의 내용이 들어가는 것이 가장 적절하다.
① 우주선 발사 횟수 증가를 초래해서
② 우주선이 충돌 영상을 포착할 수 있게 해서
④ 지구 궤도를 도는 기능을 정지한 인공 물체들을 수집해서
⑤ 지구 저궤도 내의 충돌에 대한 추가적인 연구를 요구해서

3. ④ → ⑤번 문장에서 충돌로 생성된 새로운 물체들은 추적되지 않는다고 언급했다.
① (①번 문장 참조) ② (①번 문장 참조) ③ (④번 문장 참조) ⑤ (⑦번 문장 참조)

4. 《해석》 케슬러는 추가적인 우주 쓰레기 충돌을 막기 위한 방법으로 무엇을 제안했는가? (한국어로)
⑥번 문장 참조

구문해설

④ Kessler made the pessimistic prediction that the density of space junk in orbit around the Earth **would**, by the year 2000, reach a level [at **which** random collisions were inevitable].

▷ would는 '~일 것이다'라는 의미로 추측을 나타내는 조동사이다.
▷ [ ]는 목적격 관계대명사절로 선행사 a level을 수식한다.

⑦ However, **it wasn't until** a 2009 collision between two communication satellites — one Russian, the other American — unleashed thousands of small pieces of debris into orbit and potentially set into motion Kessler's doomsday scenario, **that** international efforts [**to** authoritatively **address** the situation] were undertaken in earnest.

▷ It is ~ that ... 강조구문: '…한 것은 바로 ~이다'의 의미로 여기서 강조된 것은 until a 2009 ... scenario 이다.
▷ A is not until B: 'B에서야 비로소 A이다'
▷ [ ]는 international efforts를 수식하는 형용사적 용법의 to부정사구이다.

문화 상대주의

P.034

정답 | 1. ⑤ 2. ③ 3. ④ 4. a cross-cultural moral standard

본문 필기노트

① Cultural relativism is a form of moral relativism [that asserts (that) all ethical truth is relative to a specific culture]. ② According to cultural relativism, / it is never true [to say simply that a certain kind of behavior is right or wrong]; rather, it can only ever be true [that a certain kind of behavior is right or wrong / within a specific society].

주격 관 · 대 / ~에 따라 / ~에 따르면 / 가주어 / to 이하는 진주어 / 가주어 / that 이하는 진주어

문화 상대주의의 정의 및 개념

③ The strength of cultural relativism is [that it allows us to value our moral intuitions / without having to be judgmental about other societies [that do not share those intuitions]]. ④ If we reject cultural relativism / then we face the difficulty of having to condemn past societies [that did not conform to our modern moral code] and present societies [that do not already accept it]. ⑤ At a time [when tolerance is seen as an important value], cultural relativism certainly seems to be an attractive option.

that 이하는 보어 / S / V / allow+O+ to-v: O로 하여금 ~하게 하다 / ~일 필요 없이 / 주격 관 · 대 / condemn의 O_1 / 주격 관 · 대 / ~에 들어 맞다 / condemn의 O_2 / 주격 관 · 대 / =our modern moral code / 관계부사 / ~로서(전치사)

문화 상대주의의 강점

⑥ This strength of cultural relativism, however, is also its weakness. ⑦ Cultural relativism excuses us from judging the moral status of other cultures / when doing so seems inappropriate, but it also renders us powerless to judge the moral status of other cultures / when doing so seems to be necessary. ⑧ For example, / (Being) faced with a culture [that deems slavery morally acceptable], we need to judge that society to be morally inferior to our own (society), / for the people [who are suffering / under the unjust system] are in need of being rescued. ⑨ In order to make such a judgment, / we need a cross-cultural moral standard, which is precisely the kind of moral standard [that (cultural relativism claims) does not exist].

~로부터 면제해 주다 / ~할 때(접속사) / =judging ~ other cultures / render+O+형용사: O를 ~하게 하다 / 판단하기에(부사적 용법) / =to judge ~ other cultures / 주격 관 · 대 / ~보다 / 왜냐하면(접속사) / 주격 관 · 대 / ~하기 위해서 / 주격 관 · 대 / which의 선행사 / 주격 관 · 대 (계속적 용법) / 삽입절

문화 상대주의의 한계

본문해석

① 문화 상대주의는 모든 윤리적 진리가 특정 문화에 따라 상대적이라고 주장하는 도덕 상대주의의 한 형태이다. ② 문화 상대주의에 따르면, 단순히 특정 종류의 행동이 옳거나 그르다고 말하는 것은 결코 진실이 아니며, 오히려 특정 사회 내에서 특정 종류의 행동이 옳거나 그르다고 말하는 것만이 언제나 옳을 수 있다.

③ 문화 상대주의의 강점은 그것이 우리로 하여금 우리와 같은 도덕적 직관을 공유하고 있지 않은 다른 사회에 대하여 판단할 필요 없이 우리의 도덕적 직관을 평가할 수 있게 해준다는 것이다. ④ 만일 우리가 문화 상대주의를 거부한다면, 우리는 현대의 도덕률에 맞지 않았던 과거 사회와 아직 그것을 받아들이지 않고 있는 현재 사회를 규탄해야 하는 어려움에 직면한다. ⑤ 관용이 중요한 가치로 여겨지는 시대에 문화 상대주의는 확실히 매력적인 선택인 듯하다.

⑥ 그러나 이러한 문화 상대주의의 강점은 또한 그것의 약점이기도 하다. ⑦ 문화 상대주의는 우리로 하여금 다른 문화의 도덕적 지위를 판단하는 것이 부적절해 보일 경우 그렇게 하는 것으로부터 우리를 면제해 주지만, 다른 문화의 도덕적 지위를 판단하는 것이 필요해 보일 때 우리가 그것(다른 문화의 도덕적 지위)을 판단하는 데 있어 무력하게 만들기도 한다. ⑧ 예를 들어, 노예제도를 도덕적으로 받아들일 수 있다고 생각하는 문화와 마주쳤을 때, 우리는 그 사회를 우리의 것보다 도덕적으로 열등하다고 판단할 필요가 있는데, 왜냐하면 부당한 제도 아래에서 고통당하는 사람들은 구제될 필요가 있기 때문이다. ⑨ 그러한 판단을 하기 위해, 우리는 상호 문화적 도덕 기준이 필요한데, 그것은 바로 문화 상대주의가 주장하는 바로는 존재하지 않는 종류의 도덕적 기준이다.

본문파악

이 글은 특정 행위나 관습에 대한 도덕적 판단은 문화에 따라 달라질 수 있다는 문화 상대주의에 대한 것이다. 첫째 단락에서는 문화 상대주의의 정의와 개념을, 둘째 단락과 셋째 단락에서는 각각 문화 상대주의의 강점과 한계를 이야기하고 있다.

문제풀이

1. 《해석》 위 글의 주제는 무엇인가?
   이 글은 문화 상대주의의 개념과 장점, 그리고 그 한계에 대하여 이야기하고 있다.
   ① 도덕적 기준 수립의 필요성 ② 우리 사회의 문화 상대주의를 극복하는 방법
   ③ 문화 간 도덕적 기준의 차이점 ④ 과거 사회와 현재 사회의 차이점 ⑤ 문화 상대주의의 장점과 한계

2. ③~④번 문장에 의하면, 같은 도덕 기준을 공유하지 않는 문화에 대하여 옳고 그름을 판단할 필요가 없게 해주는 것이 문화 상대주의의 강점이라고 했으므로, 관용을 중요하게 여기는 시대에 문화 상대주의는 '③ 매력적인 선택'이 될 수 있다.
   ① 커다란 도전 ② 전통적인 의무 ④ 부적절한 길 ⑤ 어려운 선택

3. (A) 뒤에는 우리가 문화 상대주의를 '거부하면' 현대의 도덕률에 맞지 않았던 과거 사회를 비난해야 하는 어려움에 직면한다는 내용이 자연스러우므로, reject가 적절하다. (B) 뒤의 문장에서 다른 문화의 도덕적 지위를 판단하는 것이 정작 '필요할' 때 우리를 무력하게 만든다는 앞 내용과 상반되는 내용이 언급되었으므로, (B)에는 판단하는 것이 '부적절한' 때가 언급되는 것이 적절하다. 따라서 inappropriate가 오는 것이 알맞다. (C)에서는 노예제도 하에서 고통 받는 사람들은 구제될 필요가 있다는 명분이 예로 제시되었으므로, 노예 제도를 도덕적으로 용인하는 사회는 우리 사회보다 '열등한' 사회가 된다. 따라서 inferior가 적절하다.

4. ⑨번 문장 참조

구문해설

⑧ For example, (**being**) **faced** with a culture [that deems slavery morally acceptable], we need to judge that society to be morally **inferior to** our own (society), for the people [who are suffering under the unjust system] are in need of being rescued.

▷ faced 이하는 때를 나타내는 분사구문으로, 앞에 being이 생략되었다.
▷ 「inferior to」는 '~보다 열등한'의 의미로, than이 아니라 to를 쓰는 것에 유의한다.

⑨ In order to make such a judgment, we need a cross-cultural moral standard, **which** is precisely the kind of moral standard [that (**cultural relativism claims**) does not exist].

▷ which 이하는 a cross-cultural moral standard를 부연 설명하는 계속적 용법의 주격 관계대명사절이다.
▷ ( ) 표시된 cultural relativism claims는 주격 관계대명사절 속의 삽입절이다.

문화 상대주의의 성립 배경

문화 상대주의는 영국 인류학과 대비되는 미국 인류학의 특징으로 볼 수 있다. 이는 인류학자가 연구 대상에 대하여 취하는 일반적인 태도나 입장으로서, 도덕 상대주의와 인식 상대주의로 나뉘어진다. 도덕 상대주의는 어떤 행위나 사상의 옳고 그름은 문화적인 맥락에서 규정된 가치체계에 따라 판단되어야 한다는 관점이다. 인식 상대주의는 현실을 분류하고 조직하는 방식인 세계관 · 사물관 등이 문화에 의해 결정되기 때문에 인간의 사고방식은 문화적 배경에 따라 상대적으로 파악되어야 한다는 관점이다.

문화 상대주의가 하나의 학문으로 자리잡게 된 것은 보아스(Franz Boas) 등 미국 인류학자들에 의한 문화진화론 비판이 계기가 되었다. 문화진화론은 유럽 중심적인 발상으로, 인류 문화의 진보가 지식과 기술, 경제 수준에 따라 객관적으로 측정될 수 있다는 가정이었다.

문화 상대주의가 인류학의 한 분야로 자리잡은 가장 큰 이유는 자본주의의 발달로 서구의 몰락에 대한 위기감이 증대되면서 서구인들이 비서구사회의 문화적 가치에 관심을 갖게 되었기 때문이었다. 이러한 인식은 서구문명에 대한 비판적 성찰의 계기가 되었고, 미개사회를 포함하여 모든 문화의 독립적 가치는 존중되어야 한다는 견해를 낳았다.

12

SECTION 03. 사회 · 문화

미셸 푸코의 파놉티콘(the Panopticon)

P.036

정답	1. ② 2. ④ 3. 모든 움직임이 감시되고 모든 사건이 기록되는 현실 4. ④

본문 필기노트

① One of the techniques/regulatory modes of power/knowledge [cited by Michel Foucault], a French philosopher [associated with the structuralist and post-structuralist movements], was the Panopticon, an architectural design [put forth by Jeremy Bentham in the late 18th century / for prisons, insane asylums, schools, hospitals, and factories]. ② Instead of using violent methods, such as torture, the progressive and modern democratic state needed a different sort of system to regulate its citizens. ③ The Panopticon offered a powerful and sophisticated form of internalized coercion, [which was achieved through the constant observation of prisoners, [each separated from the others, allowing no interaction or no communication]]. ④ This modern structure would allow guards to continually see inside each cell / from their vantage point in a high central tower, unseen by the prisoners. ⑤ Constant observation would act as a control mechanism, a consciousness of constant surveillance [that would be internalized].

벤담의 파놉티콘: 감시의 내면화

⑥ The Panopticon was a metaphor [that allowed Foucault to explore 1) the relationship between systems of social control and people in a disciplinary situation, and 2) the power-knowledge concept]. ⑦ In his view, power and knowledge come from observing others. ⑧ It marked the transition to a disciplinary power, with every movement supervised and all events recorded. ⑨ The result of this surveillance is acceptance of regulations and docility — a normalization of sorts, [stemming from the threat of discipline]. ⑩ Suitable behavior is achieved not through total surveillance, but by panoptic discipline and inducing a population to conform by the internalization of this reality. ⑪ The actions of the observer are based upon this monitoring and the behaviors [he sees exhibited]; the more one observes, the more

본문해석

① 구조주의 및 후기 구조주의 운동과 관련 있는 프랑스 철학자 미셸 푸코가 인용한 권력/지식의 기법/규제 수단 중 하나는 제러미 벤담이 18세기 후반에 감옥, 정신병원, 학교, 병원, 공장을 위해 제안한 건축 설계인 파놉티콘이었다. ② 고문 같은 폭력적인 수단을 사용하는 대신, 진보적이고 현대적인 민주국가는 시민을 규제하는 데 다른 종류의 체제를 필요로 했다. ③ 파놉티콘은 내면화된 강압의 강력하고도 정교한 형태를 가했는데, 이것은 상호작용이나 소통이 허용되지 않은 채 서로 격리된 수감자에 대한 끊임없는 감시를 통해 이루어졌다. ④ 이 현대적인 구조는 감시자가 높은 중앙 탑의 감시 지점에서 수감자에게는 보이지 않은 채 각 감방 안을 끊임없이 관찰할 수 있게 해 주는 것이었다. ⑤ 끊임없는 감시는 통제 기제로 기능했고, 그에 따라 지속적인 감시에 대한 인식이 내면화되었다.

⑥ 파놉티콘은 푸코가 1) 사회 통제 체제와 처벌 상황에 처한 사람들 사이의 관계와 2) 권력-지식 개념을 탐구할 수 있게 한 은유였다. ⑦ 그가 보기에, 권력과 지식은 타인을 관찰하는 데서 비롯한다. ⑧ 그것은 모든 움직임이 감시되고 모든 사건이 기록되는 규율적 권력으로의 이행을 나타냈다. ⑨ 이 감시의 결과는 규제를 받아들이고 순응하는 것이다. 즉, (이 결과는) 일종의 표준화로, 이것은 규율의 위협으로부터 비롯한다. ⑩ 적합한 행동은 총체적인 감시를 통해서가 아니라, 일망감시적 통제에 의해 사람들이 이러한 현실을 내면화함으로써 순응하도록 유도하며 이루어진다. ⑪ 감시자의 행동은 이러한 감시와 드러나는 것을 관찰하는 행동을 바탕으로 한다. 더 많이 감시할수록, 그는 더 강력해진다. ⑫ 권력은 관찰자가 순환적으로 활동을 관찰하는 데서 축

powerful one becomes. ⑫ The power comes from the knowledge [the observer has accumulated from his observations of actions in a circular fashion], with knowledge and power reinforcing each other. ⑬ Foucault says [(that) "by being combined and generalized, they attained a level [at which the formation of knowledge and the increase in power regularly reinforce one another in a circular process]]."

(that) 목적격 관 · 대
with+O+분사: O가 ~한 채로
that 이하는 목적어
=knowledge and power
목적격 관 · 대

푸코의 파놉티콘: 권력과 지식

적한 지식에서 비롯하며, 지식과 권력은 서로를 강화한다. ⑬ 푸코는 "결합되고 일반화되면서, 그들은 지식의 형성과 권력의 증대가 순환 과정 속에서 서로를 꾸준히 강화하는 단계에 도달했다."라고 말한다.

본문파악 이 글은 미셸 푸코가 파놉티콘 개념을 통해 설명한 권력과 지식의 관계를 제시하고 있다. 첫째 단락에서는 제러미 벤담이 제시한 파놉티콘 개념을 설명하고, 둘째 단락에서는 파놉티콘을 통해 권력과 지식이 감시에서 비롯하며 서로 강화한다고 본 미셸 푸코의 관점을 제시한다.

문제풀이

1. ② → 물리적인 힘을 가한다는 내용은 언급된 바 없다.
   ① (①번 문장 참조)　③ (③번 문장 참조)　④ (④번 문장 참조)　⑤ (⑤번 문장 참조)

2. 《해석》 위 글에 따르면, 다음 중 일망감시적 통제가 아닌 것은?
   ⑧번 문장에서 알 수 있듯이, 일망감시적 통제란 수감자의 움직임을 낱낱이 관찰하고 기록하는 것이다. ④는 감시와 연관이 없으므로 일망감시적 통제라 볼 수 없다.
   ① 사용자가 어디에 있었는지 기록하는 교통 카드
   ② 브라우저 기록을 통해 추적할 수 있는 인터넷 사용
   ③ 사용자가 무엇을 구입했는지 보여 줄 수 있는 신용카드 내역
   ④ 사용자가 자신이 만든 동영상을 올리고 공유할 수 있게 해 주는 웹 사이트
   ⑤ 개인 정보가 포함된 칩을 내장한 전자 신분증

3. this reality는 '모든 움직임이 감시되고 모든 사건이 기록되는 현실'을 말하는 것으로, ⑧번 문장의 내용을 가리킨다.

4. ⑫번, ⑬번 문장에서 지식과 권력이 서로를 강화한다고 하였으므로, 빈칸에 각각 들어갈 말은 (A) observes, (B) powerful이다.

구문해설

⑩ Suitable behavior is achieved **not** through total surveillance, **but** by panoptic discipline and **inducing** a population to conform by the internalization of this reality.

▷ 'A가 아니라 B'를 나타내는 「not A but B」 구문에서 전치사구 through total surveillance가 A, by panoptic discipline ... this reality가 B에 해당한다.
▷ inducing 이하는 전치사 by의 목적어로 쓰인 동명사구이다.

⑪ The actions of the observer are based upon this monitoring and the behaviors [(**that**) he sees **exhibited**]; **the more** one observes, **the more** powerful one becomes.

▷ [ ]의 관계사절에 목적격 관계대명사 that이 생략되어 있으며, exhibited는 관계사절 안에서 선행사 the behaviors의 목적보어 역할을 한다.
▷ the+비교급 ~, the+비교급 ...: '~할수록 더 …한'

13 연령차별

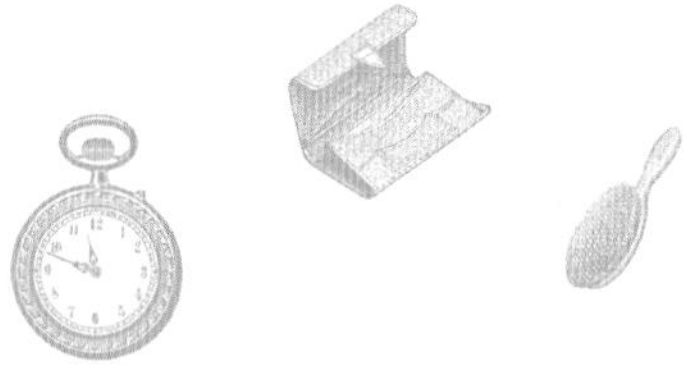

P.038

정답

1. ③ 2. prejudice 3. ③ make → made
4. 우리 모두가 늙는다는 것을 고려할 때, 연령차별은 우리 중 많은 이가 스스로의 노화에 대해 갖고 있는 내적 공포를 포함한다.

본문 필기노트

① Ageism occurs across the human lifespan / and is not limited to any particular age group. ② In fact, age is one of the first characteristics [(that) we notice about other people, whether they are young or old]. ③ From a person's perceived age, / we make assumptions about their competencies, beliefs and abilities. ④ For example, we may consider an older job applicant to be unsuitable / because we imagine (that) he or she will be forgetful, slow, or of poor health. ⑤ We see young people (in the street) and associate them with antisocial behaviors. ⑥ Ageism is the one prejudice [that we all experience, / regardless of our race, ethnicity, and gender].

(occurs: V_1 / across: ~에 걸쳐 / is: V_2 / limited to: ~에 국한되다 / whether A or B: A이든지 B이든지 간에 / about: ~에 대해 / consider+O+to-v: O가 ~하다고 여기다 / of poor health: =unhealthy / see: V_1 / associate: V_2 / with: ~와 / that: 목적격 관 · 대 / regardless of: ~에 관계없이)

연령차별이 만연된 사회

⑦ The most widespread occurrence of ageism / is that [which is directed towards older adults] : think of all the "over-the-hill" jokes [made as people approach middle age]. ⑧ It is this implicit nature of negative attitudes towards old age that makes ageism so insidious and difficult to counter. ⑨ Furthermore, society tends to highlight exceptions to the commonly held stereotypes. ⑩ Consider [how frequently the media reports on "exceptional" older adults, such as the astronaut John Glenn, or the woman [who first climbed Mt. Rainier at age 77]].

(that: 그것 / which: 주격 관 · 대 / : 부연설명 / as: ~할 때(접속사) / It is ~ that ...: …한 것은 바로 ~이다 / to counter: 대항하기에(부사적 용법) / tend to-v: ~하는 경향이 있다 / to: ~에 대해 / Consider: 생각해 보라 / on: ~에 대해 / A such as B: B와 같은 A / who: 주격 관 · 대)

연령차별의 전형적인 예: 연장자 차별

⑪ Given that we are all aging, / ageism encompasses the inner fear [that many of us / have of our own aging]. ⑫ Because humans tend to blend their personal and public attitudes, / studying and understanding ageism / is particularly complex and challenging. ⑬ Accordingly, professionals need to become aware of their own ageism / when studying and working with older adults.

(Given that: ~임을 고려[감안]하면 / ageism: S / encompasses: V / the inner fear: O / that: 목적격 관 · 대 / of: ~ 중에 / of: ~에 대해 / tend to-v: ~하는 경향이 있다 / need to-v: ~할 필요가 있다 / when studying and working: =when they study and work / with: ~와 함께)

연령차별의 심리학적 이유 및 전문가에게 요구되는 태도

본문해석

① 연령차별은 인간의 평생에 걸쳐 일어나며 특정 연령 집단에 국한되어 있지 않다. ② 사실, 사람들이 젊든지 늙든지 간에 연령은 우리가 다른 사람들에 대해 알아차리는 첫 번째 특징들 중 하나이다. ③ 겉으로 판단되는 연령으로부터, 우리는 그들의 역량, 신념, 그리고 능력을 추측한다. ④ 예를 들어, 우리는 연령이 많은 구직자는 건망증이 있고, 굼뜨며, 건강도 안 좋을 것이라고 여기기 때문에 부적합하다고 생각할지도 모른다. ⑤ 우리는 거리의 젊은 이들을 보고 그들을 반사회적 행동과 연관짓는다. ⑥ 연령차별은 인종, 민족성, 성별과 관계없이 우리 모두가 경험하는 하나의 편견이다.

⑦ 연령차별에 대해 가장 일반적인 것은 연장자들을 향한 것이다. 사람들이 중년에 가까워질 때 만들어지는 '노인들을 빗댄' 모든 농담들을 생각해 보라. ⑧ 연령차별을 그렇게 교활하고 대항하기 어렵게 만드는 것은 바로 노년을 향한 이러한 암묵적 성질의 부정적 태도이다. ⑨ 더욱이, 사회는 일반적으로 갖는 고정관념에 대한 예외를 강조하는 경향이 있다. ⑩ 매체가 얼마나 자주 우주비행사 존 글렌이나 77세에 레이니어산을 처음 등반한 여성 같은 '예외적인' 노인들에 대해 보도하는지를 생각해 보라.

⑪ 우리 모두가 늙는다는 것을 고려할 때, 연령차별은 우리 중 많은 이가 스스로의 노화에 대해 갖고 있는 내적 공포를 포함한다. ⑫ 사람에게는 개인의 태도와 대중의 태도를 섞으려는 경향이 있기 때문에, 연령차별을 연구하고 이해하는 일은 특히 복잡하고 어렵다. ⑬ 따라서, 전문가들은 노인들에 대해 연구하고 함께 일할 때 자신의 연령차별 의식을 인식할 필요가 있다.

본문파악

이 글은 연령차별(ageism)에 대한 것이다. 첫째 단락은 도입부로 사회적으로 만연된 연령차별에 대해 소개하고 있고, 둘째 단락에서는 연장자들이 전형적인 연령차별의 대상임을 밝히고 있다. 셋째 단락에서는 연령차별의 심리학적 원인에 대해 언급하면서, 전문가들에게 요구되는 태도를 밝히고 있다.

문제풀이

1. ① 연령차별은 우리의 사회문화적 잠재의식 속에 깊이 뿌리박혀 있다. (첫째 단락 참조)
   ② 연령차별은 노인들이 직업을 구하기 어렵게 만든다. (④번 문장 참조)
   ③ 젊은이들은 연령차별을 받지 않는 경향이 있다. → ①번 문장에서 연령차별은 특정 연령에 국한된 것이 아니라고 했다.
   ④ 연령차별은 노화에 대한 우리의 내적 두려움에서 비롯된다. (⑪번 문장 참조)
   ⑤ 노화에 대한 우리의 태도는 연령차별에 대한 우리의 연구에 영향을 줄 수 있다. (⑫~⑬번 문장 참조)

2. 빈칸 앞의 내용, 즉 연령만으로 그 사람의 역량, 신념, 능력을 추측하고 젊은이들을 반사회적 행동과 연관짓는 것은 일종의 '편견(prejudice)'으로 볼 수 있다.

3. 문장의 동사는 think of이므로 동사가 또 나올 수 없고 수식어구가 와야 한다. 의미상 사람들이 중년에 가까워질 때 '만들어지는' 농담들이 되어야 자연스러우므로 make는 수동의 과거분사인 made가 되어야 한다.

4. given that: '~임을 고려할 때'

구문해설

⑩ Consider [**how frequently** the media reports on "exceptional" older adults, such as the astronaut John Glenn, or the woman who first climbed Mt. Rainier at age 77].
(how frequently: 의문사(구), the media: S, reports: V)

▷ how frequently 이하는 간접의문문으로서 동사 Consider의 목적어절이다. 간접의문문의 어순은 〈의문사+주어+동사〉이다.

차별에 관한 새로운 화두, 에이지즘(Ageism)

에이지즘은 오늘날 최대의 사회문제로 떠올랐다. 미국에서는 이와 관련된 소송이 급증하고 있고, 그 배상액수 또한 인종차별이나 성차별을 능가하고 있다. 에이지즘은 1969년에 처음으로 사용된 용어로서, 연령이 들어감에 따라 사람의 지적 · 성적 능력, 생산성, 매력 등이 떨어진다는 일반적인 믿음을 근거로 하여 나이 든 사람에게 가해지는 편견과 차별을 의미한다. 인종차별이나 성차별과는 달리, 차별하는 사람들이 나이가 들면 차별을 받는 입장이 된다는 특징이 있다.
사실 에이지즘은 일상생활에 너무나 깊숙이 뿌리내리고 있어서, 우리가 그러한 편견이나 차별을 하거나 받고 산다는 것 자체를 인식하기가 힘들다. 흰 머리가 나면 염색 좀 하라는 핀잔을 듣게 된다거나, 직장에서는 정년퇴직이나 명예퇴직 등 나이와 경제활동을 연결시키는 것을 당연시하는 것 등이 그 예에 해당한다. 우리 사회에 만연된 에이지즘은 점점 늘어가는 노인 인구 활동에도 부정적인 영향을 미쳐, 그들이 사회의 건강한 일원으로서 기여하는 것을 방해한다. 이제 에이지즘은 고령화 시대의 경제적 측면만의 문제가 아니라 인권의 문제가 되었다. '늙는다'는 것에 대해 부정적인 인식이 강한 '젊은이'들은 언젠가 부메랑을 맞게 된다. 자신들이 노인이 되었을 때 스스로에 대해 부정적인 인식을 품게 되기 때문이다. 따라서 현재의 젊은이들이 나이가 들어 불행한 삶에 빠지지 않게 하기 위해서라도 만연된 에이지즘을 줄여나가기 위한 노력이 필요하다.

14

SECTION 03. 사회 · 문화

개인과 사회의 관계

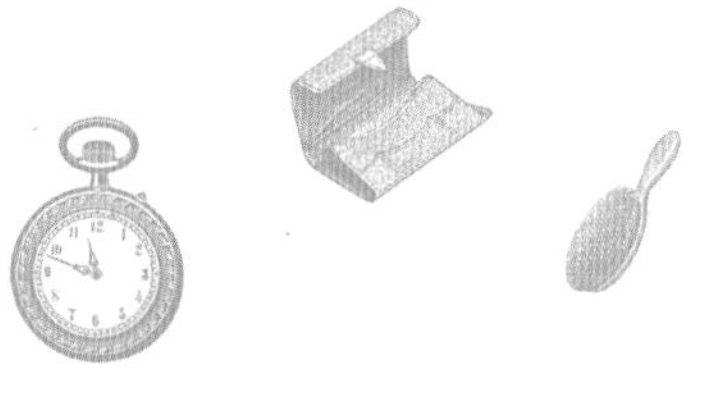

P.040

정답

1. (A)에서는 개인이 자신을 사회의 구성원으로 인식하여 집단적 이익을 행동의 목표로 삼는다. (B)에서는 개인이 자기 자신의 이익을 추구함으로써 의도와 무관하게 사회의 이익을 증진하게 된다. **2.** ② that → those **3.** ③ **4.** the interest of the society

본문 필기노트

(A)

① The social state is at once so natural, so necessary, and so habitual to man, / that, (except in some unusual circumstances) or (by an effort of voluntary abstraction), he never conceives himself otherwise than / as a member of a body. ② Now, society between human beings is manifestly impossible on any other footing than [that the interests of all are to be consulted]. ③ In this way people grow up unable to conceive (as possible to them) a state of total disregard of other people's interests. ④ They are also familiar with the fact of [cooperating with others], and [proposing (to themselves) a collective, not an individual, interest, as the aim (at least for the time being) of their actions]. ⑤ So long as they are cooperating, their ends are identified with those of others; there is at least a temporary feeling [that the interests of others are their own interests].

인간이 자신을 사회의 구성원으로 자각하고 공동의 이익을 도모한다는 입장

(B)

⑥ The annual revenue of every society is always precisely equal to the exchangeable value of the whole annual produce of its industry, or rather is precisely the same thing with that exchangeable value. ⑦ As every individual, therefore, endeavors as much as he can, both [to employ his capital in the support of domestic industry], and [so to direct that industry that its produce may be of the greatest value], every individual necessarily labors to render the annual revenue of the society as great as he can. ⑧ He generally, indeed, neither intends to promote the public interest, nor knows how much he is promoting it. ⑨ By preferring the support of domestic to that of foreign industry, he intends only his own security; and by directing that industry in such a manner as its produce may be of the greatest value, he intends

본문해석

(A)

① 사회 상태는 인간에게 동시에 너무나 자연스럽고 필요하며 타고난 것이라서, 어떤 예외적 상황 또는 고의적으로 분리하려는 노력에 의해서가 아니라면 인간은 자신을 조직의 한 구성원으로 인식하지 않을 수 없다. ② 이제 사람 간의 사회는 모든 사람들의 이익을 고려해야 한다는 기반 위가 아니라면 존재하기가 명백히 불가능하다. ③ 이렇게 하여 사람들은 타인의 이익을 완전히 무시하는 상태가 가능하다고 생각하지 못하게 된다. ④ 그들은 또한 타인과 협력한다는 사실과, 개인적 이익이 아니라 집단적 이익을 (적어도 당분간은) 행동의 목적으로서 자신에게 제안하는 것에 익숙하다. ⑤ 그들이 서로 협력하는 한, 그들의 목표는 타인의 목표와 일치하게 된다. 타인의 이익이 자신의 이익이 된다고 하는 감정이 적어도 일시적으로는 존재하는 것이다.

(B)

⑥ 모든 사회의 연간 수입은 사회 전체 노동의 연간 총 생산물의 교환 가치와 항상 정확히 동일하거나, 아니면 아예 그 교환 가치와 정확히 동일한 개념이다. ⑦ 따라서 각 개인이 최선을 다해 자기 자본을 자국 노동을 지원하는 데 사용하고, 그 생산물이 최대의 가치를 갖도록 노동을 이끌수록 필연적으로 각 개인은 사회의 연간 수입이 가능한 한 최대의 가치를 갖도록 노력하는 것이 된다. ⑧ 사실 각 개인은 일반적으로 말해서 공공의 이익을 증진하려고 의도하지도 않고, 자신이 공공의 이익을 얼마나 증진하고 있는지도 모른다. ⑨ 외국 노동의 지원보다 자국 노동의 지원을 선호함으로써, 그는 오로지 자기 자신의 안전을 의도한다. 노동 생산물이 최대의 가치를 갖도록 그 노동을 이끎으로써 오로지 자기 자신의 이익을 위한다. 이 경우, 그는 다른 많은

only his own gain; and he is (in this), as in many other cases, led by an invisible hand to promote an end [which was no part of his intention]. ⑩ By pursuing his own interest, / he frequently promotes / that of the society more effectually than / when he really intends to promote it.

촉진하게 된다(결과의 부사적 용법) / 주격 관·대 / =interest / ~할 때(접속사)

인간이 개인의 이익을 도모함으로써 의도와 무관하게 사회 전체의 이익을 늘린다는 입장

경우에서처럼, 보이지 않는 손에 이끌려 자신의 의도에는 없었던 목적을 달성하게 된다. ⑩ 자기 자신의 이익을 추구함으로써, 그는 실제로 사회의 이익을 증진하려고 의도할 때보다 더욱 효과적으로 사회의 이익을 빈번하게 증진하게 된다.

본문파악

글 (A)와 (B)는 개인의 이익과 사회의 이익의 관계에 대해 서로 다른 입장을 서술하고 있다. (A)는 개인이 집단적 이익이 곧 자신의 이익이라고 인식하고 공동의 이익을 도모한다는 입장인 반면, (B)는 개인이 자신만의 이익을 도모함으로써 의도와 무관하게 사회의 이익을 극대화하게 된다는 입장이다.

문제풀이

1. ⑤번과 ⑩번 문장을 참조하여 간략히 요약한다.

2. ②는 앞에 나온 명사의 반복을 피하기 위해 쓰는 지시대명사로, 앞의 ends를 대신하고 있으므로 복수형인 those로 고쳐야 한다.

3. (A) 빈칸 앞뒤의 내용이 개인이 자신의 이익보다 집단의 이익을 우선한다는 맥락이므로 an individual이 적절하다. (B) 빈칸 앞뒤의 내용은 개인이 자신의 이익을 추구하면서 무의식적으로 집단의 이익도 증진한다는 맥락이므로 빈칸에는 the public이 적절하다.

4. it은 앞에 나온 that of the society를 가리키고, that은 다시 앞에 나온 the interest를 가리킨다.

구문해설

⑤ So long as they are cooperating, their ends are identified with **those** of others; there is at least **a temporary feeling** [that the interests of others are their own interests].

▷ 지시대명사 those는 ends를 가리킨다.
▷ a temporary feeling과 [ ]는 동격이다.

⑦ As every individual, therefore, endeavors as much as he can, **both** [to employ his capital in the support of domestic industry], **and** [so to direct that industry **(so) that** its produce may be of the greatest value], every individual necessarily labors [to render the annual revenue of the society as great as he can].

▷ 'A와 B 둘 다'를 나타내는 「both A and B」 구문의 A, B 자리에 각각 목적을 나타내는 부사적 용법의 to부정사구가 쓰였다.
▷ that은 '~하도록'의 의미로 쓰인 목적을 나타내는 접속사로 앞에 so가 생략되었다고 볼 수 있다.
▷ 세 번째 [ ]는 목적을 나타내는 부사적 용법의 to부정사구이다.

15

SECTION 03. 사회 · 문화

이슬람 문화의 부르카 전통

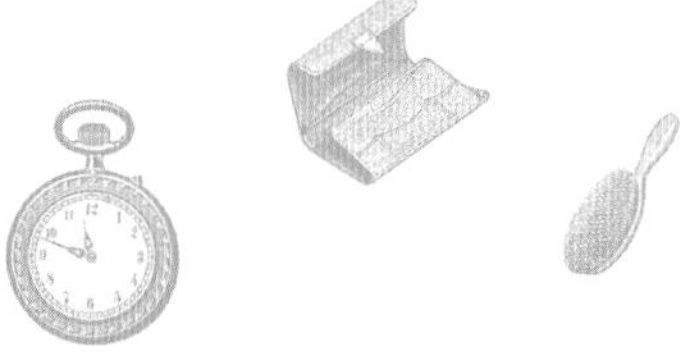

P.042

정답	1. (A) 부르카 및 그와 유사한 의복들 (B) 서양 비평가들 2. the tradition of wearing such clothing is unjustified because it greatly restricts the autonomy of women 3. 각 문화마다 여성과 여성의 선택 능력에 대한 가정이 다르기 때문에 부르카를 입는 것에 관해서 함부로 비판할 수 없다. 4. ③

본문 필기노트

① The primarily Islamic tradition [of females covering themselves from head to foot with a burqa] is an example of the intrinsic difficulty in evaluating the extent [to which cultural practices promote individual autonomy]. ② Critics of the burqa and similar garments, (especially critics from Western cultures,) deem them physically oppressive with the weight of the fabric; psychologically oppressive / in that they seem to make women devoid of distinctiveness; and emotionally oppressive / in that they are yet another manifestation of a male-dominated society [in which women are subordinate]. ③ According to this view, / the tradition of wearing such clothing is unjustified / because it greatly restricts the autonomy of women.

부르카 착용이 여성의 자율성을 제한한다고 보는 견해

④ Defenders of this practice, however, argue the opposite view. ⑤ They insist [that coverings like the burqa actually foster autonomy and liberate women for a number of reasons]. ⑥ For example, a burqa prevents women from being viewed as sexual objects; / it encourages unity among female Muslims; / and it promotes the appearance of holiness. ⑦ Proponents of the burqa / also ask questions of Western critics [which force them to examine / their own clothing culture], such as, "Why is it considered oppressive / to wear a head scarf / but liberating to wear a miniskirt?" ⑧ They insist the answer lies in the assumptions [each culture makes about the women involved and their ability to make choices]. ⑨ They say that if the assumptions are wrong, and the wearing of the burqa and its variants is actually a matter of personal preference, / then it is completely justified as a legitimate expression of individual autonomy.

부르카 착용이 여성의 자율성을 보장한다고 보는 견해

본문해석

① 여성이 머리부터 발끝까지 부르카로 자신을 감싸는 가장 이슬람적인 전통은 문화적 관습이 개인의 자율성을 증진시키는 정도를 평가하는 것에 있어서의 본질적인 어려움의 한 예이다. ② 부르카와 이에 유사한 복장을 비판하는 사람들, 특히 서구 문화비평가들은 그것들이 직물의 무게로 인해 신체적 압박을 가하고, 여성이 개성이 결여돼 보이게 한다는 점에서 심리적으로 압박하며, 여성이 종속되어 있는 남성 지배 사회의 또 하나의 표시라는 점에서 정서적으로 압박한다고 생각한다. ③ 이런 견해에 따르면, 그런 옷을 입는 전통은 여성의 자율성을 크게 제한하기 때문에 정당하지 않다.

④ 그러나 이 관습을 옹호하는 사람들은 반대되는 견해를 주장한다. ⑤ 그들은 부르카 같은 덮개는 여러 가지 이유에서 실제로 자율성을 조성하며 여성들을 자유롭게 해준다고 주장한다. ⑥ 예를 들어, 부르카는 여성이 성적 대상으로 보이는 것을 막아준다. 이는 여성 이슬람교도들 간의 단결을 장려하며, 성스러운 외모가 되도록 해준다. ⑦ 부르카 지지자들은 또 서양 비평가들에게 "왜 두건을 쓰는 것은 압박하는 것이고, 미니스커트를 입는 것은 자유롭게 하는 것으로 여겨지는 것인가?"처럼 그들로 하여금 자신들의 의복 문화를 살펴보게 하는 질문을 한다. ⑧ 그들은 그 대답이 관련된 여성들과 그들이 선택하는 능력에 대해 각 문화가 만들어 내는 가정에 있다고 주장한다. ⑨ 그들은 만일 그 가정이 잘못되었고, 부르카와 그 변형된 형태의 옷을 입는 것이 사실 개인의 선호 문제라면, 그것은 개인의 자율성에 대한 타당한 표현으로서 완전히 정당한 것이라고 말한다.

본문파악

이 글은 이슬람 여성들의 부르카 착용이 여성의 자율성을 침해하는 것인가에 대한 상반된 의견을 다룬 글이다. 첫째 단락은 부르카 착용이 여성을 신체적 · 심리적 · 정서적으로 억압하여 자율을 제한한다는 주장이며, 둘째 단락은 부르카가 여성을 성적 대상으로 보지 않게 해주는 등 오히려 여성의 자유를 보장해 준다는 주장이다.

문제풀이

1. (A) 「deem +O +OC」 구문은 'O가 ~하다고 생각하다'라는 뜻이다. 서구 문화 비평가들이 '그것들'이 여성들을 억압하는 것으로 보는 것이므로, them은 내용상 앞서 언급된 'the burqa and similar garments'이다.
   (B) which의 선행사가 questions이므로, which 이하는 '질문들은 them에게 ~하도록 강요한다'는 의미가 된다. 문맥상 '~을 살펴봐야 하는' 주체는 Western critics이다.

2. 이슬람 여성들의 부르카 착용을 반대하는 주장은 첫째 단락에 나와 있고, ③번 문장이 이 단락의 주제문이다.

3. 《해석》 위 글의 둘째 단락의 밑줄 친 질문이 암시하는 바는 무엇인가?
   바로 뒤의 ⑧번 문장을 참고한다.

4. 《해석》 다음 중 부르카 전통을 옹호하는 사람들에 의해 이루어진 언급이 아닌 것은?
   ①, ②, ④ (⑥번 문장 참조)
   ③ → 본문에서는 언급되지 않은 내용이다.
   ⑤ (⑧번 문장 참조)

구문해설

① The primarily Islamic tradition of **females covering** themselves from head to foot with a burqa is .... .

▷ females는 동명사 covering 이하의 의미상 주어이다.

⑥ For example, a burqa prevents women from **being viewed as** sexual objects; it encourages unity among female Muslims; and it promotes **the appearance of holiness**.

▷ 3개의 단문이 열거된 문장으로, ⑤번 문장에서 언급된 '여러 가지 이유들'의 예에 해당된다.
▷ view A as B: 'A를 B라고 여기다'. A에 해당하는 것이 women이므로 수동태 be viewed as로 쓴 것이다.
▷ 「of + 추상명사」는 형용사의 의미가 되므로 the appearance of holiness는 the holy appearance로 바꿔 쓸 수 있다.

⑦ Proponents of the burqa also ask questions of Western critics [which force them to examine their own clothing culture], (**such as**, "Why is it considered oppressive to wear a head scarf but liberating to wear a miniskirt?")

▷ such as 이하도 [ ] 부분의 which 이하와 같이 questions를 수식하며, such as 뒤에 콤마(,)를 붙인 것은 뒤에 큰따옴표("") 를 사용한 직접 인용의 문장이 오기 때문에 구분을 보다 명확히 하기 위해서이다.

⑨ They say that **if** the assumptions are wrong, and (if) the wearing of the burqa and its variants is actually a matter of personal preference, **then** it is completely justified as a legitimate expression of individual autonomy.

▷ if ~, then ...: '만일 ~라면, …이다'의 의미로, if절이 두 개의 단문을 이끌고 있는 구조이다.

16 SECTION 04. 정보 통신
기술 혁신이 가져올 미래

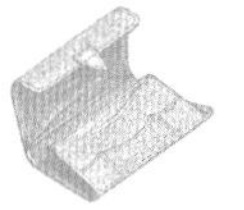

P.046

정답 1. ④ 2. ⑤ 3. ② 4. humans' capacity to construct mental models of the world will no longer be a characteristic that sets us apart from machines

본문 필기노트

① With technological innovations advancing at an exponential rate, interfacing physical reality with virtual reality is becoming more commonplace, with some experts predicting the widespread existence of virtual humans by as early as 2030.
(with+O+분사: O가 ~한 채로 / S(동명사구) / V / with+O+분사: O가 ~한 채로)

② The development of nanobots, miniature robots [as small as a human blood cell], and nonbiological intelligence / affords opportunities for [reshaping our interaction with the world].
(S / = / 형용사구 / (of) / V / 전치사 for의 목적어(동명사구))

기술 발달로 인한 물리적 현실과 가상 현실의 결합

③ Through the utilization of nanobots, experiencing a virtual world would not differ appreciably from experiencing the "real world," as external stimuli must be translated into signals in the brain. ④ Nanobots [strategically positioned in close proximity to sensory neurons] could be programmed [to modify the communication of interneuronal connections by either inhibiting or precipitating the firing of the neighboring neuron]. ⑤ The nanobots could remain present yet inactive in their position / until the person wishes to enter the virtual environment, [at which time they could be activated [to intercept sensory input and fire alternative signals].
(~을 통해, ~으로 / S(동명사구) / 가정법 과거 / 전치사 from의 목적어(동명사구) / ~로 번역되다, 바뀌다 / 조정하도록(부사적 용법) / either A or B: A 또는 B 둘 중 하나 / S / V / SC / which의 선행사 / 목적격 관·대(계속적 용법) / 가로채다(결과의 부사적 용법) / (to))

나노봇을 통한 가상 현실 체험

(B) ⑥ In addition to [creating virtual worlds], the emerging technology gives rise to nonbiological thinking, / and scientists are making inroads into [incorporating machine intelligence into human intelligence]. (A) ⑦ The hybrid of human and computer thinking / may seem like something out of a sci-fi film, but nonbiological cognition / has already made its way into humans. (C) ⑧ Neural implants are currently being used / in patients [suffering from Parkinson's disease] [to act as a replacement for cells with impaired functioning]. ⑨ As the technology progresses, humans' capacity [to construct mental models of the world] will no longer be a
(~에 더하여 / 전치사 to의 목적어(동명사구) / ~이 생기게 하다 / 전치사 into의 목적어(동명사구) / 역할을 하도록(부사적 용법) / ~을 가진 / ~함에 따라 / 구성하는(형용사적 용법) / 더 이상 ~하지 않은)

본문해석

① 기술 혁신이 급격한 속도로 발전하면서, 물리적 현실을 가상 현실과 연결하는 것이 점점 흔해지고 있으며, 몇몇 전문가들은 빠르면 2030년이면 가상 인간이 널리 존재하게 될 것이라고 예상한다. ② 인간의 혈구만큼 작은 초소형 로봇인 나노봇과 비생물학적 지능의 개발이 세상과 우리의 상호작용을 재구성할 기회를 제공한다.

③ 나노봇의 활용을 통하면, 가상 세계를 경험하는 것이 '실제 세계'를 경험하는 것과 눈에 띄게 다르지 않게 될 것인데, 외부 자극이 두뇌 속의 신호로 해석되어야 하기 때문이다. ④ 감각 뉴런 근처에 전략적으로 배치된 나노봇들은 이웃 뉴런의 발화를 억제하거나 촉진함으로써 뉴런간 연결부의 통신을 조정하도록 설정될 수 있다. ⑤ 나노봇들은 사람이 가상 환경에 들어가기를 희망할 때까지 그들의 위치에 비활성화 상태로 있을 수 있을 것이며, 그 시점에서 그것들은 활성화되어 감각 입력을 가로채고 대체 신호를 발화할 수 있을 것이다.

(B) ⑥ 가상 세계를 생성하는 것에 더해, 신흥 기술은 비생물학적 지능을 등장시켰으며, 과학자들은 기계 지능을 인간 지능에 통합시키는 데 접근하고 있다. (A) ⑦ 인간과 컴퓨터 지능의 혼성은 공상과학 영화에서 나온 것처럼 보일지도 모르지만, 비생물학적 인지는 이미 인간에게 삽입되었다. (C) ⑧ 신경 이식은 현재 파킨슨병을 앓는 환자들에게 기능 장애가 있는 세포의 대체 역할을 하도록 사용되고 있다. ⑨ 기술이 진보함에 따라, 인간의 세상에 대한 정신 모형을 구성하는 능력은 더 이상 우리를 기계와 구별하게 하는 특징이 아닐 것이다.

characteristic [that sets us apart from machines].

주격 관 · 대

비생물학적 사고의 등장

본문파악

기술 발달로 인해 물리적 현실과 가상 현실의 경계가 모호해지면서, 현실과 다름없는 가상 현실 체험이 가능해지고 비생물학적(기계) 지능이 대두될 것이라는 글이다. 첫째 단락은 도입이고 둘째, 셋째 단락에서 각각 사례를 들어 가상 현실 체험과 비생물학적 지능을 설명하고 있다.

문제풀이

1. ④번 문장에서 나노봇들이 뉴런의 발화를 억제하거나 촉진한다고 했으므로 억제만을 언급하는 ④는 글의 내용과 일치하지 않는다.
   ① (①번 문장 참조) ② (③번 문장 참조) ③ (④번 문장 참조) ⑤ (⑦번 문장 참조)

2. 빈칸 앞에서 나노봇은 근처 뉴런의 발화를 억제하거나 촉진함으로써 뉴런간 통신을 조정할 수 있다고 했다. 따라서, 사람이 가상 환경에 들어가기를 희망할 때에는 '⑤ 그것들은 활성화되어 감각 입력을 가로채고 대체 신호를 발화할 수 있을 것이다'가 문맥상 자연스럽다.
   ① 의사들이 그것들을 제거하여 생물학적 물질로 교체할 수 있을 것이다
   ② 사람이 외부 컴퓨팅 시스템을 접속기로 사용해야만 할 것이다
   ③ 신체의 예측되는 신경 과정을 변경할 필요가 없을 것이다
   ④ 그것들은 두뇌의 지시에 따라 작동하여 적절한 메시지를 발송할 것이다

3. 나노봇으로 가상 세계를 체험할 수 있다는 내용의 글 다음에, 이에 더하여 비생물학적 지능이라는 새로운 개념을 소개하는 내용의 (B)가 이어지고, 비생물학적 지능이 아마 인간에게 이용되고 있다는 내용의 (A)가 온 후, 그 예인 파킨슨 병의 신경 이식 치료법을 언급하는 (C)가 오는 것이 가장 자연스럽다.

4. 형용사적 용법의 to부정사구와 주격 관계대명사절을 이용하여 순서를 재구성할 수 있다.

구문해설

③ **Through the utilization of nanobots**, experiencing a virtual world **would** not differ appreciably from experiencing the "real world," as external stimuli must be translated into signals in the brain.

▷ 현재에 실현가능성이 희박한 일을 가정하는 가정법 과거 구문으로, 전치사구인 Through ... nanobots가 조건절을 대신한다.

⑧ Neural implants **are** currently **being used** in patients [**suffering** from Parkinson's Disease] **to act** as a replacement for cells with impaired functioning.

▷ 동사가 「be being v-ed」형태로, 현재진행 수동태 문장이다.
▷ [ ]는 patients를 수식하는 현재분사구이다.
▷ to act 이하는 목적을 나타내는 부사적 용법의 to부정사구이다.

17 SECTION 04. 정보 통신
퀀텀 컴퓨팅(quantum computing)

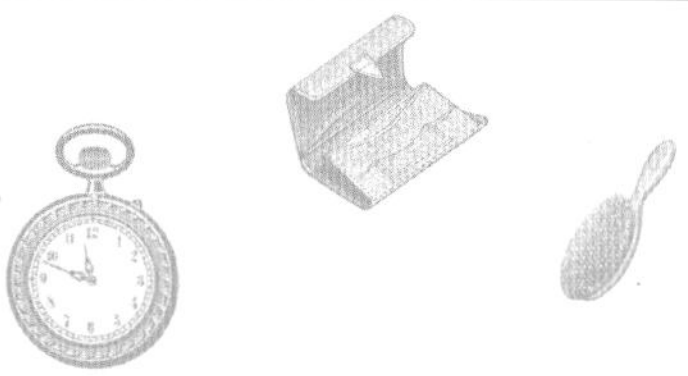

P.048

정답 | 1. ② 2. 전자가 관찰되거나 측정되지 않는 한, 두 가지 상태를 모두 띠는 것 3. ① 4. ⑤

본문 필기노트

① Advancements in quantum theory, a concept [that defines [how particles behave at the atomic and subatomic level]], can be utilized in computer technology, a practice [known as quantum computing]. ② This field has the potential [to enhance computer performance / by a billion times or more], as the simultaneous processing of tasks could be accomplished / at unprecedented speeds.

퀀텀 컴퓨팅의 개념

③ The capacity (of high-performance quantum computers) / is facilitated by quantum superposition, a phenomenon [in which electrons hold two states, for example both 0 and 1, at the same time]. ④ As long as the electrons are not observed or measured, they continue to behave / as if they were in both states. ⑤ To control superposition, scientists use the process of entanglement, [in which a force is applied to two atoms to instantaneously create an interaction between them, no matter how distantly they're separated]. ⑥ If an atom is not disturbed, its spin state will be in multiple directions. ⑦ However, if it is disrupted, it instantly begins spinning in a single direction. ⑧ Meanwhile, the other atom [it is entangled with] will begin spinning in the opposite direction. ⑨ Knowledge about one entangled atom, therefore, provides information about the other. ⑩ [Using superposition and entanglement], undisturbed pairs of qubits (quantum bits) can exhibit four states — 00, 01, 10 and 11 — at the same time, as compared to traditional computer bits, [which can only exhibit one — 0 or 1]. ⑪ Adding qubits to the system allows the computing power to increase exponentially.

퀀텀 컴퓨팅의 원리

⑫ While there are numerous potential applications of quantum computing, / these are limited / by our current technology. ⑬ Few algorithms have been devised

본문해석

① 입자들이 원자와 아원자 단계에서 어떻게 반응하는지를 정의하는 개념인 양자론의 발달은 컴퓨터 기술에 활용될 수 있는데, 이것이 퀀텀 컴퓨팅이라고 알려진 실제다. ② 작업의 동시 처리가 전례 없는 속도로 이루어질 수 있으므로, 이 분야는 컴퓨터 성능을 십억 배 이상으로 향상할 수 있는 잠재력을 가지고 있다.

③ 고성능 퀀텀 컴퓨터의 능력은 양자 중첩에 의하여 촉진되는데, 이는 전자들이 동시에 두 상태, 예컨대 0과 1을 동시에 띠는 현상이다. ④ 그 전자들은 관찰되거나 측정되지 않는 한, 계속 두 상태 모두를 띤 것처럼 행동한다. ⑤ 중첩을 제어하기 위해, 과학자들은 얽힘이라는 절차를 사용하는데, 여기에서는 두 개의 원자에 힘이 가해져 그것들이 아무리 멀리 떨어져 있더라도 순간적으로 그 사이에 상호작용을 만들어 낸다. ⑥ 원자가 간섭받지 않으면, 그것의 회전 상태는 여러 방향일 것이다. ⑦ 그러나 그것이 간섭받으면 즉시 한 방향으로 회전하기 시작한다. ⑧ 한편, 그것과 얽힌 나머지 원자는 반대 방향으로 회전하기 시작할 것이다. ⑨ 따라서 하나의 얽힌 원자에 대한 지식이 나머지 원자에 대한 정보를 제공한다. ⑩ 중첩과 얽힘을 이용해, 간섭받지 않은 큐비트(양자 비트) 쌍들은 전통적인 컴퓨터 비트가 한 개의 상태, 즉 0 또는 1을 나타낼 수 있는 데 비해, 네 개의 상태, 즉 00, 01, 10, 11을 동시에 나타낼 수 있다. ⑪ 큐비트를 시스템에 추가하는 것은 연산 능력이 기하급수적으로 증가하게 한다.

⑫ 퀀텀 컴퓨팅의 잠재적 응용이 많은 한편, 이것은 우리의 현재 기술에 의해 제한된다. ⑬ 양자 기술을 위한 알고리즘은 거의 고안되지 않았고, 과학자들

/ for quantum technology, and scientists / are still developing methods (for keeping quantum computing devices at a low enough temperature for operation). ⑭ Once these obstacles are overcome, we can fully reap the benefits of quantum computing.

keep+O+OC: O를 ~한 상태로 유지하다

일단 ~하면(접속사)

은 여전히 퀀텀 컴퓨팅 기기를 작동하기에 충분할 만큼 저온으로 유지하는 방법을 개발하고 있는 중이다. ⑭ 일단 이 장애물들이 극복되고 나면, 우리는 퀀텀 컴퓨팅의 혜택을 온전히 거둘 수 있다.

퀀텀 컴퓨팅의 한계 및 가능성

본문파악

퀀텀 컴퓨팅에 대해 설명하는 글이다. 첫째 단락에서는 퀀텀 컴퓨팅의 개념을 소개하고, 둘째 단락에서는 그 이론적인 원리를 자세히 설명하며, 셋째 단락에서는 실제 구현의 한계와 가능성에 대해 이야기한다.

문제풀이

1. 《해석》 위 글의 제목으로 가장 적절한 것은?
   퀀텀 컴퓨팅의 이론적인 원리를 설명하고 한계점 및 가능성을 이야기하는 글이므로 ②가 글의 제목으로 가장 적절하다.
   ① 새롭게 도입된 이론: 얽힘
   ② 퀀텀 컴퓨팅: 이론에서 현실까지
   ③ 퀀텀 컴퓨팅의 성공적인 적용 사례
   ④ 퀀텀 컴퓨팅을 통한 가상 세계의 새로운 가능성
   ⑤ 경제를 가속하고 있는 양자 컴퓨터

2. ④번 문장 참조

3. ⑧번 문장에서 두 개의 원자가 얽혀 있을 때 두 원자는 서로 반대 방향으로 회전한다고 하였으므로, 전자 하나의 회전 방향을 알면 나머지 전자의 회전 방향도 알 수 있을 것이다.
   ① 나머지 원자에 대한 정보를 제공한다
   ② 그 원자를 여러 개의 큐비트로 바꾼다
   ③ 나머지 원자와 얽히는 것이 불가능하다
   ④ 원자가 여러 방향으로 회전하게 만든다
   ⑤ 얽힘 과정 동안 증가한 힘을 받는다

4. 《해석》 위 글에 따르면, 다음 중 참이 아닌 것은?
   ① 양자 이론은 아원자 입자의 동작과 상호작용에 관한 것이다. (①번 문장 참조)
   ② 컴퓨터 기술은 향상된 양자론으로부터 혜택을 입을 수 있을 것이다. (①번 문장 참조)
   ③ 얽힘은 그것들이 서로 가까이 있든 아니든 원자들에게 영향을 미친다. (⑤번 문장 참조)
   ④ 큐비트는 중첩과 얽힘이 일어나는 동안 동시에 네 가지 상태를 나타낼 수 있다. (⑩번 문장 참조)
   ⑤ 양자 기술은 온도를 고정해 최적의 작동을 보장하는 알고리즘을 사용한다. → 퀀텀 컴퓨팅에서 컴퓨터를 저온으로 유지하기 위한 방법을 개발 중이라고 했다.(⑬번 문장 참조)

구문해설

① Advancements in quantum theory, a concept [**that** defines [how particles behave at the atomic and subatomic level]], can be utilized in computer technology, a practice [**known** as quantum computing].

▷ 첫 번째 [ ]는 a concept를 선행사로 하는 주격 관계대명사절이다.
▷ 두 번째 [ ]는 defines의 목적어 역할을 하는 의문사절이다.
▷ 세 번째 [ ]는 a practice를 수식하는 과거분사구이다.

④ As long as the electrons are not observed or measured, they continue to behave **as if** they **were** in both states.

▷ as if+가정법 과거: '마치 ~인 것처럼'

18

SECTION 04. 정보 통신

잊힐 권리에 대한 찬반 입장

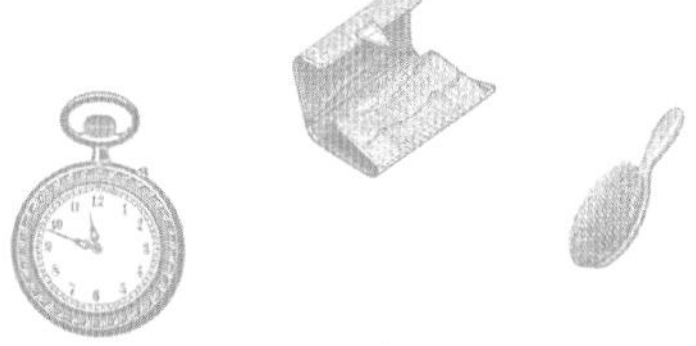

P.050

정답	1. ③ 2. ③ 3. ⓑ 4. 자유 사회의 핵심 신조인 발언의 자유에 대한 권리와 직접적으로 충돌한다. / 잊힐 권리를 위한 기술을 개발하고 구현하는 데 상당한 비용이 필요하기 때문에 실시하기 어렵다. 5. ④

본문 필기노트

(A)

① The dissemination of information in the digital age / has become increasingly rapid thanks to social networking services and cloud technology. ② However, with these advancements coexists a threat to privacy, as information [shared online] is difficult, / if not impossible, to remove. ③ The European Court of Justice / has officially conferred "the right to be forgotten" on citizens, / [safeguarding individuals' control over their personal information]. (④ The practical implication of this right / is the requirement [that search engines exclude or remove from their search results any data [that is outdated or of a deeply personal nature]].) ⑤ Without such protections in place, individuals are highly vulnerable to the erosion of personal privacy. ⑥ By putting the right to be forgotten into place, / we can expand the level of control / [people have / over their personal privacy] / and protect individual rights.

잊힐 권리에 대한 찬성 입장

(B)

⑦ The amount of personal data [available online] and the technologically advanced methods of [gathering such data] / have seen unprecedented growth in recent years. ⑧ Supporters of the right to be forgotten argue [that citizens should be able to have certain data about them removed from the public sphere]. ⑨ However, this is in direct conflict / with the right (to freedom of speech), a central tenet of a free society. ⑩ By upholding the right to be forgotten, we are denying people the right [to know] and restricting the free flow of information. ⑪ The right to be forgotten is also unfeasible / due to the considerable expenditure [needed to develop and implement technology [capable of carrying out the necessary "forgetting.]]" ⑫ Though there is a critical need for the responsible sharing of

본문해석

(A)

① 디지털 시대의 정보의 보급은 소셜 네트워크 서비스와 클라우드 기술 덕분에 점점 더 빨라지고 있다. ② 그러나, 이러한 발전과 함께 사생활에 대한 위협이 공존하는데, 온라인으로 공유되는 정보는 삭제하기가 불가능하지는 않다 해도 어렵기 때문이다. ③ 유럽사법재판소는 시민들에게 공식적으로 '잊힐 권리'를 부여하여, 자신의 개인 정보에 대한 개인의 통제를 보호해왔다. (④ 이 권리에 실제 함축된 내용은 검색 엔진이 시대에 뒤지거나 매우 사적인 성질의 정보를 검색 결과로부터 제외하거나 삭제해야 한다는 요구이다.) ⑤ 그러한 보호책의 시행 없이는, 개인은 개인적인 사생활의 침식에 매우 취약하다. ⑥ 잊힐 권리를 정립함으로써, 우리는 사람들이 개인적인 사생활에 대해 가지는 통제력을 확장하고 개인의 권리를 보호할 수 있다.

(B)

⑦ 온라인에서 입수할 수 있는 개인 정보의 양과 그러한 정보를 수집하는 기술적으로 진보된 수단은 최근 몇 년 간 유례없는 성장을 겪었다. ⑧ 잊힐 권리의 옹호자들은 시민들이 자신에 대한 특정 정보를 공공 영역으로부터 삭제할 수 있어야 한다고 주장한다. ⑨ 하지만, 이것은 자유 사회의 핵심 신조인 발언의 자유에 대한 권리와 직접적으로 충돌한다. ⑩ 잊힐 권리를 옹호함으로써, 우리는 사람들에게 알 권리를 허락하지 않고 정보의 자유로운 흐름을 방해하고 있다. ⑪ 잊힐 권리는 또한 필요한 '잊기'를 수행할 수 있는 기술을 개발하고 시행하는 데 필요한 상당한 지출 때문에 실시하기 어렵다. ⑫ 책임감 있는 정보 공유에 대한 중대한 필요성이 존재하지만, 그것은 우리의 필수적인 자유를 손상하면서 실현돼서는 안 될 것이다.

information, it should not be fulfilled to the detriment of our essential freedoms.

=the responsible sharing of information 결국 ~을 해치며

잊힐 권리에 대한 반대 입장

본문파악

글 (A), (B)는 온라인상의 개인 정보를 삭제할 권리인 잊힐 권리에 대한 찬반론이다. (A)는 개인의 사생활을 보호해야 한다는 이유로 잊힐 권리에 찬성하는 반면, (B)는 자유롭게 발언할 권리 및 개인 정보 삭제에 발생되는 비용 문제를 이유로 반대하고 있다.

문제풀이

1. 《해석》 (A)와 (B)의 쟁점은 어느 것인가?
   (A)와 (B)는 잊힐 권리에 대해 찬성하는 입장과 반대하는 입장을 각각 드러내고 있으므로, 이 글의 주제로는 ③이 가장 적절하다.
   ① IT 발달을 저해하는 정부 정책
   ② 유럽에서 온라인 사생활 문제에 대한 커져가는 우려
   ③ 잊힐 권리가 존중되어야 하는 것인지 아닌지
   ④ 법적으로 규제되는 저작권이 이득인가 저해인가
   ⑤ 소셜 네트워킹 시스템을 이용해서 정보를 믿을 만하게 공유하는 것의 장단점

2. 주어진 문장에서 this right은 잊힐 권리를 가리키며, 주어진 문장은 이를 구체적으로 설명하는 내용이므로, 잊힐 권리를 처음으로 언급하는 문장과 잊힐 권리가 없을 경우에 발생할 결과에 대해 언급하는 문장 사이인 ③에 들어가는 것이 적절하다.

3. 잊힐 권리의 지지자들이 주장한 내용이므로, 시민들이 그들에 관한 특정 정보를 공공 영역으로부터 '삭제할' 수 있어야 한다고 주장하는 것이 문맥상 자연스럽다. 따라서 ⓑ sustained는 removed로 고쳐야 한다.

4. ⑨번, ⑪번 문장 참조

5. ①번, ②번 문장을 통해 디지털 기술이 발전함에 따라 개인 정보에 대한 위협도 커졌음을 알 수 있다.

구문해설

② However, with these advancements **coexists** (V) **a threat to privacy** (S), **as** information [**shared** online] is difficult, if not impossible, to remove.

▷ 부사구 with these advancements가 앞으로 나오면서 동사 coexists와 주어 a threat to privacy가 도치되었다.
▷ as는 '~때문에'의 뜻으로 이유를 나타내는 접속사로 쓰였다.
▷ [ ]는 information을 수식하는 과거분사구이다.

④ The practical implication of this right is the requirement [**that** search engines **exclude** or **remove** from their search results any data [**that** is outdated or of a deeply personal nature]].

▷ 첫 번째 [ ]는 the requirement의 내용을 설명하는 동격의 that절이다.
▷ 주장 · 제안 · 요구를 나타내는 동사 또는 명사 뒤 that절의 동사는 「(should)+동사원형」 형태로 쓴다.
▷ 두 번째 [ ]는 any data를 선행사로 하는 주격 관계대명사절이다.

19 SECTION 04. 정보 통신
테크놀로지에 대한 시각 변화

P.052

정답 | 1. ④ 2. ④ 3. 과학기술이 인간을 지배할 것이라는 두려움 4. ③

본문 필기노트

① In the mid-1800s, / a splendid accomplishment was attained in technology, which put an end to the modern natural sciences [as represented by Newtonian mechanics]. ② At the 1851 London Fair, / so many novel and striking products were shown it seemed to prove Francis Bacon's projection [that all things could be realized]. ③ Inasmuch as technology became highly developed and played an unprecedented role in social life over the next hundred years, / many have called that period "the glorious beginning" of the technological era. ④ However, while homage was made to the technological progress, / warnings were issued.

과학기술 발전에 대한 찬사와 경고

⑤ For example, in his novel *Brave New World*, / Aldous L. Huxley described a future [dominated by technology]. ⑥ In this society / there would be great comfort, / but at the cost of freedom, beauty, and privacy. ⑦ In various science fiction novels, / technology controlled humans. ⑧ Robots [reigning over the world] indirectly reflected this fear. ⑨ The formerly popular attitude [that technology was a powerful tool for the betterment of humankind] seemed to be one-sided at best. ⑩ The view [that technology was simply harmless] / did not accord with actuality. (⑪ In reality, the arrival of so many of the latest devices has made day-to-day living more convenient for everyone.) ⑫ Slowly, the anti-technological tendency began to grow, / primarily because the tremendous destructive power of technological progress [made during wars] constituted a grave danger to the planet and to the existence of humans themselves. ⑬ It was also due to such harmful outcomes [caused by technological progress] as traffic accidents, pollution of air and water, noise, and damage to the environment. ⑭ These causes, and their negative effects, were immediately obvious. ⑮ On a much deeper level, / these negative effects were

본문해석

① 1800년대 중반에 과학기술 분야에서 눈부신 업적이 달성되어, 뉴턴 역학으로 대표되던 근대 자연과학에 종지부를 찍었다. ② 1851년 런던 박람회에는 너무나 많은 새롭고 놀라운 제품들이 전시되어, 모든 것은 실현될 수 있다는 프랜시스 베이컨의 예상을 증명하는 듯했다. ③ 향후 백 년에 걸쳐 과학기술이 고도로 발달하여 사회생활에서 전례 없는 역할을 하게 된 까닭에, 많은 이들이 그 시대를 과학기술시대의 '화려한 시작'이라고 불렀다. ④ 그러나 과학기술의 발전에 대해 경의가 표해지는 한편 경고도 나왔다.

⑤ 예를 들어, 올더스 헉슬리는 그의 소설 「멋진 신세계」에서 과학기술에 의해 지배되는 미래를 묘사했다. ⑥ 이 사회에는 굉장한 편안함이 있지만 자유, 아름다움, 사생활을 희생한다. ⑦ 많은 공상 과학 소설에서, 과학기술은 인간을 통제했다. ⑧ 세상을 지배하는 로봇들이 이러한 두려움을 간접적으로 반영했다. ⑨ 과학기술이 인류의 진보를 위한 강력한 도구였다는 이전에 널리 퍼졌던 태도는 기껏해야 편파적인 것 같았다. ⑩ 과학기술이 전혀 해가 없었다는 견해는 현실과 맞지 않았다. (⑪ 실제로, 최신 기기의 수많은 도래는 모두에게 일상생활을 편리하게 만들었다.) ⑫ 주로 전쟁 동안 이루어진 과학기술 발전의 엄청난 파괴력이 지구와 인간 자체의 존재에 심각한 위험을 야기했기 때문에, 반 과학기술적인 경향이 서서히 증가하기 시작했다. ⑬ 그것은 또한 교통사고, 대기 및 수질 오염, 소음, 그리고 환경 훼손과 같이 과학기술의 발전으로 인해 야기된 해로운 결과들 때문이었다. ⑭ 이러한 원인들, 그리고 그것들의 부정적인 결과들은 곧 명백해졌다. ⑮ 더 깊은 수준에서 본다면, 이러한 부정적인 결과들은 주로 과학기술에 의한 인간 지배 때문이었다.

mainly due to the domination of humans by technology. 반 과학기술적인 태도의 등장과 그 원인
~에 의한

본문파악

이 글은 과학기술 발전의 부정적인 측면에 초점을 맞추고 있다. 첫째 단락 전반부에서는 1800년대 과학기술이 가져온 엄청난 발전에 대한 찬사와 기대를, 후반부에서는 이에 대한 우려를 언급하고 있다. 둘째 단락에서는 구체적인 예를 통해 과학기술 발전의 폐해를 설명하면서, 이를 첫째 단락에서 언급한 우려에 대한 근거로 사용하고 있다.

문제풀이

1. 《해석》 위 글의 주제는 무엇인가?
이 글은 주로 과학기술 발전이 초래한 부정적 결과에 초점을 맞추고 있다.
① 현대 과학기술이 얼마나 더 진보할 수 있는가
② 유명 공상 과학 소설들에 대한 소개
③ 과학기술 시대가 가져온 이점들
④ 과학기술 발전의 부정적 측면들
⑤ 과학기술 시대와 소설가의 책임

2. 《해석》 위 글에 의하면 다음 중 참인 것은?
① 뉴턴이 이룩한 것은 근대 과학자들에게 비난을 받았다. → ①번 문장에서 뉴턴의 역학이 근대 자연 과학을 대표한다고는 했지만, 근대 과학자들로부터 비난을 받았다는 언급은 없었다.
② 올더스 헉슬리는 과학기술에 대한 부정적인 견해를 나타낸 최초의 사람이었다. → ⑤번 문장에서 헉슬리가 그의 소설에서 과학기술의 지배를 받는 미래 사회를 묘사했다는 언급은 있으나, 그가 과학기술에 대한 부정적인 견해를 나타낸 최초의 사람이었다는 언급은 없다.
③ 애초부터 많은 사람들은 과학기술의 힘에 대해 심각한 의구심을 가졌었다. → ③~④번 문장에서 과학기술에 대한 긍정적인 생각과 부정적인 생각이 공존했음을 알 수 있다.
④ 과학기술의 발전은 인류에게 엄청난 위험을 초래했다. (⑫번 문장 참조)
⑤ 환경오염은 과학기술의 발전과 아무런 관계가 없다. → ⑬번 문장과는 반대되는 내용이다.

3. ⑦번 문장 참조

4. 과학기술의 발전이 인류의 진보에 긍정적인 역할을 할 거라는 과거의 견해와 달리 이의 부정적 측면을 우려하는 반과학기술적 태도의 글에서 최신 기기가 일상생활을 편리하게 만들었다는 내용의 ③은 글의 흐름과 맞지 않다.

구문해설

① In the mid-1800s, a splendid accomplishment was attained in technology, **which** put an end to the modern natural sciences [**as represented** by Newtonian mechanics].

▷ which 이하는 앞 문장에 대한 부연 설명을 해주는 계속적 용법의 관계대명사로, and this로 바꾸어 쓸 수 있다.
▷ as는 이 문장에서 관계대명사와 유사한 역할을 하며, the modern natural sciences를 선행사로 받는다.

② At the 1851 London Fair, **so** many novel and striking products were shown (**that**) it seemed to prove Francis Bacon's projection that all things could be realized.

▷ so ~ that ...: '너무 ~하여 …하다'의 의미로, that이 생략된 경우이다.

과학과 기술의 만남

16~17세기의 과학혁명은 중세 전체를 거부하고 근대의 시작을 알리는 혁명적인 사건이었다. 과학혁명으로 인해 과학과 철학이 분리되었으며, 그 대신 과학과 기술이 결합하게 되었다. 여기에 응용과학의 중요성을 강조했던 베이컨(Francis Bacon)의 새로운 지식관이 큰 영향을 끼쳤다. 코페르니쿠스와 뉴턴으로 대표되는 과학혁명은 '이성의 시대'인 18세기에 과학의 대중화로 이어졌고, 18세기 후반의 산업혁명은 과학과 기술의 긴밀한 상호작용을 가능케 했다.
20세기에 들어와 과학기술은 엄청난 발전을 이룩했다. 과학은 기술의 진보를 촉진하고, 기술에서 나온 문제는 과학의 발전으로 해결되었기 때문이다. 이제 과학과 기술은 구별이 어려울 만큼 하나가 되었다. 한편으로 이러한 발전이 엄청난 부작용을 만들어내면서 인류가 살아남기 위해 과학기술을 전면 포기해야 한다는 소리도 높아지고 있다.

20 SECTION 04. 정보 통신
사물 인터넷

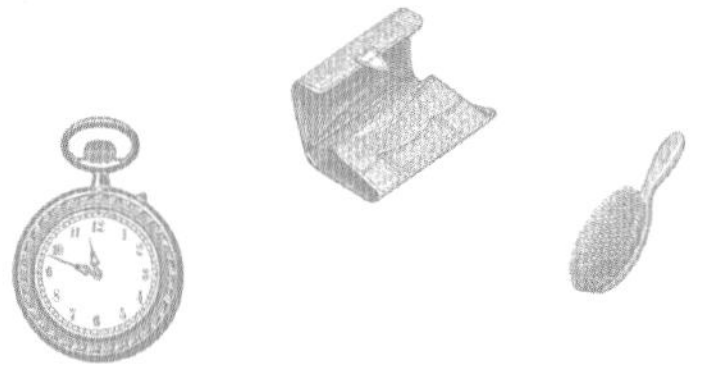

P.054

정답	1. (1) ③ (2) ② (3) ⑤　2. ③　3. (1) F (2) T (3) T (4) T　4. ②

본문 필기노트

주격 관 · 대
① Contemporary commuters [who find themselves stuck in heavy traffic on the
V' O' OC'
journey home] may pass the time contemplating all the tasks [that need to be
pass+시간+v-ing: ~하는 데 시간을 보내다 주격 관 · 대
accomplished once they reach their destination]. ② In the near future, however,
일단 ~하면(접속사) 가까운 장래에
the Internet of Things (IoT) may allow them to do much more than that. ③ While
allow+O+to-v: O가 ~하는 것을 허락하다 ~하는 동안(접속사)
their smart cars navigate the roadways, / the commuters will be able to remotely
(to)
pre-heat their ovens, / activate their washing machines, / and prompt their
(to) prompt+O+to-v: O가 ~하도록 하다
refrigerators to perform an inventory of their own contents and prepare a shopping
(to)
list based on the results.

사물 인터넷의 구현 사례

④ This may sound unrealistically futuristic, / but many of the appliances and
(that) 목적격 관 · 대 ~중에
devices [we already own] possess embedded computing systems of one degree (of
sophistication or another). ⑤ What the IoT does is [create a virtual network of these
S(관계대명사절) V SC
physical objects, [allowing them to collect and exchange a wide range of data]]. ⑥ In
부대상황의 분사구문 allow+O+to-v: O로 하여금 ~하게 하다
a sense, it serves as a bridge [that allows for the direct integration of the physical
~로(서) 주격 관 · 대
realm into cyberspace]. ⑦ It is estimated [that by 2020 there will be nearly 50
가주어 that 이하는 진주어
billion individual objects [wired into the IoT]]. ⑧ This will lead to improvements in
~로 이어지다, ~을 초래하다
countless everyday tasks / in terms of both efficiency and economy.
~면에서 both A and B: A와 B 둘 다

사물 인터넷의 원리와 그 전망

⑨ The manufacturing industry is currently at the vanguard of the IoT revolution,
which의 선행사
[which is not surprising considering the benefits (inherent in the adoption of such
주격 관 · 대(계속적 용법) ~을 고려하면(전치사) =the IoT
technology)]. ⑩ The terms "Industry 4.0" and "the fourth industrial revolution" are
=
currently being employed [to refer to the next wave of manufacturing advances and
가리키는 데(부사적 용법)
innovations [expected to accompany the advent of the IoT]]. ⑪ The factories of
~의 ~의
tomorrow will possess computer systems / [that continuously monitor and evaluate
주격 관 · 대

본문해석

① 집으로 가는 길에 교통 체증에 갇힌 현대의 통근자는 목적지에 도착하면 해야 하는 모든 일들을 생각하며 시간을 보낼지도 모른다. ② 하지만, 가까운 미래에 사물 인터넷(IoT)이 그들로 하여금 그보다 훨씬 더 많은 것을 할 수 있게 해 줄지도 모른다. ③ 자동 운전 승용차가 길을 찾는 동안, 통근자는 원격으로 오븐을 예열하고, 세탁기를 작동시키고, 냉장고가 자신의 내용물 재고 조사를 하도록 하고 그 결과를 바탕으로 쇼핑 목록을 준비하도록 할 수 있을 것이다.

④ 이것은 비현실적으로 미래적인 것처럼 들릴지도 모르지만, 우리가 이미 소유하고 있는 가전제품과 기기 중 다수가 다양한 정도의 정교함을 지닌 내장 전산 시스템을 가지고 있다. ⑤ 사물 인터넷이 하는 일은 이러한 물체의 가상 네트워크를 만들어서, 그것들이 광범위한 데이터를 수집하고 교환할 수 있게 하는 것이다. ⑥ 어떤 의미에서, 그것은 물리 세계를 사이버 공간에 직접 통합할 수 있게 하는 다리 역할을 한다. ⑦ 2020년이면 사물 인터넷에 연결된 개별 물체가 거의 500억 개일 것으로 추정된다. ⑧ 이것은 효율과 절약 면에서 모두 수많은 일상 작업의 개선으로 이어질 것이다.

⑨ 현재 제조업계가 사물 인터넷 혁명의 선두에 있는데, 그러한 기술의 채용에 따르는 내재하는 이득을 고려하면 이는 놀라운 일이 아니다. ⑩ '산업 4.0'과 '네 번째 산업혁명'이라는 용어는 현재 사물 인터넷의 도래와 함께 찾아올 것으로 예상되는 제조업 발전 및 혁신의 차기 물결을 가리키는 데 사용되고 있다. ⑪ 미래의 공장들은 끊임없이 물리적 성능을 감시하고 평가하는 컴퓨터 시스템을 소유하여, 이 정보를 이용해 분권화된 결정을 내릴 것이

physical performance], / [using this information to make decentralized decisions,
부대상황의 분사구문 which의 선행사
[which is expected to boost efficiency]].
주격 관 · 대(계속적 용법)

며, 그것은 효율을 높일 것으로 예상된다.

사물 인터넷을 이용하는 산업 4.0이 이끌 제조 혁신

본문파악

사물 인터넷의 원리와 전망을 설명하고, 사물 인터넷의 발달과 함께 도래할 제조업계의 혁신(산업 4.0)에 대해 설명한 글이다.

문제풀이

1. 《해석》 각 단락의 요지는 무엇인가? 아래의 상자 안에서 알맞은 선택지를 고르시오.
본문 필기노트의 단락 요약을 참조한다.
① 사물 인터넷이 소기업에 무엇을 의미하는가
② 사물 인터넷이 기능하는 원리와 그것의 미래에 대한 관측
③ 사물 인터넷이 사람들의 삶에 어떻게 영향을 미칠 수 있는지에 대한 실례들
④ '산업 4.0' 내 성공적인 사업 모델의 예시
⑤ '산업 4.0'의 정의와 사물 인터넷이 제조업계를 변혁할 방식

2. ⑤번 문장에서 사물 인터넷이란 가상 네트워크를 통해 물리 세계에 있는 사물을 서로 연결하는 것이라고 했으므로, 빈칸에는 ③이 가장 적절하다.
① 인류 ② 정보 교환 ③ 사이버 공간 ④ 정신 세계 ⑤ 개별 물체

3. 《해석》 다음 진술에 대해 T(참) 또는 F(거짓)로 표시하시오.
(1) 물리적으로 멀리 있는 문제들은 사물 인터넷 시대에 쉽게 피할 수 없는 장애물이 될 것이다. → ③번 문장에 따르면 출근 중에도 사물 인터넷을 통해 집의 가전제품을 제어할 수 있다고 하였으므로 물리적 거리는 중요하지 않다는 것을 알 수 있다.
(2) 사람들은 이미 많은 전자 기기를 소유하고 있으며, 이들 기기가 가까운 미래에 사물 인터넷에 연결될 것으로 예상된다. (④번 문장 참조)
(3) 제조업계가 사물 인터넷을 받아들이는 데 있어서 모든 업계의 선두에 있다. (⑨번 문장 참조)
(4) 네 번째 산업혁명은 사물 인터넷 시대 내에서의 제조업의 발달 단계를 나타낸다. (⑩번 문장 참조)

4. 원격으로 냉장고가 자신의 내용물 재고 조사를 하고, 그 결과를 바탕으로 쇼핑 목록을 준비'하도록 한다'라는 내용이 되어야 하므로, ② impede(방해하다)는 '~하도록 하다'라는 의미의 prompt 등으로 고치는 것이 적절하다.

구문해설

③ While their smart cars navigate the roadways, the commuters will be able **to** remotely **pre-heat** their ovens, **(to) activate** their washing machines, and **(to) prompt** their refrigerators **to perform** an inventory of their own contents and **(to) prepare** a shopping list based on the results.

▷ pre-heat과 activate, prompt는 모두 remotely 앞의 to에 병렬연결되어 있다.
▷ to perform과 (to) prepare는 모두 동사 prompt의 목적격보어로 접속사 and로 병렬연결되어 있다.

⑤ [What the IoT does] is **create** a virtual network of these physical objects, allowing them to collect and exchange a wide range of data.
S V SC

▷ [ ]는 선행사를 포함하는 관계대명사 what이 이끄는 명사절로 문장의 주어로 쓰였다.
▷ what, all, the only thing, the first thing 등이 이끄는 절이 do 동사를 포함하고 있을 때, 주격보어로는 흔히 to가 생략된 원형부정사가 온다.

21

SECTION 05. 철학

철학이 필요한 이유

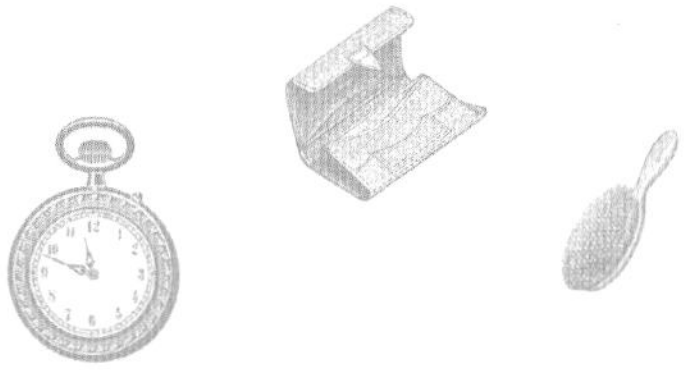

P.058

정답

1. By studying philosophy we can achieve very profound and very significant insights into the world and the nature of the human condition. 2. would[could/might] have been

본문 필기노트

① If philosophy is just "a residue" of unanswered questions / or a pursuit of unanswerable questions, / why should we keep doing it? ② One may say why bother with problems [we cannot solve]? ③ Because just dealing with the puzzle / increases our understanding of the problem and the difficulties [involved in it]. ④ Without philosophical curiosity [displayed in this way], many important issues (in the past) would have been overlooked or forgotten. ⑤ By continuing to raise questions and study their implications, / we keep theoretical interest alive / no matter whether it can yield positive results or not. ⑥ Many questions [that are now unanswered] could turn one day into new areas of study. ⑦ Those [that are unanswerable in principle] are still meaningful and important both intellectually and humanly. ⑧ Thus, despite the fact [that philosophy does not provide definitive answers], it is not a futile activity of the human mind. ⑨ By studying philosophy / we can achieve (very profound and very significant) insights (into the world and the nature of the human condition).

(=philosophy / keep v-ing: ~하는 것을 계속[유지]하다 / (that) / (which/that) / (we) / (It's) / S (동명사구) / V(단수동사) / O / ~에 대한 / O / by v-ing: ~함으로써 / (to) / keep+O+형용사: O를 ~하게 유지하다 / (no matter) whether+S+V+or not: ~이든 아니든 간에 / 주격 관 · 대 / turn into: ~으로 변하다 / 분야 / 주격 관 · 대 / 동격의 that / both A and B: A와 B 둘 다 / ~에도 불구하고 / = / =philosophy / S / V / O / ~에 대한[대해])

철학이 필요한 이유

본문해석

① 만일 철학이 단지 대답할 수 없는 질문들의 '나머지'이거나 대답할 수 없는 질문들을 추구하는 것이라면, 왜 우리는 그것을 계속해야 하는가? ② 혹자는 왜 우리가 풀 수 없는 문제들로 고민하느냐고 말할지도 모른다. ③ 단지 어려운 문제를 다루는 것만으로도 문제와 그에 수반된 어려움에 대한 우리의 이해를 높여 주기 때문이다. ④ 이런 식으로 표현된 철학적 호기심이 없었다면 과거의 많은 중요한 문제들은 간과되거나 잊혔을 것이다. ⑤ 의문을 제기하고 함축된 뜻을 연구하는 것을 계속함으로써, 우리는 그것이 긍정적 결과를 가져오든 아니든 이론적 관심이 계속 살아 있도록 유지한다. ⑥ 지금 대답되지 않은 많은 질문들은 언젠가 새로운 연구 분야로 변할 수 있다. ⑦ 원칙적으로 대답할 수 없는 질문들도 지적으로나 인간적으로나 여전히 의미 있고 중요하다. ⑧ 이렇게 철학이 명확한 답변을 주지 않는다는 사실에도 불구하고, 그것은 인간의 쓸데없는 정신 활동이 아니다. ⑨ 철학을 공부함으로써 우리는 세상과 인간 상태의 본질에 대한 아주 심오하고 아주 중요한 통찰력을 얻을 수 있다.

본문파악

철학이 필요한 이유에 대해 질문하고 그것에 대해 답변해 나가는 귀납적 형식의 글이다.

문제풀이

1. 철학이 필요한 이유를 제시한 문장을 찾되 글 전체의 내용을 포괄할 수 있는 문장을 선택한다.

2. 빈칸을 포함한 문장은 '이런 식으로 표현된 철학적 호기심이 없었다면 과거의 많은 중요한 문제들은 ~되었을 것이다'라는 뜻으로, 과거의 일에 대한 가정임을 알 수 있다. 가정법 과거완료의 주절은 「주어+조동사의 과거형+have v-ed」가 되어야 한다.

구문해설

④ **Without** philosophical curiosity displayed in this way, many important issues in the past **would have been** overlooked or forgotten.

▷ 이때의 without은 조건절을 대신하는 것으로 주절 시제에 따라 '~이 없다면, ~이 없었다면'으로 해석하는데, 여기서는 동사 형태가 would have been이므로 가정법 과거완료인 것을 알 수 있고, 따라서 '~이 없었다면'으로 해석한다.

22

SECTION 05. 철학

실용주의(pragmatism)

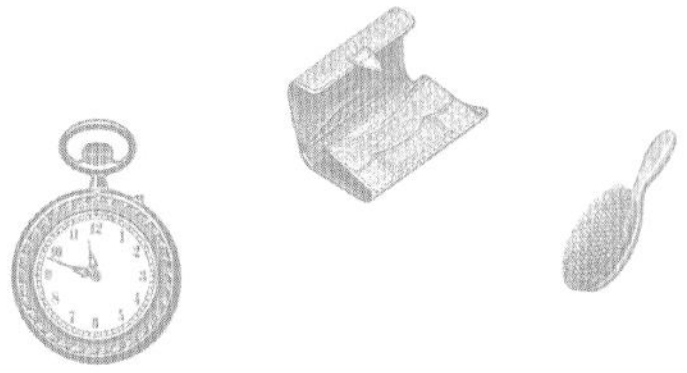

P.059

정답	1. ②, ⑤

본문 필기노트

① Pragmatism is a philosophical approach [that was developed in America during
주격 관 · 대 ~ 동안에
the late nineteenth and early twentieth centuries]. ② It is the only philosophical
~에서
tradition [to originate on American soil]. ③ So it reflects ideas [implicitly accepted
시작된(형용사적 용법) S V O
in the United States]. ④ Because pragmatism's highest ideal is action, / it
주격 관 · 대
corresponds with the attitude of an egalitarian nation [built by immigrants [who
~와
were eager to abandon the restrictive traditions of the old world]]. ⑤ Pragmatism
be eager to-v: ~하기를 열망하다
advocates only those ideas [that can be practically applied], / thus denying
주격 관 · 대 = it denies(결과의 분사구문)
philosophy's reputation of being idealistic and abstract. ⑥ Pragmatism states [that
동격 S V that 이하는 목적어
the meaning of ideas lies in their consequences rather than in the ideas themselves].
~에 놓여 있다 A rather than B: B라기보다는 오히려 A
⑦ Accordingly, pragmatists believe in the importance of trying different methods
따라서 ~의 존재[가치]를 믿다
and ways of life / and then evaluating their effectiveness. ⑧ Pragmatism finds fault
~을 흠잡다[비난하다]
with philosophy's insistence on truth and certainty. ⑨ According to pragmatists, /
~에 대한
truth does not correspond to any ideals. ⑩ Rather, truth exists in a theoretical
~에 ~에
relationship of meaning [that is constantly changing according to the practical
주격 관 · 대 ~에 따라
necessities (of the present moment and at a particular age)]. 실용주의의 개념 및 그 특징

본문해석

① 실용주의는 19세기 후반과 20세기 초반 동안 미국에서 발전된 하나의 철학적 접근이다. ② 그것은 미국 땅에서 시작된 유일한 철학 전통이다. ③ 따라서 그것은 미국에서 암묵적으로 용인되는 생각들을 반영한다. ④ 실용주의의 최고 이상은 행동이기 때문에, 그것은 구세계의 구속적인 전통을 버리기를 열망하는 이민자들에 의해 세워진 평등주의 국가에 대한 태도와 일치한다. ⑤ 실용주의는 실질적으로 적용될 수 있는 개념들만을 옹호하며, 따라서 이상적이고 추상적이라는 철학의 명성을 거부한다. ⑥ 실용주의는 사고의 의의가 사고 자체보다 오히려 그 결과에 있다고 말한다. ⑦ 따라서 실용주의자들은 여러 가지의 방법과 생활 방식을 시도해 보고 나서 그것들의 효과를 평가해 보는 것의 중요성을 믿는다. ⑧ 실용주의는 진실과 확실성에 대한 철학의 주장을 비난한다. ⑨ 실용주의자들에 따르면, 진리는 어떠한 이상에도 일치하지 않는다. ⑩ 오히려 진리는 당시의 순간과 특정 시대의 실질적인 필요에 따라 끊임없이 변하는 의미의 이론적 관계 속에서 존재한다.

본문파악 이 글은 철학의 한 사조인 실용주의에 관해 쓴 글이다. 실용주의가 발생한 미국과 실용주의의 관계에 대해 설명하고 실용주의 사상의 주요 개념들에 대해서도 자세히 언급하고 있다.

문제풀이 1. ② → 이 글에 언급되어 있는 내용이 아니다.
⑤ → ⑩번 문장에서 진리는 실질적인 필요에 따라 끊임없이 '변하는' 것이라고 했다.
① (②번 문장 참조) ③ (⑤번 문장 참조) ④ (⑦번 문장 참조)

구문해설 ⑦ Accordingly, pragmatists believe in the importance (**of trying** different methods and ways of life and then **evaluating** their effectiveness).

▷ ( ) 부분의 of 이하가 the importance를 수식하고 있고, 동명사 trying과 evaluating이 and로 병렬연결되어 있다.

23

SECTION 05. 철학

데카르트와 프로타고라스의 회의주의

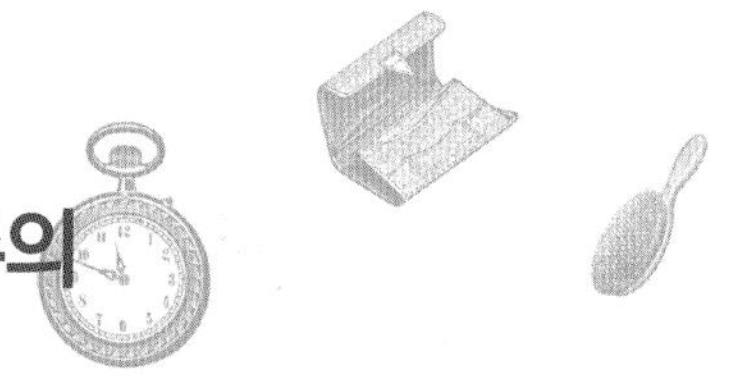

P.060

정답	
	1. skeptical, absolute[ultimate] 2. cogito ergo sum [I think, therefore I am.] 3. 두 사람이 믿을 수 있는 중립적이고 객관적인 척도가 존재하기만 한다면, 한 사람의 의견이 옳은지 그른지를 알 수 있는 방법이 있다.

본문 필기노트

(A)

① Descartes began his philosophical meditations from(~에서부터) a position of absolute skepticism. ② In his search for(~에 대한) a rational philosophical foundation, / he attempted(attempt to-v: ~하려고 시도하다) to eliminate anything [that(목적격 관 · 대) he could not know with 100% surety(100% 확신을 가지고)]. ③ He wanted to construct a foundation for knowledge [that(주격 관 · 대) could not be doubted], just like(마치 ~처럼) the principles of mathematics. ④ From this philosophical foundation / Descartes thought (that) he could deduce all other truths. ⑤ The method [(that) he came up with] was that(=the method) of doubting the existence of all things / until(~할 때까지) he arrived at(~에 도착하다) the point [where(관계부사) he could not doubt [that(that 이하는 목적어) he was doubting], and (he) should therefore exist in order to doubt]. ⑥ This knowledge led to(~에 이르게 하다) one of philosophy's most famous sayings:(즉, 다시 말해) "cogito ergo sum" — "I think, therefore I am."

데카르트의 방법적 회의

(B)

⑦ The ancient Greek philosopher Protagoras taught [that(that 이하는 목적어) "man is the measure of all things]." ⑧ This follows from the idea [that all (that) we know(S) is(V) our thoughts(C)]. ⑨ If all (that) I can know(S) is(V) what I think(C(내가 생각하는 것)) / then I can never escape into(~ (속으)로) reality. ⑩ Thus, whatever I think(S) is(V) all [(that) there is for me to know]. ⑪ If all individuals are trapped in(~ 안에 갇히다) their own thought life / then it(가주어) is not possible [to judge between alternative views](to 이하는 진주어) — (결과) and there is no ultimate truth. ⑫ Only if there is a neutral, objective measure [that(목적격 관 · 대) two individuals can look to], is(V) there any way(S) [to know(알(형용사적 용법)) whether one's views are correct or not(whether ~ or not: ~인지 아닌지)]. ⑬ Protagoras was so skeptical that(so ~ that ...: 너무 ~해서 …하다) he refused to believe [that(that 이하는 목적어) we could ever really know anything].

프로타고라스의 상대주의

본문해석

(A)

① 데카르트는 절대적인 회의주의의 입장에서 그의 철학적인 명상을 시작했다. ② 합리적인 철학적 기초를 찾으려는 노력 속에서, 그는 100% 확신을 가지고 알 수 없는 것은 무엇이든지 제거하려고 시도했다. ③ 그는 마치 수학의 법칙들처럼 의심될 수 없는 지식을 위한 기초를 세우기를 원했다. ④ 이러한 철학적 기반으로부터 데카르트는 다른 모든 진리를 추론해 낼 수 있다고 생각했다. ⑤ 그가 생각해 낸 방법은 자신이 의심하고 있다는 것을 의심할 수 없어서 의심하기 위해 존재해야 하는 지점에 도달할 때까지 모든 사물의 존재를 의심하는 것이었다. ⑥ 이러한 지식은 철학의 가장 유명한 명언들 중 하나인 "cogito ergo sum," 즉 "나는 생각한다, 고로 나는 존재한다."로 이어졌다.

(B)

⑦ 고대 그리스 철학자인 프로타고라스는 "인간은 만물의 척도다."라고 가르쳤다. ⑧ 이것은 우리가 알고 있는 모든 것이 곧 우리가 사고하는 것이라는 생각에서 나온다. ⑨ 만약 내가 알 수 있는 모든 것이 내가 생각하는 것이라면, 나는 절대 현실 속으로 탈출할 수가 없다. ⑩ 따라서 내가 생각하는 것은 무엇이든지 내가 알아야 하는 모든 것들이다. ⑪ 만약 개개인 모두가 자기 자신만의 사고 생활에 갇혀 있다면, 양자택일해야 하는 의견들 사이에서 판단하는 것은 불가능하다. 그리고 결국 궁극적인 진리란 존재하지 않게 된다. ⑫ 두 사람이 믿을 수 있는 중립적이고 객관적인 척도가 존재하기만 한다면, 한 사람의 의견이 옳은지 그른지를 알 수 있는 방법이 있다. ⑬ 프로타고라스는 너무나 회의적이어서 우리가 어떤 것이라도 도대체 진정으로 알 수 있다고 믿기를 거부했다.

본문파악

글 (A)와 글 (B)는 각각 데카르트와 프로타고라스의 철학 사상을 다루고 있다. 데카르트와 프로타고라스는 둘 다 회의주의 철학자였지만, 진리에 대한 태도에는 차이가 있었다. 데카르트가 '방법적 회의(methodological skepticism)'를 통해 절대적인 진리를 찾으려고 했다면, 프로타고라스는 인간 개개인을 척도로 보고 진리라는 것은 상대적이라고 믿는 상대주의자였다. 그래서 그는 절대 진리가 존재한다는 것에 '회의적(skeptical)'이었다.

문제풀이

1. 《해석》 위 글 (A)와 (B)에 따르면, 데카르트와 프로타고라스 모두 지식에 회의적이었다. 그러나 그들 사이의 차이점은, 데카르트가 절대적인 지식을 이해할 수 있게 될 거라고 믿었던 반면, 프로타고라스는 진리 자체가 도대체 존재할 수 있는지에 대해 의심했다는 것이었다. (각 단어는 본문에서)
④번 문장에서 데카르트가 모든 진리를 도출해 낼 수 있는 '철학적인 기초'를 세우기를 원했다는 것과, ⑤번 문장에서 '자신이 의심한다는 것조차 의심할 수 없는 지점'에 도달할 때까지 모든 것을 의심했다는 것으로 보아 데카르트는 '절대적인(absolute)' 지식을 찾으려 했던 것을 알 수 있다. 반면, 프로타고라스는 ⑬번 문장에서 알 수 있듯이 인간이 어떤 것에 대한 진정한 지식을 얻을 수 있다는 것 자체에 '회의적'이었다. 하지만 이 두 철학자 사이의 공통점이 있다면, 데카르트가 절대적인 지식 외의 다른 지식에 대해 '회의적'이었던 것과 마찬가지로, 프로타고라스도 진리의 존재 자체에 '회의적'이었다는 것이다.

2. 데카르트가 도달하고자 했던 '지식의 기초(a foundation for knowledge)'는 어떤 사실을 더 이상 의심할 수 없는 지점(⑤번 문장)이었고, 그것은 글 (A)의 마지막 문장(⑥번 문장)에서 알 수 있듯이 'cogito ergo sum [I think, therefore I am.]'이다.

3. Only if ... look to까지가 조건절이고, 주절의 there와 is가 도치된 구문이다. (구문해설 참조)

구문해설

⑧ This follows from the idea **that** all (that) we know (S) is (V) our thoughts (C).

▷ that 이하의 절에서, all (that) we know가 주어이고, is가 동사에 해당한다. we 앞에 생략된 that은 all을 선행사로 하는 주격 관계대명사이다.

⑫ Only if there is a neutral, objective measure that two individuals can look to, **is** (V) **there** (S) any way to know whether one's views are correct or not.

▷ Only와 같은 부사어(부사, 부사구, 부사절 등)가 문두에 나와 주어처럼 쓰인 there와 동사 is가 도치된 문장이다.
▷ Only if ~: '만약 ~이기만 하다면'

회의주의(skepticism)

회의주의는 인간이 보편적인 진리를 인식하는 것이 불가능하다고 주장한다. 서양철학사에서 회의주의는 프로타고라스의 개인주의적 상대론에서 시작되었고, 모든 일에 대해 확실한 판단을 내리는 것은 불가능하므로 판단 자체를 유보해야 한다고 주장한 피론(Pyrron)에 의해 체계화되었다. 판단을 유보하는 것은 불안의 근원인 오류에서 해방되어 마음의 평화(ataraxia)를 구하기 위한 것으로 여겨졌다.
이후 고대 그리스의 회의론은 신이 세계를 지배한 중세시대에 자취를 감추었다가 근대초 몽테뉴(Montaigne)와 베일(Beyle)에 의해 부활되었다. 이 시대의 회의론은 중세교회의 권위에 도전하는 데 중요한 사상적 원천이 되었다.
회의주의의 정점은 데카르트라 할 수 있다. 그는 '방법적 회의'라는 표현을 통하여, 전통적으로 확실하다고 인정되어 온 모든 명제를 의심해 볼 필요가 있다고 주장하였다. 그의 이러한 회의론은 근대 사상의 전환점을 마련하였다.
이외에도 회의주의자로 파스칼(B. Passcal), 흄(D. Hume), 칸트(I. Kant) 등이 있다. 회의주의는 불가지론, 상대론, 실증주의, 실용주의, 허무주의 등 다양한 근대 사상에 영향을 끼쳤다.

24

SECTION 05. 철학

동양철학 vs. 서양철학

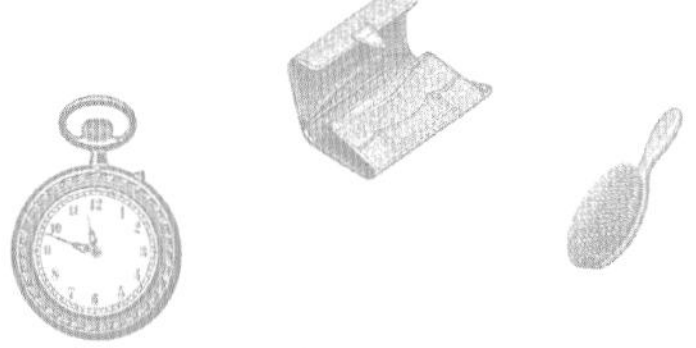

P.062

정답 | 1. 서양철학에서는 종교와 철학의 구분이 분명한 반면, 동양철학에서는 그렇지 않다. 2. ④ 3. 동양철학과 종교와의 관계는 서양신학과 기독교 같은 종교들과의 관계와 같다 4. ②

본문 필기노트

① In the West, / there has always been a sharp distinction between philosophy and religion. ② Philosophy started out as a reaction against religion on the one hand, and against myth and magic on the other. ③ Thales (c. 600 BC) was the first philosopher / in ancient Greek times. ④ A noted scientist as well, / he was the first person [to explain the nature of the universe in solely physical terms, / saying that water was the substance [out of which the entire universe was made]]. ⑤ Thales was famous for his questioning approach to the understanding of natural phenomena / and for allowing his scientific observations and reasoning to govern his behavior / instead of relying on myth and magic. ⑥ In the West, philosophy has always tended to be a rational endeavor, cut off from superstition, faith or godly intervention of any kind.

- has always been: 현재완료(계속)
- between A and B: A와 B 사이에
- as: ~로서
- on the one hand: 한편으로는
- and (a reaction)
- on the other: 또 다른 한편으로는
- ④ (Being)
- as well: 게다가, 마찬가지로
- to explain: 설명한(형용사적 용법)
- saying: =and he said
- out of which: 목적격 관 · 대
- was famous for: ~으로 유명하다
- to: ~에 대한
- and (famous) for
- allowing: allow+O+to-v: O에게 ~하는 것을 허락하다
- relying on: rely on: ~에 의존하다
- tended to be: tend to-v: ~하는 경향이 있다
- endeavor, (being) cut off

서양철학의 특징

⑦ In Eastern philosophy, in contrast, there is no sharp distinction between philosophy and religion. ⑧ From the beginning, / there was never a conflict between them. ⑨ Rather, / Eastern philosophy actually heightened the meditative aspects of religion, / while at the same time providing a theoretical framework and justification for the basic concepts of religion. ⑩ It is even said that Eastern philosophy is to religion as Western theology is to religions like Christianity. ⑪ Only it should also be noted [that there are elements of Eastern philosophy [that represent unique modes of perceiving reality, different from what religions generally teach]]. ⑫ Furthermore, these modes are not based on such essentials of religion as ritual, belief or faith.

- in contrast: 그와 대조적으로
- From the beginning: 시작부터, 애초에
- Rather: 오히려
- heightened: 강화시키다
- while: ~하면서
- It is even said that: 심지어 ~라고도 한다
- A is to B as C is to D: A와 B의 관계는 C와 D의 관계와 같다
- it: 가주어
- that: that 이하는 진주어
- that: 주격 관 · 대
- reality, (being) different
- what: (=the thing which)
- be based on: ~을 기반으로 하다
- such A as B: B와 같은 A

동양철학의 특징

본문해석

① 서양에서는 철학과 종교 간에 항상 분명한 구분이 있어 왔다. ② 철학은 한편으로는 종교에 대해 또 한편으로는 신화 및 마법에 대한 반발로 시작되었다. ③ 탈레스(기원전 600년경)는 고대 그리스 시대 최초의 철학자였다. ④ 유명한 과학자이기도 했던 그는 우주의 본질을 오직 물리적인 용어로 설명한 최초의 사람으로서, 물이 우주 전체가 거기에서 만들어진 물질이라고 말했다. ⑤ 탈레스는 자연 현상을 이해하는 데 질문하는 방식의 접근을 한 것과 신화나 마법에 의존하지 않고 과학적인 관찰과 추론이 그의 행동을 통제하도록 한 것으로 유명했다. ⑥ 서양에서 철학은 미신, 신앙 또는 모든 종류의 신적 개입과도 분리되어, 항상 이성적 시도인 경향이 있었다.

⑦ 그와 대조적으로 동양철학에서는 철학과 종교 간에 분명한 구분이 없다. ⑧ 애초부터, 그 둘 사이에는 대립이 전혀 없었다. ⑨ 오히려, 동양철학은 종교의 기본 개념에 대한 이론적 틀과 정당성을 제공하면서, 종교의 명상적인 측면을 실제로 강화시켰다. ⑩ 심지어 동양철학과 종교와의 관계는 서양신학과 기독교 같은 종교들과의 관계와 같다고도 한다. ⑪ 또한 종교들이 일반적으로 가르치는 것과 달리, 현실을 인지하는 독특한 양식을 나타내는 동양철학의 요소들이 있다는 것만은 주목해야 한다. ⑫ 더욱이 이 양식들은 의식, 믿음 또는 신앙과 같은 종교의 필수 요소들을 기반으로 하지 않는다.

본문파악

이 글은 서양철학과 동양철학의 차이점에 대해 쓴 것으로, 서양철학에서는 철학과 종교의 구분이 명확한 반면, 동양철학은 그 둘을 완전히 구분하기 어렵다는 것이다. 첫째 단락에서는 탈레스의 철학 사상을 예로 들어 서양철학의 성격에 대해 설명하고 있다. 둘째 단락에서는 서양철학과 동양철학을 비교하면서 동양철학의 특징에 대해 말하고 있다.

문제풀이

1. ①, ⑦번 문장을 참조하여 간략히 요약한다.

2. ④ → ⑧번 문장에서 동양철학은 처음부터 종교와 대립이 전혀 없었다고 했다.
① (②번 문장 참조) ② (④번 문장 참조) ③ (⑤번 문장 참조) ⑤ (⑨번 문장 참조)

3. 「A is to B as C is to D」는 'A와 B의 관계는 C와 D의 관계와 같다'라는 의미이다.

4. (A)에는 선행사 the substance와 같으면서 전치사 out of의 목적어 역할을 하는 관계대명사 which가 와야 하며, (B)에는 앞에 being이 생략된 부대상황의 분사구문을 만들어주는 cut이 와야 하고, (C)에는 선행사인 주어 elements of Eastern philosophy가 복수이므로, 동사는 represent가 와야 한다.

구문해설

④ **(Being)** A noted scientist as well, he was the first person to explain the nature of the universe in solely physical terms, **saying** that water was the substance out of which the entire universe was made.

▷ (Being) A noted scientist as well은 Being이 생략된 분사구문으로, 주어 he를 부연 설명해 준다.
▷ saying 이하는 동시동작의 분사구문으로, and he said that ...의 의미이다.

⑨ Rather, Eastern philosophy actually heightened the meditative aspects of religion, **while** at the same time **providing** a theoretical framework and justification for the basic concepts of religion.

▷ providing 이하는 동시동작을 나타내는 분사구문으로 '~하면서'라고 해석한다. while은 뜻을 명확히 하기 위해 분사구문 앞에 접속사를 밝혀준 것으로, while it provided ...의 의미이다.

⑪ Only it should also be noted that there are elements of Eastern philosophy that represent unique modes of perceiving reality, **(being)** different from what religions generally teach.

▷ different 이하는 앞에 being이 생략된 분사구문으로, 의미상 and they are different ...로 바꿔 쓸 수 있다.

철학(philosophy)의 어원

philosophy라는 말은 그리스어의 'philosophia'에서 유래한 것으로, '사랑하다, 좋아하다'라는 뜻의 접두사 'philo'와 '지혜'라는 뜻의 'sophia'가 합쳐진 말이다. 따라서 philosophia는 지(知)를 사랑하는 것, 즉 '애지(愛知)의 학문'을 뜻한다. 철학(哲學)의 '哲'이라는 글자도 '賢' 또는 '知'와 같은 뜻이다. 따라서 철학이라는 글자 그대로의 뜻으로 보아서 단순히 지를 사랑한다는 것일 뿐, 그것만으로는 무엇을 연구하는 학문인지 알 수가 없다. 경제학이나 물리학 등의 학문과는 달리, 철학이라는 이름만 듣고는 철학이라는 학문의 내용을 이해할 수 없는 것이다. 이는 철학이라는 학문의 대상이 결코 일정하지 않다는 뜻이기도 하다.

25

SECTION 05. 철학

플라톤과 이데아론

P.064

정답	1. ① 2. ⑤ 3. (1) T (2) F (3) F

본문 필기노트

① Plato (c. 400 BC) was a famous Greek philosopher and prized student of Socrates. ② In 385 BC, he founded a school [called the Academy], where rich young men, and even some women, studied philosophy and other subjects. ③ Plato was both an idealist and a rationalist. ④ He divided reality into two: On the one hand we have *idea* or *ideal*. ⑤ This is ultimate reality, which is eternal and spiritual. ⑥ On the other hand, there are *phenomena*, which are an imperfect manifestation of the ideal because they appear in the material, physical world, and are associated with matter, time, and space.

실재에 관한 플라톤의 구분: 이데아와 현상

⑦ Whereas phenomena are illusions [which decay and die], ideals are unchanging and perfect. ⑧ Phenomena are inferior to ideals. ⑨ For example, the idea (of a triangle) — the properties of its form — is eternal. ⑩ Any individual triangle [found in the everyday world] is never quite perfect: they may be a little crooked, or the lines a little thick, or the angles not quite right. ⑪ They are only ever an approximation of the ideal. ⑫ Ideals are the basis of science: the law of gravity, $E=mc^2$, and so on — these are the unchanging laws of the universe. ⑬ Ideals are available to us through thought, while phenomena are experienced through our senses. ⑭ So, naturally, thought is a vastly superior means [to get to the truth]. ⑮ This is what makes Plato a rationalist, as opposed to an empiricist. ⑯ Senses can only give you information about the ever-changing and imperfect world of phenomena, / and so can only provide you with implications about ultimate reality, not reality itself.

이데아와 현상의 비교 · 대조

본문해석

① 플라톤(기원전 400년경)은 유명한 그리스 철학자였고 소크라테스의 소중한 학생이었다. ② 그는 기원전 385년에, 아카데미라고 불리는 학교를 설립했는데, 여기서 부유한 젊은 청년들과 심지어 일부 여성들까지 철학 및 기타 과목들을 공부했다. ③ 플라톤은 이상주의자면서 합리주의자였다. ④ 그는 현실을(세계를) 둘로 나누었는데, 한편으로 우리는 이데아, 즉 이상을 가지고 있다. ⑤ 이것은 궁극적인 현실(세계)로, 영원하며 정신적이다. ⑥ 다른 한편으로 현상들이 있는데, 그것들은 물질적이고 물리적인 세계에서 나타나며, 물질, 시간, 그리고 공간과 관련되어 있기 때문에 이상의 불완전한 표현이다.

⑦ 현상은 쇠퇴하다 사라지는 환영인 반면에, 이상은 불변하며 완전하다. ⑧ 현상은 이상보다 열등하다. ⑨ 예를 들어, 삼각형의 이상, 즉 그 형태의 속성들은 영원하다. ⑩ 일상 세계에서 발견되는 어떠한 개별 삼각형도 결코 절대적으로 완벽하지 않다. 즉 약간 굽었거나, 선들이 약간 두껍거나, 혹은 각도가 전혀 맞지 않을 수 있다. ⑪ 그것들은 항상 이상에 근접한 것일 뿐이다. ⑫ 이상은 과학의 기초로, 중력의 법칙, $E=mc^2$ 등은 우주의 변하지 않는 법칙들이다. ⑬ 이상은 사고를 통해 우리가 접할 수 있는 반면에, 현상은 우리의 감각을 통해 경험된다. ⑭ 그러므로 당연히 사고는 진리에 도달하게 하는 매우 우수한 수단이다. ⑮ 이것이 플라톤을 경험주의자와 대조되는 것으로서의 합리주의자로 만드는 것이다. ⑯ 감각은 당신에게 현상이라는 변화무쌍하고 불완전한 세계에 대한 정보만을 줄 수 있을 뿐이며, 따라서 당신에게 실재 그 자체가 아닌 궁극적 실재에 대한 암시만을 제공할 수 있을 뿐이다.

본문파악

이 글은 고대 그리스의 철학자 플라톤과 그의 철학 사상인 이데아론에 대한 것이다. 첫째 단락에서는 플라톤에 대해 소개하면서 세계를 이데아와 현상으로 구분한 그의 이데아론에 대해 설명하고 있다. 둘째 단락에서는 현상과 이데아의 개념에 대해 좀더 구체적으로 짚어보고, 사고를 통해 진리에 도달할 수 있다고 보는 플라톤의 합리주의자적인 면모에 대해 언급하고 있다.

문제풀이

1. 이 글은 플라톤과 그의 이데아론에 대해 다루고 있다. 따라서 주제로는 '① 플라톤의 세계관: 이원론'이 적절하다.
   ② 진리를 찾는 과정 ③ 세계를 이해하는 다양한 방법 ④ 고대 그리스인들의 견해 ⑤ 철학에서의 플라톤의 뛰어난 업적

2. ⑬~⑭ 번 문장에 현상은 '감각(sense)'을 통해 경험되고, 진리는 '사고(thought)'를 통해 도달할 수 있다는 내용이 나오므로, ⑤에서는 sense와 thought의 위치가 바뀌어야 한다.
   ①~④ (⑤~⑦번 문장 참조)

3. 《해석》 다음 진술에 대해 T(참) 또는 F(거짓)로 표시하시오.
   (1) 플라톤의 아카데미에서는 남자와 여자 모두 철학을 공부할 수 있었다. (②번 문장 참조)
   (2) 삼각형의 이상은 일상생활의 제한된 조건 하에서 실현될 수 있다. → ⑨~⑪번 문장을 보면 틀린 내용임을 알 수 있다.
   (3) 플라톤은 진리에 도달하는 수단으로 사고와 감각에 동등한 비중을 두었다. → ⑭번 문장을 보면 사고가 진리에 도달하는 우수한 수단이라고 했고 ⑧번 문장에서 현상(감각)이 이상(사고)보다 열등하다고 했다.

구문해설

⑥ ... because they **appear** in the material, physical world, and **are** associated with matter, time, and space.

▷ 앞 문장의 which 이하의 내용에 대한 이유에 해당하는 절이다.
▷ 주어 they에 동사 appear와 are가 and로 병렬연결되어 있다.

⑯ Senses can only give you information (**about** the ever-changing and imperfect world of phenomena), **and so** can only provide you with implications (**about** ultimate reality, **not** reality itself).

▷ ( ) 표시된 2개의 about 이하는 '~에 대한'의 의미로 각각 information, implications를 수식한다.
▷ and so는 '따라서'의 의미로 결과를 나타낸다.
▷ not 이하는 '~이 아닌'의 의미로 ultimate reality를 부연 설명한다.

플라톤의 이데아

이데아는 플라톤 철학의 기본 개념으로 동사 '이데인(idein: 보다, 알다)'의 파생어이다. 원래는 '보이는 것', 모양 · 모습, 그리고 물건의 형식이나 종류를 의미했지만, 플라톤 철학에서는 육안(肉眼)이 아니라 영혼의 눈으로 볼 수 있는 형상을 의미한다. 그것은 아이데스(Aides: 보이지 않는 것)라고 불리며, 끊임없이 변하는 잡다한 감각 세계의 사물과 달리 이성(理性)만이 파악할 수 있는 영원불변하고 단일한 세계이다. 감각세계의 사물은 이데아를 본떠 이루어지는 것이지만, 그것은 진실한 존재가 아니고, 이데아야말로 진실한 존재이며 철학의 궁극적 목적이다. 이데아는 우리의 마음이나 정신 가운데에 있는, 즉 우리의 사고가 만들어 낸 하나의 관념이나 개념에 그치는 단순한 사유물이 아니라 객관적 실재이다. 그것은 사물뿐만 아니라 자연적 사물이나 예술품, 가치 있는 것들과 나쁘고 쓸모없는 것들에도 그들의 이데아가 있다. 순수하고 독립적이고 실재인 이데아들은 현상계의 원형이자 이상적 세계인 이데아계를 구성한다. 다시 말해 경험적인 감각의 세계는 생성, 변화, 운동, 소멸하는 유동의 세계로 단지 현상(現像)에 불과하지만, 이데아계는 현상의 배후에 존재하는 참된 실재이다.

26 SECTION 06. 미디어
매스미디어의 영향력

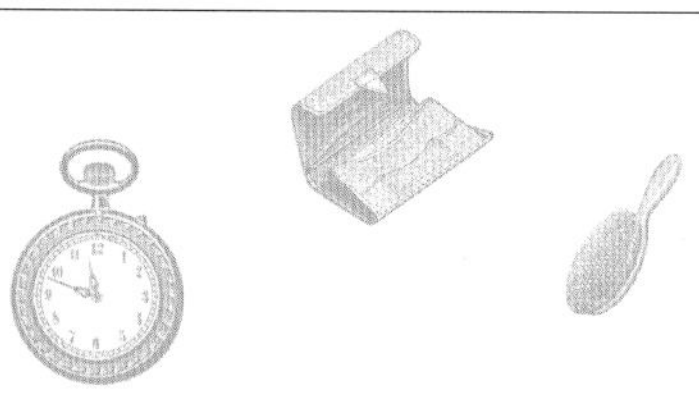

P.070

정답 | 1. (1) ④ (2) ② (3) ③ (4) ① 2. (1) T (2) T (3) F (4) F

본문 필기노트

① The modern industrialized world is saturated with the mass media. ② The
~으로 가득 차 있다
television in the living room, the magazines on the coffee table, the radio in the
~에 ~(위)에 ~에
car, and the billboards by the roadside / are just a few of the outlets [used by the
~ 곁에[옆에] 있는 V ~ 중의
mass media to deliver their constant stream of advertising, news, opinion, and other
전달하기 위해서(부사적 용법)
forms of mass communication].

현대 산업사회의 범람하는 매스미디어

③ Because the mass media are so firmly established in industrialized countries, they
S
strongly influence how those populations view the world. ④ In the United States, /
V O
nearly all the news stations and newspapers are owned by one major news network.
~에 의해 소유되다
⑤ Thus the American public now experiences all major news events through the
V ~을 통해서
interpretative eyes (of one powerful newsgroup).

거대 언론사의 매스미디어 독점

not only A (but) also B: A뿐만 아니라 B도 역시
⑥ Of course, not only do news media interpret the news, they also create the news
V S (but)
by choosing what events to report. ⑦ The "top story" of the day is selected from the
by v-ing: ~함으로써 =what events they should report
millions of things [that happen each particular day]. ⑧ After a news story is selected,
주격 관 · 대
managerial decisions are made on how much time or space to give it, / whom
~에 대해 =the news story
to interview, / and what pictures to use. ⑨ All of these decisions create the
~에 대한 V
audience's view of the world, putting those [who influence the decision-making]
=and they put(분사구문) 주격 관 · 대
in an extremely powerful position.
~에, ~로

뉴스 결정권을 가진 언론기관의 영향력

⑩ The media, therefore, have enormous importance to conflict resolution /
~에 대해
because they are the primary source of information regarding conflicts in society.
~에 관한(전치사)
⑪ If a situation doesn't make the news, / it simply does not exist for most people.
뉴스가 되다
⑫ When peaceful options (such as negotiation and other collaborative problem-
S A such as B: B와 같은 A

본문해석

① 현대의 산업화된 세상은 매스미디어로 가득 차 있다. ② 거실에 있는 텔레비전, 커피테이블 위의 잡지, 차량 내 라디오, 그리고 길가의 광고판은 광고, 뉴스, 의견 및 기타 매스컴의 끊임없는 흐름을 전하기 위해 매스미디어에 의해 사용되는 표현 수단 중 몇 가지 예일 뿐이다.

③ 매스미디어는 산업국가들 내에서 매우 확고한 입지를 구축하고 있기 때문에, 그것은 그 나라 사람들이 세계를 보는 방식에 강한 영향을 미친다. ④ 미국에서는, 거의 모든 뉴스 방송사와 신문사들이 한 대형 뉴스 네트워크에 의해 소유되어 있다. ⑤ 따라서 미국 국민은 현재 뉴스거리가 되는 모든 주요한 사건들을 하나의 강력한 언론그룹이 해석한 시각을 통해 경험한다.

⑥ 물론 뉴스매체는 뉴스를 해석할 뿐만 아니라, 어떤 사건을 보도할지 선택함으로써 뉴스를 만들어 내기도 한다. ⑦ 그날의 '톱기사'는 각각의 특정한 날에 일어나는 수백만 건의 사건들 중에서 선택된다. ⑧ 기사가 선정되면 거기에 얼마나 많은 시간이나 지면을 할애할지, 누구를 인터뷰할지, 그리고 어떤 사진을 사용할지에 대해 관리자선의 결정이 이루어진다. ⑨ 이 모든 결정들은 세계에 대한 시청자(독자)의 시각을 형성시켜 주고, 의사 결정에 영향을 미치는 사람들을 매우 권력 있는 지위에 있게 만든다.

⑩ 그러므로 미디어는 사회 내의 갈등에 관한 정보의 주요한 원천이므로 갈등 해결에 막대한 중요성을 갖는다. ⑪ 만일 어떤 상황이 뉴스가 되지 못하면, 그것은 다수의 사람들을 위해 존재하는 것이 전혀 아니다. ⑫ 협상과 기타 상호 협력적인 문제 해결 기법들과 같은 평화적인 대안들이 다뤄지지 않

solving techniques) are not covered, / or their successes are not reported, / they become invisible and are not likely to be considered or even understood (as) possible options in the management of a conflict.

V (are) / V_1 (become) / V_2 (are not likely to) be likely to-v: ~일 것 같다 / as: ~로서

거나, 그것들의 성공(성공사례)이 보도되지 않으면, 그 평화적인 대안들은 자취를 감추게 되고, 따라서 그것들은 갈등을 처리하는 데 있어 가능한 대안들로 고려되거나 심지어는 인식되지도 않을 것이다.

사회 갈등 해결을 위한 매스미디어의 역할과 영향력

본문파악

이 글은 현대 산업사회에 미치는 매스미디어의 영향력에 관한 것이다. 첫째 단락은 도입부로 매스미디어가 범람하는 현대 산업사회에 대해 묘사하고 있다. 둘째 단락에서는 미국을 예로 들면서 뉴스가 대형 언론 · 방송사에 의해 독점되어 있음을 설명하고 있다. 셋째 단락은 뉴스와 뉴스 관계자들의 영향력에 관한 내용이고, 넷째 단락은 사회적 갈등 해결자로서의 미디어의 역할 또는 영향력에 대한 내용이다.

문제풀이

1. 《해석》 각 단락의 요지는 무엇인가? 아래의 상자 안에서 알맞은 선택지를 고르시오.
   필기노트의 단락 요약을 참조한다.
   ① 사회의 갈등을 해결하는 데 있어 매스미디어의 중요한 역할 ② 주요 뉴스그룹들에 의한 매스미디어의 독점
   ③ 뉴스를 만드는 사람들의 엄청난 영향력 ④ 매스미디어로 넘쳐나는 현대 사회

2. 《해석》 다음 진술에 대해 T(참) 또는 F(거짓)로 표시하시오.
   (1) 산업화된 국가에서는 매스미디어가 모든 사람들이 그것을 통해 세상을 바라보는 창의 역할을 한다. (③번 문장 참조)
   (2) 뉴스 사건들은 시청자에게 제시되기 전에 먼저 영향력 있는 뉴스그룹에 의해 선택된다. (⑥~⑦번 문장 참조)
   (3) 뉴스는 우리가 공정하고 객관적인 태도로 실제 세상을 바라볼 수 있게 해준다. → ③, ⑨번 문장에서 대중은 매스미디어에 의해 형성된 시각으로 세상을 보기 때문에 비판적이거나 공정할 수 없을 것임을 추론할 수 있다.
   (4) 매스미디어는 사회적 갈등에 직접적인 해결책을 제시한다. → ⑩번 문장에 매스미디어가 갈등 해결을 위해 중요한 역할을 한다고 언급되어 있지만, 직접적인 해결책을 제시한다는 언급은 없다.

구문해설

⑥ Of course, **not only** do news media interpret the news, (**but**) they **also** create the news by choosing what events to report.

(not only: 부정어구 / do: V / news media: S)

▷ 「not only A (but) also B」는 'A뿐만 아니라 B도'의 의미로, 여기서는 but이 생략되었으며, 부정어구 not only가 문두에 강조되어 나감에 따라 주어와 동사가 도치되었다.

어젠다 세팅(agenda setting)

우리말로는 '의제설정'이라고도 하며 매스미디어가 의식적 또는 무의식적으로 현행 이슈에 대한 공중의 생각과 토론을 설정하는 방식을 나타내는 데 사용되는 용어다. 매스미디어의 의제설정 기능이란 미디어가 뉴스나 시사 프로그램 등을 통해 중요하다고 보도하는 주제(미디어의제)가 공중에게도 중요한 주제(공중의제)로 되는 것을 말한다. 어떠한 사회적 문제를 강조, 보도함으로써 그것을 사회의 중요한 이슈(issue)로 부각시켜 주는 기능으로서 의제설정 기능은 1950-1960년대에 매스미디어가 수용자의 태도 변화에 거의 효과가 없다는 제한효과 이론(limited-effect theory)이 지배적인 상황에서 매스미디어가 태도 변화에는 효과가 적지만 지적 측면에는 효과가 있다는 주장의 일환으로 제기되었다.

27

SECTION 06. 미디어

뉴미디어와 기자의 역할

P.072

정답	1. ④ 2. monopoly, information 3. 전문가적 수준을 유지하고 질 중심의 자료를 제공하기 위해 기술의 변화를 받아들여야 한다. 4. ③

본문 필기노트

① There has been considerable change in (~에 (있어)) the nature (본질) of journalism and employment for journalists in recent years (최근 몇 년 동안). ② Most notably, the growth of online media / is encouraging newspapers and broadcasting companies to launch their own successful Internet ventures, (encourage+O+to-v: O를 ~하도록 장려하다) / creating (=and it creates(분사구문)) more jobs for journalists. ③ Despite (~에도 불구하고) some predictions [that (동격의 that) online technology / would reduce journalists' employment / by automating (by v-ing: ~함으로써) their jobs], the demand for (~에 대한) reporters and editors has risen. ④ Technological developments such as (A such as B: B와 같은 A) the Internet / are in many respects (여러 가지 면에서) helping journalists do (help+O+동사원형: O가 ~하도록 돕다) their jobs better and more efficiently.

온라인 매체의 발달이 저널리즘의 본질과 기자들의 채용에 미친 영향

⑤ However, technological change does present (do[does, did]+동사원형: 동사 강조(정말로)) some concerns and challenges. ⑥ Freelancers are becoming increasingly concerned about (become[be] concerned about: ~에 대해 걱정하다) electronic re-publication rights for (~에 대한) their stories. ⑦ Journalists have reason to be concerned (have reason to-v: ~할 이유가 있다) that as (~함에 따라(접속사)) new media and technology change the way [news is gathered and distributed] (관계부사절), ethics could be ignored in the rush (그에 휩쓸려), / their (=journalists') independence could be threatened, / and public trust in (~에 대한) the news media could decline further.

기술 발달이 가져올 수 있는 문제점

⑧ The monopoly [that newspapers and broadcasters once enjoyed] (목적격 관·대) has rapidly been eroded by online media, and now anybody (with access to (~로의 접근) a computer) can become a reporter. ⑨ As a result (결과적으로), media institutions / are having to answer more questions / from their audiences / in regard to (~에 관한[관하여]) accuracy. ⑩ This loss of exclusivity (with regard to (~에 관한) information), and the weakening of the role of the media as (~로서) news arbitrators, began (V_1) in the 1990s, and continues (V_2) to bring further changes to (bring A to B: A를 B에 가져오다) the professional and social functions of the journalist. ⑪ Journalists need to embrace (need to-v: ~할 필요가 있다) the technological changes in order to (~하기 위하여) retain their professional standards and provide quality-oriented materials; otherwise (그렇지 않으면), / they may be severely challenged / by (~에 의해 도전을 받다) the great influx of other news sources.

온라인 매체가 확산되는 환경 속에서 기자들에게 요구되는 점

본문해석

① 최근 몇 년간 저널리즘의 본질과 기자 채용에 상당한 변화가 있어 왔다. ② 가장 주목할 만한 것은, 온라인 매체의 성장이 신문사와 방송사들을 그들 자신의 성공적인 인터넷 신규 사업에 착수하도록 고무시키고 있으며, 이는 기자들에게 보다 많은 일자리를 창출한다. ③ 온라인 기술이 기자의 업무를 자동화하여 그들의 고용을 감소시킬 것이라는 일부 예측에도 불구하고, 기자 및 편집자에 대한 수요는 증가해왔다. ④ 인터넷 같은 과학기술의 발전은 기자들이 자신의 일을 보다 우수하고 효율적으로 하도록 여러 면에서 돕고 있다.

⑤ 그러나 과학기술의 변화는 진정 몇 가지 근심거리와 문제들을 제시한다. ⑥ 프리랜서들은 그들의 기사에 대한 전자 재출판권에 대해 점점 더 우려하고 있다. ⑦ 기자들에게는 새로운 매체와 기술이 뉴스가 수집되고 배급되는 방식을 변화시킴에 따라 그에 휩쓸려 윤리가 무시되고, 그들의 독립이 위협받으며, 뉴스 매체에 대한 대중의 신뢰가 보다 더 줄어드는 것을 걱정할 이유가 생겼다.

⑧ 한때 신문사와 방송사가 누렸던 독점은 온라인 매체에 의해 급속히 침식되었고, 이제는 컴퓨터에 접근할 수 있는 사람이라면 누구나 다 기자가 될 수 있다. ⑨ 그 결과, 매체기관들은 정확성에 관하여 대중들로부터의 보다 많은 질문들에 답해야 할 것이다. ⑩ 정보에 관한 이와 같은 독점권의 손실과 뉴스 중재자로서의 매체 역할의 약화는 1990년대에 시작되었고, 기자의 직업적이고 사회적인 역할에 더 큰 변화를 계속해서 가져오고 있다. ⑪ 기자들은 그들의 전문가적 수준을 유지하고 질에 중점을 둔 자료를 제공하기 위하여 기술의 변화를 받아들일 필요가 있는데, 그렇지 않으면 다른 뉴스 출처들의 대량 유입에 의해 심각하게 도전을 받을 수 있다.

본문파악

이 글은 온라인 매체의 발달로 인한 저널리즘의 본질 및 기자들의 역할 변화에 대해 설명하고 있다. 첫째 단락은 온라인 매체의 발달이 언론 · 방송에 미친 긍정적 영향에 대해 언급하고 있고, 둘째 단락은 인터넷 확산과 같은 기술 발달이 야기할 수 있는 문제점들에 대해 언급하고 있다. 셋째 단락은 마무리 단락으로, 변화된 매체 환경 속에서 기자들에게 요구되는 자질이 무엇인지에 대해 언급하고 있다.

문제풀이

1. 《해석》 위 글의 제목으로 가장 적절한 것은?
이 글은 새로운 매체의 발달로 저널리즘의 본질과 기자들의 역할에 변화가 생겼다는 내용이다. 따라서 제목으로는 '④ 새로운 매체와 기자의 역할'이 가장 적절하다.
① 새로운 매체: 그것이 우리에게 무엇을 가져다주는가?
② 왜 우리는 새로운 매체에 적응해야 하는가
③ 인터넷 시대의 대중 저널리즘
⑤ 매체기관들과 그들의 공적 의무

2. 《해석》 위 글에 따르면, 인터넷의 확산으로 신문사와 방송사들이 한때 가졌던 독점권이 약화되었는데, 이제는 컴퓨터를 가진 사람이라면 누구나 정보를 자유롭게 이용할 수 있기 때문이다. (각 단어는 본문에서)
⑧, ⑩번 문장 참조

3. ⑪번 문장 참조

4. (A)에는 '상당한' 변화라는 의미가 문맥상 자연스러우므로 considerable이 와야 하고, (B)에는 앞에 언급된 내용의 결과 뉴스 매체에 대한 대중의 신뢰가 '줄어드는' 것이 적절하므로 decline이 와야 하며, (C)에는 컴퓨터에 대한 '접근'이라는 의미의 access가 와야 한다.
cf. considerate(사려 깊은) / incline(기울다) / assess(평가하다)

구문해설

⑦ Journalists have reason **to be concerned that** [**as** new media and technology **change** the way [news is gathered and distributed]], ethics could be ignored in the rush, ...

▷ to be concerned 이하는 reason을 수식하는 형용사적 용법의 to부정사구이다.
▷ that 이하는 concerned의 목적어 역할을 하는 명사절이다.
▷ [ ] 부분의 as ... distributed는 that절 속에 쓰인 부사절로, 이때의 as는 '~함에 따라'의 의미이고, as절의 동사는 change이다.
▷ [ ] 표시된 news ... distributed는 선행사 the way를 수식하는 관계부사절이다. 선행사 the way와 관계부사 how는 같이 쓰지 않는다.

⑨ As a result, media institutions **are having to answer** more questions (**from** their audiences) (**in regard to** accuracy).

▷ are having to-v는 have to-v의 현재진행형으로 '~해야 할 것이다'의 의미이다. 이와 같이 현재진행형은 가까운 미래를 나타내기도 한다.
▷ ( ) 표시된 두 개의 전치사구는 각각 앞에 있는 more questions를 수식한다.

인터넷의 발달이 가져온 기자와 언론사의 역할 변화

지금까지 우리는 신문과 라디오, TV 등의 매스미디어를 통해 정보를 접해왔다. 이러한 종류의 대중매체들은 대기업들의 후원을 받았는데, 그것은 기업들이 자신의 상품과 서비스를 소비자에게 판매하기 위해 매스미디어에 제공한 광고비였다. 또한 국가라는 통치기구의 권력 역시 매스미디어가 표현할 수 있는 방향과 한계를 규정짓고 제한하는 역할을 해왔다. 궁극적으로 언론은 자본과 권력의 영향 하에 놓여 있었던 것이다.
그러나 인터넷의 등장은 언론에 혁명적인 변화를 가져왔다. 기존에는 정보의 수집과 전달이 매스미디어에 한정되어 있었지만, 모든 사람이 정보의 생산, 가공, 그리고 유통에 참여할 수 있는 시대로 바뀌면서 누구나 인터넷을 통해 자신을 알리고 소식과 정보, 광고를 전할 수 있게 되었다. 이에 따라 기자들의 역할에도 변화가 필요하게 되었다. 기자들은 민감한 네티즌 독자들의 반응에 대응하기 위해 속보의 전달뿐만 아니라 도표, 사진 등 다양한 멀티미디어 기술을 기반으로 양과 질에서 기존 신문방송에 실린 뉴스 그 이상의 뉴스를 만들어 전달하도록 요구되고 있다.

28 SECTION 06. 미디어

매스미디어와 문화적 신화

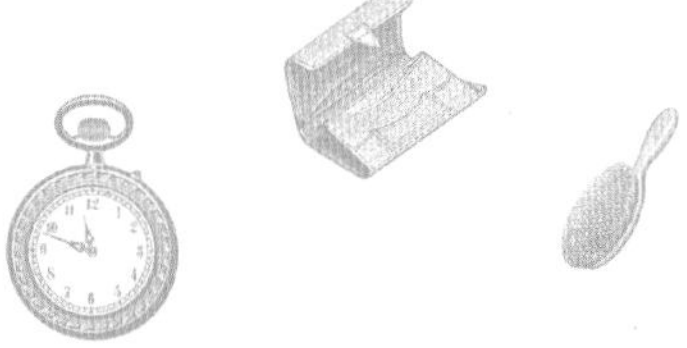

P.074

정답	1. ③　2. ③　3. 문화적 신화가 소비자들의 사고와 가치관에 영향을 미쳐, 문화적 신화에 의해 지배당하는 것을 모른 채 대중들이 상품을 소비하는 것　4. ② composed of → are composed of

본문 필기노트

① The mass media is responsible for creating cultural symbols, which greatly impact our society. ② As well as having overt primary meanings, / these cultural symbols also have secondary, hidden meanings [which are charged with psychological, emotional or ideological values]. ③ It is through the constant production of these symbols that cultural myths are produced.

~에 대해 책임이 있다 / which의 선행사 / 주격 관 · 대(계속적 용법) / ~할 뿐만 아니라 / 주격 관 · 대 / ~로 가득 차 있다 / It is ~ that ... 강조구문: …한 것은 바로 ~이다

매스미디어에 의해 생산된 문화적 상징과 신화

④ These myths are composed of stories, stereotypes, and images [that symbolize the main aspects of culture]. ⑤ (B) For example, the mass media bombards us with images of female physical perfection. ⑥ (C) Through these, the modern woman has been taught the cultural myth [that unless she is able to improve every feature of her face and body, she will never be considered successful as a woman]. ⑦ (A) Thus, women have been conditioned to spend their money on expensive clothes and cosmetic products.

~으로 구성되다 / 주격 관 · 대 / bombard A with B: A에게 B를 퍼붓다 / 동격의 that / 배워 왔다(현재완료 계속) / = / 만약 ~이 아니라면(=if ~ not) / ~로서(전치사) / be conditioned to-v: ~하도록 조건화되다 / ~에

문화적 신화의 구성 요소와 그 예

⑧ Far from being a true representation of society, / cultural myths are created by advertisers, journalists, television producers and movie directors. ⑨ These myths influence consumers' thoughts and values, working to create a society [in which people consume products / without thinking about the origins of the myths]. ⑩ Critics of mass culture consider it to be basic conditioning and manipulation. ⑪ They think cultural producers use myths to make large profits. ⑫ When viewed this way, / mass culture is nothing more than an illusion [created by cultural industries].

~이 아닌, ~이기는커녕 / S / V / O / =and they work(결과의 분사구문) / 목적격 관 · 대 / consider+O+to-v: O를 ~하다고 여기다 / (that) / use+O+to-v: ~하기 위해 O를 사용하다, O를 사용하여 ~하다 / (it is) / ~에 지나지 않는

문화적 신화와 대중문화

본문해석

① 매스미디어는 문화적 상징을 만들어 내는 것에 대해 책임이 있는데, 그것은 우리 사회에 크게 영향을 미친다. ② 이러한 문화적 상징들은 명시적인 1차적 의미를 지니고 있을 뿐만 아니라 심리적, 정서적, 또는 이데올로기적인 가치들로 가득 차 있는 부차적이고 숨겨진 의미 또한 지니고 있다. ③ 문화적 신화가 만들어지는 것은 바로 이러한 상징들의 끊임없는 생산을 통해서이다.

④ 이러한 신화들은 문화의 주요 측면을 상징하는 이야기, 고정관념, 그리고 이미지들로 구성되어 있다. ⑤ (B) 예를 들어, 매스미디어는 우리에게 육체적으로 완벽한 여성의 이미지들을 퍼붓는다. ⑥ (C) 이것들을 통해, 현대 여성은 만일 그녀가 자신의 얼굴과 신체의 모든 특징을 개선할 수 없다면 결코 여성으로서 성공한 것으로 여겨지지 못할 것이라는 문화적 신화를 배워 왔다. ⑦ (A) 따라서 여성들은 값비싼 옷과 화장품에 그들의 돈을 쓰도록 조건화 되었다.

⑧ 사회의 사실적 표현이기는커녕, 문화적 신화는 광고주, 기자, 텔레비전 프로듀서 및 영화감독들에 의해 만들어진다. ⑨ 이러한 신화들은 소비자의 사고와 가치관에 영향을 미쳐, 사람들이 그 신화의 기원에 대해서는 생각지도 않고 제품을 소비하는 사회를 만들도록 작용한다. ⑩ 대중문화 비평가들은 그것을 기본적인 조건화와 조작이라고 여긴다. ⑪ 그들은 문화 생산자들이 큰 이익을 내기 위해 신화를 이용한다고 생각한다. ⑫ 이런 식으로 볼 때, 대중문화는 문화산업에 의해 만들어진 환상에 지나지 않는다.

본문파악

이 글은 문화적 신화가 대중과 대중문화에 미치는 영향력에 대해 이야기하고 있다. 첫째 단락은 매스미디어가 문화적 상징을 만들어 내고 이것들이 모여서 문화적 신화를 만들어 낸다는 내용이며, 둘째 단락은 예시를 통해 문화적 신화를 구체적으로 설명하고 있다. 셋째 단락은 문화적 신화의 생산 주체가 매스미디어 관계자들이라는 것을 언급하면서, 대중문화는 결국 문화산업이 만들어 낸 환상이라고 이야기하고 있다.

문제풀이

1. 《해석》 위 글의 주제는 무엇인가?
   이 글은 매스미디어가 만들어 낸 문화적 신화의 영향력에 대해 이야기하고 있으므로, 주제로는 '③ 매스미디어에 의해 만들어진 문화적 신화'가 가장 적절하다.
   ① 매스미디어와 사회적 가치　　② 매스미디어와 대량생산
   ④ 대중문화의 다양한 특징　　⑤ 문화적 신화가 현대 여성에 미치는 영향

2. (A)~(C)는 ④번 문장의 예에 해당하므로 For example이 들어간 (B)가 맨 처음에 와야 하고, (C)의 these는 (B)의 images of female physical perfection을 가리키므로 (C)가 (B) 다음에 와야 한다. (A)는 (C)와 (B)에 이어서 일어난 결과에 해당하므로 맨 마지막에 오는 것이 적절하다.

3. 「consider+O+to-v」는 'O를 ~하다고 여기다'의 의미이다. it은 '문화적 신화가 소비자들의 사고와 가치관 및 소비문화에 영향을 미친다'는 앞 문장의 내용을 가리킨다. (⑨번 문장 참조)

4. ② 「be composed of」는 '~으로 구성되다'라는 의미이며, 현재의 사실을 나타내기 때문에 현재시제를 사용하여 are composed of로 고치는 것이 알맞다.

구문해설

⑨ These myths influence consumers' thoughts and values, **working** to create a society [in which people consume products **without thinking** about the origins of the myths].

▷ working 이하는 결과의 분사구문이다.
▷ without v-ing: '~하지 않고'

⑫ **When (it is) viewed** this way, mass culture is **nothing more than** an illusion [created by cultural industries].

▷ When과 viewed 사이에는 it is가 생략된 것이며, 이와 같이 때를 나타내는 부사절의 주어가 주절 주어와 동일할 경우 부사절의 〈주어+be동사〉는 생략이 가능하다.
▷ nothing more than ~: '~에 불과한', '~에 지나지 않는'

29 SECTION 06. 미디어
게이트키퍼(gatekeeper)

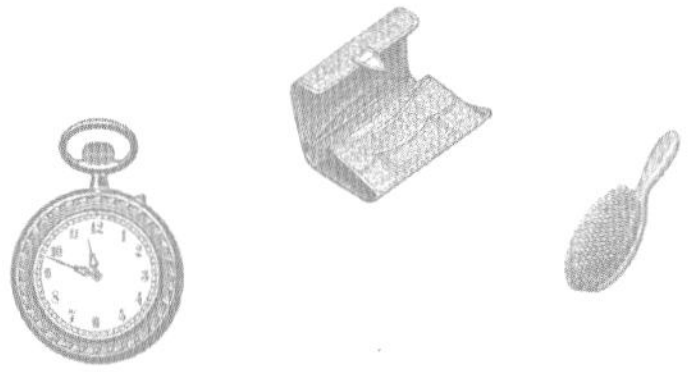

P.076

정답 1. 어떤 경기를 방송으로 내보낼지 선택하고 결정하는 사람 2. ④ 3. ② 4. 시청자 사전 수요, 중계 비용, 국민의 성향

본문 필기노트

① Many different sports events / take place in the Olympics, / and each appeals to
개최되다(=are held) ~에게
a different audience. ② For example, while track events appeal to some viewers,
~인 반면에 some ~, others ...:
/ archery appeals to others. ③ If both events are taking place simultaneously, /
몇몇은 ~, 다른 나머지는 …
then it is the job of gatekeepers [to decide which event to televise]. ④ Gatekeepers
가주어 ~의 to 이하는 진주어
estimate / [whether the demand for track events / is greater than the demand
whether(~인지 아닌지) 이하는 목적어 ~에 대한 ~보다 더 크다
for archery]. ⑤ If the demand [to see both] is equal, / then gatekeepers consider
~에 대한 보려는(형용사적 용법) consider v-ing: ~하는 것을 고려하다
broadcasting both events by continually switching between the two. ⑥ However, if
by v-ing: ~함으로써
possible, gatekeepers try to avoid this option / as it costs twice as much as covering
가능하면 try to-v: ~하려고 노력하다 ~이기 때문에(접속사) 두 배만큼이나 많은(두 배 더 많은)
just one event. ⑦ As a result, the majority of Olympics television coverage is of a
~의 =about
single event at a time. ⑧ Events such as table tennis / are given a lot of coverage
A such as B : B와 같은 A 주어진다
/ because they last for hours, / and television companies only have to pay a lump
몇 시간 동안 only have to-v: ~하기만 하면 된다
sum / to cover them. ⑨ Shorter events such as pole-vaulting / are avoided by
중계하기 위해서(부사적 용법)
smaller TV channels / because they are relatively more expensive to cover.
중계하기에(는)(부사적 용법)

올림픽 중계방송 시 게이트키퍼의 결정에 영향을 미치는 요인: 시청 수요, 비용

⑩ Another way [that gatekeepers make their decisions] is according to nationality
관계부사(방법) ~에 따라
bias. ⑪ For example, Chinese channels tend to give Chinese gymnasts considerable
tend to-v: ~하는 경향이 있다 give A B: A에게 B를 주다
coverage. ⑫ English-speaking channels tend to give a lot of coverage to athletes
give A to B: A를 B에게 주다
(from the U.S.A. and Great Britain). ⑬ All networks cover famous athletes in order to
S V O ~하기 위해서
increase the audience. ⑭ For example, in the 2000 Olympics, / Hong Kong channels
gave extensive coverage / to the local 1996 gold-medalist windsurfer Lee San San.
=
⑮ However, when it became evident [that she was not going to win another
가주어 that 이하는 진주어
medal], / windsurfing coverage decreased considerably. ⑯ In the end, gatekeepers
결국
have to try to decide / [who the events will appeal to / and how many people will
간접의문문1 간접의문문2
watch them]. ⑰ This sometimes results in two or three channels covering the same
~의 결과를 초래하다

본문해석

① 올림픽에서는 많은 다양한 운동 경기가 열리며, 각 경기마다 좋아하는 시청자가 따로 있다. ② 예를 들어, 어떤 시청자들은 트랙 경기를 좋아하는 반면, 다른 시청자들은 양궁을 좋아한다. ③ 만일 두 경기가 동시에 개최되고 있다면, 어떤 경기를 방송으로 내보낼지를 결정하는 게 게이트키퍼의 일이다. ④ 게이트키퍼는 트랙 경기에 대한 수요가 양궁에 대한 수요보다 더 큰지 아닌지를 추정한다. ⑤ 만일 두 경기 모두를 보려는 수요가 같을 경우, 게이트키퍼들은 두 경기를 계속 번갈아 가면서 방송하는 것을 고려한다. ⑥ 그러나 이것은 한 경기만 중계하는 것보다 비용이 두 배가 들기 때문에 게이트키퍼들은 가능하면 이러한 선택을 피하려고 노력한다. ⑦ 결과적으로, 올림픽 TV 중계의 대부분은 한 번에 한 경기를 방송하고 있다. ⑧ 탁구와 같은 경기들은, 몇 시간씩 계속되고 그 경기들을 중계하기 위해 텔레비전 방송사들은 돈을 일괄 지급하기만 하면 되기 때문에, 중계 방송을 많이 한다. ⑨ 장대높이뛰기 같이 경기 시간이 보다 짧은 경기는 소규모 TV 방송사들이 회피를 하는데, 이는 중계 비용이 상대적으로 더 비싸기 때문이다.

⑩ 게이트키퍼들이 결정을 내리는 또 하나의 방법은 국민들의 성향을 따르는 것이다. ⑪ 예를 들어, 중국 방송사들은 중국 체조 선수들에게 상당한 시간을 할애하는 경향이 있다. ⑫ 영어 방송사들은 미국과 영국 선수들에게 많은 양의 방송 시간을 할애하는 경향이 있다. ⑬ 모든 방송사들은 시청률을 높이기 위해 유명 선수들을 방송한다. ⑭ 예를 들어, 2000년 올림픽 당시, 홍콩 방송사들은 자국 출신의 1996년 윈드서핑 금메달리스트인 리산산을 집중적으로 방송했다. ⑮ 그러나 그녀가 메달을 더 따지 못할 것이 분명해지자, 윈드서핑 방송이 상당량 줄었다. ⑯ 결국, 게이트키퍼들은 경기들이 누구에게 인기를 끌 것인지 그리고 얼마나 많은 사람들이 그 경기를 볼 것인지를 결정하기 위해 노력해야 한다. ⑰ 이것은 때때로 두 개 혹은 세 개 방송사가 시

event in the hope of attracting viewers.
~를 기대하여

청자를 사로잡기를 기대하여 동일한 경기를 방송하는 결과를 초래하기도 한다.

게이트키퍼들의 결정에 영향을 미치는 또 다른 요인: 국민의 성향

본문파악

이 글은 올림픽 경기 방송 시 게이트키퍼(gatekeeper)의 역할에 대해 설명한 것이다. 첫째 단락에서는 게이트키퍼의 결정에 영향을 미치는 요인으로 시청 수요 및 중계 비용을 언급하고, 둘째 단락에서는 또 다른 요인으로 국민의 성향을 들고 있다.

문제풀이

1. ③번 문장 참조

2. 빈칸 앞의 내용이 한 번에 두 경기를 방송하면 비용이 두 배로 든다는 내용이고, 빈칸 뒤의 내용이 올림픽 중계 대부분이 한 번에 한 경기를 중계한다는 내용이므로, (A)에는 결과를 나타내는 연결어구인 '④ As a result'가 적절하다.
① 예를 들어 ② 부가적으로 ③ 사실상 ⑤ 그럼에도 불구하고

3. 바로 앞의 ⑯번 문장에 게이트키퍼들이 시청자들에게 인기가 있을 경기를 선택하려고 노력한다는 내용이 나오고, 빈칸이 있는 문장에서 여러 방송사가 동시에 같은 경기를 중계한다는 내용이 나오므로, 빈칸에는 '② 시청자를 사로잡기'가 가장 적절하다.
① 비용 줄이기 ③ 더 나은 방송 ④ 일관성 유지하기 ⑤ 승리하기

4. 올림픽 경기 보도 시 게이트키퍼의 결정에 영향력을 미치는 요인으로 시청자의 사전 수요와 중계 비용이 첫째 단락에서 언급되었고, 둘째 단락에서 국민의 성향이 언급되었다.

구문해설

③ If both events are taking place simultaneously, then it is the job of gatekeepers to decide **which event to televise**.

▷ which event to televise는 decide의 목적어로 '어떤 경기를 방송해야 하는지'의 의미이며, 간접의문문인 which event they should televise를 〈의문사+to-v〉로 줄여 쓴 표현이다.

⑯ In the end, gatekeepers have to try to decide **who(m)** the events will appeal to and **how** many people will watch them.

▷ who(m) ... to와 how 이하는 동사 decide의 목적어 역할을 하는 명사절로, 어순이 〈의문사+주어+동사〉인 간접의문문이다.

⑰ This sometimes results in **two or three channels covering** the same event in the hope of attracting viewers.

▷ 동명사 covering의 의미상의 주어는 two or three channels이다.

30

SECTION 07. 역사

역사가는 사실을 기록한다

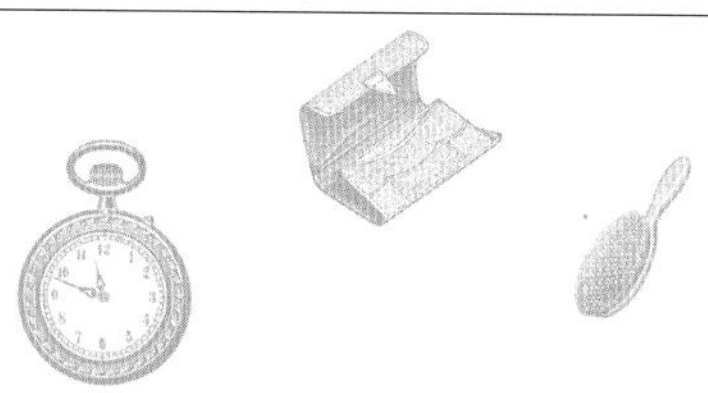

P.080

정답 | 1. 포스트모더니스트들은 사실과 허구 사이에 명백한 차이가 없다는 입장이고, 필자는 둘 사이에 분명한 차이가 있다는 입장이다.

본문 필기노트

① We historians have a responsibility to historical facts in general, and for
= have a responsibility to[for]: ~에 책임이 있다 일반적으로
criticizing the abuse of history in particular. ② I need say little about the first
특히, 특별히 조동사 거의 ~않다
of these responsibilities. ③ I would not have to say anything, but for two
one ~, the other ...: 하나는 ~, 다른 하나는 … =except
developments. ④ One is the current fashion [for novelists to base their plots
사태(=events) 의미상의 주어 기초를 두는(형용사적 용법)
on recorded reality / rather than inventing them, / thus fudging the border
~에 =사료, 역사 ~라기보다는 오히려 =they fudge(분사구문)
between historical fact and fiction]. ⑤ The other is the rise of "postmodernist"
which의 선행사
intellectual fashions in universities, (particularly in departments of literature and
삽입구
anthropology), [which imply / that all "facts" [claiming objective existence] are
주격 관·대(계속적 용법) that 이하는 목적어
simply intellectual constructions — in short, that there is no clear difference
부연설명 요컨대, 한마디로 말해서
between fact and fiction]. ⑥ But there is. ⑦ And for historians, the ability [to
between A and B: A와 B 사이에 (a clear difference ...) ~에게 있어서
distinguish between the two] is absolutely fundamental. ⑧ We cannot invent our
구별하는(형용사적 용법)
facts. ⑨ Either Elvis Presley is dead or he isn't. ⑩ The question can be answered
either A or B: A 또는 B 둘 중 하나 (dead)
unambiguously / on the basis of evidence, / in so far as reliable evidence is
~을 근거로 ~하는 한
available.

역사를 객관적으로 기술해야 할 필요성

본문해석

① 우리 역사가들은 일반적으로 역사적 사실에 책임이 있으며, 특히 역사의 오용을 비판할 책임이 있다. ② 책임들 중에서 첫 번째 것에 대해서는 거의 말할 필요가 없다. ③ 나는 두 가지 사태를 제외하고는 어떤 것도 말할 필요가 없을 것 같다. ④ 하나는 소설가들이 소설의 줄거리를 창작하기보다는 기록된 실제에 기초를 두어 역사적 사실과 허구 사이의 경계를 왜곡시키는 오늘날의 경향이다. ⑤ 다른 하나는 대학, 특히 문학과 인류학 분야에서의 '포스트모던적' 지적 경향의 발생인데, 이것(포스트모던적 지적 경향)은 객관적 존재임을 주장하는 모든 '사실들'이 단지 지적 구성물에 불과하다는, 한마디로 말해서 사실과 허구 사이에 명백한 차이가 존재하지 않는다는 것을 의미한다. ⑥ 하지만 분명한 차이가 있다. ⑦ 그리고 역사가에게 있어서, 그 둘을 구별하는 능력은 절대적으로 기본적인 것이다. ⑧ 우리는 사실을 창작해 낼 수 없다. ⑨ 엘비스 프레슬리는 죽었거나, 또는 죽지 않았거나 둘 중 하나다. ⑩ 이 문제는 믿을 만한 증거를 구할 수 있는 한 증거를 근거로 하여 분명하게 해결될 수 있다.

본문파악

이 글은 에릭 홉스봄(Eric Hobsbawm)의 「역사론(*On History*)」의 일부분으로, 역사가는 사료나 유물 등의 역사적 증거를 통해 역사를 객관적으로 기술해야 한다고 주장하는 글이다. ①번 문장과 ⑦번 문장에서 역사가의 책임에 대한 홉스봄의 견해를 알 수 있다.

문제풀이

1. 필자는 포스트모던적인 학문 경향에서는 사실과 허구 사이에 명백한 차이가 없는 것으로 여겨지지만(⑤번 문장), '그 둘의 차이는 있고(⑥번 문장), 역사가에게 그 둘을 구별하는 능력은 아주 기본적인 것이다'라고 말하고 있다(⑦번 문장).

구문해설

② I **need** say little about the first of these responsibilities.

▷ need(조동사)+동사원형: '~할 필요가 있다'
cf. need가 일반동사로 쓰이게 되면 같은 의미로 「need to-v」를 쓴다.
(예) He **need** not do the work. vs. He doesn't **need to do** the work. (그는 그 일을 할 필요가 없다.)

31 SECTION 07. 역사
역사는 '사실'인가?

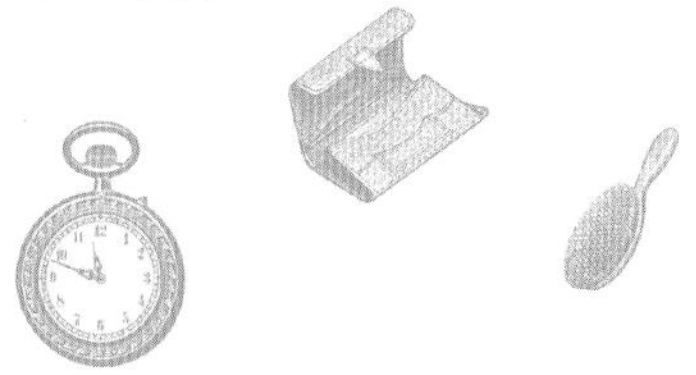

P.081

정답 | 1. 역사의 해석은 과거의 기록과 증거를 바탕으로 역사가 각 개인의 신념을 통해 이루어지는 것이기 때문이다.

본문 필기노트

① In a speech [delivered at the University of Oxford in 1957], British historian Hugh Trevor-Roper said there are two essential functions of human history : to be useful and to be controversial. ② According to him, history [that cannot teach lessons to those in the present] is nothing more than a diamond in the rough. ③ And history [that is not controversial] is completely dead, for no subject is more open to interpretation than history.

(~에서 / ~에 / = / (that) / 부연설명 / ~(인) 것(명사적 용법) / 주격 관 · 대 / ~에게 / 현재에 있는 사람들 / 단지(=only) / 왜냐하면(접속사) / 주격 관 · 대 / no A is more ~ than B: 어느 A도 B보다 더 ~하지 않다, A에서 B가 가장 ~하다)

역사의 두 가지 필수기능: 유용성과 논란성

④ By its very nature, / human history is a subject [that cannot be unbiased or factual]. ⑤ It is the study of man's past, specifically the past [that is relevant to the present]. ⑥ But the past is mute, / and so it doesn't tell us much at all. ⑦ We can only try to analyze and reconstruct it / on the basis of the records and evidence [that have been preserved / in one form or another]. ⑧ And this is where the controversial aspects of history arouse and provoke us. ⑨ The analyses [made by historians] and the conclusions [they come to] are all based on their own personal interpretations, which are based on their own individual beliefs.

(본질적으로 / 주격 관 · 대 / ~에 관련이 있다 / not ~ at all: 전혀 ~않다 / try to-v: ~하려고 노력하다 / ~을 토대로 / 여기가 ~한 지점이다 / S' / V'₁ / V'₂ / (which/that) / V / be based on: ~에 기초를 두다 / which의 선행사 / 주격 관 · 대(계속적 용법))

역사에 논란이 생길 수밖에 없는 이유

본문해석

① 1957년에 옥스퍼드 대학에서 있었던 한 연설에서, 영국의 역사가 휴 트레버-로퍼는 인간의 역사에는 유용성과 논란성이라는 2가지 필수적인 기능이 있다고 말했다. ② 그에 의하면, 현재에 있는 이들에게 교훈을 줄 수 없는 역사는 가공하지 않은 다이아몬드에 지나지 않는다. ③ 그리고 논란의 여지가 없는 역사는 완전히 죽은 것인데, 왜냐하면 어떤 주제도 역사만큼 해석에 있어 열려 있지 않기 때문이다.

④ 본질적으로, 인간의 역사는 편견에 치우치지 않거나 사실일 수 없는 대상이다. ⑤ 그것은 인간의 과거, 특히 현재와 관련이 있는 과거에 관한 연구이다. ⑥ 그러나 과거는 말이 없어서, 우리에게 결코 많은 이야기를 해주지 않는다. ⑦ 우리는 이런 저런 형태로 보존되어 온 기록과 증거를 토대로 과거를 분석하고 재구성하려고 노력할 수 있을 뿐이다. ⑧ 그리고 여기가 바로 역사의 논란이 되는 면이 발생하여 우리를 자극하는 지점이다. ⑨ 역사가들에 의한 분석과 그들이 도달하는 결론은 모두 역사가들 자신의 개인적 해석을 토대로 하는데, 그 해석은 그들 자신의 개인적인 신념을 바탕으로 한다.

본문파악 이 글은 역사의 특성에 대한 필자의 생각을 밝힌 글이다. 첫째 단락은 역사가 휴 트레버-로퍼(Hugh Trevor-Roper)의 연설을 인용하면서 역사에 유용성과 논란성이 있음을 언급하고 있다. 둘째 단락에서는 역사는 기록과 증거에 대한 분석과 재구성을 통해 쓰여질 수밖에 없는데, 여기에 역사가의 주관이 반영되기 때문에 역사의 사실 여부는 논란이 생길 수밖에 없다고 이야기하고 있다.

문제풀이 1. 역사의 논란성에 대해 언급하고 있는 ⑦, ⑨번 문장에 그 이유가 나와 있다.

32 SECTION 07. 역사
역사의 법칙화는 가능한가?

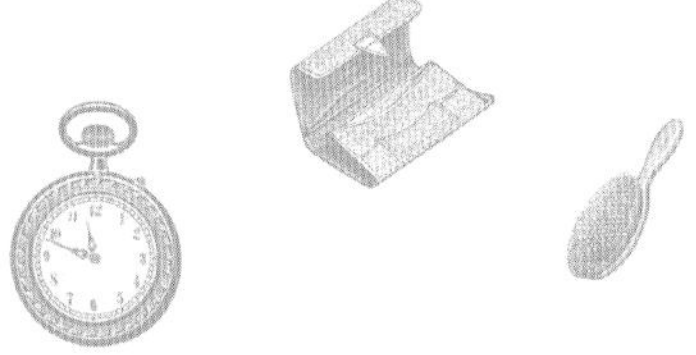

P.082

정답 | 1. ④ 2. ⓐ 역사적 법칙에 대해 논할 가치가 있다는 것 (역사를 법칙화할 수 있다는 것) ⓑ 과학적 법칙을 이용해 역사를 예측하는 것
3. historical laws, human behavior 4. ②

본문 필기노트

(A)

① Some historians emphasize / the necessity of constructing formulas / in history. ② They insist [that it is possible [to ascertain historical laws and draw meaningful lessons from them, / much the same as we do with scientific laws (such as the laws of Kepler, the laws of wave theory, and so on)]]. ③ A historical law might specify [that "whenever x happens, y is certain to follow"] so that, for instance, "whenever a nation's resources are insufficient to maintain its population, that nation turns to war" / is a historical law. ④ For those [who suppose [that it is meaningful to talk of such laws]], / systematic historical investigation / would be the way [to validate the claim].

역사의 법칙화가 가능하다고 보는 입장

(B)

⑤ Can anyone show [that history develops according to historical laws]? ⑥ Karl Popper, [one of the greatest social and political philosophers of 20th century], doubts it. ⑦ According to him, the error lies in assuming [that history is similar to science], / when in fact, it differs greatly : scientific laws apply to closed systems, whereas history, (which is composed of the actions of many individuals), is neither closed nor even a system at all. ⑧ Moreover, since the growth of scientific knowledge affects human behavior and hence history, / the use of scientific laws [to predict history] is only possible / if we can also predict the growth of the scientific knowledge. ⑨ If we could do that, however, we would already know it. ⑩ As a result, there can be no historical laws.

역사의 법칙화가 불가능하다고 보는 입장

본문해석

(A)

① 일부 역사가들은 역사에 있어 공식을 세울 필요성을 강조한다. ② 그들은 우리가 케플러의 법칙, 파동 이론의 법칙 등과 같은 과학적 법칙에 대해 하는 것과 마찬가지로, 역사적 법칙들을 알아내어 그것들로부터 의미 있는 교훈을 도출해 내는 게 가능하다고 주장한다. ③ 한 역사적 법칙은 "x가 일어날 때마다 y가 반드시 뒤따른다"라고 명시할 수도 있으므로, 예를 들어 "한 나라의 자원이 그 나라 인구를 유지하는 데 부족할 때마다, 그 나라는 전쟁을 일으킨다"라는 것이 하나의 역사적 법칙이 된다. ④ 그와 같은 법칙에 대해 논하는 것이 의미 있는 일이라고 생각하는 사람들에게는 체계적인 역사연구가 그 주장의 정당성을 입증하는 방법일 것이다.

(B)

⑤ 역사가 역사적 법칙에 따라 발전해 나간다는 것을 누군가 입증해 보일 수 있을까? ⑥ 20세기 최고의 사회 정치 철학자들 중 한 명인 칼 포퍼는 이를 의심한다. ⑦ 그에 따르면, 역사가 과학과 유사하다고 가정하는 것에 오류가 있는데, 사실 역사는 (과학과) 많이 다른 것이 과학적 법칙은 폐쇄된 조직에 적용되는 반면, 수많은 개인들의 행동들로 구성된 역사는 폐쇄적이지도 않을 뿐더러 조직도 전혀 아니기 때문이다. ⑧ 더욱이, 과학적 지식의 성장이 인간의 행동과 그리하여 역사에 영향을 미치기 때문에, 역사를 예측하기 위한 과학 법칙의 이용은 우리가 과학적 지식의 성장도 예측할 수 있는 경우에만 가능한 것이다. ⑨ 그러나 만약 우리가 그렇게 할 수 있다면 우리는 이미 그것(역사)을 알고 있는 것이 된다. ⑩ 결과적으로, 어떠한 역사적 법칙도 존재할 수가 없는 것이다.

본문파악

글 (A), (B)는 각각 역사를 법칙화할 수 있는지에 대해서 상반된 입장을 취하고 있다. 글 (A)는 역사도 과학처럼 법칙화가 가능하다는 입장으로, 역사가 법칙화될 수 있는 예를 제시하고 있다. 글 (B)는 역사는 폐쇄된 조직이 아닌 인간을 대상으로 하는 것이기 때문에 법칙화가 불가능하다고 보고, 역사를 법칙화하는 데 과학적 지식을 이용하기 위해서는 과학적 지식의 성장도 예측 가능해야 한다는 모순을 그 근거로 제시하고 있다.

문제풀이

1. 《해석》 위 글 (A)와 (B)의 주제로 가장 적절한 것은?
   글 (A)는 역사의 법칙화가 가능하다고 보는 입장이고, 글 (B)는 그렇지 않다는 입장이므로, 두 글의 공통 주제는 '④ 역사의 법칙이 있는가 없는가?'가 가장 적절하다.
   ① 역사를 예측하는 방법 ② 법칙에 대한 역사적 필요성 ③ 인간 행동과 역사 ⑤ 역사에 있어 과학 법칙의 유용성

2. ⓐ의 the claim은 바로 앞의 it is meaningful to talk of such laws, 즉 역사의 법칙화를 논하는 것이 의미있다는 주장을 가리키며, ⓑ의 that은 앞문장의 the use of scientific laws to predict history, 즉 과학적 법칙을 이용해 역사를 예측하는 것을 가리킨다.

3. 《해석》 글 (B)에 따르면 칼 포퍼는 역사 법칙의 존재에 대해 회의적인데, 왜냐하면 과학과 달리 역사는 인간 행동과 관련되어 있다고 생각하기 때문이다. (본문에서)
   글 (B)에서 칼 포퍼는 과학적 법칙은 폐쇄된 조직에 적용되는 반면, 수많은 인간들의 행동으로 구성된 역사는 그렇지 않으므로 과학적 법칙을 역사에 적용할 수 없으며, 따라서 역사의 법칙화는 불가능하다고 주장한다.

4. (A)의 빈칸 뒤의 내용은 빈칸 앞에 제시된 역사 법칙의 예에 해당되므로, (A)에는 예시를 위한 연결어구인 for instance가 적절하다. (B)의 빈칸 뒤의 내용은 역사에는 법칙이 있을 수 없다는 빈칸 앞의 주장을 뒷받침하기 위한 또 하나의 추가 설명이므로, (B)에는 '더욱이, 게다가'라는 뜻의 접속부사인 Moreover가 와야 문맥상 자연스럽다.

구문해설

② They insist [**that** it is possible to ascertain historical laws and draw meaningful lessons from them, much the same as we **do** with scientific laws such as the laws of Kepler, the laws of wave theory, and so on].

▷ that 이하는 동사 insist의 목적어 역할을 하는 명사절로서, insist that은 '~라는 것을 주장하다'라고 해석한다.
▷ do: draw (meaningful lessons from them)를 지칭하는 대(代)동사이다.

③ A historical law might specify [that "whenever x happens, y is certain to follow"] **so that**, for instance, "whenever a nation's resources are **insufficient** [**to maintain** its population], that nation turns to war" (S') is a (V') historical law (C').

▷ so that+S+V: 주절 내용에 대한 결과를 나타내며 '그래서 [그 결과] ~이다'의 의미이다.
▷ to maintain은 insufficient(형용사)를 수식하는 부사적 용법의 to부정사로 '~을 유지하기에'의 의미이다.

역사 인식의 유형

• 순환론적 역사 인식
4계절이 순환하는 것처럼 역사도 순환한다고 보는 관점으로, 그리스와 로마의 역사 인식이 여기에 속한다. 중국 또한 왕조와 문명에 대해 순환론적 역사관의 입장을 취하고 있고, 인도는 왕조와 문명뿐만 아니라 우주까지 포함하는 순환론적 역사관을 가지고 있다.

• 직선적 역사 인식
가장 보편적인 역사관으로, 원시주의, 유태기독교 역사관, 계몽주의, 유물론적 역사관 등이 여기에 속한다. 그 중 계몽주의 역사 인식은 18세기에 프랑스와 영국을 중심으로 출현한 역사관으로, 계몽주의 철학자들에 의해 기독교적 역사관이 대치된 것이다. 계몽주의 역사 인식은 신(神)을 역사의 인도자로 보지 않고 인간을 역사의 주체로 간주한다.

• 변증법적 역사 인식
헤겔(Georg Hegel)에 의하면, 역사의 동력은 세계정신(weltgeist; world spirit)이다. 모든 것은 완전하지 않기 때문에 그 자체에 모순을 내포하고, 그것이 발전할수록 모순 또한 커져서 부정이 출현하고, 다시 부정의 부정으로 지향되어간다. 반대되는 모순의 해결을 통한 변화의 철학이다.

33

SECTION 07. 역사

역사는 승자의 기록이다

P.084

정답	1. ② 2. ① 3. ④ 4. 역사에서 소외되거나 버림받은 사람들

본문 필기노트

① Have you ever heard [that history is the story of the winners]? ② If this is true, / what should be considered / is not just the accuracy of history textbooks, but the actual influence [that goes along with being the ones [who get their story heard]]. ③ It is the history of the dominant group that gets to be told, / and it is their story that is often the one [that becomes normalized, while the stories of everyone else get 'othered' or ignored]. ④ Minority groups and outcasts in society / don't get to tell their side of the story.

(that 이하는 목적어 / ~하는 것 / V / not just[only] A but (also) B: A뿐만 아니라 B도 / (also) / ~에 따르다 / 되는 것 / get+O+v-ed: O가 ~되다 / It is ~ that ... 강조구문: …한 것은 바로 ~이다 / get to-v: ~하게 되다 / 주격 관·대 / ~인 반면에 / =become)

승자 중심의 역사

⑤ A classic example is the history of the Stolen Generation in Australia. ⑥ Until recently, the fact [that 100,000 aboriginal children were taken from their families and raised in the homes of white families] was not considered an important part of European history in Australia, and so there was no way [for those [to whom it happened] to tell their story]. ⑦ Only with the increasing rise of pluralism in Australia / has it become possible for members of the Stolen Generation [to speak out and be heard by the general public].

(동격의 that / S / = / ~로부터 데려가지다 / (were) / V / 그래서, 그 결과로 / 부사구 / V / S(가주어) / 의미상의 주어 / to 이하는 진주어)

승자 중심의 역사의 예: 호주의 도둑맞은 세대

⑧ Because history is ultimately linked to power, it is extremely difficult [to develop ways of using and managing resources] when the historical stories / make the owners of those resources invisible. ⑨ (C) Consider the Penan people of the Borneo rain forest. ⑩ (A) As long as these people go unrecognized, it is a legitimate activity [to cut down their forests and sell their timber to First World nations]. ⑪ (B) It is also legitimate [to ensure [that the profits from such activity flow directly to the lumber companies / without any recognition being given to the Penan / for their prior ownership of the trees]].

(~와 연결되어 있다 / 가주어 / to 이하는 진주어 / make+O+OC: O을 ~하게 하다 / ~하는 한 / go+형용사: ~한 상태에 있다 / 가주어 / to 이하는 진주어 / that 이하는 목적어 / 가주어 / to 이하는 진주어 / ~로 흐르다[통하다] / with(out)+O+v-ing: O가 ~해(지 않)는 채로)

승자 중심의 역사와 자원 수탈의 예: 페낭인들

본문해석

① 당신은 역사가 승자들의 이야기라는 말을 들어 본 적이 있는가? ② 만일 이것이 사실이라면, 고려되어야 하는 것은 역사 교과서의 정확성뿐만이 아니라, 이야기가 들려지는 대상이 되는 것에 따르는 실질적인 영향력이다. ③ 들려지는 것은 바로 지배 집단의 역사이며, 다른 모든 사람들의 이야기는 흔히 '기타의 것으로 취급'되거나 무시되는 반면에, 표준이 되는 것은 바로 그 지배 집단의 이야기이다. ④ 사회의 소수 집단과 버림받은 사람들은 그들의 입장에서 바라본 이야기를 하지 못하게 된다.

⑤ 전형적인 예가 호주의 도둑맞은 세대에 관한 역사이다. ⑥ 최근까지, 10만 명의 호주 원주민 아동들이 자신들의 가정에서 축출되어 백인 가정에서 길러진 사실이 호주 내 유럽 역사의 중요한 부분으로 여겨지지 않아, 그런 일을 당한 사람들이 자신들의 이야기를 할 방법이 전혀 없었다. ⑦ 호주에서 다원주의가 점차적으로 증가하면서 겨우 도둑맞은 세대의 구성원들이 거리낌 없이 이야기하고 일반 대중들이 그들의 이야기를 듣는 것이 가능해졌다.

⑧ 역사는 궁극적으로 권력과 연결되어 있기 때문에, 역사상의 이야기들이 그 자원의 소유자를 명시하지 않는 상황에서 자원을 이용하고 관리하는 방법을 개발하는 것은 매우 어렵다. ⑨ (C) 보르네오 열대우림의 페낭인들을 생각해 보라. ⑩ (A) 이 사람들이 인정을 받지 못하는 상태에 있는 한, 그들의 열대우림을 벌목하고 선진국에 목재를 판매하는 것은 합법적인 활동이다. ⑪ (B) 페낭인들에게 그들의 삼림 우선 소유권을 전혀 인정해 주지 않은 채, 그런 활동으로부터 얻어지는 수익이 제재회사로 곧장 들어가게 하는 것을 보장하는 것 또한 합법적이다.

본문파악

이 글은 역사 기술이 승자 중심으로 이루어져 왔다는 것을 호주의 도둑맞은 세대와 보르네오 섬의 페낭인들의 예를 통해 설명하고 있다.

- 단락 1(문제제기) – 승자 중심의 역사 기록이 소외된 개인이나 집단에 미치는 영향
- 단락 2(예시 1) – 역사 기록에서 소외된 호주의 도둑맞은 세대
- 단락 3(예시 2) – 역사 기록이 소유권을 명시해 주지 않아 자원수탈을 당한 페낭인들

문제풀이

1. 《해석》 다음 중 위 글의 제목으로 적절하지 않은 것은?
   이 글은 역사가 승자의 기록이며, 이로 인해 소수 집단이 입게 된 피해에 관해 이야기하고 있다. 따라서 ①, ③, ④, ⑤는 제목이 될 수 있으나, '② 믿을 만한 목격자로서의 역사'는 이 글의 내용과 무관하다.
   ① 그것은 누구의 역사인가? ③ 역사와 진정한 권력 ④ 승자들만을 위한 역사 ⑤ 역사와 소수 집단

2. 둘째 단락과 셋째 단락에서 각각 언급된 호주의 도둑맞은 세대와 보르네오 섬의 페낭인들의 예는 승자 위주의 역사로 피해를 입은 소수 집단의 이야기이다. 따라서 역사가 승자 중심의 기록이라면 역사적 사실의 정확성뿐만 아니라, 역사가 소수 집단에게 실제적으로 미치는 '① 영향(influence)'까지도 고려되어야 한다는 내용이 와야 글 전체를 포괄할 수 있다.
   ② 명성 ③ 피해 ④ 위엄 ⑤ 사실

3. 글을 배열하는 문제는 단락 첫 부분의 지시어나 연결어에 유념한다. (A) 문장의 these people은 (C) 문장의 the Penan people을 가리키므로 (C)가 (A) 앞에 와야 한다. (A)의 주절에서 it is a legitimate activity라고 했고 (B)에서 It is 'also legitimate'이란 표현이 나오므로 (B)는 (A) 뒤에 오는 것이 자연스럽다. 따라서 적절한 순서는 (C) – (A) – (B)이다.

4. 둘째 단락의 도둑맞은 세대와 셋째 단락의 페낭인들은 승자 위주의 역사 기록으로 인하여 역사에서 소외된 소수 집단의 예로 제시되었다.

구문해설

② If this is true, **what** should be considered is not just the accuracy of history textbooks, but (also) the actual influence that goes along with being **the ones who get their story heard**.

▷ what은 선행사를 포함하는 관계대명사로 '~하는 것(=the thing which)'의 의미이다.
▷ the ones who get their story heard는 역사에서의 승자, 혹은 지배 집단을 가리킨다.

⑦ [Only with the increasing rise of pluralism in Australia] **has it** (V S) become possible **for members of the Stolen Generation** to speak out and be heard by the general public.

▷ [ ] 부분은 문두로 나간 부사구로, 이에 따라 주어와 동사가 도치되었다.
▷ for members of the Stolen Generation은 뒤에 나오는 to부정사구의 의미상의 주어이다(The members of the Stolen Generation speak out and are heard by the general public.).

다원주의(pluralism)

사회는 여러 독립적인 이익집단이나 결사체로 이루어져 있으므로 권력 엘리트에 의하여 지배되기보다 그 집단의 경쟁 · 갈등 · 협력 등에 의하여 민주주의적으로 운영되어야 한다고 보는 사상이다. 다원주의자들의 명제에 따르면, 어떤 단일한 제도 또는 제도적 집합체도 지배적인 것은 없다. 사회는 오히려 여러 상충하는 목표를 가진 수많은 이익집단들로 구성되거나 특별한 문제를 중심으로 일시적으로 연합하는 변화무쌍한 연합체로 구성되어 있다는 것이다.
다원주의자들의 견해로는, 상충적인 이익집단이 정치적 영역에서 서로 경쟁하거나 협상하는 과정 속에서 권력은 다소 민주주의적으로 운영된다. 그리고 공공정책이라는 것은 경쟁하는 집단들이 내린 타협과 협상의 결과로 나타나는 것이며, 대중은 선거와 조직적인 참여를 통하여 엘리트에 대해 상당한 영향을 미칠 수 있다고 본다.

34 SECTION 07. 역사

도스 법이 몰고 온 인디언의 참상

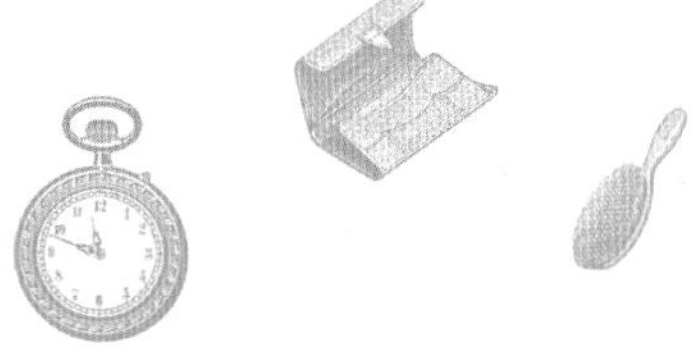

P.086

정답 | 1. ② 2. the avarice of settlers and the government for ever-increasing control of land 3. ③ 4. ⑤

본문 필기노트

① The early nineteenth century constituted a period of massive migration in the United States as white settlers moved westward in droves. ② The U.S. government enacted the forced relocation (of Native American tribes) (to government-established reservations), but continued settlement further raised the demand for land. ③ However, the Native American practice of communal use of land made it nearly impossible to acquire reservation land from tribes.

as: ~함에 따라(접속사) / The U.S. government: S₁ / enacted: V₁ / continued settlement: S₂ / 동격 / raised: V₂ / for: ~에 대한 / the Native American practice: S / of: = / it: 가목적어 / to acquire reservation land from tribes: 진목적어

백인의 대규모 이주에 따른 아메리카 원주민의 강제 이주

④ The avarice (of settlers and the government) (for ever-increasing control of land) ultimately led to the General Allotment Act of 1887, (which is) often referred to as the Dawes Act, as the legislation was sponsored by Senator Henry Dawes. ⑤ Under the Dawes Act, land [that had previously been held collectively by tribes] was parceled out into allotments and then (was) distributed to individual members of the tribe. ⑥ The territory of the reservations was not fully distributed, however, and the remaining "surplus" — often the most well-positioned or mineral-rich land — was sold off to the highest bidder, [who was usually a non-Indian settler or company].

The avarice: S / led: V / as the Dawes Act: ~로서(전치사) / as: ~하기 때문에(접속사) / that: 주격 관·대 / was parceled out: V₁ / distributed: V₂ / to: ~에게 / The territory: S / was: V / "surplus": S, = / to: ~에게 / the highest bidder: who의 선행사 / who: 주격 관·대(계속적 용법)

백인의 토지 소유권을 확보하기 위한 일반 토지 할당법 제정

⑦ The division of communal lands forced Native Americans to assimilate into mainstream American culture, [leading to the unwitting abdication of tribal sovereignty and the loss of cultural identity]. ⑧ The dramatic shift in lifestyle for Native Americans, [moving from working together as a closely tied community to individually cultivating small farms], was not only unwanted but also unfeasible. (⑨ Many plots [allotted to Native Americans] were ill-suited for farming (on a small scale), and those [caring for the land] lacked basic agricultural necessities.) ⑩ The allotment system was abolished in 1934, but its far-reaching adverse effects

force+O+to-v: O에게 ~할 것을 강요하다 / leading: 결과의 분사구문 / moving: 부대상황의 분사구문 / from A to B: A에서 B로 / not only A but also B: A뿐만 아니라 B도 역시 / Many plots: S / were: V

본문해석

① 19세기 초는 백인 이주민들이 무리 지어 서쪽으로 이동함에 따라 미국의 대규모 이주 기간이 되었다. ② 미국 정부는 아메리카 원주민 부족에 대해 정부가 설립한 보호구역으로의 강제 이주를 규정했지만, 계속되는 정착은 토지에 대한 수요를 더욱 끌어올렸다. ③ 그러나, 토지 공동 사용이라는 아메리카 원주민의 관행은 부족으로부터 보호구역 토지를 취득하는 것을 거의 불가능하게 만들었다.

④ 계속 증가하는 토지 지배권에 대한 정부와 이주민들의 탐욕은 결국 1887년의 '일반 토지 할당법'으로 이어졌는데, 그 법률이 상원의원 헨리 도스에 의해 발의되었기 때문에 도스 법이라고 흔히 불린다. ⑤ 도스 법 하에서, 이전에 부족이 집단으로 소유했던 토지가 할당으로 나뉘어 부족의 개별 구성원들에게 배분되었다. ⑥ 하지만, 보호구역의 영토가 전부 배분되지는 않았고, 보통 가장 위치가 좋거나 광물이 풍부한 땅이었던 남은 '여분'은 최고 입찰자에게 팔렸는데, 그것은 주로 인디언 계열이 아닌 이주민 또는 회사였다.

⑦ 공동 토지의 분할로 아메리카 원주민들은 주류 미국 문화에 동화될 수밖에 없었고, 그 결과 자기도 모르게 부족의 자주권을 포기하고 문화적 정체성을 잃었다. ⑧ 친밀하게 연결된 공동체로서 협업하는 것에서부터 개인적으로 작은 농장들을 경작하는 것으로 바뀐 아메리카 원주민들의 생활방식의 극적인 변화는 원치 않는 것이었을 뿐만 아니라 실행할 수도 없었다. (⑨ 아메리카 원주민에게 할당된 많은 대지는 소규모 농업에는 부적합했고, 토지를 돌보는 사람들에게는 기본적인 농업적 필수품이 없었다.) ⑩ 그 할당 제도는 1934년에 폐지되었지만, 그 광범위한 악영향은 오늘날에도 감지된다. ⑪ 이것

are still felt today. ⑪ This is evidenced by the significant changes [that the Indian way of life has undergone] and the fact [(that) some reservations still have more non-Indian than Indian residents].

동격의 that / 목적격 관 · 대 / = / 일반 토지 할당법으로 미국 사회에 동화된 아메리카 원주민

은 인디언들의 삶의 방식이 겪은 엄청난 변화와 몇몇 보호구역에는 여전히 인디언 주민보다 인디언이 아닌 주민이 더 많다는 사실로 입증된다.

본문파악

19세기 초 미국의 대규모 이주에 따른 일반 토지 할당법 제정에 따라 아메리카 원주민이 토지를 빼앗기고 자주권과 문화적 정체성을 잃은 경위를 설명한 글이다. 첫째 단락에서 일반 토지 할당법 제정의 배경을, 둘째 단락에서 그 구체적인 내용을, 셋째 단락에서 그것이 원주민들에게 끼친 영향에 대해 설명하고 있다.

문제풀이

1. 《해석》 위 글의 제목으로 가장 적절한 것은?
   일반 토지 할당법의 제정 배경과 내용, 그리고 아메리카 원주민에게 미친 파괴적인 영향을 설명하는 글이므로 '② 아메리카 원주민 문화를 파괴한 법률'이 제목으로 가장 적절하다.
   ① 헨리 도스: 최초의 아메리카 원주민 상원의원
   ③ 미국 농업에 대한 아메리카 원주민의 기여
   ④ 아메리카 원주민의 공동 토지 사용의 발단
   ⑤ 아메리카 원주민은 어떻게 법을 이용해 그들의 토지를 보호했는가

2. 《해석》 일반 토지 할당법을 야기한 것으로 저자가 제시하는 것은 무엇인가? (본문의 단어를 사용하시오.)
   ④번 문장 참조

3. ⑧번 문장에서 개인적으로 작은 농장을 경작하는 것은 실행할 수 없었다고 언급하였으므로, 그 이유를 설명하는 주어진 문장은 ⑧번 문장 다음에 들어가야 한다.

4. ⑤ → 할당 제도는 1934년에 폐지되었으나 그 악영향은 지금도 감지된다고 하였다. (⑩번 문장 참조)
   ① (③번 문장 참조)　② (④번 문장 참조)　③ (⑥번 문장 참조)　④ (⑦번 문장 참조)

구문해설

④ The avarice (**of** settlers and the government) (**for** ever-increasing control of land) ultimately led to the General Allotment Act of 1887, [often referred to as the Dawes Act **as** the legislation was sponsored by Senator Henry Dawes].

▷ ( )의 전치사구 두 개가 주어 The avarice를 수식한다.
▷ [ ]는 the General Allotment Act of 1887을 부연 설명하는 과거분사구이다.
▷ as는 '~때문에'의 의미로 이유를 나타내는 접속사이다.

35 SECTION 08. 환경 · 생태 · 의학
인간 중심의 진화

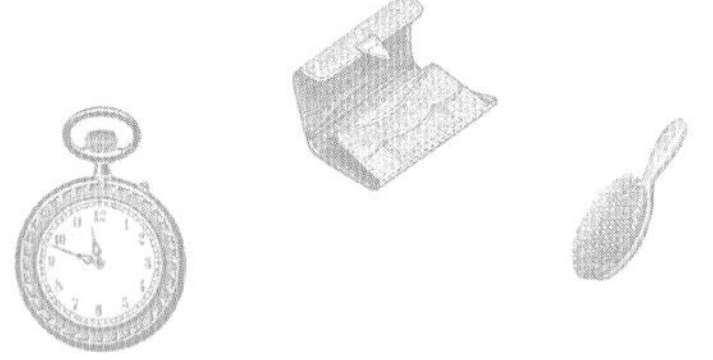

P.090

정답

1. ④ 2. ② 3. ③
4. 현대 인류가 고의적이든 아니든 몇몇 종의 생존을 장려할 때조차도 우리는 더 많은 종들의 생존을 위협하고 있다.

본문 필기노트

① Human activity has greatly affected the survival of Earth's plant and animal species. ② For millions of years, / life evolved without significant impact (from human beings). ③ As early as the first settlements in Australia and North America, / human beings caused the extinction of species through hunting or the use of fire. ④ Since the nineteenth century, / the role [that human beings play in species survival] has increased so much that many species survive / only because human beings allow it.

상당히 영향을 미쳐왔다(현재완료: 계속) / ~동안 / ~없이 / 일찍이 ~에 / ~(안)에 / ~으로(수단) / ~이래로(전치사) / 목적격 관 · 대 / ~에서 / so ~ that ...: 너무 ~해서 ···하다

동식물의 생존에 영향을 미치는 인간

⑤ Certain animal species survive in large numbers thanks to humans. ⑥ For example, / today there are about 10 billion chickens on Earth, or about fifteen times as many as there were a hundred years ago. ⑦ This is because so many chickens are bred for human consumption. ⑧ Similarly, we raise cattle, sheep, goats, and other domesticated animals in order to make use of them. ⑨ In addition, / modern civilizations have unintentionally ensured the survival of other species. ⑩ Pests such as rats and cockroaches live on the food waste [created by humans]. ⑪ Squirrels prosper in suburban landscapes [where there are few predators].

다수의 / ~ 때문[덕분]에 / 약, 대략 / 즉 / 배수사+as+원급+as ~: ~보다 몇 배 더 ···한 / ~을 위해 사육되다 / ~하기 위하여 / ~을 이용하다 / A such as B: B와 같은 A / ~을 먹고 살다 / ~에 / 관계부사 / 거의 없는

인간의 편의에 의해 생존 · 번식하게 된 동물들

⑫ Even as modern human beings intentionally or unintentionally promote the survival (of a few species), we threaten many more (species). ⑬ Thanks to technology, / hunting has become vastly more efficient, pushing animals (such as the blue whale and the North American bison) to the brink of extinction. ⑭ Many other animals, (especially tropical forest species), suffer from destruction of their habitats through logging trees by humans.

~할 때에(조차) / S′ / V′ / O′ / push A to B: A를 B로 밀어내다 / 직전 / S / 무연설명 / V / ~로 인해 (원인) / ~에 의한

인간에 의해 멸종 위기에 처한 동식물들

본문해석

① 인간 활동은 지구의 동식물 종들의 생존에 엄청난 영향을 미쳐 왔다. ② 수백만 년 동안 생물은 인간에게서 큰 영향을 받지 않고 진화했다. ③ 일찍이 호주와 북미의 초기 정착 시대에, 인간은 사냥이나 불의 사용으로 종의 멸종을 초래했다. ④ 19세기 이후에 인간이 종들의 생존에서 행하는 역할이 너무 많이 증가해서, 많은 종들이 단지 인간이 허용하기 때문에 생존한다.

⑤ 어떤 동물 종들은 인간 덕분에 다수로 살아남았다. ⑥ 예를 들어, 오늘날 지구상에 약 100억 마리, 즉 100년 전보다 약 15배가 더 많은 닭이 있다. ⑦ 이것은 인간의 소비를 위해 그렇게 많은 닭들이 길러지기 때문이다. ⑧ 비슷한 이유로, 우리는 그것들을 이용하기 위해 소, 양, 염소 및 기타 가축을 키운다. ⑨ 게다가, 현대 문명은 부지불식간에 다른 종들의 생존도 보장했다. ⑩ 쥐와 바퀴벌레 같은 유해 생물들은 인간에 의해 만들어진 음식 쓰레기를 먹고 산다. ⑪ 다람쥐들은 포식자들이 거의 없는 교외의 전원 속에서 번식한다.

⑫ 현대 인류가 고의적이든 아니든 몇몇 종들의 생존을 장려할 때조차도 우리는 더 많은 종들의 생존을 위협한다. ⑬ 과학기술 덕분에, 사냥은 훨씬 더 효율적이 되었고, 그리하여 흰긴수염고래와 아메리카 들소 같은 동물들을 멸종 직전까지 내몰았다. ⑭ 기타 많은 동물들, 특히 열대우림 종들이, 인간에 의한 삼림 벌채로 서식지가 파괴되는 고충을 겪는다.

본문파악

인간 중심적인 생활이 동식물의 생존에 커다란 영향을 미쳐왔다는 내용의 글이다. 첫째 단락에서는 인간이 동식물의 생존에 큰 영향을 미쳐 왔음을 설명하고 있으며, 둘째와 셋째 단락에서는 각각 인간에 의해 생존·번식하게 된 동물들의 예와 인간에 의해 멸종 위기에 처한 동식물들의 예를 들고 있다.

문제풀이

1. 《해석》 위 글의 제목으로 가장 적절한 것은?
이 글은 인간 중심적인 생활이 동식물의 생존에 커다란 영향을 미쳐 왔다는 내용이므로, 제목으로 가장 적절한 것은 '④ 인간 중심 진화의 결과'이다.
① 야생 동식물 ② 동물 수의 변화
③ 동물 사육의 기원 ⑤ 환경 파괴의 원인들

2. 《해석》 다음 중 첫째 단락의 빈칸에 들어갈 말로 가장 적절한 것은?
빈칸이 포함된 문장에서 19세기부터 인간이 종의 생존에 미치는 영향력이 커졌다고 했으므로, 많은 종들이 살아남게 된 것은 결국 '② 인간이 그것을 허용하기' 때문일 것이다.
① 자연이 요구하다 ③ 그들이 식단을 바꾸었다
④ 그들이 인간을 닮으려고 노력하다 ⑤ 그들이 사육되었다

3. 《해석》 위 글에 따르면, 다음 중 참이 아닌 것은?
① 동물들은 오랫동안 사육되어 왔다. (⑦~⑧번 문장 참조)
② 현대 문명이 쥐를 번식시켰다. (⑨~⑩ 번 문장 참조)
③ 살아 남은 동물들은 모두 인간의 소비를 위해 이용된다. → 이 내용은 언급된 바 없다.
④ 현대의 과학기술은 많은 동식물들을 위협한다. (⑬번 문장 참조)
⑤ 아메리카들소들은 거의 멸종되었다. (⑬번 문장 참조)

4. even as는 '~하는 동안에(조차)', '마침 ~할 때에'라는 의미이고, more 뒤에는 species가 생략되었다.

구문해설

⑬ Thanks to technology, hunting has become vastly more efficient, **pushing** animals (such as the blue whale and the North American bison) **to the brink of** extinction.

▷ pushing 이하는 결과를 나타내는 분사구문으로, pushing은 and it has pushed의 의미이다.
▷ to the brink of: '~의 직전까지'

멸종 위기에 처한 아메리카들소(American bison)

유럽인들이 북아메리카에 정착하기 전인 1500년에는 약 6천에서 1억 2천마리의 아메리카들소들이 대륙을 누비며 살고 있었다. 아메리카들소는 원주민들에게 생존을 위한 수단이었는데, 이들은 들소의 고기는 식량으로, 가죽은 천막집과 의복으로 이용하였고, 심지어 배설물도 건조시켜 연료로 사용했다.
그러나 1900년대 초에 이르러서는 지나친 사냥으로 아메리카들소의 활동 영역이 매우 좁은 지역으로 축소되었고 거의 멸종 위기에 처해졌다. 사냥과 관련하여 들소의 감소를 가속화시킨 가장 큰 요인은 1860년대 말 동서를 연결하는 철도를 부설하면서 건설 인부들에게 육류를 공급하기 위해 전문사냥꾼들이 들소 포획에 나선 것이다. 게다가 남북전쟁 이후 미합중국 군대는 원주민들이 거주하던 평원을 차지하기 위해 그들의 주요 식량공급원인 들소를 도살하기 시작했다. 엄청난 수로 감소한 아메리카들소는 1893년에 통과된 국립공원 내의 야생동물 학살금지법에 의해 보호받기 시작했다.

36 SECTION 08. 환경 · 생태 · 의학

심층 생태학(deep ecology)

정답 | 1. ③ 2. ② 3. These include socio-economic problems[concerns] as well as the usual physical and scientific environmental concerns[problems]

본문 필기노트

(A)

① So-called shallow environmentalism / still dominates the mainstream. ② It encourages continuous economic growth and environmental protection through technological ideas, resources management (such as replanting forests and recycling), and small changes in lifestyles. ③ In contrast, the Deep Ecology approach / aims to achieve a major ecological change of our socio-cultural systems, collective actions, and lifestyles. ④ The Deep Ecology approach says [that we must rethink our present culture and character, which threatens the earth]. ⑤ Deep Ecology does not separate humans from the natural environment. ⑥ It sees the world as a network [where all living things are connected]. ⑦ It calls for the protection of natural areas and areas of biodiversity in order to protect and sustain the environment and the value of everything in it.

So-called: 소위, 이른바 / dominates: V / It: S / encourages: V / continuous economic growth: O_1 / environmental protection: O_2 / through: ~을 통하여(수단) / such as: A such as B: B와 같은 A / in: ~에서 / aim to-v: ~하는 것을 목표로 삼다 / that: that 이하는 목적어 / our present culture and character: which의 선행사 / which: 주격 관 · 대(계속적 용법) / separate A from B: A를 B와 분리시키다 / see A as B: A를 B로 보다 / where: 관계부사 / calls for: ~을 요구하다 / in order to: ~하기 위해서 / it: = the environment

심층 생태학의 개념

(B)

⑧ The Sustainable Environmental System / manages all of nature's problems / at all levels. ⑨ These include socio-economic problems as well as the usual physical and scientific environmental concerns. ⑩ The environment is complex and has many different dimensions to it. ⑪ As such, any attempt [to resolve environmental problems] must also have many dimensions. ⑫ For instance, air pollution is not just a problem of cars, but also of people [using cars too much and too often]. ⑬ People drive for many reasons, [ranging from commuting to work to grocery shopping]. ⑭ So a solution to this cause of air pollution / must also include alternatives to driving. ⑮ We could also provide economic incentive systems [to discourage too much driving], / or the location of services and employment could be changed so as to minimize the need [to drive long distances]. ⑯ The Sustainable

These: 앞문장 전체 / as well as: A as well as B: B뿐만 아니라 A도 / The environment: S / is: V_1 / has: V_2 / As such: 그런 만큼 / to resolve: 해결하려는(형용사적 용법) / not just ~ but also: not just[only] A but also B: A뿐만 아니라 B도 / but also (a problem) of / for: ~ 때문에(이유) / ranging from ~ to: range from A to B: 범위가 A에서 B까지 이르다 / a solution to: ~에 대한 해결책 / alternatives to: ~에 대한 대안 / to discourage: 억제하기 위해(부사적 용법) / so as to-v: ~하도록, ~하기 위해 / to drive: 운전하려는(형용사적 용법)

본문해석

(A)

① 소위 얄팍한 환경 보호주의가 아직도 대세를 좌우하고 있다. ② 그것은 끊임없는 경제 성장과 과학기술적 사고, 삼림 이식과 재활용 같은 자원 관리, 생활양식의 작은 변화를 통한 환경 보호를 장려한다. ③ 이와는 반대로, 심층 생태학적 접근은 사회 문화적 구조, 집단적 행동 및 생활양식의 주요한 생태학적 변화를 달성하는 것을 목표로 삼고 있다. ④ 심층 생태학적 접근에서는 우리가 지구를 위협하는 현재의 문화와 성격을 재고해야 한다고 한다. ⑤ 심층 생태학은 인간을 자연환경과 분리하지 않는다. ⑥ 그것은 세상을 모든 생물들이 연결되어 있는 그물망으로 본다. ⑦ 그것은 환경과 그 안에 있는 모든 것의 가치를 보호하고 유지하기 위해 자연 지역과 다양한 생물이 있는 지역의 보호를 요구한다.

(B)

⑧ 지속가능한 환경제도는 모든 자연 문제를 모든 차원에서 관리한다. ⑨ 이것은 보통의 물리 · 과학적인 환경 문제뿐만 아니라 사회 경제적인 문제들도 포함한다. ⑩ 환경은 복잡하고 다양한 상(相)을 가진다. ⑪ 그런 만큼, 환경 문제를 해결하려는 어떠한 시도도 다양한 상을 가져야 한다. ⑫ 예를 들면, 대기 오염은 자동차 문제일 뿐만 아니라 자동차를 너무 많이 그리고 너무 자주 사용하는 사람들에 대한 문제이기도 하다. ⑬ 사람들은 직장 출퇴근에서 식료품 구매에 이르는 여러 가지 이유로 운전을 한다. ⑭ 따라서 대기 오염의 이러한 원인에 대한 해결책은 운전에 대한 대안도 포함하고 있어야만 한다. ⑮ 우리는 또한 너무 많은 운전을 억제하기 위해 경제적 보상 제도를 제공할 수 있고, 또는 장거리 운전의 필요를 최소화하기 위해 서비스와 직장의 위치를 변화시킬 수 있다. ⑯ 지속가능한 환경제도는 기본적으로 환경 문제로 이어지는 모든 원

Environmental System is basically about trying to change all of the causes [that lead to environmental problems].

try to-v: ~하려고 시도[노력]하다

주격 관·대

인을 변화시키려고 노력하는 것에 관한 것이다.

지속가능한 환경제도의 개념

본문파악 글 (A)는 심층 생태학에 대해 설명하고 있고, 글 (B)는 지속가능한 환경제도의 개념을 소개하고 있다.

문제풀이

1. 심층 생태학에서는 인간과 자연을 함께 공존하는 대등한 관계로 본다. (⑤~⑦번 문장 참조)

2. (A)에서, 빈칸의 앞부분에서는 얄팍한 생태학에 대해 이야기하고 있고, 빈칸의 뒷부분에서는 그와는 반대 개념인 심층 생태학에 대해 이야기하고 있으므로, 빈칸에는 대조를 표현하는 연결어인 In contrast가 적절하다. 글 (B)의 빈칸 뒤에는 ⑪번 문장에서 언급된 환경문제 해결을 위한 다양한 예가 나오므로 For instance가 적절하다.
   ① 그러나 – 게다가 ③ 이와는 반대로 – 다시 말해서
   ④ 다른 한편으로는 – 결과적으로 ⑤ 마찬가지로 – 예를 들면

3. 'B뿐만 아니라 A도'라는 뜻의 「A as well as B」 구문을 이용한다.

생태학이란?

1869년 헤켈(Ernst Haeckel)에 의해 처음으로 사용된 용어인 생태학은 환경과의 관계 및 생물들 상호 간의 관계를 규명하는 학문이다. 그는 생태학을 '생물과 환경 및 함께 생활하는 생물과의 관계를 논하는 과학'이라고 정의하였다. 생태학은 박물학과 개(個)생태학에서 출발하여, 행동학, 동물사회학으로 이어져 개체군 내의 개체 간의 관계와 사회구조의 연구가 이루어지게 되었다. 또한 생태학은 육지 · 해양 · 담수역의 생물군의 기능적인 문제, 특히 자연의 구조와 기능에 관해 보다 현대적으로 정의하고 있으며, 오늘날에는 인간도 자연의 일부라는 생각이 바탕이 되어 인간생태학에 관한 연구도 활발하게 전개되고 있다.
최근의 생태학의 성과는 응용부문에 직접 이용되고 있는데, 어족자원의 유지나 해충의 발생 예방이 그 예이다. 또, 자원관리나 자연보호에서도 큰 공헌을 하고 있다. 앞으로 지구 전체의 인구 증가 및 식량 확보와 더불어 자연자원의 합리적인 이용 관리, 인간 생존을 위협하는 대기오염, 수질오염, 해양오염, 열오염, 소음오염, 토양오염, 농약 오염 등의 많은 문제가 생태학적인 접근으로 다루어질 것이다.

37

SECTION 08. 환경 · 생태 · 의학

동물 사육과 환경 오염

P.094

정답 | 1. ② 2. ③ 3. ③ 4. ⑤

본문 필기노트

① The planet is approaching an energy crisis, and governments are spending more money on research (into alternative energy sources). ② However, in the midst of our panic, an ancient practice presents itself as a solution: vegetarianism.

spend A on B: A를 B에 소비하다[쓰다] / ~의 한가운데에 / ~로 / present oneself: 나타나다 / 부연설명

에너지 위기에 대한 해결책으로서 채식주의가 대두됨

③ The meat and dairy industries use huge amounts of natural gas, electricity, and fossil fuels / to house, heat, ventilate, water, feed, clean, transport and slaughter the billions of animals [consumed by humans every year]. ④ In total, raising animals for food uses more than one-third of all materials and fossil fuels ; a vegetarian diet would require only 2 percent of raw materials. ⑤ So excessive is the amount of energy [used by having a meat-based diet] that if the world switched to a plant-based one, / current petroleum reserves would easily last for another 360 years. ⑥ The creation of a single hamburger patty / uses enough fossil fuel [to power a car 20 miles] or (to) heat water for seventeen showers.

V / 엄청난 양의 / 이하의 to 부정사는 모두 '~하기 위해(부사적 용법)' / S / V / ~ 이상 / 대조되는 문장을 연결 / ~일 것이다(예측) / C / V / S / so ~ that ...: 너무 ~하여 …하다 / ~로 전환하다 / 유지하다 / 움직이기 위한(형용사적 용법)

채식을 할 때 절약되는 자원의 양

⑦ In fact, / if water [used by the meat industry] were not covered by taxpayers, / ordinary hamburger meat / would cost $35 a pound. ⑧ Whereas it takes 25 gallons of water to produce a pound of wheat, it takes 2,500 gallons to generate a pound of meat.

S' / V' / ~인 반면에 / S / V / it takes ~ to-v: …하는 데 ~가 들다

육류업에 필요한 많은 양의 물

⑨ In addition to the energy costs of meat production, / it is estimated [that 60 percent of America's waterways have been polluted by livestock industries, which create three times more water pollution than other industrial sources combined]. ⑩ The places (where) most animals are kept produce toxic methane and ammonia fumes / so that poultry workers have to wear gas masks.

가주어 / that 이하는 진주어 / ~에 의해 오염되어 왔다 / which의 선행사 / (=and they) / 배수사+비교급+than ~: ~보다 몇 배 더 …한 / V / so that ~: 그 결과 ~, 그러므로 ~

축산업으로 인한 수질오염과 대기오염

⑪ There are so many energy-wasting practices [connected with eating animals]. ⑫ We can ease some of our own burden by adopting sensible eating habits.

완화시키다 / by v-ing: ~함으로써

채식 위주 식단의 필요성 강조

본문해석

① 지구가 에너지 위기에 가까워지고 있어, 각국 정부는 대체 에너지원 연구에 보다 많은 돈을 쓰고 있다. ② 그러나 우리가 허둥지둥하는 가운데, 옛관행이었던 채식주의가 해결책으로 나오고 있다.

③ 육류업과 낙농업은 사람들에 의해 매년 소비되는 수십억 마리의 동물들을 수용하고, 난방을 하고, 통풍을 시키고, 물을 주고, 먹이를 주고, 씻기고, 수송하고, 그리고 도살하는 데 엄청난 양의 천연가스, 전기, 화석연료를 사용한다. ④ 통틀어, 식용 동물을 사육하는 데는 모든 원료와 화석연료의 1/3 이상을 사용하는데, 채식주의자의 식단은 불과 2%의 원료만을 필요로 할 것이다. ⑤ 육식을 기초로 한 식사를 함으로써 사용되는 에너지의 양이 너무 지나쳐서, 만일 세계가 채식 위주의 식단으로 바꾼다면 현재의 석유 매장량은 앞으로 360년간은 거뜬히 지속될 것이다. ⑥ 햄버거 고기 1개를 만드는 데는 자동차를 20마일 움직이거나 17번의 샤워를 위해 물을 데우기에 충분한 화석 연료를 사용한다.
⑦ 사실, 육류업에 사용된 물이 납세자들에 의해 충당되지 않는다면 일반 햄버거 고기는 1파운드에 35달러일 것이다. ⑧ 1파운드의 밀을 생산하는 데는 25갤런의 물이 필요한 반면에, 1파운드의 고기를 만들어 내는 데는 2,500갤런이 필요하다.

⑨ 육류 생산의 에너지 비용뿐만 아니라, 미국 수로의 60%가 축산업으로 오염되었는데, 축산업은 다른 산업을 합친 것보다 3배 더 많은 수질오염을 일으킨다고 추정된다. ⑩ 대부분의 동물들이 갇혀있는 장소들은 유독한 메탄가스와 암모니아 가스를 발생시키므로, 축산업 종사자들은 방독면을 꼭 착용해야 한다.

⑪ 육식을 하는 것과 관련된 너무 많은 에너지 낭비 관행이 있다. ⑫ 우리는 현명한 식습관을 취함으로써 우리 자신의 짐의 일부를 덜 수 있다.

본문파악

에너지 위기로 인하여 전 세계적으로 대체 에너지 개발에 전력을 쏟는 상황에서 육식 위주의 식단을 채식 위주로 바꾸면 에너지 절약 및 환경 보호도 할 수 있다는 내용의 글이다. 첫째 단락은 도입부이고, 둘째, 셋째, 넷째 단락에서는 육류업으로 인한 자원 낭비 및 환경 오염에 대해 구체적으로 이야기하고 있다. 마지막 단락은 결론으로 채식 위주의 현명한 식단을 선택할 것을 강조하고 있다.

문제풀이

1. 《해석》 위 글의 주제는 무엇인가?
   이 글에서는 육식으로 인한 자원 낭비와 환경오염을 언급하면서 채식의 필요성을 주장하고 있으므로, 주제로는 '② 육식을 기초로 한 식단을 바꿔야 할 필요성'이 가장 적절하다.
   ① 동물로 인한 환경 오염 ③ 채식의 건강상의 이로움
   ④ 에너지 비용 절감에 대한 해결책 ⑤ 에너지 낭비 없이 동물을 사육하는 방법

2. 빈칸이 포함된 문장은 글 전체의 핵심 요지로, 에너지 위기에 대한 해결책으로 채식을 제시하고 있다. 첫째 단락에 뒤이어 나오는 네 단락에서 육식의 부작용을 언급하고 있으므로, 빈칸에 들어갈 적절한 말은 '③ vegetarianism'이 적절하다.
   ① 재활용 ② 에너지 절약 ④ 환경 관리 ⑤ 천연자원 개발

3. ③ → 현재 석유 보유량으로 360년 이상을 쓸 수 있다는 것이 아니라 육식 위주에서 채식 위주의 식단으로 바꾸면 그렇게 될 것이라는 것이다. (⑤번 문장 참조)
   ① (①번 문장 참조) ② (④번 문장 참조) ④ (⑨번 문장 참조) ⑤ (⑩번 문장 참조)

4. 넷째 단락은 육류 생산으로 인한 에너지 비용 문제 외에도 수질 및 대기오염 등의 환경문제도 있다는 내용이므로, 빈칸에는 '~ 뿐만 아니라'의 의미인 '⑤ In addition to'가 가장 적절하다.
   ① ~때문에 ② ~에도 불구하고 ③ ~덕분에 ④ ~와 반대로

구문해설

③ The meat and dairy industries use huge amounts of natural gas, electricity, and fossil fuels **to house, heat, ventilate, water, feed, clean, transport** and **slaughter** the billions of animals [consumed by humans every year].

▷ to house 이하는 목적을 나타내는 부사적 용법의 to부정사구로, house, heat, ... slaughter가 접속사 and에 의해 병렬연결된 형태이다.

④ In total, [**raising** animals for food] (S) **uses** (V) more than one-third of all materials and fossil fuels; a vegetarian diet would require only 2 percent of raw materials.

▷ [ ]는 주어로 사용된 동명사구이며, 단수 취급하므로 단수동사 uses가 왔다.

⑤ **So excessive** (C) **is** (V) **the amount of energy** (S) [used by having a meat-based diet] **that if** the world **switched** to a plant-based one, current petroleum reserves **would** easily **last** for another 360 years.

▷ so ~ that ...: '너무 ~하여 …하다'의 의미로, 보어인 so excessive가 문두에 강조되어 나오면서 주어 동사가 도치되었다.
▷ that절 속에는 가정법 과거(If+주어+과거동사 ~, 주어+조동사의 과거형+동사원형 ...) 문장이 들어 있다.

38

SECTION 08. 환경 · 생태 · 의학

소음 공해

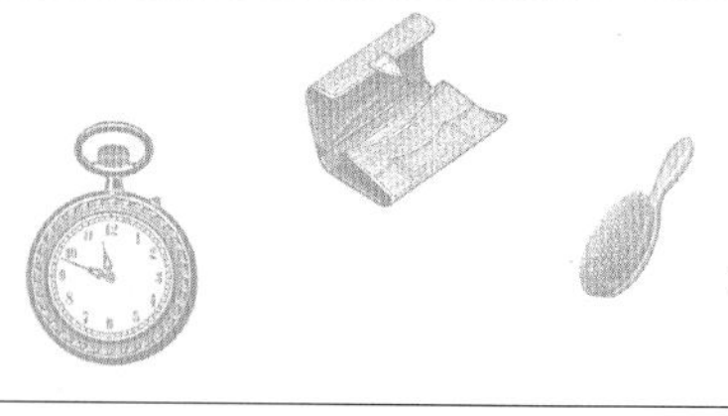

P.096

정답	1. Accordingly, practical action to limit and control human exposure to environmental noise is essential. 2. ③, ⑤ 3. (환경) 소음에 대한 규정의 부족, (환경) 소음이 인간에게 미치는 영향에 대한 지식 부족 4. intend → intended

본문 필기노트

① Noise has always been a chief environmental problem for humans. ② In ancient Rome, / rules existed to limit the noise [emitted from the ironed wheels (of wagons) [which rattled over the stone roads, / causing irritating sleep disturbance to citizens]]. ③ In Medieval Europe, / horse carriages and horseback riding / were prohibited / during nighttime in certain cities / to ensure a peaceful sleep / for the inhabitants. ④ However, the noise problems of the past are incomparable with those of modern times. ⑤ Day and night, / an enormous number of cars, trucks and buses / regularly pass through cities and the countryside. ⑥ On top of this / is the high level of noise [created by aircraft, trains, and industrial machinery].

has always been: 항상 ~이었다(현재완료: 계속) / to limit: 제한하기 위해(부사적 용법) / which: 주격 관 · 대 / causing: =so they caused(결과의 분사구문) / during: ~동안에 / to ensure: 보장하기 위해서(부사적 용법) / for: ~에게 / are incomparable with: ~와 비교가 안되다 / those: =the noise problems / On top of this: 부사구(더군다나) / is: V / high level of noise: S

현대에 더욱 심각해진 소음 공해

⑦ In comparison to other pollutants, / the control of environmental noise has been ignored because of insufficient knowledge of its effects on humans, as well as a lack of defined criteria. ⑧ While it has been suggested [that noise pollution is simply a "luxury" problem for developed countries], / one cannot ignore the fact [that the exposure to noise is often higher in developing countries, where there are less regulations]. ⑨ Regardless of where it exists, / noise pollution's effects are widespread and damaging. ⑩ Accordingly, practical action [to limit and control human exposure to environmental noise] is essential.

In comparison to: ~와 비교하여 / of: ~에 대한 / on: ~에 미치는 / has been ignored: 무시되어 왔다 / because of: ~ 때문에 / as well as: A as well as B: B뿐만 아니라 A도 / it: 가주어 / that: that 이하는 진주어 / that: 동격의 that / developing countries: where의 선행사 / where: 관계부사(계속적 용법) / where it exists: 전치사 of의 목적어절 / practical action: S / to limit and control: 제한하고 통제하는 (형용사적 용법) / exposure to: ~에의 노출 / is: V

소음 공해에 대한 조치의 필요성

⑪ Such action is now taking place in Europe, where it is estimated [that 40 percent of residents, or 150 million people, are exposed to road traffic noise [exceeding 55 decibels], and (it is estimated that) over 30 percent / suffer sleep-disturbing noise levels at night]. ⑫ Authorities are surveying areas [to discover where noise levels are the highest], and (are) producing computerized maps [(which are) available on the Internet] to warn

taking place: take place: 일어나다 / it: 가주어 / that: that 이하는 진주어 / or: 즉(부연설명) / are exposed to: ~에 노출되다 / Authorities: S / are surveying: V_1 / to discover: 발견하기 위해(부사적 용법) / where noise levels are the highest: 목적어절 / producing: V_2 / to warn: 경고하기 위해(부사적 용법)

본문해석

① 소음은 항상 인간에게 주요 환경 문제였다. ② 고대 로마에서는, 돌길을 덜컹거리며 달려서 시민들에게 짜증나는 수면 장애를 일으키는 짐마차의 철제 바퀴에서 나오는 소음을 제한하기 위해 규정이 존재했다. ③ 중세 유럽에서는 일부 도시에서 주민들에게 평화로운 잠을 확보해 주기 위해 밤 동안에는 마차와 승마가 금지되었다. ④ 그러나 과거의 소음 문제는 현대의 그것과는 비교가 되지 않는다. ⑤ 밤낮으로 엄청난 수의 자동차, 트럭, 그리고 버스가 정기적으로 도시와 시골을 지나 다닌다. ⑥ 더군다나 비행기, 기차, 그리고 산업용 기계에서 나오는 높은 수준의 소음도 있다.

⑦ 다른 오염물질들과 비교했을 때, 환경 소음에 대한 통제는 규정된 기준의 부족뿐만 아니라, 인간에게 미치는 영향에 대한 불충분한 지식 때문에 무시되어 왔다. ⑧ 소음 공해는 그저 선진국의 '사치스러운' 문제라고 여겨져 왔지만, 우리는 소음에 대한 노출이 종종 개발도상국에서 더 심각하고 거기서는 규제가 덜하다는 사실을 무시할 수 없다. ⑨ 그것이 발생하는 장소에 관계없이, 소음 공해의 영향은 광범위하고 해롭다. ⑩ 따라서, 환경 소음에 대한 인간의 노출을 제한하고 통제하는 실질적인 조치가 필수적이다.

⑪ 그러한 조치가 현재 유럽에서 이루어지고 있는데, 주민의 40%, 즉 1억 5천만 명이 55데시벨을 초과하는 도로 교통 소음에 노출되어 있고, 30% 이상이 밤에 수면을 방해하는 소음 수준을 겪고 있는 것으로 추정된다. ⑫ 관계당국은 소음 수준이 가장 높은 곳을 발견하기 위해 지역을 조사하고 있으며, 인터넷으로 이용 가능한 컴퓨터 지도를 사람들에게 경고하기 위해 제작하고 있다. ⑬ 그 지도는 데시벨

people. ⑬ The maps are color-coded according to decibel range, from green, the quietest, through to yellow, red and dark blue. ⑭ These maps will be followed by E.U. legislation [intended to reduce the noise levels in the worst, dark-blue areas].

~에 따라 / from A through to B: A에서 B까지 죽 / 뒤따를 것이다

소음 문제 해결을 위한 유럽의 노력

범위에 따라 가장 조용한 지역인 초록부터 노랑, 빨강, 그리고 남색까지의 색으로 분류되어 있다. ⑭ 이 지도 다음에는 가장 심한 남색 지역의 소음 단계를 줄이기 위해 의도된 유럽 연합의 법률이 나올 것이다.

본문파악 이 글은 소음 공해 문제의 심각성을 알리고 이에 대한 조치가 필요하다고 주장하는 글이다. 첫째 단락에서는 과거부터 있었던 소음 공해가 현대에는 더욱 심각해졌음을 알리고 있다. 둘째 단락에서는 소음 공해의 심각성이 상대적으로 등한시되었으나, 이에 대한 조치가 필요하다는 내용이며, 셋째 단락에서는 소음 공해를 줄이기 위한 유럽의 노력을 예시로 들며 마무리하고 있다.

문제풀이 1. 이 글은 현대 산업사회에서의 소음 공해의 심각성을 알리고 이에 대한 조치가 필요하다고 주장하는 글이다.

2. ① (②~③번 문장 참조)
② (⑤~⑥번 문장 참조)
③ → 종종 소음 공해 문제가 더 심각한 것은 개발도상국이라고 했다. (⑧번 문장 참조)
④ (⑪번 문장 참조)
⑤ → 소음이 가장 심한 지역은 남색으로 표시된다. (⑭번 문장 참조)

3. ⑦번 문장 참조

4. 앞부분에 이미 주어와 동사(These maps will be)가 있으므로 intend 이하는 E.U. legislation을 수식하는 구조가 되어야 한다. 내용상 E.U. legislation과 intend는 수동관계가 자연스러우므로 과거분사 intended가 되어야 한다. (⑭번 문장 해석 참조)

구문해설 ⑥ **On top of this** is the high level of noise [created by aircraft, trains, and industrial machinery].

부사구 / V / S

▷ 부사구인 On top of this가 문두로 나감에 따라 주어와 동사가 도치된 문장이다.

'소음과의 전쟁'에 나선 정부

소음은 다른 환경오염과 달리 우리의 생명과 건강에 직접적인 위협을 주지는 않는다. 그러나 만성적인 소음 공해는 스트레스를 유발하고 불안 · 초조 등의 신경장애를 일으킬 뿐만 아니라 심장병 발생률을 증가시킨다. 이러한 악영향을 끼치는 소음을 줄이기 위해, 전 세계 대도시들은 많은 노력을 기울이고 있다. 뉴욕의 경우 소음 기준을 위반할 경우의 벌금을 2~3배 강화하였고, 유럽연합(EU) 회원국들은 '소음지도'를 작성하고 있다. 우리나라에서도 다양한 소음 관련 사례들이 증가함에 따라 소음 방지가 중요한 이슈가 되고 있다.

이에 따라, 2004년에 제정된 공동주택 건설 기준에서 정부는 층간 소음을 50~58데시벨(dB) 이하로 규제했다. 또한 중앙 환경분쟁 조정위원회를 설치하여 공동주택의 층간 소음 조사 방법 및 배상 기준을 마련하여 분쟁 해결에 적용하고 있다. 이러한 노력을 시작으로 하여 정부는 더욱 체계적이고 강화된 소음관리대책을 수립하고 실행하여 모두가 쾌적한 환경에서 건강하게 살 수 있도록 노력하고 있다. 정부의 노력뿐만 아니라 소음을 유발하는 기관의 협력 또한 절실하다. 지방자치단체는 공공시설을 건설하기에 앞서 책임 있는 환경영향평가를 실시해야 하고, 인구밀도가 높은 수도권에서 도로를 건설할 때는 주거지역과의 거리 및 앞으로 증가할 차량이나 차종까지도 고려하여 교통소음 증가에 대비해야 한다.

39 SECTION 08. 환경 · 생태 · 의학
이원론과 일원론

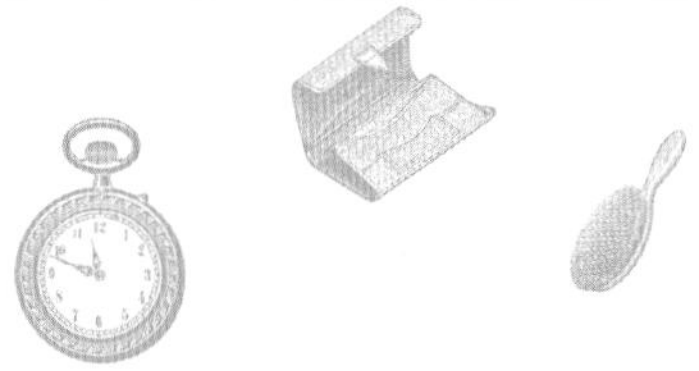

P.098

정답 | 1. ⑤ 2. ④ 3. (1) F (2) T (3) F

본문 필기노트

(A)

① Hippocrates (c. 460–377 BC) believed in the dualistic nature of mind and body.
~의 존재 · 정당성을 믿다
② He radically proposed [(that) disease occurred in the body and (that) this process
V / that 이하는 목적어 / O_1 / O_2
was independent of the mind]. ③ Hippocrates suggested [(that) the body contained
~와 관계없는 / that 이하는 목적어
four specific fluids, [called humors]]. ④ According to Hippocrates, / a person
experienced health (when) these humors were balanced. ⑤ However, when the
~일때(접속사)
fluids were out of balance, disease occurred. (⑥ Treatment therefore involved an
균형을 잃은
attempt [to balance the four fluids].) ⑦ This approach to health and disease / was
균형을 | 이루려는(형용사적 용법) / ~에 대한 접근법
radical (for) its time / because disease had previously been thought / to be the result
~으로서는 / ~의 결과
of demons or spirits possessing the body. ⑧ Hippocrates challenged this view and
V_1
established a physical approach to health and disease. ⑨ For this reason / he is
V_2 / 이런 이유로
often described as the "father of medicine."
~로서 묘사되다

신체의 질병이 정신과는 무관하다는 히포크라테스의 관점

(B)

⑩ I hope [(that) you can now understand [(that) there is an extensive and significant
that 이하는 목적어 / that 이하는 목적어
relationship between mind and health]]. ⑪ This relationship is controlled by our
between A and B: A와 B사이의 / ~에 의해 지배되다
behavior together with the biological connections [which exist between the brain
~와 더불어 / 주격 관 · 대
and the immune system]. ⑫ These connections work in both directions, / meaning
작용하다 / =and it means(부연설명의 분사구문)
[(that) our physical health is able to influence our mental state, and vice-versa].
that 이하는 목적어 / 역도 또한 같음
⑬ In other words, all illnesses have psychological consequences as well as causes.
A as well as B: B뿐만 아니라 A도
⑭ Stress, depression and other psychological factors / can affect our immunity to
~에 대한 면역성
many diseases, (including) bacterial and viral infections, heart disease and cancer.
~을 포함하여(전치사)
⑮ Thus, our mental and emotional states are highly important (in) the maintenance
=very, extremely / ~에서, ~하는 데
of health. ⑯ In that sense, our dualistic habit of contrasting mind and body, (as
그런 의미에서 / a habit of v-ing: ~하는 습관 / 삽입절
though they were two separate entities,) is deeply misleading.
as though+가정법 과거: 마치 ~인 것처럼 / V

정신 상태와 신체 건강은 서로 관련이 있다고 보는 관점

본문해석

(A)

① 히포크라테스(기원전 약 460–377년)는 정신과 신체의 이원성을 믿었다. ② 급진적이게도 그는 질병은 신체 내에서 생기며 이 과정은 정신과 관련이 없다고 주장했다. ③ 히포크라테스는 신체는 체액이라고 불리는 네 가지 특정 액체를 포함하고 있다고 주장했다. ④ 히포크라테스에 따르면, 사람은 이 체액들이 균형을 이루고 있을 때 건강하다고 느꼈다. ⑤ 그러나 체액들이 균형을 잃으면 병이 생겼다. (⑥ 그러므로 치료는 그 네 가지 체액의 균형을 이루기 위한 시도와 관련된 것이었다.) ⑦ 이전에는 질병이 악마나 유령이 들린 결과라고 생각되었기 때문에, 건강과 질병에 대한 이러한 접근법은 그 당시로서는 급진적인 것이었다. ⑧ 히포크라테스는 이러한 견해에 도전하여 건강과 질병에 대한 신체적인 접근법을 정립했다. ⑨ 이런 이유로 그는 종종 '의학의 아버지'라고 묘사된다.

(B)

⑩ 나는 이제 여러분이 정신과 건강 사이에 광범위하고 중요한 관계가 있다는 것을 이해할 수 있기를 희망한다. ⑪ 이 관계는 뇌와 면역체계 사이에 존재하는 생물학적 연관성과 더불어 우리의 행동에 의해 지배를 받는다. ⑫ 이러한 연관성은 양방향으로 작용하는데, 이는 우리의 신체적 건강이 우리의 정신 상태에 영향을 미칠 수 있으며, 또 그 반대일 수도 있다는 것을 의미한다. ⑬ 다시 말해, 모든 질병에는 심리적 원인뿐만 아니라 (심리적) 결과도 있다. ⑭ 스트레스, 우울증 및 기타 심리적 요인들은 세균성이나 바이러스성 감염, 심장병, 그리고 암을 포함한 많은 질병들에 대한 면역성에 영향을 미칠 수 있다. ⑮ 이렇게 우리의 정신적 그리고 감정적 상태는 건강을 유지하는 데 매우 중요하다. ⑯ 그런 의미에서 볼 때, 정신과 신체를 마치 두 개의 별개의 개체인 것처럼 대비시키는 우리의 이원론적 습관은 매우 잘못된 것이다.

본문파악

글 (A)는 건강과 질병에 대한 히포크라테스의 관점을 소개하고 있고, 글 (B)는 정신과 신체가 유기적으로 연관되어 있어 정신상태가 건강유지에 중요하다고 보는 관점을 소개하고 있다.

문제풀이

1. 주어진 문장에서 '그 네 가지 체액(the four fluids)'의 균형을 이루기 위한 '치료(Treatment)'가 언급되고 있으므로, 체액의 균형이 깨지면 병이 생긴다는 내용(⑤번 문장) 뒤에 오는 것이 적절하다.

2. 《해석》 히포크라테스와 글 (B)의 필자는 정신과 신체 사이의 연관성에 대해 다른 관점을 가지고 있다.
글 (A)에서 히포크라테스는 질병은 신체의 문제이지 정신과는 아무 관련이 없다고 했고, 글 (B)의 필자는 신체의 건강을 유지하는 데 정신 상태가 아주 중요하다고 했다. 따라서 둘은 '④ 정신과 신체 사이의 관련성'에 대한 관점이 다른 것이다.
① 바이러스성 질병의 원인 ② 건강과 질병의 정의 ③ 신체 구조의 구성 요소 ⑤ 병을 유발하는 심리적인 요인들

3. 《해석》 다음 진술에 대해 T(참) 또는 F(거짓)로 표시하시오.
(1) 히포크라테스에 의하면, 질병은 체액의 부족으로 인해 발생한다. → ⑤번 문장에서 체액의 부족이 아니라 불균형 때문이라고 했다.
(2) 글 (B)에 의하면, 불안감이나 슬픔 및 기타 부정적 감정이 병을 유발할 수 있다. (⑭번 문장 참조)
(3) 히포크라테스처럼 생각하는 사람은 우리가 신체를 건강하게 유지하기 위해서는 정신 및 감정 상태를 돌봐야 한다고 주장할 수 있다. → ②번 문장에서 히포크라테스는 질병은 정신과 관련이 없다고 했다.

구문해설

⑦ This approach to health and disease was radical for its time because disease **had** previously **been thought to be** the result of **demons or spirits possessing** the body.

▷ 종속절의 시제는 과거완료로, 그 행동이나 상황이 주절 시제인 특정 과거 시점까지 계속되어 온 것을 의미한다.
▷ be thought to-v: '~인 것으로 여겨지다'
▷ demons 이하는 전치사 of의 목적어로, demons or spirits는 동명사구 possessing the body의 의미상 주어이다.

⑩ I hope [**that** you can now understand [**that** there is an extensive and significant relationship between mind and health]].

▷ 두 개의 that절 모두 명사절로서, 첫 번째 that 이하는 동사 hope의 목적어이고, 두 번째 that 이하는 동사 understand의 목적어이다.

⑫ These connections work in both directions, meaning that our physical health is able to influence our mental state, and **vice-versa**.

▷ vice-versa: '역도 또한 같음'이라는 뜻으로, our mental state is able to influence our physical health too의 의미이다.

40 SECTION 09. 경제 · 경영

자유 무역 이론과 현실

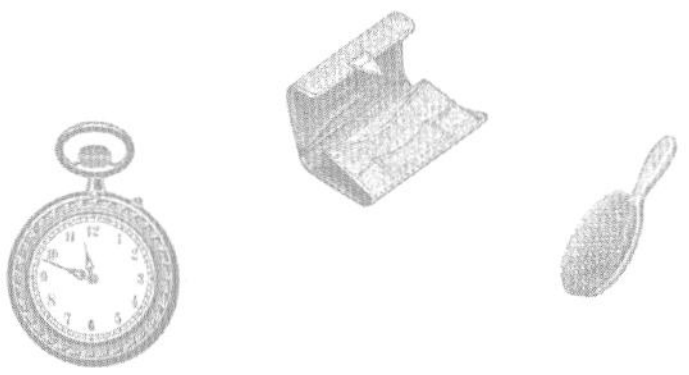

P.102

정답

1. ⑤ 2. ① 3. (1) F (2) T (3) T
4. (소비자들이) 가격이 변동해도 같은 양의 자원을 소비하기 때문에 자원이 풍부한 나라들이 수익을 내기 힘들다.

본문 필기노트

① In the study of development and international trade, most controversies revolve around the question of [who wins / when trade is being conducted between countries with different national endowments]. ② According to the conventional free-trade theory, / countries [fated by climate, geography, and history] / are to specialize in agricultural (bananas and coffee) / or certain mineral (oil and gas) commodities,/ whereas countries (rich in capital and technology)/ are expected to produce capital-intensive, high-technology products and export them / in exchange for commodities and low-skill, labor-intensive products. ③ The theory argues [that free trade provides for optimal benefits for all parties [while increasing world output overall]]. ④ [Taken to extremes], it holds [that countries should specialize in a narrow bundle of products], or [that agriculturally based economies should stick to agriculture rather than trying to industrialize].

자유 무역 이론의 내용

⑤ The specialization strategy (under the assumption of comparative advantage), / however, / has had very little practical use / for most mineral-specializing countries. ⑥ Traditionally,/ abundant natural resources / have been regarded as / contributing to the successful development of Western countries,/ such as Australia, the US and Canada. ⑦ However, during the past three decades, the star performers (among developing countries), such as Korea and Taiwan, have been resource-poor, while the majority of the resource-rich countries, such as Argentina, Mexico, Peru, Saudi Arabia and Venezuela, have had lower than average annual growth rates overall.

자유 무역 이론에 대한 반증

⑧ What are the growth-retarding factors for a large number of resource-abundant countries? ⑨ These countries are usually poor / because the demand (for their

본문해석

① 개발과 국제 무역에 대한 연구에서, 대부분의 논란은 서로 다른 국가 재원을 지닌 국가들 간에 무역이 이루어지고 있을 때 누가 득을 보느냐는 문제에 초점을 맞춘다. ② 종래의 자유 무역 이론에 따르면, 기후, 지리, 역사에 의해 운명 지어진 국가는 농산물(바나나와 커피) 또는 특정 광물(석유와 가스) 원자재를 특화해야 하며, 반면 자본과 기술이 풍부한 국가는 자본 집약적인 첨단 기술 제품을 생산하여 원자재와 낮은 기술, 노동 집약적 제품과 교환하여 수출할 것으로 예상된다. ③ 그 이론은 자유 무역이 세계 생산량을 전반적으로 증대시키면서 모든 당사자에게 최적의 이익을 제공한다고 주장한다. ④ 극단적으로는, 그것은 국가들이 폭이 좁은 몇 가지 제품을 특화해야 한다고, 즉 농업 기반의 경제는 산업화하려고 노력하기보다는 오히려 농업을 고수해야 한다고 주장한다.

⑤ 그러나, 비교 우위라는 전제 하의 특화 전략은 광물을 특화한 대부분의 국가에는 실제적인 효과가 거의 없다. ⑥ 전통적으로, 풍부한 천연자원은 호주, 미국, 캐나다와 같은 서양 국가들의 성공적인 발전에 기여하고 있는 것으로 여겨져 왔다. ⑦ 그러나, 지난 30년 동안 한국과 대만과 같은 개발도상국 중 주역 국가들은 자원이 빈약한 반면, 아르헨티나, 멕시코, 페루, 사우디아라비아, 베네수엘라와 같이 자원이 풍부한 국가의 대다수는 전체적으로 평균 미만의 연 성장률을 지녀왔다.

⑧ 자원이 풍부한 국가 다수의 성장을 지연시키는 요인은 무엇일까? ⑨ 이 국가들은 보통 그들의 제품에 대한 수요가 상대적으로 비탄력적이기 때문에

products) is relatively inelastic : ⑩ People consume about the same amounts of resources even as their prices fluctuate. ⑪ In addition, / the costs (of making these products) / tend to rise / as production increases because poorer natural resources have to be brought into production / as the better ones are used up.

V₁ / 부연설명 / 거의 / ~일 때(접속사) / 게다가 / ~함에 따라(접속사) / ~함에 따라(접속사) / =natural resources

자원이 풍부한 국가의 성장이 더딘 이유

가난하다. ⑩ 즉, 사람들이 그것의 가격이 변동할 때도 거의 같은 양의 자원을 소비한다. ⑪ 게다가, 생산이 증가함에 따라 이런 제품들을 만드는 데 드는 비용이 오르는 경향이 있는데, 더 나은 천연자원이 고갈됨에 따라 비교적 빈약한 천연자원이 생산에 투입되어야 하기 때문이다.

본문파악

이 글은 비교 우위에 근거한 자유 무역 이론에 관한 글이다. 첫째 단락에서는 국제무역에서 각국은 자국에서 생산이 유리한 재화를 특화해야 한다는 비교 우위 이론의 내용을 소개하고 있다. 둘째 단락에서는 광물 자원이 풍부한 저성장 국가들의 예를 들어 그 이론이 현실적으로 맞지 않음을 반증한다. 셋째 단락에서는 이러한 자원이 풍부한 국가들의 성장을 저해하는 원인에 대해 설명하고 있다.

문제풀이

1. (A)에는 문맥상 자본과 기술이 풍부한 국가가 첨단 기술 제품을 생산하여 그것들을 노동집약적 제품과 교환하여 '수출하는' 것이 자연스러우므로, export가 적절하다. (B)에는 앞의 while로 보아 앞절과는 반대되는 내용이 나와야 하므로, 자원이 풍부한 국가들의 연 성장률은 '낮다'는 내용이 와야 한다. 따라서 lower이 알맞다. (C)에는 because 뒤의 내용으로 미루어보아 빈약한 천연자원도 지속적으로 생산되고 있으므로, 생산이 '증가함에' 따라 제조 비용도 오른다가 문맥상 자연스럽다. 따라서, increases가 적절하다.
   cf. import (수입하다) / higher (더 높은) / decline (감소하다)

2. 《해석》 다음 중 빈칸에 들어갈 말로 가장 적절한 것은?
   앞의 내용을 바꾸어 말할 때 쓰는 or 뒤에 나오는 내용이므로, '폭이 좁은 몇 가지 제품을 특화하는 것'에 대한 설명이 되어야 한다. 빈칸은 농업에 기반을 둔 예시이므로 ①이 가장 적절하다.
   ① 산업화하려고 노력하기보다는 오히려 농업을 고수해야 한다고
   ② 농업의 성장에 대한 예측을 고려해야 한다
   ③ 농업과 첨단 기술 산업 모두에서 뛰어나기 위해 노력해야 한다
   ④ 자국의 농업 제도를 산업화 제도로 바꾸어야 한다
   ⑤ 다른 나라에 대한 자국의 농업 우위에 만족해서는 안 된다

3. 《해석》 다음 진술에 대해 T(참) 또는 F(거짓)로 표시하시오.
   (1) 종래의 자유 무역 이론에 따르면, 양측의 이익을 보장하지 않고 비교 우위가 있는 물품을 교역하는 것이 이상적이다. → ③번 문장에 따르면 자유 무역 이론은 비교 우위가 있는 물품을 전문으로 취급하는 것이 결국 양측에도 최적의 이익이라고 했다.
   (2) 역사적으로, 일부 서양 국가는 천연자원이 풍부했기 때문에 상당한 경제 성장을 겪었다. (⑥번 문장 참조)
   (3) 비교 우위 이론은 자원이 풍부한 국가들과 관련해서는 최근에 적용되지 않았다. (⑦번 문장 참조)

4. 《해석》 위 글에 따르면, 자원이 풍부한 국가의 제품에 대한 비탄력적 수요가 그 국가들에 어떤 영향을 미치는가? (한국어로)
   바로 뒤의 ⑩번 문장을 참고한다.

구문해설

④ [Taken to extremes], **it** holds [that countries should specialize in a narrow bundle of products], or [that agriculturally based economies should stick to agriculture rather than trying to industrialize].

▷ 첫 번째 [ ]는 조건을 나타내는 분사구문으로, If it is taken to extremes로 바꾸어 쓸 수 있다.
▷ it은 앞 문장의 주어인 the theory를 가리킨다.
▷ that이 이끄는 두 번째와 세 번째 [ ]는 모두 동사 holds의 목적어로 쓰인 명사절이다.

41

SECTION 09. 경제 · 경영

미국 초기 이주민들과 '보이지 않는 손'

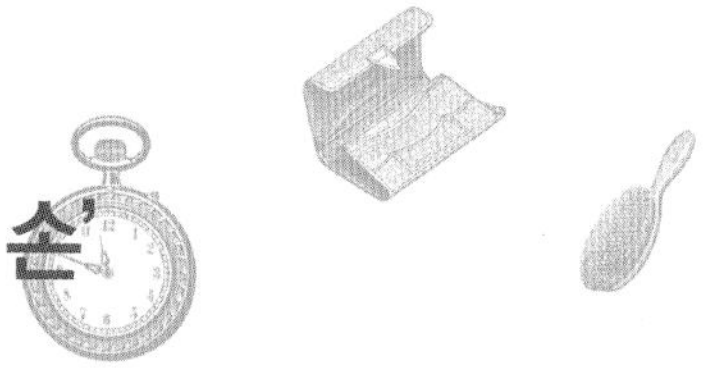

P.104

정답 | 1. ② 2. private property[appropriate incentives] 3. ③ 4. ⑤

본문 필기노트

① Thanksgiving is a time [to gather with family and friends / and eat a huge feast /
모이는(형용사적 용법) (to) 먹는
like the Pilgrims did in 1623]. ② We often forget, however, how extremely poor
~인 것처럼 =gathered ~ and ate a huge feast 간접의문문(의문사+주어+동사)
they once were.
추수감사절의 의미

③ Half the Pilgrims died or returned to England / in their first year. ④ Those [who
주격 관 · 대
remained] went hungry. ⑤ Despite religious convictions, the Pilgrims stole from
~에도 불구하고
one another. ⑥ Finally, facing starvation for the fourth winter, Governor Bradford
서로서로 =when they faced(때의 분사구문)
and others began to think of ways to grow corn more efficiently. ⑦ One of the
(which/that) ~을 생각해 내다 재배하는(형용사적 용법)
traditions [the Pilgrims had brought with them from England] was a practice
(that)
[known as "communal farming]." ⑧ Everything [they produced] was put into a
common pool and rationed among them. ⑨ This tradition, however, was challenged
(was)
in light of the perilous conditions of the time. ⑩ Young men, in particular, thought
~에 비추어 볼 때 think A B:
it an injustice to receive the same allotment of food as those [who didn't pull their
A를 B라고 여기다 받는 것(명사적 용법) the same A as B: B와 똑같은 A 주격 관 · 대 역할을 다하다
weight]. ⑪ Incentives were sorely needed. ⑫ Thus, Bradford decided to experiment
decide to-v: ~하기로 결정하다
/ in the spring of 1623. ⑬ He set aside a plot of land for each family so that they
~을 따로 떼어두다 ~에게 so that ~ can ...: ~가 …할 수 있도록
could grow their own crop and rely on themselves. ⑭ The results were nothing short
~에게 의지하다 아주 ~한
of miraculous. ⑮ Those [who previously claimed they were too old or ill to work]
주격 관 · 대 (that) too ~ to-v: …하기에 너무 ~하다
accepted the idea of private property and enjoyed the fruits of their labor. ⑯ Given
V_1 동격 V_2 성과, 열매 (Being)
appropriate incentives, / the Pilgrims produced and enjoyed a bountiful harvest in
the fall of 1623 / and set aside "a day of thanksgiving" to thank God for their good
감사하기 위해서(부사적 용법)
fortune.
청교도들에 의해 추수감사절이 생겨난 배경

⑰ However, according to 18th-century economist, Adam Smith, the Pilgrims
merely responded to the "invisible hand" — a kind of enlightened self-interest
~에 반응하다 부연설명
[which directs people's actions and serves the interest of the whole society]. ⑱ It
V_1 V_2
provided them with the incentive [to produce a bountiful harvest], which they then
provide A with B: A에게 B를 제공하다 생산하는(형용사적 용법) which의 선행사 목적격 관 · 대(계속적 용법)
celebrated in a feast, which we call Thanksgiving Day.
which의 선행사 목적격 관 · 대(계속적 용법)
풍작의 원인에 대한 애덤 스미스의 해석

본문해석

① 추수감사절은 청교도들이 1623년에 그랬던 것처럼 가족 및 친구들이 모여 잘 차린 진수성찬을 먹는 때이다. ② 그러나 우리는 종종 그들이 한때 얼마나 빈곤했는지를 잊는다.

③ 첫 해에 청교도들의 절반이 사망하거나 영국으로 돌아갔다. ④ 남은 사람들은 굶주렸다. ⑤ 종교적인 신념에도 불구하고 청교도들은 서로 도둑질을 했다. ⑥ 결국 네 번째 겨울에 기아에 직면하게 되자, 브래드포드 총독과 다른 사람들은 더 효율적으로 옥수수를 재배하는 방법을 생각해 내기 시작했다. ⑦ 청교도들이 영국에서 가져온 전통들 중의 하나가 '공동 농작'이라고 알려진 관습이었다. ⑧ 그들이 생산한 모든 것은 공동 저장소에 보관되었다가 그들에게 배급되었다. ⑨ 그러나 이 전통은 당시의 위기 상황에 비추어 볼 때 문제가 제기되었다. ⑩ 특히 청년들은 역할을 다하지 않는 사람들과 똑같은 양의 음식을 배급받는 것을 부당한 처사라고 생각했다. ⑪ 동기유발책이 절실히 필요해졌다. ⑫ 그리하여, 브래드포드는 1623년 봄에 실험을 하기로 결정했다. ⑬ 그는 자기 소유의 농작물을 재배하여 자급자족할 수 있도록 각 가정에게 약간의 토지를 할당해 주었다. ⑭ 결과는 아주 기적적이었다. ⑮ 이전에는 너무 늙거나 병들어 일을 할 수 없다고 주장한 사람들이 사유 재산의 개념을 받아들였고 그들의 노동의 성과를 누렸다. ⑯ 적절한 동기유발책이 주어지자, 청교도들은 1623년 가을에 풍성한 수확을 거두어 이를 누렸으며, 그들의 행운에 대해 하나님께 감사드리기 위해 '감사하는 날'을 따로 정했다.

⑰ 그러나 18세기 경제학자인 애덤 스미스에 의하면 청교도들은 '보이지 않는 손,' 즉 사람들의 행동을 지배하고 사회 전체의 이익에 보탬이 되는 일종의 진보된 이기심에 반응했을 뿐이다. ⑱ 그것이 그들에게 풍성한 수확을 생산할 동기를 제공했고, 그리고 나서 그들은 그것을 축제로 축하를 했으며, 이것을 우리는 추수감사절이라고 부른다.

본문파악

미국 추수감사절의 유래를 설명한 글이다. 첫째 단락은 도입부로 추수감사절의 의미를 말하고 있고, 둘째 단락은 추수감사절이 생겨난 과정에 대해 자세히 설명하고 있다. 셋째 단락에는 풍작의 원인에 대한 경제학자 아담 스미스의 해석이 부연되어 있다.

문제풀이

1. 《해석》 둘째 단락의 those who didn't pull their weight는 무슨 뜻인가?
pull one's weight는 '역할(직무)을 다하다'라는 뜻이다.
① 일하기에 충분히 튼튼했던 사람들 ② 마땅히 해야 하는 만큼 열심히 일하지 않은 사람들
③ 동기부여를 받지 못한 사람들 ④ 영국의 전통을 따르지 않은 사람들
⑤ 공동 농작에 대해 몰랐던 사람들

2. 이 글에 따르면 '보이지 않는 손(invisible hand)'은 '이기심(self-interest)'을 의미하며, 이것이 청교도들에게는 '사유 재산(private property)'이었다.

3. ③ 청교도들이 영국을 떠난 이유 → 청교도들이 왜 영국을 떠나 미국으로 건너왔는지는 언급되어 있지 않다.
① 추수감사절의 유래 (⑯번 문장 참조) ② 청교도들에 대한 동기부여의 효과 (⑭~⑯번 문장 참조)
④ 브래드포드 총독이 만든 정책 (⑫~⑬번 문장 참조) ⑤ 청교도들이 직면했던 궁핍한 환경 (③~⑤번 문장 참조)

4. (A)에는 문맥상 영국으로 돌아가지 않고 '남은' 사람들이라는 뜻의 remained가 적절하다. (B)에는 예전에는 나이가 많거나 몸이 아프다는 이유로 일을 안 했던 사람들도 사유 재산제를 '받아들였다'는 내용이 자연스러우므로 accepted가 적절하다. (C)에는 보이지 않는 손을 따라 사람들이 진보된 이기심에 반응하는 것을 보면 사람들의 행동을 '지배하다'는 내용이 어울리므로 directs가 적절하다.
cf. remind(상기시키다) / oppose(반대하다) / liberate (자유롭게 하다)

구문해설

⑩ Young men, in particular, thought **it** an injustice **to receive** the same allotment of food as those [who didn't pull their weight].

▷ it은 가목적어, to receive 이하가 진목적어이다.

⑱ **It** provided them with the incentive [**to produce** a bountiful harvest], **which** they then celebrated in a feast, **which** we **call Thanksgiving Day**.

▷ It은 앞문장의 the invisible hand를 가리키는 대명사이다.
▷ which로 시작하는 두 개의 관계대명사절은 각각 앞의 a bountiful harvest와 a feast를 부연 설명하는 계속적 용법의 목적격 관계대명사절이다.
▷ call A B: 'A를 B라고 부르다'의 의미로, A에 해당하는 말이 'a feast'를 선행사로 하는 관계대명사 which이다.

애덤 스미스의 「국부론(*An Inquiry into the Nature and Causes of the Wealth of Nations*)」

영국의 사회과학자이자 고전경제학의 창시자인 애덤 스미스는 「국부론」에서 우리가 저녁 식사를 기대할 수 있는 것은 정육점 주인, 양조업자, 제빵업자의 자비심 덕분이 아니라, 그들이 자신의 이익을 추구하기 때문이라고 이야기한다. 그는 인간의 이기심을 긍정적이고 발전적으로 해석함으로써 자유시장경제가 윤리적으로 정당화될 수 있는 길을 열었다.
그는 개인의 이익추구가 사회 전체의 이익에도 기여하기 때문에 도덕적으로 정당하며, 따라서 개인의 의사결정은 존중되어야 하고, 그 결정에 정부를 포함한 제삼자가 개입하려고 해서는 안 된다고 말한다. 자신의 경제적 상황을 고려하여 어떤 일에 투자하면 좋을지, 어떤 물건을 생산하는 것이 큰 이익을 가져올 것인지 등에 대해서는 정치가나 국가보다 개인 스스로 판단하는 것이 더 낫기 때문이다. 그가 주장한 바람직한 국가의 역할은 국가가 국민의 경제활동에 간섭하지 않고 자유로운 경제활동이 안전하게 이루어질 수 있도록 국방과 사법을 담당하는 것이다. 또한 교육과 토목 등의 각종 공공사업을 담당하여 자유경쟁사회가 안전하고 순조롭게 존속하도록 노력해야 한다고 주장한다.

42

SECTION 09. 경제 · 경영

정보 비대칭으로 인한 도덕적 위험

p.106

정답 | 1. ③ 2. ④ gathering → gather 3. 여러 경제 주체가 보유한 정보의 양에 불균형이 있기 때문이다. 4. ③

본문 필기노트

① Economic agents base decisions about a trade / on the information [(that) they possess]. ② There may exist, however, an inequality / in the amount of information [held by various agents], [providing an advantage to one or more sides], a situation [referred to as asymmetric information]. ③ An illustration of this condition is [(the time) when the buyer (of a used vehicle) utilizes market averages as a reference point while the seller has specific information (regarding the quality and maintenance history, and therefore the true value, of the vehicle), [thus creating an imbalance of power].

(providing: =and it provides (결과의 분사구문) / buyer: S₁ / utilizes: V₁ / as: ~로(서) / while: ~하는 반면 / regarding: ~에 관한(전치사) / thus creating: 결과의 분사구문)

경제 행위에서 정보의 비대칭이 발생하는 상황

④ While the previous example highlights the presence of asymmetric information prior to completion of a transaction, the principle also applies to actions [taken after a contract is in effect], a scenario [known as a moral hazard]. ⑤ One framework for evaluating this premise / is the principal-agent problem, in which an agent is contracted by a principal to carry out a task]. ⑥ Following the contract's finalization, the agent may perform an action without the principal's knowledge or gather information (unavailable to the principal). ⑦ For instance, in the car insurance industry, the insurance provider, the principal, is unable to monitor the actions of the insured driver, the agent. ⑧ Consequently, the hidden actions of the agent, such as careless or reckless driving, have an adverse monetary effect on the principal, [who must cover the costs [associated with accidents]].

(While: ~인 반면에(접속사) / prior to: ~에 앞서 / applies to: ~에 적용되다 / for: ~을 위한 / the principal-agent problem: which의 선행사 / in which: 목적격 관 · 대(계속적 용법) / to carry out: 수행하도록(부사적 용법) / Following: ~후에(전치사) / without: ~이 없는, ~이 없이 / the insurance provider = the principal / the insured driver = the agent / principal: who의 선행사 / who: 주격 관 · 대(계속적 용법))

정보의 비대칭으로 인해 발생하는 도덕적 위험 현상

⑨ When asymmetric information causes a moral hazard, the principal must provide incentives and disincentives to counterbalance the effect. ⑩ Instituting deductibles in insurance policies and increasing insurance premiums for drivers [involved in repeated accidents] / are some actions [taken to encourage drivers to be careful].

(to counterbalance: 상쇄하기 위해(부사적 용법) / for: ~에 대해)

도덕적 위험을 상쇄하기 위한 조치

본문해석

① 경제 주체들은 자신이 소유한 정보를 근거로 거래에 대한 결정을 내린다. ② 그러나, 정보의 양에 있어서 한쪽 또는 그 이상을 유리하게 하는 불평등이 다양한 주체들에 의해 생기는데, 이것이 비대칭 정보라고 불리는 상황이다. ③ 이 상황의 한 예시로는 중고 차량의 구매자는 시장 평균값을 기준으로 이용하는 반면 판매자는 그 차량의 품질과 정비 내역, 즉 진짜 가치에 대한 구체적인 정보를 보유하고 있기 때문에 권력의 불균형을 낳는 경우다.

④ 앞의 예시가 거래 완료 전의 비대칭 정보의 존재를 강조하는 반면, 이 원리는 또한 계약이 효력을 발휘한 후에 취해지는 행동에도 적용되는데, 이것은 도덕적 위험이라고 알려진 시나리오다. ⑤ 이 전제를 평가하는 하나의 틀이 주인-대리인 문제인데, 이것은 대리인이 주인으로 인해 업무를 수행하도록 고용되는 경우이다. ⑥ 계약 체결 후에, 대리인은 주인이 모르게 행동을 하거나 주인이 손에 넣을 수 없는 정보를 수집할 수 있다. ⑦ 예를 들어, 자동차 보험 업계에서 보험 제공자, 즉 주인은 보험에 가입한 운전자, 즉 대리인의 행동을 감시할 수 없다. ⑧ 결과적으로, 대리인의 숨겨진 행동, 즉 부주의하거나 무모한 운전처럼 주인에게 금전적으로 불리한 영향을 끼치고 주인은 사고와 연관된 비용을 지급해야만 한다.

⑨ 비대칭 정보가 도덕적 위험을 야기할 때, 주인은 그 효과를 상쇄하기 위하여 유인책과 역유인책을 제공해야 한다. ⑩ 보험 정책에 자기 부담금을 도입하는 것과 반복되는 사고에 휘말리는 운전자에게 보험료를 할증하는 것이, 운전자들을 보다 조심성 있게 만들기 위해 취해진 몇몇 조치이다.

본문파악

이 글은 경제 상황에서 정보의 불균형에 따른 정보 비대칭 현상과, 그로 인해 발생할 수 있는 도덕적 위험에 대해 설명하는 글이다. 첫째 단락에서는 중고차 시장의 예를 들어 정보의 비대칭이 발생하는 상황을 설명하고 있다. 둘째 단락에서는 이로 인해 야기되는 도덕적 위험의 개념을 보험 계약 체결 이후의 상황을 예시로 들며 설명하고 있다. 마지막 단락에서는 도덕적 위험 현상을 상쇄하는 방편으로 유인책과 역유인책을 제공해야 한다는 결론을 내리고 있다.

문제풀이

1. ≪해석≫ 위 글에 따르면, 다음 중 도덕적 위험이 아닌 것은?
둘째 단락에서 도덕적 위험은 계약이 효력을 발휘한 뒤, 대리인이 비대칭 정보를 이용해 개인의 이익을 취하는 것이라고 하였으므로 (b),(c)는 이에 해당하지 않는다.
(a) 근무 시간 중에 관리자 모르게 주식 투자를 하는 직원
(b) 보통 많은 음식을 먹으려고 하는 고객이 그렇지 않는 고객보다 더 많은 뷔페 식당들
(c) 오작동을 일으킨 스마트폰을 수리해서 중고 폰 시장에 판매하는 유통업자
(d) 개인 이득을 극대화하기 위해 고객의 자금을 투자함으로써 위험을 무릅쓰는 펀드 매니저들

2. ④는 조동사 may 뒤의 perform과 함께 접속사 or로 병렬연결된 동사 자리이므로 gathering이 아닌 gather가 와야 한다.

3. 《해석》 위 글에 따르면, 힘의 불균형은 왜 일어나는가? (한국어로)
②번 문장 참조

4. 대리인이 도덕적 위험으로 정보를 공개하지 않아 주인이 손해를 보는 상황이므로, 대리인이 정보를 숨기지 못하도록 조치를 취해야 할 것이다. 따라서 그러기 위한 방편을 제시하는 ③이 빈칸에 가장 적절하다.
① 최대의 수익을 보장하는 다른 대리인을 찾아야
② 결과를 이해하면서도 더 많은 위험을 무릅써야
③ 그 효과를 상쇄하기 위하여 유인책과 역유인책을 제공해야
④ 얼마나 많은 이익을 얻을 수 있는지에 대한 더 나은 정보를 확보해야
⑤ 대리인에게 지금까지 일어난 모든 일에 대한 정보를 제공해야

구문해설

③ An illustration of this condition is **when** the buyer of a used vehicle utilizes market averages as a reference point while the seller has specific information (**regarding** the quality and maintenance history, and therefore the true value, of the vehicle), thus **creating** an imbalance of power.

▷ when 이하는 문장의 보어로 쓰인 명사절이다.
▷ ( )는 specific information을 수식하는 전치사구이다.
▷ creating 이하는 결과를 나타내는 분사구문이다.

⑩ [Instituting deductibles in insurance policies] and [increasing insurance premiums for drivers **involved** in repeated accidents] **are** some actions **taken** to encourage drivers to be careful.

▷ 첫 번째 [ ]와 두 번째 [ ]는 모두 동명사구로 문장의 주어 역할을 한다. 주어가 복수이므로 be동사로 복수동사 are가 쓰였다.
▷ involved와 taken은 각각 drivers와 some actions를 수식하는 과거분사이다.

43

SECTION 09. 경제 · 경영

크라우드소싱(crowdsourcing)

P.108

정답 | 1. ③ 2. ③ 3. ④ 4. customers

본문 필기노트

① The term "crowdsourcing" is a blending of the words "crowd" and "outsourcing," and it refers to the business strategy of [obtaining work, ideas or funding from a variety of collaborators]. ② It is considered a type of open innovation, meaning [it acts as a catalyst for innovative development by combining ideas, efforts and materials / from both internal and external sources]. ③ The advent of this process / has been facilitated by advances in networking technology, as a dedicated web platform — an Internet-accessible base [upon which technologies and processes can be built] — often serves as the focal point of crowdsourcing efforts.

크라우드소싱의 개념과 대두 배경

④ Strategically speaking, the primary appeal of crowdsourcing / can be found in the superior quality of the results [it produces], [the idea being [that it allows businesses to selectively handpick the "cream of the crop" / from a vast pool of proposals]]. ⑤ This offers an inherent advantage over the traditional method of [relying on a single provider of services or an internal research and development department]. ⑥ What's more, the external contributors (in a crowdsourcing effort) / need not be limited to freelancers and professional partners — customers are also being included, and are, in fact, somewhat sought after for their unique perspective on the brands [they favor] and the products [they purchase].

크라우드소싱의 이점

⑦ LEGO, for example, has launched a website [onto which individuals can upload innovative ideas for future LEGO products]; these ideas are then judged by the online LEGO community. ⑧ If a proposal obtains 10,000 "likes," the product is slated for development and release, with the originator of the idea receiving one percent of the sales [subsequently generated].

크라우드소싱 적용 사례

본문해석

① '크라우드소싱'이라는 용어는 '대중(crowd)'과 '외주(outsourcing)'의 혼성어이며, 다양한 협력자들로부터 일, 아이디어, 또는 자금을 얻는 경영 전략을 가리킨다. ② 그것은 오픈 이노베이션의 일종으로 여겨지는데, 이는 곧 그것이 내부 자원과 외부 자원의 아이디어, 노력, 자료를 모두 결합함으로써 혁신적인 발전을 위한 촉매제로서 기능한다는 뜻이다. ③ 이 과정의 도래는 네트워킹 기술의 발전으로 인해 용이해졌는데, 전용 웹 플랫폼, 즉 기술과 프로세스가 구축될 수 있는 인터넷 접근 기반이 흔히 크라우드소싱 활동의 중심 역할을 하기 때문이다.

④ 전략적으로 말해, 크라우드소싱의 주요 매력은 그것이 생산하는 결과물의 우수한 품질에서 찾아볼 수 있는데, 이는 그것이 기업으로 하여금 방대한 제안의 집합으로부터 '알짜'를 선택적으로 골라내도록 하기 때문이다. ⑤ 이것은 단일 서비스 공급자 또는 내부 연구 개발 부서에 의존하는 전통적인 방법에 비해 고유한 이점을 제공한다. ⑥ 게다가, 크라우드소싱 활동에서의 외부 기여자들은 프리랜서와 전문 동업자에 한정될 필요가 없다. 고객 역시 포함되고 있으며, 실제로 고객은 그들이 선호하는 브랜드와 구매하는 제품에 대한 특별한 관점 때문에 다소 수요가 많다.

⑦ 예를 들어 레고사는, 사람들이 향후의 레고 제품을 위한 혁신적인 아이디어를 올릴 수 있는 웹사이트를 개시했다. 이 아이디어들은 그다음 온라인 레고 커뮤니티에 의해 평가된다. ⑧ 한 제안이 10,000개의 '좋아요'를 얻으면, 그 제품은 개발 및 출시 대상으로 선발되고, 그 아이디어의 창시자는 그에 따라 발생되는 매출의 1퍼센트를 받는다.

본문파악

이 글은 크라우드소싱에 관한 글이다. 첫째 단락에서는 크라우드소싱의 개념 및 도래 배경을 소개하고 있으며, 둘째 단락에서는 제한되지 않은 외부 자원을 활용하여 향상된 품질의 결과물을 창출한다는 크라우드소싱의 이점에 대해 설명하고 있다. 셋째 단락에서는 크라우드소싱의 실제 사례인 레고사의 경우를 들어 설명하고 있다.

문제풀이

1. 《해석》 위 글의 제목으로 가장 적절한 것은?
   크라우드소싱의 개념 및 특징을 설명하는 글이므로, 글의 제목으로는 ③이 가장 적절하다.
   ① 크라우드소싱의 여러 유형
   ② 오픈 이노베이션의 부정적인 면
   ③ 제한 없는 출처, 향상된 결과
   ④ 크라우드소싱이 자기자본의 자산을 늘린다
   ⑤ 고객 설문 조사: 없어서는 안 되는 수단

2. 《해석》 다음 중 크라우드소싱에 대해 참이 아닌 것은?
   ① (①번 문장 참조) ② (①번 문장 참조)
   ③ → ②번 문장에서 내부 자원과 외부 자원을 모두 활용한다고 했다.
   ④ (③번 문장 참조) ⑤ (⑤번 문장 참조)

3. 《해석》 필자가 두 번째 단락에서 'cream of the crop'을 언급하는 이유는 무엇인가?
   'cream of the crop'은 '가장 좋은 것, 알짜'라는 뜻으로, 이것을 언급하는 이유로는 ④가 가장 적절하다.
   ① 크라우드소싱이라는 용어가 적절한 이유를 설명하기 위해
   ② 크라우드소싱의 부정적인 면에 대한 예시를 제공하기 위해
   ③ 오늘날에는 전통적인 방법이 효과적이지 않다는 것을 강조하기 위해
   ④ 크라우드소싱으로 나온 결과물의 탁월한 품질을 강조하기 위해
   ⑤ 기업이 양이 아니라 질을 통해 인기를 얻을 수 있다는 것을 제시하기 위해

4. 《해석》 레고는 고객들의 유용한 브랜드 통찰력을 가장 잘 활용했다는 사실에 근거하여 크라우드소싱을 성공적으로 활용한 기업으로 소개된다. (본문에서)
   (⑥~⑧번 문장 참조)

구문해설

④ Strategically speaking, the primary appeal of crowdsourcing can be found in the superior quality of the results [(**which/that**) it produces], [**the idea being** that it allows businesses to selectively handpick the "cream of the crop" from a vast pool of proposals].

▷ 첫 번째 [ ]는 the results를 선행사로 하는 목적격 관계대명사절로 앞에 which 또는 that이 생략되었다.
▷ the idea는 분사구문의 의미상 주어로, 분사구문에서 분사구문의 주어(the idea)가 주절의 주어(the primary appeal)와 다를 때는 이와 같이 분사구문 앞에 그 주어를 밝혀 준다.

⑧ If a proposal obtains 10,000 "likes," the product is slated for development and release, **with the originator of the idea receiving** one percent of the sales [subsequently generated].

▷ 「with+O+분사」는 'O가 ~한 채로, ~하면서'라는 뜻의 분사구문으로, 이때, 목적어인 the originator of the idea와 분사가 능동 관계이므로 현재분사인 receiving이 쓰였다.
▷ [ ]는 the sales를 수식하는 과거분사구이다.

44 SECTION 09. 경제 · 경영

윤리적 소비(ethical consumption)

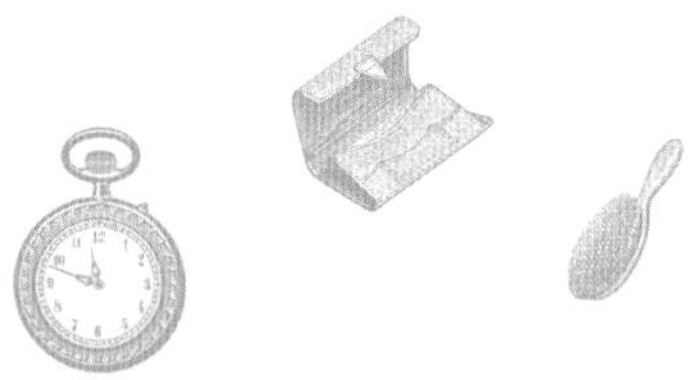

P.110

정답 | 1. ③ 2. ④ 3. 정부 감독이 더욱 줄어들고, 소비자들은 책임감 있는 경제 정책을 정부에 청원하기를 단념한다. / 경제적, 사회적 지위가 비교적 낮은 많은 소비자들은 윤리적 소비에 참여하는 데서 배제된다. 4. ②

본문 필기노트

① Over the past few decades, consumers in wealthy nations have begun practicing ethical consumption, [making informed purchasing decisions to support or avoid certain brands based on the company's record on human rights, fair labor practices, animal protection, and environmental sustainability].

(Over: ~동안, ~에 걸쳐 / practicing: 동사 have begun의 목적어로 쓰인 동명사 / making ~: 부대상황의 분사구문 / to support or avoid: 지지하거나 기피하기 위해(부사적 용법))

윤리적 소비의 실천 현황

② While ethical consumption has its merits, critics argue [that concentrating exclusively on consumer behavior at the individual level will only absolve governments and corporate entities of accountability]. ③ By emphasizing autonomy in consumer decision-making, the decrease (in governmental oversight) is reinforced, and consumers sacrifice the petitioning of the government to enact responsible economic policies.

(While: ~하는 반면 / that: that 이하는 목적어 / concentrating ~ level: S'(동명사구) / absolve A of B: A에게서 B를 면제하다 / by v-ing: ~함으로써 / the decrease: S / is reinforced: V)

윤리적 소비의 한계점 1

④ Furthermore, the practice of ethical consumption / is not solely determined by the individual's motivation [to create a robust market for ethical goods and services]. ⑤ The ability [to make such choices, such as buying organic food or expensive green products], is dependent upon a number of socio-economic factors, including household income and symbolic capital — that is, one's social status and reputation. ⑥ As a result, many consumers (with lower levels of economic and social status) are excluded from participating in ethical consumption.

(to create: 만들려는(형용사적 용법) / for: ~을 위해 / to make: (선택을) 할 수 있는(형용사적 용법) / A such as B: B와 같은 A / is dependent upon: ~에 의존하다 / including: ~를 포함하여(전치사) / that is: 즉 / As a result: 결과적으로 / from: ~로부터 / participating in: ~에 참가[참여]하다)

윤리적 소비의 한계점 2

⑦ Nevertheless, ethical consumption serves as a cultural force [that initiates change in the market and, more importantly, raises important questions regarding the relationships among ethics, commerce, and politics, as well as the sustainability of these systems]. ⑧ This trend should not be dismissed / as simply a passing fad or marketing tactic; instead, it should be treated /as an opportunity [to reshape consumer perspectives /on the meaning of living "the good life]."

(as: ~로(서) / that: 주격 관 · 대 / initiates: V'_1 / raises: V'_2 / regarding: ~에 관한(전치사) / A as well as B: B뿐만 아니라 A도 / as: ~로서 / instead: 그 대신에 / it: =this trend / to reshape: 재형성할(형용사적 용법))

윤리적 소비의 의의

본문해석

① 지난 몇 십 년 간, 부유한 나라의 소비자들은 인권, 공정한 노동 관행, 동물 보호, 환경 지속 가능성에 대한 그 회사의 내력을 기반으로 특정 브랜드를 지지하거나 기피하기 위해 정보에 근거한 구매 결정을 내리며 윤리적 소비를 실천하기 시작했다.

② 윤리적 소비에도 그 나름의 장점이 있는 한편, 비판자들은 개인적 수준의 소비자 행동에만 집중하는 것은 정부와 기업 법인의 책임을 면제해 줄 뿐이라고 주장한다. ③ 소비자 의사 결정의 자율성을 강조함으로써, 정부 감독의 축소가 강화되고, 소비자들은 책임감 있는 경제 정책을 제정하라는 정부에 대한 청원을 단념한다.

④ 게다가, 윤리적 소비의 관행은 윤리적 상품 및 용역을 위한 활발한 시장을 만들고자 하는 개인의 동기만으로 결정되는 것이 아니다. ⑤ 유기농 식품 또는 비싼 친환경 제품을 사는 것과 같은 그러한 선택을 할 수 있는 능력은, 가계 소득과 상징적 자산, 즉 개인의 사회적 지위 및 평판을 포함하는 여러 가지 사회경제학적 요인에 달려있다. ⑥ 결과적으로, 경제적, 사회적 지위가 비교적 낮은 많은 소비자들은 윤리적 소비에 참여하는 데서 배제된다.

⑦ 그럼에도 불구하고, 윤리적 소비는 시장의 변화를 촉발하고 더 중요하게는 윤리와 상업, 정치의 관계뿐만 아니라 이 체계들의 지속 가능성에 대해서도 중요한 의문을 제기하는 문화적 힘으로 기능한다. ⑧ 이 추세는 단순히 지나가는 유행이나 마케팅 전술로 일축되어서는 안 된다. 대신, '올바른 삶'을 산다는 것의 의미에 대한 소비자의 관점을 재형성할 기회로서 다루어져야 한다.

본문파악

이 글은 윤리적 소비를 소개하고 그 한계점 및 의의를 설명하는 글이다. 첫 번째 단락에서 윤리적 소비를 실천하고 있는 현황을 소개하고 있다. 두 번째와 세 번째 단락에서는 윤리적 소비가 가지는 한계점에 대해서 짚고 있으며, 마지막 단락에서는 올바른 삶을 산다는 것에 대한 관점을 형성할 기회로서의 윤리적 소비의 의의를 설명하고 있다.

문제풀이

1. 《해석》 위 글의 주제는 무엇인가?
   윤리적 소비의 문제점과 의의를 하나씩 살펴보고 있으므로, 글의 주제로는 ③이 가장 적절하다.
   ① 현대 소비자 행동의 특징
   ② 윤리적 소비가 널리 퍼진 이유
   ③ 윤리적 소비의 가치와 부정적 영향
   ④ 소비와 삶의 질의 관계
   ⑤ 경기 부양에서 정부 역할의 중요성

2. (A) 빈칸 앞에서 윤리적 소비의 한계점을 언급하고, 빈칸 뒤에서는 추가적인 내용을 덧붙이고 있으므로, '게다가'라는 의미의 Furthermore가 적절하다.
   (B) 빈칸 앞에서 윤리적 소비의 한계점에 대해 말한 반면, 빈칸 뒤에서는 윤리적 소비가 가지는 의의를 설명하고 있으므로, 빈칸에는 '그럼에도 불구하고'를 뜻하는 Nevertheless가 적절하다.
   ① 게다가 — 마찬가지로　　② 예를 들어 — 더욱이
   ③ 그러나 — 그럼에도 불구하고　　⑤ 그러나 — 더욱이

3. ③번, ⑥번 문장 참조

4. 윤리적 소비자는 인권, 공정한 노동 관행, 동물 보호, 환경 지속 가능성을 중시한다는 ①번 문장의 내용을 바탕으로, 윤리적 소비는 '② 올바른(good)' 삶과 관련이 있음을 알 수 있다.
   ① 특이한　　③ 융통성 있는
   ④ 반항적인　　⑤ 물질주의적인

구문해설

⑤ The ability [**to make** such choices, such as buying organic food or expensive green products], is dependent upon a number of socio-economic factors, including household income and symbolic capital — that is, **one's social status and reputation**.

▷ to make 이하는 The ability를 수식하는 형용사적 용법의 to부정사구이다.
▷ that is 뒤의 one's social status and reputation은 symbolic capital의 부연 설명이다.

⑦ Nevertheless, ethical consumption serves as a cultural force [**that initiates** change in the market and, more importantly, **raises** important questions (**regarding** the relationships among ethics, commerce, and politics, **as well as** the sustainability of these systems)].

▷ [ ]는 선행사 a cultural force를 수식하는 주격 관계대명사절로 동사 initiates와 raises가 접속사 and로 병렬연결되어 있다.
▷ ( )는 전치사구로 앞의 명사구 important questions를 수식하다.
▷ A as well as B: 'B뿐만 아니라 A도'

45 SECTION 10. 윤리

왜 직업윤리가 필요한가?

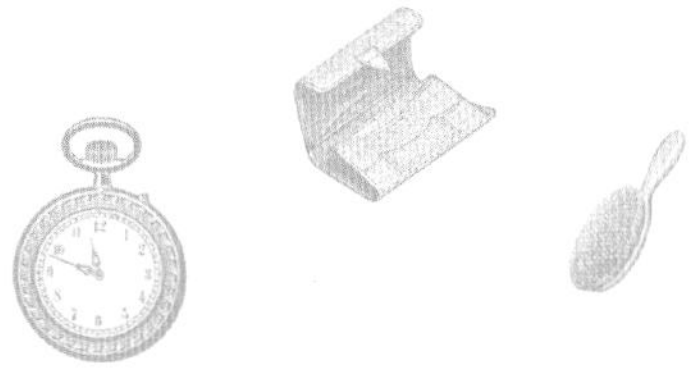

P.116

정답	1. professional ethics 2. ② 3. 인류에게 막대한 피해를 주는 것을 피해야 한다는 가치 판단 4. 전문직에 종사하는 사람이 관련 분야에 대해 윤리적 책임 의식을 갖는 것

본문 필기노트

① Before the explosion of the first atomic bomb, / the scientist [who created it] must have been confused ; the common understanding of a scientist's duties / includes neither an obligation [to consider the actual or prospective consequences of one's scientific findings] nor a duty [to warn the public]. ② But nevertheless, the scientist should not follow the same understanding as regards the development of nuclear power. (③ For there is no one other than him/her [who can know the destructive consequences of it].) ④ This reasoning is simple and straightforward, / and I think it can be regarded as a basic pattern for deriving duties and responsibilities of the scientist. ⑤ The reasoning assumes a value judgment [that we should try to avoid grave harm to mankind], and anyone should be able to agree on this. ⑥ And I wish to emphasize [that the duties and responsibilities derived / are closely connected with the scientist's role as a scientist, as a specialist of knowledge in a specific field].

(주격 관·대 / ~였음에 틀림없다 / 왜냐하면(=for) / V / neither A nor B: A도 B도 아닌 / 고려할(형용사적 용법) / 경고할(형용사적 용법) / ~해야 한다(의무·당연) / ~에 관한 한 / 왜냐하면(접속사) / =except / 주격 관·대 / regard A as B: A를 B로 여기다 / ~를 위한(전치사) / 동격의 that / V / O / = / ~에 동의하다 / that 이하는 목적어 / S' / V' / ~와 관련되어 있다 / ~로서 / =)

과학자가 지녀야 할 직업윤리

⑦ If we change the phrase "the scientist's role as a scientist" to other phrases such as "the carpenter's role as a building constructor" or "the physician's role as a medical specialist," / the same reasoning can be applied ; thus it should be used as a basis for professional ethics.

(~로 / A such as B: B와 같은 A / 부연설명 / ~로(서))

다른 전문 직종으로 확대 가능한 과학자의 직업윤리

본문해석

① 최초의 원자폭탄 폭발 이전에 그것을 만든 과학자는 틀림없이 혼란스러웠을 것이다. 왜냐하면 과학자의 의무에 대한 일반적인 지식은 과학적 발견으로 인한 실제의 혹은 예상되는 결과를 고려해야 할 의무도 대중에게 경고해야 할 의무도 포함하고 있지 않기 때문이다. ② 그러나 그럼에도 불구하고 과학자는 원자력의 개발에 대해서는 동일한 인식을 따라서는 안 된다. (③ 왜냐하면 그것의 파괴적인 결과를 아는 사람은 그/그녀 외에 다른 사람은 없기 때문이다.) ④ 이런 논리는 단순하고 간단한 것이어서, 나는 이것이 과학자의 의무와 책임을 끌어내기 위한 기본적인 전형으로 간주될 수 있다고 생각한다. ⑤ 이 논리는 우리가 인류에게 커다란 해를 끼치지 않도록 노력해야 한다는 가치 판단을 나타내며, 누구나 이것에 동의할 수 있어야만 한다. ⑥ 그리고 나는 도출된 의무와 책임감은 과학자로서의, 즉 특정 분야 지식에 대한 전문가로서의 과학자의 역할과 밀접히 관련되어 있다는 것을 강조하고 싶다.

⑦ 만일 우리가 '과학자로서의 과학자의 역할'이라는 어구를 '빌딩 건설자로서의 목수의 역할'이나 '의료 전문가로서의 의사의 역할'과 같은 다른 어구로 바꾼다면, 이 동일한 논리가 적용될 수 있고, 이렇게, 그것은 직업윤리의 기본으로 사용될 수 있다.

본문파악

이 글은 전문직에 종사하는 사람들이 가져야 할 직업윤리에 대한 것이다. 첫째 단락에서는 원자 폭탄을 개발한 과학자를 예로 들면서 과학자가 지녀야 할 직업윤리에 대해 언급하고 있고, 둘째 단락에서는 이와 같은 직업윤리가 다른 직업 분야에도 확대 적용될 수 있다고 주장하고 있다.

문제풀이

1. 《해석》 위 글의 주제는 무엇인가? (본문에서 두 단어)
   이 글의 요지는 과학자를 비롯한 전문직 종사자들이 자신의 직업에 걸맞은 윤리 의식을 지녀야 한다는 것이다. 따라서 주제로는 둘째 단락의 맨 마지막 문장에 나와 있는 '직업윤리(professional ethics)'가 적절하다.

2. 주어진 문장이 '왜냐하면 그것의 파괴적인 결과를 아는 사람은 그/그녀 외에 다른 사람은 없기 때문이다.'라는 뜻이므로 이 문장이 앞 문장에 대한 이유로 쓰였다는 것과 '그것(it=nuclear power)'이 앞 문장에서 이미 언급된 바 있다는 것을 짐작할 수 있다.

3. 《해석》 첫째 단락의 this가 가리키는 바는 무엇인가? (한국말로)
   ⑤번 문장에서, and 앞의 문장 참조

4. the same reasoning은 앞 단락에서 언급된 과학자의 예시와 같은 것으로, 전문직 종사자들이 자신의 일이 사회적으로 미칠 부정적 영향까지도 고려해야 한다는 것이다.

직업과 직업윤리

직업은 한 인간의 생계유지를 위한 수단이자, 자신의 이상을 실현하기 위한 도구가 되는 것이다. 직업에는 귀천이 없다는 말이 있듯이, 직업은 어떠한 종류의 것이라도 사회에서 필요한 것이며 신성한 것이다. 인간은 누구나 직업을 가지고 있으며, 또한 그에 맞는 직업윤리를 가지고 있어야 한다.
윤리적 존재로서의 인간이 지켜야 할 윤리에는 한 사회의 모든 구성원의 상호작용 관계를 지배하며 사회질서를 유지하고 통합시키는 보편적인 윤리와 부분적 집단 구성원 간의 행위 관계를 지배하는 특수한 윤리가 있다. 현대와 같이 노동이 분화되고 새로운 직업이 생겨나며 수많은 조직이 구성되는 사회에서 살고 있는 우리는 사회 전체에서 요구하는 보편적 윤리 외에 집단과 조직에서 요구하는 특수 윤리에 의해서도 행위 관계를 통제받게 되었다. 더구나 필연적으로 집단에 소속되지 않으면 안 되는 현대인들은 그 대부분의 행위 관계가 집단의 목표와 과업의 성취를 겨냥하지 않으면 안 되기 때문에 보편적 윤리보다 특수 윤리에 의해 지배될 가능성이 더욱 커졌다. 이와 같이 현대인의 행위 관계를 크게 지배하는 특수 윤리 가운데 특정한 직업에 종사하는 이들의 윤리를 직업윤리라 한다.

46

SECTION 10. 윤리

윤리의 궁극적 목적

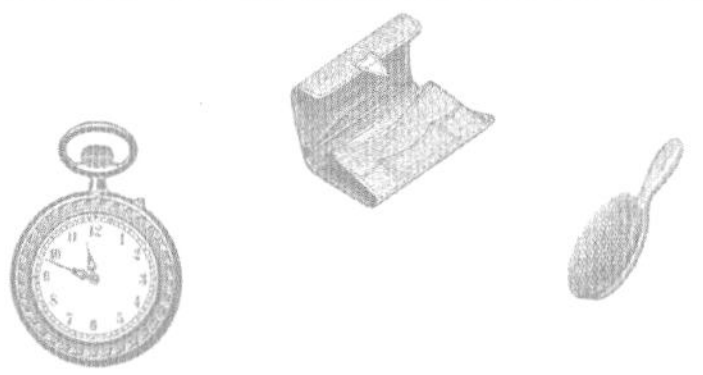

P.118

정답 | 1. ③ 2. ② 3. ④, ⑤

본문 필기노트

① The purpose of ethics is [to define a person's proper values and interests and the actions [which he should take in regard to those interests]]. ② If an individual has no interests, no values [with which to concern himself], / then any discussion regarding ethics / becomes as useless as contemplation of how many angels will fit on the head of a pin. ③ To begin this exploration, / we first need to ask, "What are values?"

- to define: 정의하는 것(명사적 용법)
- which: 목적격 관 · 대
- in regard to: ~에 관해서
- with which: 목적격 관 · 대
- regarding: ~에 관한(전치사)
- as useless as: as+형+as ~: ~만큼 …한
- of: ~에 대한
- on: ~위에
- To begin: 시작하기 위해서(부사적 용법)
- need to ask: need to-v: ~할 필요가 있다

윤리의 목적

④ A value is something [for which a person is willing to take some action in order to obtain and/or to keep that something — whether that something is a physical object such as a house or a nonphysical existent such as love]. ⑤ It is important [to emphasize here [that some "action" is involved]]. ⑥ This serves conceptually to distinguish between values and desires (wants or wishes). ⑦ I may want or desire a million-dollar home, / but unless I am willing to take some action [to try to obtain it], it is not a value. ⑧ Values presuppose someone [who values and acts].

- for which: 목적격 관 · 대
- is willing to: 기꺼이 ~하다
- in order to: ~하기 위해서
- —: 부연설명
- whether ... or: whether A or B: A이든 B이든 간에
- such as: A such as B: B와 같은 A
- It: 가주어
- to emphasize: to 이하는 진주어
- that: that 이하는 목적어
- serves to: serve to-v: ~하는 데 도움이 되다
- between ... and: between A and B: A와 B 사이의
- unless: ~하지 않는다면
- to try: 노력하는(형용사적 용법)
- who: 주격 관 · 대

가치의 개념

⑨ But should this "acting person" be the one [to benefit from what he does]? ⑩ And what are these values for? ⑪ One popular answer to these questions / comes from the proponents of altruism. ⑫ Altruism is the doctrine [which states that only an action [taken for others' benefit] is the good, that is, constitutes proper behavior]. ⑬ According to altruism, anything [done for one's self] has no moral sanction. ⑭ Any hint of selfish benefit [received by the "acting person"] is immoral by this credo.

- what: ~한 것
- to benefit: 이득을 얻는(형용사적 용법)
- for: ~을 위한
- to: ~에 대한
- which: 주격 관 · 대
- is: V'_1
- that is: 즉
- constitutes: V'_2
- is: V
- by: ~에 의하면

가치 실현과 이타주의

본문해석

① 윤리의 목적은 한 사람의 적절한 가치 및 관심과 그러한 관심에 관해 그 사람이 취해야 하는 행동을 정의하는 것이다. ② 만일 한 개인이 어떠한 관심 또는 자기 자신과 관련된 어떠한 가치도 지니고 있지 않다면, 윤리에 관한 어떠한 논의도 얼마나 많은 천사들이 못의 머리에 들어앉을 수 있는지에 대해 예상하는 것만큼이나 쓸모없게 된다. ③ 이러한 탐구를 시작하기 위해서 우리는 우선 "가치란 무엇인가?"라는 질문을 할 필요가 있다.

④ 가치란 어떤 것, 즉 그 어떤 것이 집과 같은 물질적인 대상이든 사랑과 같은 비물질적인 존재물이든 간에, 그것을 얻고/얻거나 간직하기 위해 한 개인이 기꺼이 어떤 조치를 취하려는 것이다. ⑤ 여기서 어떤 '행동'이 수반된다는 것을 강조하는 것이 중요하다. ⑥ 이것은 개념상으로 가치와 욕망(욕구 또는 소망)을 구분하는 데 도움이 된다. ⑦ 내가 백만 달러짜리 집을 원하거나 바랄 수는 있지만, 만약 내가 그것을 얻으려고 노력하는 어떤 조치를 기꺼이 취하지 않는다면 그것은 가치가 아니다. ⑧ 가치는 소중히 여기고 행동에 옮기는 누군가를 전제로 한다.

⑨ 그러나 이 '행동하는 사람'은 그가 행하는 것으로부터 이득을 얻는 당사자이어야 하는가? ⑩ 그리고 이 가치는 무엇을 위한 것인가? ⑪ 이 질문들에 대한 한 가지 잘 알려진 대답은 이타주의 옹호자들에게서 나온다. ⑫ 이타주의란 다른 사람들의 이익을 위해 행해지는 행동만이 선이라고, 즉 적절한 행위를 구성한다고 말하는 주의이다. ⑬ 이타주의에 의하면 자신을 위해 행해지는 것은 무엇이든지 도덕적 인정을 받지 못한다. ⑭ '행동하는 사람'이 얻는 어떠한 이기적인 이득도 이 신조에 의하면 비도덕적인 것이다.

본문파악

이 글은 윤리의 목적을 가치의 개념과 이타주의 정신을 통해 설명한 것이다. 첫째 단락에서는 윤리의 목적에 대해 설명하고 있고, 둘째 단락에서는 가치의 개념에 대해 설명하면서 가치의 성립 조건으로 행동이 수반되어야 함을 이야기하고 있다. 셋째 단락에서는 행동이 수반된 가치라도 그것이 타인을 위한 것이어야 도덕적으로 인정받는다는 내용이 언급되어 있다.

문제풀이

1. (A)에는 「as ~ as ...」 구문이 쓰인 것으로 보아 두 번째 as 뒤의 내용이 결정적 단서가 된다. 못의 머리 부분에 얼마나 많은 천사들이 들어앉을 수 있을지 고민하는 것은 '쓸모없는(useless)' 일이다. (B) 앞문장의 내용을 보면 자신을 위해 행해진 행동은 도덕적으로 인정되지 못한다 했으므로, 행동을 하는 사람 자신이 득을 보게 된다면 '비도덕적인(immoral)' 것이다.

2. 《해석》 위 글에 의하면 다음 중 참인 것은?
① 오로지 물질적인 대상만이 진정한 가치를 지녔다고 할 수 있다. → ④번 문장에 의하면 가치의 대상은 물질적인 것도 될 수 있고 비물질적인 것도 될 수 있다.
② 가치와 욕망 사이에는 큰 차이가 있다. → ⑥~⑧번 문장에 의하면 가치와 욕망은 행동의 수반 여부에서 구별될 수 있다고 했으므로 옳다.
③ 가치는 자기 이익을 추구할 때 가장 정당화될 수 있다. → ⑬~⑭번 문장에 의하면 가치의 실현은 타인을 위한 것일 때 의미가 있는 것이다.
④ 행동하는 것이 어떤 것을 바라는 것보다 더 중요하다. → 언급된 바가 없다.
⑤ 이기심은 이타주의자들에게 하나의 가치가 될 수 있다. → ⑬~⑭번 문장에 의하면 이기적인 행동은 이타주의자들에게는 비도덕적인 것이므로 가치가 될 수 없다.

3. 위 글에 따르면, 윤리적 가치는 행동이 수반되어야 하며, 행동이 수반된 가치라도 그 행동이 타인을 위한 것이어야 한다. 따라서 타인을 위한 행동을 한 사람을 찾으면 된다.

구문해설

② If an individual has no interests, <u>no values</u> [**with <u>which</u> to concern himself**], then ... .

▷ [ ] 부분은 with which he should concern himself의 의미이다.

인간에게 내재된 이타주의

과학자들은 왜 인간이 아무런 대가를 바라지 않고 남을 도와주는 이타적인 행동을 하는가에 대해 논쟁을 벌여 왔다. 많은 과학자들과 심리학자들이 이타주의는 인간만이 지닌 고유한 신념이라고 여기고 인간에게만 존재하는 것이라고 주장했다. 바르네켄(Felix Warneken)을 비롯한 독일의 심리학자들의 연구에 의하면 이타주의는 18개월 된 유아도 지니고 있는 덕목으로 나타났다.
「사이언스(Science)」에 게재된 그들의 논문에 의하면, 18개월 된 유아는 이타주의적인 행동을 보이며, 이것은 인간이 태어날 때부터 자연적으로 다른 사람을 돕는 경향을 가지고 있다는 증거라고 볼 수 있다. 실험에 참가한 24명의 유아들은 책을 쌓아올리거나 빨래집게를 줍는 것과 같은 일을 완수하기 위해 다른 사람을 도와준다. 이 실험에서, 바르네켄이 유아들에게 도움을 청하지도 않았고 고맙다는 말을 하지도 않았는데 유아들은 도움을 제공했다. 게다가 그가 고의로 책장에서 책을 빼서 던지거나 빨래집게를 던지면 유아들은 도움을 주지 않으려고 했다고 한다.
이를 계기로 아직 사회적인 기술을 익히지 않은 아주 어린 아기들도 타인을 도우려는 의지가 있음이 밝혀졌다. 이타주의는 사회의 일원으로 살아가는 인간이 어릴 때부터 지니고 있는 윤리적 가치인 것이다.

47

SECTION 10. 윤리

소극적 자유와 적극적 자유

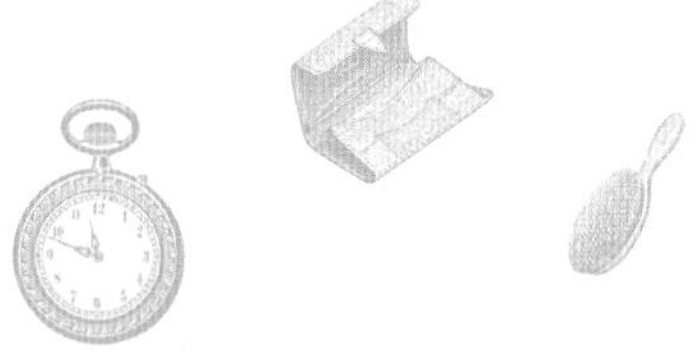

P.120

정답 | 1. 외부로부터의 장애가 전혀 없는 상태, 자기 결정력이 있어 자신을 통제할 수 있는 상태 2. ⑤ 3. ③

본문 필기노트

① Imagine you are driving your car. ② You come to a fork in the road and turn right. ③ Next you come to a crossroads and turn left. ④ There is no traffic to speak of, and there are no roadblocks. ⑤ You seem to be completely free. ⑥ This view of your situation / might change dramatically, however, / if we consider [that the reason (why/that) you turned right and then left] is because you're addicted to smoking, and you're desperate to get to the nearest store to buy more cigarettes]. ⑦ Rather than driving, / it's like you are being driven, / as your urge to smoke causes you uncontrollably to turn the wheel / first in one direction and then the other. ⑧ Moreover, you know [that your turning left at the crossroads / means (that) you'll be late for an important appointment], but you do it anyway.

Imagine: 상상해 보라(명령형) / come to: ~에 이르다 / to speak of: ~에 대해 말할(형용사적 용법) / seem to-v: ~인 듯 보이다 / that: that 이하는 목적어 / we: S′ / consider: V′ / be addicted to v-ing: ~에 중독되다 / get to: ~에 도착하다 / to buy: 사기 위해(부사적 용법) / Rather than: ~라기보다는 오히려 / like: 접속사(~인 것 같이) / as: ~때문에(접속사) / cause O to-v: O로 하여금 ~하게 하다 / one ~ the other ...: (둘 중) 하나는 ~ 다른 하나는 … / that: that 이하는 목적어 / your turning left at the crossroads: S′ / means: V′ / be late for: ~에 늦다 / it: =turning left at the crossroads

흡연 중독인 운전자의 예를 통한 화두 제시

본문해석

① 당신이 당신의 자동차를 운전하고 있다고 상상해 보라. ② 갈림길에 이르러 우회전을 한다. ③ 그 다음에는 교차로에 이르러 좌회전을 한다. ④ 특별히 언급할 만한 교통량도 없고, 장애물도 전혀 없다. ⑤ 당신은 완벽하게 자유로운 것처럼 보인다. ⑥ 그러나 만약 당신이 우회전하고 나서 좌회전을 한 이유가 당신이 흡연에 중독되어 담배를 더 사러 가장 가까운 가게에 필사적으로 가는 것이라고 생각한다면, 당신의 상황에 대한 이러한 관점은 극적으로 바뀔 수 있다. ⑦ 담배를 피우고 싶은 충동이 당신으로 하여금 자제력 없이 핸들을 처음에는 이쪽으로 그다음에는 반대쪽으로 돌리게 하기 때문에, 그것은 운전을 한다기보다는 오히려 운전 당하고 있는 것과 같다. ⑧ 게다가 당신은 교차로에서의 좌회전이 중요한 약속에 늦게 할 거라는 의미인 것을 알고 있지만, 어쨌든 당신은 그렇게 한다.

⑨ This story presents us with two contrasting ways of thinking about liberty. ⑩ On the one hand, liberty is the absence of external restraints or obstacles. ⑪ You are free / if no one is stopping you from doing / whatever it is you want to do. ⑫ In the above story / you appear, (in this sense), to be free. ⑬ On the other hand, one can think of liberty as the presence of control on the part of the person. ⑭ To be free, / you must be self-determined, which is to say that you must be able to control your own destiny / in your own interests. ⑮ In the above story / you appear, (in this sense), to be unfree: you are not in control of your own destiny. ⑯ That is to say, you are failing to control an addiction, which is preventing you from realizing your true interests. ⑰ While in the first view / liberty is simply about how many doors are open, in the second view / it is more about going through the right doors for the right reasons.

present A with B: A에게 B를 제공[제시]하다 / On the one hand: 한편으로는 / stop+O+from v-ing: O가 ~하는 것을 막다 / whatever: 복합관계대명사(=anything that) / appear to-v: ~인 것처럼 보이다 / On the other hand: 다른 한편으로는 / think of A as B: A를 B로 여기다 / on: ~에 / To be free: 자유롭기 위해서(부사적 용법) / which is to say that: 다시 말하면 that 이하의 내용이다 / in this sense: 이런 의미에서 / (:): 이유 / in control of: ~을 통제하다 / That is to say: 즉, 다시 말해서 / which: =and it / prevent+O+from v-ing: O가 ~하지 못하게 하다 / While: ~인 반면에 / the first view: ⑩번 문장의 내용 / about: ~에 관한 / the second view: ⑬번 문장의 내용 / more: 오히려 / for: ~ 때문에

자유의 두 가지 개념

⑨ 이 이야기는 우리에게 자유에 대한 2가지 대조적인 사고방식을 제시한다. ⑩ 한편으로 자유란 외부의 저지나 장애가 없는 상태이다. ⑪ 어느 누구도 당신이 원하는 것이 무엇이든 그것을 못하게 하지 않는다면 당신은 자유롭다. ⑫ 이런 의미로 볼 때 위의 이야기에서 당신은 자유로운 듯하다. ⑬ 다른 한편으로는 자유를 당사자에게 통제력이 있는 상태로 생각할 수 있다. ⑭ 자유롭기 위해서 당신은 스스로 결정해야 하는데, 그것은 다시 말하면 당신이 당신 자신의 이해관계 내에서 당신 자신의 운명을 통제할 수 있어야 한다는 것이다. ⑮ 이런 의미에서 볼 때, 위의 이야기에서 당신은 자유롭지 못한 듯하다. 왜냐하면 당신은 당신 자신의 운명을 통제하지 못하고 있기 때문이다. ⑯ 즉 당신은 중독을 통제하지 못하고 있는데, 이것이 당신으로 하여금 당신의 진정한 이해관계를 파악하지 못하게 하고 있다. ⑰ 첫 번째 견해에서 자유란 그저 얼마나 많은 문이 열려 있는가에 관한 것인 반면에, 두 번째 견해에서는 자유란 오히려 올바른 이유로 올바른 문을 통과하는 것에 관한 것이다.

본문파악

이 글은 소극적 자유와 적극적 자유의 개념에 대한 것으로서, 첫째 단락은 흡연 중독자인 운전자의 예를 들어 소극적 자유와 적극적 자유에 대한 화두를 꺼내고, 둘째 단락에서는 소극적 자유와 적극적 자유의 의미에 대해서 구체적으로 설명하고 있다.

문제풀이

1. 이 글에는 아무런 외부 장애가 없는 자유인 소극적 자유와, 자기 결정력이 있어 자신을 통제할 수 있는 적극적 자유가 언급되어 있다. (⑩, ⑬번 문장 참조)

2. 「be addicted to v-ing」는 '~에 중독되다'란 뜻으로 (A)에는 동명사에 해당하는 smoking이 와야 하고, (B)에는 앞에 '운전을 한다기보다는 오히려'의 의미인 Rather than driving이 왔으므로 빈칸에는 의미상 driving과 대조를 이루는 수동형 동명사구인 being driven이 적절하다. 주어로 쓰인 동명사구는 단수 취급하므로 (C)에는 means가 적절하다.

3. ⑭번 문장에서 「which is to say that ~」은 '앞의 말을 다시 표현하자면 ~이다'의 의미이므로, 빈칸에는 ~ 부분의 내용을 집약해주는 '③ self-determined(스스로 결정하는)'이 가장 적절하다.
① 자명적인　② 자기찬양의　④ 자포자기의　⑤ 자기 생각에 몰두한

구문해설

⑧ Moreover, you know that [**your turning** left at the crossroads] **means** (that) you'll be late for an important appointment, but you do it anyway.

▷ [ ] 표시된 your turning 이하는 주어로 사용된 동명사구이며, 주어로 쓰인 동명사구는 단수 취급을 하므로 동사로 means를 썼다. 동명사구인 turning ...의 의미상 주어는 you이다.

⑪ You are free if no one is stopping you from doing **whatever it is you want to do**.

▷ whatever는 '~하는 것은 무엇이든지'라는 뜻으로 whatever 이하는 doing의 목적어이다.

⑭ To be free, you must be self-determined, **which is to say that** you must be able to control your own destiny in your own interests.

▷ 「which is to say that+S+V」는 '그런데 그것은 다시 말하면 ~이다'의 의미로, 이때의 which는 앞 문장 전체를 선행사로 받는 계속적 용법의 관계대명사이다.

⑰ While in the first view liberty is simply **about** [**how** many doors are open], in the second view it is more **about** [**going** through the right doors for the right reasons].

▷ 두 개의 about은 각각 how 이하의 간접의문문과 going 이하의 동명사구를 목적어로 취하고 있다.

에리히 프롬의 「자유로부터의 도피」

에리히 프롬(Erich Fromm)은 자신의 저서인 「자유로부터의 도피」에서 자유를 소극적 자유(~로부터의 자유)와 적극적 자유(~을 향한 자유) 두 가지로 구분하였다. 먼저 소극적 자유는 어떤 속박으로부터의 탈출을 의미하는 것으로, 서구사회에서 중세 이후 인간이 획득한 종교적 · 정치적 · 경제적 자유가 이에 속한다. 그러나 인간은 이러한 소극적 자유를 얻음으로써, 고독과 무력감, 공포, 불안 등에 사로잡히게 되었고 현대에 들어와서 인간관계는 사람들 사이의 '인간적'인 관계가 아니라 '기계적', '소외적' 관계로 변화되면서 인간은 더욱 무력해지고 고독해지게 되었다.
이러한 상황에서 인간이 선택할 수 있는 길은 두 가지뿐인데, 하나는 이 상황을 극복하고 적극적인 자유로 나아가 참된 의미의 자유를 얻는 것이며, 다른 하나는 자유를 아예 포기하는 것이다. 이와 같은 도피의 예로 히틀러의 나치즘에 복종한 경우를 들 수 있다. 독일인들은 히틀러의 사상에 복종함으로써 기쁨을 느끼고, 다른 한편으로는 자신들보다 열등한 유대인을 학대함으로써 욕구 불만과 열등감을 해소하려고 했다는 것이 프롬의 견해이다.
그의 주장에 따르면, 인간이 자발적으로 사회에 참여하고 개인의 자유와 개성이 억압받지 않는 완전한 민주사회를 이룬다면 적극적 자유의 실현이 가능하다. 물론 그에 앞서 사회제도의 개혁이 선행되어야 한다고 그는 주장했다.

48

SECTION 10. 윤리

절대론적 윤리설과 상대론적 윤리설

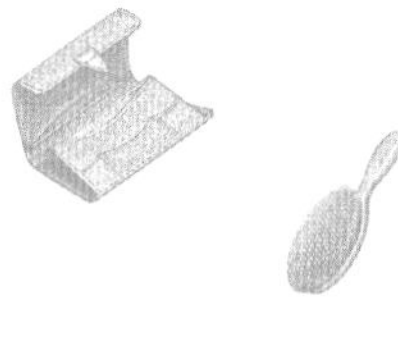

p.122

정답	1. ④ 2. ④ 3. (1) undesirable (2) right

본문 필기노트

① Suppose a daughter (from a religious family) deceives her dying father by promising him [that she will not marry someone (from a different religion)]. ② By lying to her father, / has she done something good or bad?

거짓말의 선악 여부를 통한 화두 제시

③ Strict adherents (of the Kantian view) would first examine the daughter's motive for lying. ④ They would find [that she lied in order to reassure her dad and prevent him from suffering even more / in his final hours on earth]. ⑤ She also lied to relieve herself of any guilt [associated with the anger [her father would have felt towards her had he known she was going to deny his final wish]]. ⑥ Followers of Kant would be critical of the girl for lying. ⑦ From their point of view, / wanting to minimize suffering or guilt / is not sufficient reason to lie. ⑧ In other words, / the daughter should tell the truth no matter what the consequences. ⑨ It is a moral obligation to tell the truth / and that is the standard [we must all uphold].

칸트학파의 윤리적 관점

⑩ The strict utilitarian, on the other hand, would first look at the results of the daughter's deceitful action. ⑪ By promising not to marry a man (from another religion), she has made her father happy so that he can now die in peace. ⑫ At the same time, by lying, she has kept herself free of any feelings of guilt for having caused her dad additional suffering / in his final days. ⑬ Utilitarians would find no fault with this action / since it leads to preventing the pain and anguish [the dying father would have experienced / from knowing the truth]. ⑭ To them, / the daughter has brought the greatest amount of happiness to everyone involved, and that is a good thing.

공리주의 학파의 윤리적 관점

본문해석

① 어느 독실한 집안의 딸이 종교가 다른 사람과는 결혼하지 않겠다고 약속함으로써 죽어가는 아버지를 속이는 것을 가정해 보라. ② 아버지에게 거짓말을 함으로써, 그녀는 선한 행동을 한 것인가, 아니면 악한 행동을 한 것인가?

③ 칸트학파적 관점의 엄격한 신봉자들은 거짓말 하는 것에 대한 딸의 동기를 먼저 검토할 것이다. ④ 그들은 그녀가 아버지를 안심시키고 그가 이 세상에서의 마지막 시간들을 더 고통스럽지 않게 하기 위해서 거짓말을 했다는 것을 알게 될 것이다. ⑤ 그녀는 또한 아버지가 딸이 자기의 마지막 소망을 거절할 것이라는 것을 알았다면 딸에게 느꼈을 분노와 관련된 어떤 죄의식을 자신에게서 경감시키기 위해 거짓말을 했다. ⑥ 칸트의 추종자들은 거짓말을 했다는 이유로 소녀에 대해 비판적일 것이다. ⑦ 그들의 관점에서는, 고통이나 죄의식을 최소화하기를 원하는 것은 거짓말을 할 만한 충분한 이유가 아니다. ⑧ 다시 말해서, 딸은 어떤 결과이든지 간에 진실을 얘기해야 한다. ⑨ 진실을 말하는 것은 도덕적인 의무이고 그것은 우리 모두가 유지해야 하는 기준이다.

⑩ 반면에 엄격한 공리주의자들은 딸의 거짓된 행동의 결과를 먼저 볼 것이다. ⑪ 종교가 다른 남자와 결혼하지 않겠다고 약속함으로써, 그녀는 그녀의 아버지를 행복하게 했고 그래서 아버지는 평화롭게 죽을 수 있다. ⑫ 동시에, 거짓말을 함으로써, 그녀는 아버지 최후의 날들 동안 아버지에게 고통을 가중한 데 대한 그 어떤 죄책감으로부터 자신을 자유롭게 유지했다. ⑬ 그것(거짓말을 하는 것)은 죽어가는 아버지가 진실을 앎으로 인해 경험했을 고통과 고뇌를 예방하는 결과를 가져오기 때문에, 공리주의자들은 이 행동을 비난하지 않을 것이다. ⑭ 그들에게 있어서 딸은 관련된 모든 사람에게 엄청난 행복을 가져다주었고, 그래서 그것은 선한 행동이다.

본문파악

이 글은 하나의 상황을 가정하여 칸트학파와 공리주의 학파 간의 윤리적 견해의 차이에 관해 설명하고 있다. 첫째 단락은 도입부이고, 둘째 단락과 셋째 단락에서 각각 칸트학파와 공리주의 학파의 윤리적 관점에 대해 설명하고 있다.

문제풀이

1. 《해석》 위 글의 주제는 무엇인가?
이 글은 한 가지 상황을 가정하여 칸트학파와 공리주의 학파 간의 윤리적 관점의 차이를 설명한 글이다.
① 칸트와 그의 엄격한 도적적 기준
② 현대 사회에서 도덕학자들의 역할
③ 칸트학파의 도덕과 공리주의 학파의 도덕에 대한 찬반 입장
④ 칸트 추종자와 공리주의 추종자의 반대되는 견해
⑤ 우리 일상생활에서 도덕 기준의 중요성

2. 둘째 단락의 칸트학파의 윤리 관점을 종합해 보면, 어떤 행동의 '동기'를 중요시하는 것을 알 수 있다. 이와 대조적으로 공리주의 학파의 윤리 관점에서는 동기보다 '결과'가 중시된다.

3. 《해석》 다음 상황을 읽고, 괄호 안에서 알맞은 단어에 동그라미 치시오.
둘째 단락과 셋째 단락을 참고한다.
(1) 칸트학파의 견해에 따르면, 어떤 사람이 배고픈 사람들에게 주려고 빵을 훔쳤다면, 그 사람의 행동은 (바람직하다 / 바람직하지 않다).
(2) 공리주의 학파에 따르면, 어떤 사람이 어린아이가 자동차에 치이지 않도록 구하기 위해 빨간 신호등을 지키지 않았다면, 그 또는 그녀는 도덕적으로 (옳다 / 그르다).

구문해설

⑤ She also lied to **relieve** herself **of** any guilt (that/which is) associated with the anger (that/which) her father **would have felt** towards her **had he known** (that) she was going to deny his final wish.

▷ relieve A of B: 'A에게서 B를 덜어주다[경감시키다]'
▷ had he known 이하는 가정법 과거완료의 조건절로, if가 생략되면서 주어인 he와 동사 had가 도치된 구문이다. 가정법 과거완료는 「If+주어+had v-ed, 주어+조동사의 과거형+have v-ed」 형태로 쓴다.

⑪ By promising **not to marry** a man from another religion, she **has made her father happy so that** he can now die in peace.

▷ to부정사의 부정은 그 앞에 not 또는 never를 둔다.
▷ make+O+OC(형용사): 'O를 ~하게 만들다'
▷ so that은 결과의 부사절을 이끌고, '그 결과, 그래서'라는 뜻이다.

윤리설과 철학사상의 만남

서양의 윤리설은 철학사상과도 흐름을 같이 하는데, 크게 절대론적 윤리설과 상대론적 윤리설로 나뉜다.
첫째, 절대론적 윤리설은 이성 중심의 철학과 함께 발전해 왔다. 이성 중심의 철학은 말 그대로 이성이 사고의 중심에 있으므로 절대적이고 보편적인 것을 중시한다. 이것은 소크라테스, 플라톤, 아리스토텔레스, 그리고 스토아학파 등의 고대 그리스에서 시작되어 근대 합리주의와 계몽주의, 그리고 독일의 관념론까지 연결된다. 이와 함께 발전해 온 절대론적 윤리설은 인간을 이성적 존재로 보고, 윤리의 기준이 보편적이고 절대적이라고 생각하기 때문에 누구나 지켜야 하는 의무론적 윤리설을 포함한다.
둘째, 상대론적 윤리설은 감각과 경험 중심의 철학과 연결되는데, 고대 그리스의 소피스트와 에피쿠로스 학파, 근대 경험론, 실존주의, 그리고 실용주의 등과 호응한다. 경험 철학은 개별적 감각을 중시하기 때문에 상대적이고 주관적인 것이 특징이다. 따라서 상대론적 윤리설은 인간을 감성적인 존재로 보고, 쾌락을 추구하고 실용적인 것을 찾는 현실적인 모습 그대로를 중시한다. 목적주의, 결과주의, 자연주의 윤리설 등으로도 불리며, 여기서 목적은 결과와 같은 의미로 사용된다.

49

SECTION 11. 정치

플라톤과 아리스토텔레스의 이상 국가

P.126

정답	1. ③ 2. 플라톤은 철학자나 현명함을 갖춘 왕이 지배하는 도시를 이상적으로 보았고, 아리스토텔레스는 각자 맡은 바 일에 충실한 시민 개개인이 모여 전체를 이루는 도시를 이상적이라고 보았다.

본문 필기노트

① Another example was the role of power [distributed and issued within the state].
② Plato held the belief (of) the philosopher king. ③ He believed [that (to ensure
~에 대한 / 보장하기 위해서는(부사적 용법)
the ideal state) "either philosophers become kings in their countries, or those [who
either A or B: A이거나 B이거나 / 주격 관 · 대
are now called kings and rulers] come to be sufficiently inspired with a desire for
~하게 되다
wisdom"]. ④ Plato believed (that) only the wise could execute proper justice. ⑤ A just
(that) / 현자들(the+형용사=복수명사)
city is an ideal city for Plato, one [in which the philosopher was in total control].
=a city
⑥ On the other hand, Aristotle's views greatly differ from Plato's (views). ⑦ Aristotle
반면에 / ~와 다르다 / (views)
believed [(that) each individual made an important contribution to the polis].
that 이하는 목적어 / make a contribution to: ~에 기부[공헌]하다
⑧ He compares the polis to an extended and all-encompassing family, with each
compare A to B: A를 B에 비유하다 / with+O+분사: O가 ~한 채로
individual acting (as) a part of it. ⑨ This describes individuals [working as a whole
~로서 / = the extended ~ family / 전체로서
to better the polis]. ⑩ (By) including all citizens / Aristotle believed (that) he had created
향상시키기 위해서(부사적 용법) / by v-ing: ~함으로써 / (that)
the ideal city.

이상 국가에 대한 플라톤과 아리스토텔레스의 견해 차이

본문해석

① 또 하나의 예는 국가 내에서 분배되고 발휘되는 권력의 역할이다. ② 플라톤에게는 철인 왕에 대한 신념이 있었다. ③ 그는 이상 국가가 되려면 '철학자가 그 나라의 왕이 되거나, 오늘날 왕이나 지배자라고 불리는 사람들이 지혜에 대한 욕구로 충분히 고무되어야 한다'고 믿었다. ④ 플라톤은 현자만이 올바른 정의를 실현할 수 있다고 믿었다. ⑤ 플라톤에게는 정의로운 도시가 이상 도시인데, 이는 철학자가 전권을 쥐고 있던 도시이다. ⑥ 반면에, 아리스토텔레스의 견해는 플라톤의 견해와 상당히 다르다. ⑦ 아리스토텔레스는 각 개인이 폴리스에 중대한 공헌을 한다고 믿었다. ⑧ 그는 폴리스를 각 개인이 한 부분으로서 역할을 하는 확대되고 포괄적인 가족에 비유했다. ⑨ 이것은 폴리스를 향상시키기 위해 전체로서 기능하는 개개인들을 묘사한다. ⑩ 모든 시민들을 다 포함함으로써 아리스토텔레스는 자신이 이상 도시를 고안해 냈다고 믿었다.

본문파악

이 글은 이상 국가에 대한 플라톤과 아리스토텔레스의 견해를 소개한 글이다. 플라톤은 철학자나 현자가 통치하는 국가를, 아리스토텔레스는 개개인이 각자 맡은 역할을 수행함으로써 결국은 전체를 위해 기능하는 국가를 이상적으로 보았다.

문제풀이

1. 첫 문장이 Another example로 시작되고, 본문에서 이상 국가에 대한 플라톤과 아리스토텔레스의 견해 차이에 대해 말하고 있으므로, 이 글 앞에서도 플라톤과 아리스토텔레스의 견해 차이가 언급되었음을 짐작할 수 있다.

2. 플라톤은 철학자나 현자가 통치하는 국가를 이상적으로 보았고(③, ⑤번 문장 참조), 아리스토텔레스는 맡은 바 일에 충실한 시민 개개인이 전체를 위해 기능하는 국가를 이상적이라고 보았다(⑧, ⑨번 문장 참조).

구문해설

③ He believed that **to ensure** the ideal state "**either** philosophers become kings in their countries, **or** those who are now called kings and rulers come to be sufficiently inspired with a desire for wisdom."

▷ to ensure는 목적을 나타내는 부사적 용법의 to부정사이다.
▷ 「either A or B」는 'A 또는 B'의 의미로, A, B 자리에 문장이 온 경우이다.

⑧ He compares the polis to an extended and all-encompassing family, **with each individual acting** as a part of it.

▷ 「with+O+분사」는 'O가 ~한 채로'라는 뜻의 분사구문으로, an extended and all-encompassing family를 부연 설명해준다.

⑩ By including all citizens Aristotle believed (that) he **had created** the ideal city.

▷ had created는 과거완료로 주절 시제보다 앞서 일어난 일임을 나타낸다.

플라톤 「국가론」

「국가론」은 민주주의가 변질되고 쇠퇴해가는 조국 아테네를 구하려던 플라톤의 고민에서 출발하여 쓰여졌다. 철인이 통치하는 정의로운 국가를 추구했던 플라톤은, 이 책에서 민주주의의 불합리성과 비효율성을 비판한다. 그는 민주주의가 다수의 난폭하고 무도한 개인들로 구성된 집단이 벌이는 '중우정치'로 전락할 수 있음을 꼬집었다. 정치의 목적은 국가의 이데아인 정의의 실현이며 이를 가장 잘 아는 철학자가 통치하는 국가를 이상적인 정치 형태로 생각했다. 철인정치는 지덕체로 몸과 마음을 갈고 닦은 현명한 지식인에 의해 지배되는 형태로, 재산도 가정도 포기한 철학자의 희생으로 이루어지는 것이다. 이러한 플라톤의 이상 국가론은 윤리적 정치관을 벗어나지 못한 채, 피지배자보다도 지배자의 덕의 명목으로 계승되어 왔다는 비판을 받기도 한다.

아리스토텔레스 「정치학」

정치학이 학문의 한 분야로 독립된 이름을 얻고 체계를 갖추게 된 시초가 바로 아리스토텔레스의 「정치학」이다. 「정치학」에서 그는 정치공동체로서의 국가의 기원과 본질, 민주정, 귀족정, 군주정 등 다양한 정체체제의 성격과 장단점을 다루고 당시 국가 체제들에 대한 비판과 이상적인 국가 체제를 언급한다.
「정치학」에서 그는 사람은 본질적으로 국가에서 살 수 있는 동물이므로 국가가 개인이나 가족에 선행한다고 주장한다. 국가의 형태는 그 사회의 성격에 따라 선택되어야 하며, 한 사람이 지배하더라도 공동의 이익을 지향하면 그것은 올바른 정치이고, 다수가 지배하더라도 소수의 이익만을 추구하는 것은 잘못된 정치라고 말한다. 지배 형태가 어떠하든 정치적 사회의 최선의 형태는 권력의 중심이 중간계급인에 있는 사회이며, 중간계급이 많은 국가가 좋은 정부를 이룰 수 있다고 주장한다.

50

SECTION 11. *정치*

리프먼이 보는 민주주의와 대중

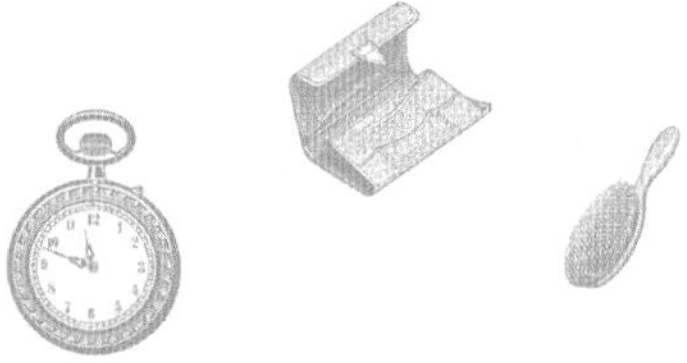

P.127

정답 | 1. 불완전한 언론과 미디어를 통해 얻어진 왜곡된 상으로 세상을 보기 때문에 / (인간의) 편견, 고정관념, 부주의함, 무지로 인해 진실을 이해하는 능력이 떨어지기 때문에

본문 필기노트

① In 1922, Walter Lippmann published an influential book [entitled *Public Opinion*]. ② In this book, Lippmann was very suspicious (of) and critical of any model of democracy [that placed excessive faith and power in the hands of the public].

(of) / of: ~에 대해 / that: 주격 관·대 / in: ~에

민주주의에 대한 리프먼의 부정적 견해

③ People, (he insisted), mostly know the world only indirectly, / through "pictures [(which/that) they make up / in their heads]." ④ And they receive these mental pictures largely through the media. ⑤ The problem, (Lippmann argued), is [that the pictures [(which/that) people have in their heads] are hopelessly distorted and incomplete, / (being) marred by the irredeemable weakness of the press]. ⑥ Just as bad is the public's ability [to comprehend the truth]. ⑦ Even if people happened to come across it, their understanding was undermined / by human bias, stereotypes, inattentiveness, and ignorance. ⑧ In the end, Lippmann thought (that) citizens are like theatergoers [who "arrive in the middle of the third act and leave before the last curtain, staying just long enough to decide / who is the hero and who is the villain]."

People: S / know: V / make up: 형성하다, 구성하다 / that 이하는 보어 / largely through: 주로 ~을 통해 / is: V / the pictures: S' / are: V' / marred 이하는 분사구문(이유) / Just as bad: SC / is: V / the public's ability: S / to comprehend: 이해하는(형용사적 용법) / Even if: 비록 ~일지라도 / happen to-v: 우연히 ~하다 / it = the truth / In the end: 결국에(는) / arrive: V'₁ / in the middle of: ~의 도중[중간]에 / leave: V'₂ / staying: =and so they stay(분사구문) / to decide: 결정하기에(부사적 용법) / who is the hero and who is the villain: 목적어절

리프먼이 대중을 불완전하다고 보는 이유

본문해석

① 1922년에 월터 리프먼은 「여론」이라는 제목의 영향력 있는 책을 출판했다. ② 이 책에서 리프먼은 대중의 수중에 과도한 신뢰와 힘을 부여하는 어떤 형태의 민주주의에 대해서도 매우 의심스러워하고 비판적이었다.

③ 그는 사람들이 대부분 그들이 '머리 속에서 만드는 이미지'를 통해 세상을 간접적으로만 안다고 주장했다. ④ 그리고 그들은 주로 미디어를 통해 이러한 마음속 이미지들을 얻는다. ⑤ 문제는 사람들이 그들의 머리 속에 갖고 있는 이미지들이 언론의 구제할 수 없는 결점에 의해 손상되어 돌이킬 수 없을 정도로 왜곡되어 있고 불완전하다고 리프먼은 주장했다. ⑥ 진실을 이해하는 대중의 능력 또한 심각하다. ⑦ 사람들이 우연히 진실을 이해하게 되었을지라도, 그들의 이해는 사람들의 편견, 고정관념, 부주의함, 그리고 무지에 의해 손상되었다. ⑧ 결국 리프먼은 시민들이 '3막 중간에 도착해서 마지막 커튼이 내려지기 전에 떠나는, 그래서 누가 영웅이고 누가 악당인지 결정하는 데 충분할 만큼만 머무는' 관객과 같다고 생각했다.

본문파악

이 글은 리프먼의 저서인 「여론」에 나오는 민주주의를 부정적으로 보는 그의 견해를 소개하고 있다. 첫째 단락에서는 대중을 과도하게 신뢰하는 민주주의에 대한 리프먼의 부정적 견해에 대해 언급하고, 둘째 단락에서는 리프먼이 대중을 불완전하게 생각하는 이유를 밝히고 있다. 결국 이러한 불완전한 대중에게 과도한 신뢰와 힘을 부여하는 민주주의는 바람직할 수 없다는 내용이다.

문제풀이

1. 리프먼은 불완전한 언론과 미디어에 의해 대중의 시각이 왜곡될 수밖에 없다는 점과, 편견이나 무지 등과 같은 대중의 인간적 한계로 인해 대중이 진실을 완전히 이해할 수 없다는 점을 언급하였다. (⑤~⑦번 문장 참조)

구문해설

⑥ Just as bad (SC) is (V) the public's ability to comprehend the truth (S).

▷ 주격보어인 Just as bad가 문두에 나와 강조되면서 주어와 동사가 도치되었다.

⑧ In the end, Lippmann thought (that) citizens are like theatergoers [**who** "arrive in the middle of the third act and leave before the last curtain, **staying** just long enough to decide **who** is the hero and **who** is the villain]."

▷ who 이하는 선행사 theatergoers를 수식하는 주격 관계대명사절이다.

▷ staying 이하는 결과의 분사구문으로 staying은 and so they stay로 바꿔 쓸 수 있다.

▷ who가 이끄는 두 개의 의문사절은 decide의 목적어이다.

여론의 역사적 변천

고대에는 여론이란 용어가 사용되지는 않았지만 오늘날 여론이라고 부르는 것과 비슷한 말들이 고대 이집트의 문서나 역사서 속에서 언급되어 있다. 고대 그리스에서는 부 · 명성 · 존경이 모두 국민의 의사에 달려 있다고 생각했다.

중세의 서유럽은 신분에 의해 행동이 결정되는 전형적인 봉건사회였기 때문에 농노들은 자유로운 여론을 형성하기가 힘들었고, 주로 종교적 · 문화적 · 정치적 엘리트들이 여론을 형성했다. 그러나 13세기에 이르러 이탈리아를 선두로 시작된 인본주의 운동은 일반 대중에게 교육의 폭을 넓혀주었고, 15세기의 이동식 활자 인쇄술의 발명과 16세기의 종교개혁은 당대의 쟁점들을 여론화할 수 있는 가능성을 높여주었다. 마틴 루터의 독일어판 성서 번역 작업은 일반대중에게 더 많은 지적 기회를 갖게 해주었고, 인쇄술의 발달은 대중이 새로운 소식에 더 빨리 접할 수 있게 해주었으며, 선전책자의 발행과 정기간행물의 출판을 촉진시켰다. 이러한 사실은 중세말에 여론을 형성할 수 있는 대중의 수를 크게 증가시켰다.

근세초의 중요한 정보통은 금융시장이었다. 유급 공무원제와 직업군인제가 도입되면서 제후들은 돈을 빌리게 되었고, 금융업자들은 제후들의 신용, 그들의 정치적 전망, 그리고 그들에 대한 신민들의 평판에 따라 돈을 대출해주었다. 온갖 종류의 정치적 · 경제적 정보가 금융시장으로 흘러들어갔으며, 그 정보가 금융계에서 일반 여론을 형성했다.

오늘날에는 여론에 대한 논의가 분분히 이루어지고 있으면서도 그에 대한 정확한 정의는 정립되고 있지 않다. 사회학적 관점에 의하면 여론은 특정 문제에 이해관계를 갖고 있는 사회구성원들의 의사교환 없이는 형성될 수 없는 것으로서, 그러한 사회구성원들의 의사교환은 신문 · 라디오 · 텔레비전과 같은 대중매체와 대면토론을 통해서 이루어진다. 여론이 형성되려면, 첫째로 쟁점이 있어야 하고, 둘째로 그 쟁점에 관해 의견을 표명하는 상당수의 개인이 있어야 하며, 셋째로 그 의견에 대한 최소한의 동의가 이루어져야 하고, 넷째로 그 일치된 의견이 직접 또는 간접으로 영향력을 발휘해야 한다.

51

SECTION 11. 정치

투표제도의 한계

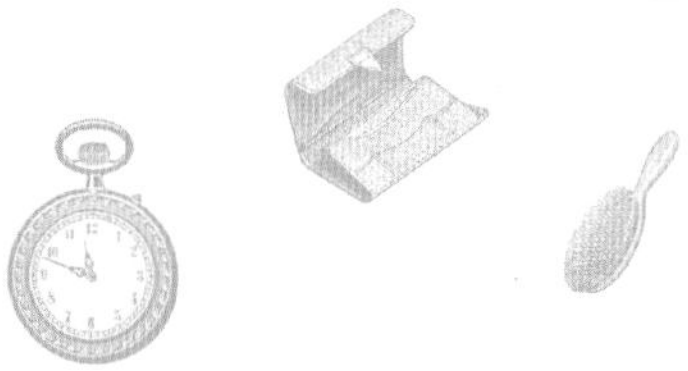

P.128

정답 | 1. ③ 2. ② 3. D의원

본문 필기노트

① Usually voting is proposed as a reasonably democratic way of reaching a consensus. ② But voting is not a meeting process, it is simply a procedure. ③ The goal of carrying out a vote is [to record the preferences of a group of people / and in some logical, fair, and equitable way come up with a good decision]. ④ Kenneth Arrow, a Nobel Prize winner in 1972, proved [it was impossible to do this / except under very simple circumstances; for example, situations [when there are only two possible options]]. ⑤ Furthermore, the act of voting necessarily ignores [how strongly each individual feels about the matter [being voted on] / or the consequences [that a final decision may impose]]. ⑥ And even under the best of circumstances, / voting necessarily means [that some group of people will not get what they want and (if severely beaten by the majority), may leave the group or retaliate].

as: ~로서 / is: V / to record: 기록하는 것(명사적 용법) / in some logical, fair, and equitable way: 어떤 논리적이고 공정하고 평등한 방식으로 / (to) / Kenneth Arrow: S / proved: V / (that) / it: 가주어 / to do this: 진주어 / under circumstances: ~의 상황 하에서 / when: 관계부사 / how 이하는 목적어 / (about) / that: 목적격 관·대 / even: 조차도 / that 이하는 목적어 / will: V_1 / what: ~한 것(=the thing which) / (they are) / may: V_2

투표 제도의 한계

⑦ Voting can therefore only produce satisfying decisions / where there is unanimity of opinion. ⑧ Unanimity can sometimes be achieved / if one person or group can persuade everyone else of the validity of their perspective and proposed solution. ⑨ But [if the problem has no clear solution, / some people are personally devoted to a particular solution, / or there is competition for power in the group], / the process will quickly bog down, factionalize, and/or revert to coercion.

where: ~할 때, ~인 경우에 / be achieved: 성취되다 / persuade A of B: A에게 B를 설득시키다 / (if) / be devoted to: ~에 전념하다 / (if)

투표가 만족스러운 결정을 이끌어낼 수 있는 경우

본문해석

① 보통 투표는 합의에 도달하는 상당히 민주적인 방식으로서 제안된다. ② 그러나 투표는 합의 과정이 아니라, 단순히 하나의 절차일 뿐이다. ③ 투표를 실시하는 목적은 한 무리의 사람들의 선호도를 기록하여 어떤 논리적이고, 바르고, 공정한 방법으로 훌륭한 결정을 내리는 것이다. ④ 1972년 노벨상 수상자인 케네스 애로우는 예를 들어 선택할 수 있는 것이 두 가지만 있는 상황과 같이 아주 단순한 상황 하에서를 제외하고는 이렇게 하는 것이 불가능하다는 것을 증명했다. ⑤ 더욱이, 투표라는 행위는 필연적으로 표결되고 있는 문제나 최종 결정이 가져올 수 있는 결과에 대해 각 개인이 어느 정도 강하게 느끼고 있는지를 간과한다. ⑥ 그리고 가장 좋은 상황에서조차도, 투표란 필연적으로 어떤 무리의 사람들은 그들이 원하는 것을 얻지 못할 것이고, 만일 다수에 의해 심한 패배를 당한다면 그 무리를 떠나거나 복수할 수도 있다는 것을 의미한다.

⑦ 그러므로 투표는 의견의 만장일치가 있을 때에만 만족스러운 결정을 이루어 낼 수 있다. ⑧ 만일 한 사람이나 한 무리가 모든 사람들에게 그들의 견해와 제시된 해결책에 대한 타당성을 설득시킬 수 있다면 때때로 만장일치가 이루어질 수 있다. ⑨ 그러나 만일 문제에 대한 명료한 해결책이 전혀 없거나, 어떤 사람들이 개인적으로 특정 해결책에 몰두하고 있거나, 무리 내에 권력 경쟁이 있다면, 그 방법은 금방 막다른 길에 봉착하고, 파벌이 형성되거나, 강압으로 되돌아가게 될 것이다.

본문파악

일반적으로 투표제도를 민주적인 해결책으로 생각하지만, 실제로는 투표제도에 한계가 있음을 설명한 글이다. 첫째 단락에서는 투표제도의 한계를 노벨상 수상자인 케네스 애로우의 정리를 통해 구체적으로 설명하고 있다. 둘째 단락에서는 투표제도가 효과적인 의사 결정 절차가 될 수 있는 제한적인 경우에 대해 언급하고 있다.

문제풀이

1. 《해석》 위 글의 주제는 무엇인가?
이 글은 민주적인 절차로 여겨지는 투표제도가 지닌 한계에 대해 설명하고 있으므로, 주제로는 '③ 투표제도의 근본적 한계'가 알맞다.
① 공정한 투표 절차를 수립하는 방법 ② 투표 결과에 대한 다양한 반응
④ 소수 의견을 존중해야 할 필요성 ⑤ 민주주의의 필수 요소로서의 투표제도

2. (A)에는 is의 보어인 앞의 to record와 and로 연결되어 record와 병렬구조가 될 수 있는 부정사가 와야 하므로, come up with가 적절하며, (B)에는 문제가 표결에 '부쳐지는' 것이므로 수동형인 분사구 being voted on이 적절하고, (C)에는 뒷부분이 완전한 문장이므로 관계부사 where가 오는 것이 적절하다.

3. D의원은 자신이 지지한 의견이 아닌데도 불구하고 채택된 의견을 수용하겠다는 의지를 보였으므로, 만장일치가 있을 때만 만족스러운 결정을 이끌어 낼 수 있다는 이 글의 내용과 다르다.
A의원(⑤번 문장 참조) / B의원(⑥번 문장 참조) / C의원(⑨번 문장 참조)

구문해설

④ Kenneth Arrow, a Nobel Prize winner in 1972, proved [(**that**) it was impossible to do this except under very simple circumstances; for example, situations [**when** there are only two possible options]].

▷ 생략된 접속사 that 이하는 동사 proved의 목적어 역할을 하는 명사절이다.
▷ when 이하는 situations를 수식하는 관계부사절로, '상황'이란 뜻의 situations를 때로 보았다는 점에 유의한다.

⑤ Furthermore, the act of voting necessarily ignores [**how strongly**(의문사(구)) each individual(S') feels(V') about the matter [being voted on] or (about) the consequences [that a final decision may impose]].

▷ how 이하는 동사 ignores의 목적어로 쓰인 간접의문문이다. 간접의문문의 어순은 〈의문사(구)+주어+동사〉이다.

애로우(Arrow)의 불가능성 정리

민주주의적 의사 결정 과정이 불가능하다는 것을 증명한 이론이다.
예를 들어, 한 사회 내에서 A, B, C라는 정당에 대한 선호가 A 〉 B이고 B 〉 C라면, A 〉 C이어야 한다. 그런데 '가'라는 사람은 A 〉 B 〉 C 순으로 좋아하고, '나'라는 사람은 B 〉 A 〉 C 순으로, 그리고 '다'라는 사람은 C 〉 A 〉 B 순으로 좋아한다고 가정해 보자. 여기서 투표 방법은 두 가지 중 하나를 선택하게 한 뒤 그 중 선택된 것을 나머지 하나와 놓고 비교하는 방식이다. 이 방식은 '가'라는 사람에게 물어보았다면 'A, B 중 선호하는 것은 A,' 'A, C 중 선호하는 것은 A' 이 과정을 거쳐 A를 선택하는 방식이다. 이를 사회 전체로 확대해서 생각해 보자. 'A, B 중 선호하는 것은?'이라고 질문할 때 '가'와 '다'는 A를, '나'는 B를 선택함으로써 결과적으로는 A가 선택된다. 그리고 'A, C 중 선호하는 것은?'의 경우에는 '가'와 '나'는 A, '다'는 C를 선택함으로써 A가 선택된다. 또한 'B, C 중 선호하는 것은?'이라고 묻는다면 '가'와 '나'는 B를, '다'는 C를 선택하여 B가 최종적으로 선택된다. 이는 투표 순서에 따라 특정 개인의 선호가 투표 결과에 나타나게 된 것이고, 따라서 '특정 개인의 선택이 다른 사회 구성원의 선택을 무시하고 결과를 결정해서는 안 된다'는 민주주의 선거 제도의 일반적인 원칙을 어기는 셈이 된다.
이와 같은 애로우의 이론은 현대 정치학자들에게 엄청난 충격이었고, 반박하고자 했던 시도들을 모두 실패로 돌아가게 했다.

52

SECTION 11. 정치
차별 철폐 조처(affirmative action)

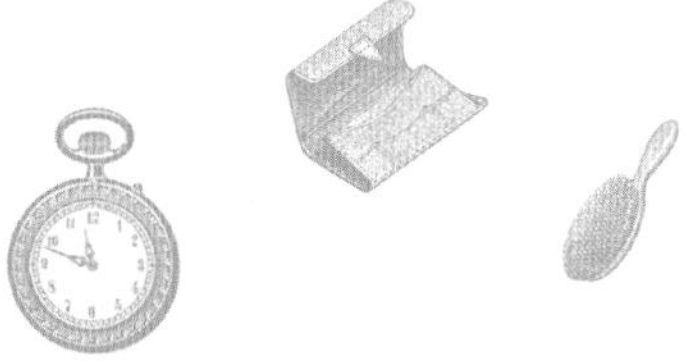

P.130

정답 1. discrimination, educational, employment 2. ③ 3. 경제적 격차를 상쇄하여 소수 집단과 특권층이 아닌 배경 출신이며 또한 저소득인 경향이 있는 학생들과 근로자들이 특권층의 또래들과 정당하게 경쟁할 수 있도록 해야 한다. 4. ⑤

본문 필기노트

① A controversial issue (in many countries around the globe), affirmative action is essentially the policy of [bestowing benefits / upon groups [that have traditionally faced discrimination]. ② The specific policies vary from nation to nation, but their focal point tends to be the provision of impartial educational and employment opportunities.

Note: 동격; 주격 관 · 대; from A to B: A에서 B까지; tend to-v: ~하는 경향이 있다; ~의

차별 철폐 조처의 취지

③ In France, for example, the constitution expressly forbids discrimination [based on race, religion or gender]. ④ To ensure this, certain low-income neighborhoods (with a high concentration of minority groups) have been classified "Priority Education Zones," a designation [which entitles them to supplemental government funding]. (⑤ In addition, the French government makes educational support available to all citizens in a variety of forms, including grants, loans, and special scholarships [earmarked for returning expatriates].) ⑥ South Africa has also implemented affirmative action policies. ⑦ Since transitioning into a democracy in 1994, the nation has endeavored to rectify racial imbalances in employment through legislation [compelling employers to hire non-white workers]. ⑧ There have also been government-backed efforts [to enhance the employment opportunities of women and disabled people from all racial groups].

Note: 보장하기 위해(부사적 용법); S; 주격 관 · 대; make+O+OC: O을 ~하게 하다; ~에게; ~을 포함하여(전치사); ~이래로; 현재완료(계속); ~을 통해; 확대하기 위한(형용사적 용법); ~의; ~로부터

차별 철폐 조처의 사례

⑨ Advocates of affirmative action argue [that it is imperative [to offset economic disparities, [capacitating students and workers from minority and underprivileged backgrounds, [who tend to also be low-income], to properly compete with their more privileged peers]]]. ⑩ Opponents, however, charge [that affirmative action unnecessarily harms people [who happen to come from a privileged social group]]. ⑪ Some go so far as to label affirmative action a form of reverse discrimination,

Note: that 이하는 목적어; 가주어; to 이하는 진주어; 부대상황의 분사구문; who의 선행사; 주격 관 · 대(계속적 용법); ~와 경쟁하다; that 이하는 목적어; 주격 관 · 대; V'; O'; OC'

본문해석

① 전 세계 여러 나라에서 논란이 많은 쟁점인 '차별 철폐 조처'는 근본적으로 전통적으로 차별을 직면했던 집단들에 혜택을 부여하는 정책이다. ② 구체적인 정책은 국가마다 다르지만, 그들의 초점은 공정한 교육 및 고용 기회의 제공인 경향이 있다.

③ 예를 들어 프랑스에서는, 헌법이 인종, 종교 또는 성별에 기반을 둔 차별을 명시적으로 금지한다. ④ 이것을 보장하기 위해, 소수 집단의 밀집도가 높은 특정 저소득 지역이 '우선 교육 지역'으로 분류된 바 있는데, 이것은 그들에게 추가적인 정부 자금을 받을 권리를 부여하는 지정이다. (⑤ 추가로, 프랑스 정부는 보조금, 대출금, 귀국하는 국외 거주자에게 배당된 특별 장학금을 포함하여 모든 시민에게 다양한 형태로 교육적 지원을 제공한다.) ⑥ 남아프리카 공화국 또한 차별 철폐 조처 정책을 시행해 오고 있다. ⑦ 1994년에 민주주의로 이행한 이후로, 그 국가는 고용주가 백인이 아닌 근로자를 고용하도록 강제하는 법률을 통해 고용의 인종 불균형을 바로잡기 위해 노력해 왔다. ⑧ 또한 모든 인종 집단의 여성과 장애인의 고용 기회를 확대하기 위한 정부 지원 노력도 있어 왔다.

⑨ 차별 철폐 조처의 옹호자들은 경제적 격차를 상쇄하여, 소수 집단과 혜택을 못 받는 배경 출신이며 또한 저소득인 경향이 있는 학생들과 근로자들이 특권층의 또래들과 정당하게 경쟁할 수 있도록 해야 한다고 주장한다. ⑩ 그러나 반대자들은 차별 철폐 조처가 공교롭게 특권 사회 집단 출신인 사람들에게 불필요하게 해를 끼친다고 주장한다. ⑪ 일부는 차별 철폐 조처에 역차별의 한 형태라는 꼬리표를 붙이기까지 하며, 그것이 단순히 과거의 불평등

[claiming that it simply replaces past injustices with new injustices, [fostering resentment without actually ameliorating the living standard of those [it seeks to aid]]].

부대상황의 분사구문 / replace A with B: A를 B로 바꾸다 / 부대상황의 분사구문 / ~없이 / (whom/that) / 차별 철폐 조처에 대한 찬반 양론

을 새로운 불평등으로 바꾸어 그것이 돕고자 하는 사람들의 생활 수준을 실제로 개선하지는 않으면서 분노를 조장한다고 주장한다.

본문파악

이 글은 차별 철폐 조처의 취지와 실례, 그리고 이에 대한 찬성과 반대 의견을 다루고 있다. 첫째 단락에서는 차별받는 집단에게 교육 및 고용의 평등한 기회를 제공한다는 정책의 취지를 설명하고 있다. 둘째 단락에서는 이 정책을 시행하고 있는 프랑스와 남아프리카 공화국의 예시를 보여주고 있다. 셋째 단락에서는 이 정책에 대한 찬성과 반대 입장의 논거를 짚고 있다.

문제풀이

1. 《해석》 위 글에 따르면, 차별 철폐 조처는 공평한 교육 및 고용 기회를 제공함으로써 문화권 내에서 차별을 겪은 집단의 구성원들에게 혜택을 주는 정책이다. (각 단어는 본문에서)
①번, ②번 문장 참조

2. ③은 프랑스 시민 전체를 대상으로 하는 교육적 지원에 대한 내용으로, 차별받는 집단에게 혜택을 부여하는 정책인 차별 철폐 조처와는 무관하므로 글의 흐름과 관계가 없다.

3. ⑨번 문장 참조

4. 차별 철폐 조처가 특권층에게 거꾸로 해를 끼친다는 빈칸 앞 문장으로 미뤄 보아, 빈칸에는 '⑤ 역차별'이 들어가는 것이 알맞다.
① 사회 복지 ② 비폭력 저항 ③ 불법 입법 ④ 국가적 치유

구문해설

④ **To ensure** this, certain low-income neighborhoods (S) with a high concentration of minority groups have been classified (V) "**Priority Education Zones**," **a designation** [**which** entitles them to supplemental government funding].

▷ To ensure은 목적을 나타내는 부사적 용법의 to부정사이다.
▷ "Priority Education Zones"와 a designation ... funding은 동격이다.
▷ which 이하는 선행사 a designation을 수식하는 주격 관계대명사절이다.

⑪ Some go so far as to label affirmative action a form of reverse discrimination, **claiming that** it simply replaces past injustices with new injustices, **fostering** resentment without actually ameliorating the living standard of those [(**whom/that**) it seeks to aid].

▷ claiming 이하와 fostering 이하는 부대상황의 분사구문이다.
▷ that 이하는 동사 claim의 목적어 역할을 하는 명사절이다.
▷ [ ]는 those를 선행사로 하는 목적격 관계대명사절로 관계대명사 whom이나 that이 생략되었다.

53

SECTION 11. 정치

에드워드 사이드의 오리엔탈리즘

P.132

정답	1. ② 2. ② 3. 동양으로 간주된 이슬람에 대해 적대적이고 두려운 태도를 갖는 것 4. ② to → than ④ which → where[in which, when]

본문 필기노트

① From at least the end of the eighteenth century until our own day, / modern Occidental reactions to Islam have been dominated by a type of thinking [that may still be called Orientalist]. ② The general basis of Orientalist thought is an imaginative geography [dividing the world into two unequal parts: the larger and *different* one called the Orient, / the other, also known as our world, called the Occident or the West]. ③ Such divisions always take place / when one society or culture thinks about another one, different from it, / but it is interesting [that even when the Orient has uniformly been considered an inferior part of the world, it has always been endowed both with far greater size and with a greater potential for power than the West]. ④ In so far as Islam has always been seen as belonging to the Orient, / its particular fate (within the general structure of Orientalism) / has been to be looked at / with a very special hostility and fear. ⑤ There are, of course, many obvious religious, psychological and political reasons for this, / but all of these reasons derive from a sense [that so far as the West is concerned, Islam represents not only a formidable competitor but also a late-coming challenge to Christianity].

~로부터 / ~까지 / S / ~에 대한 / V / ~에 의하여 / 주격 관·대 / V / divide A into B: A를 B로 나누다 / (which is) / ~로서 알려진 / (which is) / 일어나다 / ~할 때(접속사) / = society or culture / = one society or culture / 가주어 / that 이하는 진주어 / ~할 때조차도 / be considered: ~로 여겨지다 / = the Orient / both A and B: A와 B 둘 다 / ~로서(전치사) / ~하는 한 / belong to: ~에 속하다 / S / 보아지다 / ~으로 / 동격의 that / ~에서 기인하다 / = / so far as A is concerned: A에 관한 한 / ~에 대하여 / not only A but also B: A뿐만 아니라 B도

이슬람에 대한 서양의 왜곡된 시각과 그 이유

⑥ I have not been able to discover any period (in European or American history since the Middle Ages) [where Islam was generally discussed or thought about outside a framework [created by passion, prejudice and political interests]]. ⑦ This may not seem like a surprising discovery, but included in the indictment is [the entire gamut of scholarly and scientific disciplines [which, (since the early nineteenth century), have either called themselves Orientalism or tried systematically to deal with the Orient]].

~ 이래로 / any period를 선행사로 하는 관계부사 / 앞 문장 전체 / SC / V / S / 주격 관·대 / 삽입구 / either A or B: A나 B 둘 중 하나 / try to-v: ~하려고 노력하다 / ~을 다루다

중세 이후 서양 역사와 학문에서 이슬람에 대한 올바른 시각의 부재

본문해석

① 최소한 18세기 말엽부터 오늘날까지, 이슬람에 대한 현대 서양의 태도는 여전히 동양학으로 불리우고 있을지 모르는 사고 유형에 의해 지배되어 왔다. ② 동양학적 사고의 일반적인 기준은 세계를 두 개의 불평등한 지역으로 나누는 가상의 지리학으로, 즉 동양이라고 불리는 보다 넓고 특별한 지역과 '우리' 세계로 알려진 서양이라고 불리는 지역이다. ③ 어떤 사회나 문화가 그들과는 다른 또 하나의 사회나 문화에 대해 생각할 때 그러한 구별이 항상 생기는데, 동양이 한결같이 세계에서 열등한 지역으로 여겨질 때조차도 늘 서양에 비해 규모가 훨씬 크고, 또 훨씬 더 큰 잠재력을 지니고 있었다는 것은 흥미롭다. ④ 이슬람이 항상 동양에 속해 있는 것으로 여겨져 왔던 만큼, 동양학의 전체적인 구조 내에서의 이슬람의 특별한 운명은 아주 독특한 적대감과 두려움을 갖고 보아져 왔다. ⑤ 물론 이에 대한 명백한 종교적, 심리적, 정치적 이유들이 있긴 하지만, 이런 이유 모두는 서양에 관한 한 이슬람은 만만치 않은 경쟁자일 뿐만 아니라 기독교에 대해 최근에 나타난 도전을 의미한다는 의식에서 기인한다.

⑥ 나는 중세시대 이후 유럽이나 미국 역사에서, 격렬한 감정, 편견, 정치적 이익에 의해 만들어진 틀 밖에서 이슬람이 일반적으로 논의되거나 사고되었던 어떤 기간도 발견할 수 없었다. ⑦ 이것은 놀라운 발견처럼 보이지 않을 수도 있지만, 그 비난에는 19세기초 이후로 그것들 자체를 동양학이라고 불렀거나 동양을 체계적으로 다루려 했던 학문적 및 과학적 부문의 전분야가 포함되어 있다.

본문파악

이 글은 에드워드 사이드가 쓴 「서구인의 눈을 통해 본 이슬람(*Islam Through Western Eyes*)」이라는 논문의 일부분으로, 동양, 특히 이슬람 문화에 대한 서양의 왜곡된 시각에 대해 비판하고 있다.

문제풀이

1. 이 글은 서구인들의 왜곡된 눈에 비친 이슬람 문화에 대해 비판하고 있으므로, 빈칸에는 '② 서양의 시각을 통한 이슬람'이 가장 적절하다.
   ① 종교와 문화 충격 ③ 서양 역사와 기독교
   ④ 서양 역사에서 이슬람교의 영향력 ⑤ 이슬람과 동양 문명

2. 《해석》 위 글에 따르면, 서구의 이슬람에 대한 태도는 왜곡되어 있다.
   첫째 단락 중반에 필자가 생각하는 이슬람에 대한 서양의 시각이 드러나 있다. (②, ④, ⑤번 문장 참조)
   ① 우호적인 ② 왜곡된 ③ 무관심한 ④ 중립적인 ⑤ 의존적인

3. ④번 문장 참조

4. ② → 앞에 비교급인 greater가 있으므로 to를 than으로 고쳐야 알맞다.
   ④ → which 이하가 완전한 문장이므로 관계대명사 which 대신 any period를 선행사로 하는 관계부사 또는 in which를 써야 한다. 원문에서는 관계부사 where가 쓰였는데, 이때 where는 물리적인 장소가 아닌 어떤 지점이나 경우, 상황 등의 추상적 의미를 갖는다. 같은 의미에서 where 대신 when도 가능하다.

구문해설

③ Such divisions always take place when one society or culture thinks about another one, [(that is) **different from it**], but it is interesting that [even when the Orient has uniformly been considered an inferior part of the world], it has always been endowed both with **far** greater size and with a greater potential for power than the West.

▷ different from it은 another one을 수식하는 형용사구로, different 앞에 〈주격 관계대명사+be동사〉인 that is가 생략되어 있다.
▷ 두 번째 [ ] 부분의 even when ... of the world는 진주어 that절 속에 들어가 있는 때를 나타내는 부사절이다.
▷ far는 비교급을 강조하는 부사로 still, even, much, a lot 등과 함께 '훨씬'의 뜻을 나타낸다.

④ In so far as Islam has always **been seen as** belonging to the Orient, its particular fate (within the general structure of Orientalism) has been [**to be** looked at with a very special hostility and fear].

▷ see A as B는 'A를 B로 보다'의 의미로, 여기서는 수동태로 쓰였으며, B 자리에는 형용사(belonging)가 온 경우이다.
▷ to be 이하는 be동사(has been)의 보어로 쓰인 명사적 용법의 to부정사구이다.

⑦ This may not seem like a surprising discovery, but included in the indictment (SC) is (V) [the entire gamut of scholarly and scientific disciplines which, since the early nineteenth century, have either called themselves Orientalism or tried systematically to deal with the Orient] (S).

▷ 주격보어 included in the indictment가 문두로 나와 강조되면서 주어 the entire gamut ... the Orient와 동사 is가 도치되었다.

54

SECTION 12. 교육 · 심리 · 언어

교육과 직업의 진정한 의미

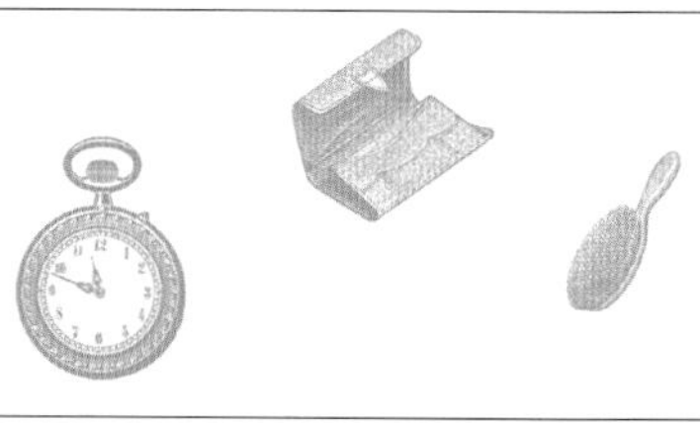

p.138

정답

1. ② 2. 자신의 적성에 맞지 않는 일을 하고 있는 사람들 3. (1) F (2) T (3) F
4. The situation clearly calls for a process-oriented education instead of an input-oriented one

본문 필기노트

① Considering the modern-day obsession with knowledge and so-called "decent"
~을 고려하면, ~을 감안하면
occupations, / the original meaning of education and occupation / should tell us
당연히 ~일 것이다
something. ② Originally, the word "education" comes from two Latin terms *ek*
중요한 것 / ~에서 유래하다
and *ducere*. ③ *Ek* means "out" and *ducere* means "to draw." ④ Therefore, true
education means to draw out knowledge from within. ⑤ This is quite different from
동격 / 안으로부터
the established practice today [(of) "stuffing in" knowledge], (as) somebody pointed
= / ~인 것처럼(접속사) / ~을 지적하다
out sarcastically (:) "The world is full of educated derelicts."
=that

교육의 진정한 의미

⑥ And what does occupation mean? ⑦ Literally, it implies something [that
주격 관 · 대
"occupies" you]. ⑧ However, finding the appropriate occupation [to suit a person's
맞는(형용사적 용법)
temperament] / is not an easy task. ⑨ Often times / we see that somebody [who
V / 주격 관 · 대
could have been a musician] is a doctor and somebody [who could have been a
주격 관 · 대
good doctor] is a businessman. ⑩ The importance (of identifying the right job / for
the right person) /can only be gauged / (when) you see the agony (of such square
~할 때(접속사) / (형용사적 용법)
pegs in round holes). ⑪ Only (an) Albert Einstein could have the wisdom [to reject
~와 같은 사람 / 거절할
an offer [to become President of Israel]] because he argued [(that) he did not have
되는(형용사적 용법) / S′ / V′ / that 이하는 목적어
enough experience (in working with human beings)].

올바른 직업 선택의 중요성

⑫ Therefore, it would be appropriate [(if) the right knowledge came to the right
가주어(또는 상황의 it) / ~라면 / if 이하는 진주어 / 가정법 과거
individual / with the active participation of the teacher / at an early age]. ⑬ In
이른 나이에
addition, (in) determining one's occupation, / one should above all focus on innate
~에 있어 / 무엇보다 / ~에 초점을 맞추다
potential and interest. ⑭ The situation clearly calls for a process-oriented education
~을 요구하다
instead of an input-oriented one.
~ 대신에 / =education

바람직한 교육과 직업 선택

본문해석

① 지식과 소위 '좋은' 직업에 대한 현대의 강박 관념을 고려하면, 교육과 직업의 본래 의미가 우리에게 중요한 것을 말해 줄 것이다. ② 원래, 'education'이란 말은 두 라틴 단어 ek와 ducere에서 유래한다. ③ ek는 'out'을 의미하고 ducere는 'to draw'를 의미한다. ④ 그러므로 진정한 교육은 안에서부터 밖으로 지식을 끌어내는 것을 의미한다. ⑤ 이것은 누군가가 "세상은 교육받은 낙오자들로 가득 차 있다."라고 풍자적으로 지적한 바와 같이, 지식을 '주입하는' 오늘날의 굳어진 관행과는 상당히 다르다.

⑥ 그렇다면 occupation은 무엇을 뜻하는가? ⑦ 글자 그대로 보면, 그것은 당신을 '점유하는' 어떤 것을 의미한다. ⑧ 그러나 한 사람의 기질에 맞는 적절한 직업을 찾는 것은 쉬운 일이 아니다. ⑨ 종종 우리는 음악가가 될 수 있었던 사람이 의사이거나, 좋은 의사가 될 수 있었던 사람이 기업인인 것을 본다. ⑩ 적합한 사람에게 적합한 직업을 찾아주는 것의 중요성은 자신에게 맞지 않는 직업을 가진 사람들의 고뇌를 보게 될 때만 파악될 수 있다. ⑪ 앨버트 아인슈타인 같은 사람만이 자신은 사람들과 같이 일한 경험이 충분하지 않다는 주장을 이유로 이스라엘 대통령이 되어 달라는 제의를 거절할 수 있는 지혜를 가질 수 있다.

⑫ 그러므로 올바른 지식이 이른 나이에 교사의 적극적인 참여로 올바른 개인에게 주어진다면 적절할 것이다. ⑬ 또한 자신의 직업을 결정하는 데 있어서 무엇보다도 타고난 잠재력과 흥미에 초점을 두어야 한다. ⑭ 상황은 확실히 주입 중심의 교육 대신에 과정 중심의 교육을 요구한다.

본문파악

적성에 맞는 직업 선택과 과정 중심의 교육의 중요성을 강조한 글이다. 첫째 단락에서는 education의 어원을 설명하면서 교육의 진정한 의미에 대해 언급하고 있다. 둘째 단락에서는 올바른 직업 선택의 중요성에 대해 이야기하고 있다. 셋째 단락은 결론으로서 올바른 교육의 정의와 직업 선택 시 고려할 점에 대해 정리하고 있다.

문제풀이

1. 《해석》 위 글에 따르면, 오늘날의 교육과 직업 선택의 관행에 대한 필자의 태도는 어느 것인가?
   필자는 오늘날의 교육이 그것의 진정한 의미와 거리가 먼 주입식 교육이며, 직업 선택 시 본인의 잠재력과 흥미를 고려하기가 쉽지 않다고 했다. 따라서 '② critical'이 가장 적절하다.
   ① 중립적인　③ 무관심한　④ 낙관적인　⑤ 만족한

2. a square peg in a round hole은 '둥근 구멍에 있는 사각형 모양의 못'이라는 뜻으로, 이 글에서는 자신의 적성에 맞지 않는 일을 하는 사람을 비유한 말이다.

3. 《해석》 다음 진술에 대해 T(참) 또는 F(거짓)로 표시하시오.
   (1) 오늘날의 교육은 주입 중심이라기보다 오히려 과정 중심이다. → 오늘날의 교육은 주입식 교육이라고 했다. (④~⑤번 문장 참조)
   (2) 오늘날 많은 사람들은 자신에게 맞는 직업을 갖고 있지 않다. (⑧~⑩번 문장 참조)
   (3) 앨버트 아인슈타인은 잠깐 동안 이스라엘 대통령이 되기를 꿈꾸었다. → 아인슈타인은 이스라엘 대통령이 되어 달라는 제의를 거절했다. (⑪번 문장 참조)

4. call for: '~을 요구하다' / instead of: '~ 대신에'

구문해설

⑧ However, **finding** the appropriate occupation to suit a person's temperament **is** not an easy task.

▷ finding ... temperament는 주어로 사용된 동명사구로 '~하는 것'으로 해석하며, 동명사(구)는 단수 취급하기 때문에 동사는 is를 썼다.

⑨ Often times we see [**that** somebody [who **could have been** a musician] is a doctor and somebody [who **could have been** a good doctor] is a businessman].
(somebody = S'_1, is = V'_1; somebody = S'_2, is = V'_2)

▷ that 이하는 동사 see의 목적어이다.
▷ could have v-ed: '~이었을 수도 있었다'

⑫ Therefore, **it would** be appropriate **if** the right knowledge **came to** the right individual (**with** the active participation of the teacher) (**at** an early age).

▷ it은 if절을 가리키는 가주어 또는 상황의 it이다. would와 came to는 가정법 과거 동사로, 필자가 그렇게 되기 어렵다고 가정하고 있음을 말해 준다.
▷ come to: '~에 달하다, ~에 이르다'
▷ ( ) 표시된 with는 '~와 함께'의 의미이다.
▷ ( ) 표시된 at은 때를 나타내며 '~에'의 의미이다.

55

SECTION 12. 교육 · 심리 · 언어

도제 제도가 주는 교훈

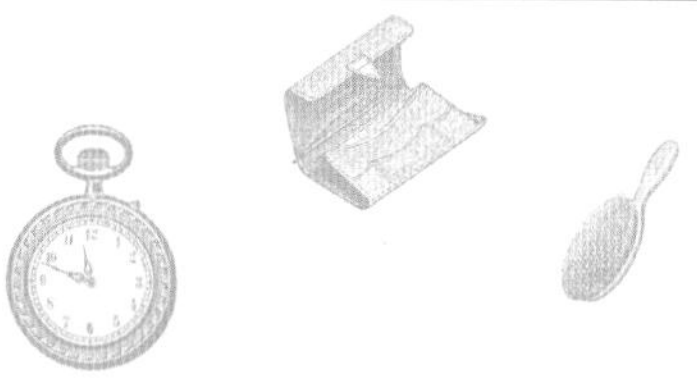

P.140

정답	1. ④ 2. 실습을 먼저 해 봄으로써 실제적인 문제점을 미리 파악해 이론 공부 시 지적 흥미를 갖게 해준다. 3. ④ 4. ② that of civilized life → those of civilized life ③ was recognizing → was recognized

본문 필기노트

① Logically we should learn about things before doing them / and that is presumably why the pundits enforce this in our educational system. ② But it is not the natural way, (nor), (I venture to think,) the best way. ③ The adolescent wants to do things first, / and only then does he appreciate the problems involved and want to learn more about them.

(that's why ~: 그것이 ~한 이유이다 / =learn about things before doing them / nor: ~역시 아니다 / 삽입절 / only then: 부사구, does: V, he: S)

이론보다 경험이 선행되어야 할 필요성

④ They do these things better in primitive life, (for) there at puberty / the boy joins his father in making canoes, patching huts, going out fishing or hunting, and preparing weapons of war. ⑤ He is serving his apprenticeship / in the actual accomplishments of life. ⑥ It is not surprising [(that) anthropologists find [(that) the adolescents of primitive communities do not suffer from the same neurotic 'difficulties' as those of civilized life]]. ⑦ This is not, (as) some assume, because they are permitted / more sexual freedom, but because they are given / more natural outlets / for their native interests and powers / and are allowed to grow up freely / into a full life of responsibility / in the community.

(for: ~이기 때문에(접속사) / join+O+in v-ing: ~하는 데 있어 O에 합류하다 / It: 가주어 / that 이하는 진주어 / anthropologists: S, find: V / that 이하는 find의 목적어 / suffer from: ~으로 고통받다 / the same A as B: B와 같은 A / those: =the adolescents / This: =⑥번 문장 내용 / as: ~이듯이(접속사) / not because A but because B: A 때문이 아니라 B 때문에 / be allowed to-v: ~하는 것을 허락받다)

원시사회 청소년들의 교육 방식

⑧ In the last century / this was recognized / in the apprenticeship system, which allowed the boy to go out with the master carpenter, thatcher, or ploughman to engage in the actual work of carpentry, roof-mending, or ploughing, and so to learn his trade. ⑨ It was the same in medicine, in which a budding young doctor of sixteen / learnt his job / by going round with the general practitioner / and (by) helping with the blood-letting and other treatments. ⑩ In our agricultural colleges (at) the present time / young men have to do a year's work (on) a farm / before their

(which의 선행사 / allow+O+to-v: O가 ~하는 것을 허락하다 / to engage in: ~에 가담하기 위해서(부사적 용법) / and so: 그래서 / to learn: 배우기 위해서(부사적 용법) / medicine: which의 선행사 / in which: 목적격 관 · 대(계속적 용법) / by v-ing: ~함으로써 / at: ~에 / on: ~에서)

본문해석

① 논리적으로 우리는 뭔가를 하기 전에 그것에 대해 배워야 하는데, 그것이 아마도 현인들이 이것을 우리의 교육 제도에 도입하는 이유인 것 같다. ② 그러나 그것은 자연스러운 방법도 아니고, 생각해 보건대 최선의 방법도 아니다. ③ 청소년은 뭔가를 먼저 해보고 싶어하는데, 그제야 그는 수반된 문제점들을 알게 되고 그것에 대해 더 많이 배우고 싶어 한다.

④ 원시생활에서 그들은 이런 것들을 더 잘하는데, 왜냐하면 거기에서는 사춘기 때 소년이 아버지가 카누를 만들고, 오두막을 짓고, 낚시하거나 사냥을 하고, 전쟁 도구를 만드는 데 같이 참여하기 때문이다. ⑤ 그는 생활의 실제 수행에서 도제의 신분을 다하고 있는 것이다. ⑥ 인류학자들이 원시 사회 청소년들이 문명사회 청소년들과 같은 스트레스로 고통받지 않는다는 점을 발견하는 것은 놀랄 만한 일이 아니다. ⑦ 이것은 혹자가 추정하듯이 그들이 더 많은 성적 자유를 허락받기 때문이 아니라, 그들의 타고난 관심과 힘을 위한 자연스러운 배출구들이 더 많이 주어지고 사회에서 책임감 있는 성인으로 자유롭게 성장하도록 허락받았기 때문이다.

⑧ 지난 20세기에 이것은 도제 제도에서 찾아볼 수 있는데, 도제 제도는 소년이 대장 목수, 지붕 이는 사람, 또는 농부와 함께 나가 목수일, 지붕 고치는 일, 밭갈이와 같은 실제적인 일에 참여함으로써 자신의 일을 배울 수 있도록 허락하였다. ⑨ 이것은 의학 분야에서도 마찬가지로, 16세의 신참 의사는 전문의를 따라다니면서 방혈 및 기타 치료를 도와줌으로써 일을 배웠다. ⑩ 현재 농대에서는 신입생들이 대학에서 이론 교육을 받기 전에 농장에서 1년간 일을 해야 한다. ⑪ 이 제도의 커다란 장점은 그것이 수습생으로 하여금 문제를 푸는 방법을 배우

theoretical training (at) college. ⑪ The great advantage of this system is [(that) it lets the apprentice see the practical problems / before he sets to work learning how to solve them, / and he can therefore take a more intelligent interest in his theoretical work].

~에서 / that 이하는 보어 / V / let+O+동사원형: O에게 ~하게 하다 / ~하기 시작하다 / take an interest in: ~에 관심[흥미]을 갖다

는 일에 착수하기 전에 실제적인 문제들을 볼 수 있게 해주어서, 그가 자신의 이론 수업에 더 많은 지적 흥미를 가질 수 있다는 것이다.

20세기에 실시된 도제 제도의 예와 그 장점

본문파악

청소년 교육에 있어 이론보다 실습이 우선시 되어야 한다고 주장하는 글이다. 첫째 단락에서 필자는 이론 중심의 교육에 대해 의구심을 제기하고 있다. 둘째 단락에서는 도제 제도와 유사한 원시사회 청소년들의 교육 방식을 소개하고 있고, 셋째 단락에서는 20세기의 도제 제도의 예를 들면서 그 장점을 설명하고 있다.

문제풀이

1. 이론을 먼저 배우는 것보다는 도제 제도처럼 실습을 먼저 해 보는 것이 청소년 교육에 더 효과적이라는 내용의 글이다.

2. ⑪번 문장 참조

3. 《해석》 셋째 단락에서 필자는 그의 의견을 명확히 표현하기 위해 예를 주로 사용하고 있다.
필자는 이론보다 실습을 먼저 하는 것이 교육상 더 효과적이라는 주장을 하기 위해 다양한 분야에서 실시되고 있는 도제 제도를 '④ 예(example)'를 들어 설명하고 있다.
① 은유 ② 대조 ③ 비교 ⑤ 시간 순서

4. ②의 that은 the adolescents가 복수 형태이므로 those가 되어야 하고, ③의 recognizing은 주어가 사람이 아닌 this이므로 수동의 의미인 recognized가 되어야 옳다.

구문해설

③ The adolescent wants to do things first, and **only then** **does** **he** appreciate the problems involved and want to learn more about them.
(only then: 부사구, does: V, he: S)

▷ 강조를 위해 부사구인 only then을 문두로 보내면서 주어(he)와 동사(does)가 도치된 구문이다.

⑪ The great advantage of this system is [**that** it lets the apprentice see the practical problems before he sets to work learning how to solve them, **and** he can therefore take a more intelligent interest in his theoretical work].
(The great advantage of this system: S, is: V)

▷ 접속사 that 이하는 동사 is의 보어절이며 '~하는 것'이라는 뜻이다. 접속사 that이 '그래서'란 뜻의 and로 연결되는 두 개의 절을 이끌고 있다.

56

SECTION 12. 교육 · 심리 · 언어

자존감(self-esteem)

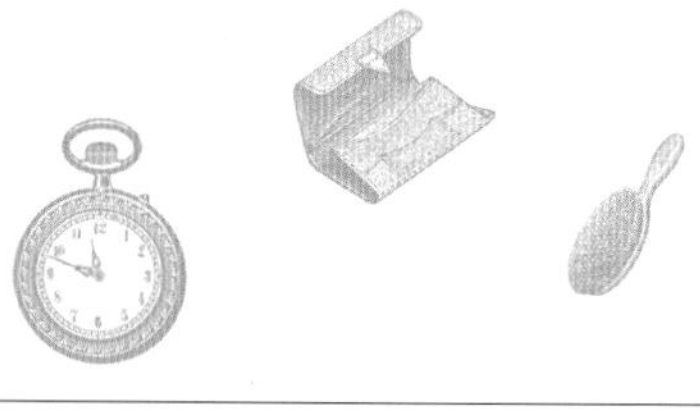

p.142

정답	1. ③ 2. ④ 3. 어릴 때 형성된 낮은 자존감은 성인이 되어서도 계속되고 이는 심한 정서적 고통을 주기 때문이다. 4. ⑤

본문 필기노트

① How you feel about yourself as a person / is called self-esteem. ② People with high self-esteem / believe they are capable, strong and worthy of a good life, while those with low self-esteem / feel inadequate and worthless. ③ Low self-esteem often develops in childhood and continues throughout adulthood, causing severe emotional pain. ④ Therefore, it is important [to develop a healthy, positive sense of self from an early age].

~로서(전치사) / V / (that) / ~의 가치가 있는 / ~인 반면에(접속사) / feel+형용사: ~하게 느끼다 / V_1 / V_2 / =and it causes(분사구문) / 가주어 / to 이하는 진주어

자존감의 의미와 중요성

⑤ Many people base their self-esteem on external factors such as how much money they earn, how much they weigh, and whether others like and appreciate them. ⑥ If one of these external factors changes, their self-esteem can be greatly shaken. ⑦ For example, if your self-esteem is based on the fact [that someone else loves you], / then you risk feeling vulnerable and worthless / if that person's love ends. ⑧ By the same token, / building self-esteem is not an easy task / if you have been hurt by others or have suffered years of personal, academic or professional failure.

~에 / V / O / ~ such as A, B, and C: A, B, C와 같은 ~ / ~ 중의 하나 / 동격의 that / ~에 근거를 두다 / = / risk v-ing: ~할 위험을 무릅쓰다 / 마찬가지로 / (if you) / 현재완료(경험)

낮은 자존감 형성에 영향을 주는 외적 요소들

⑨ To build up your self-esteem, / you need to take an honest look at your strengths and weaknesses. ⑩ Being at peace with yourself, with who you are and what you have to offer others, / is a major part of having high self-esteem. ⑪ This inner peace does not mean [that you are ignorant of your weaknesses]; rather, it means [that you accept who you are and genuinely like the person [you have become]].

형성하기 위해서(부사적 용법) / take a look at: ~을 보다 / ~인 것 / ~에 대하여 / ~해야만 한다 / V / 부연설명 / that 이하는 목적어 / ~에 무지하다, ~을 모르다 / 오히려 / that 이하는 목적어 / V'_1 / V'_2

자존감 형성에 필요한 요소들

본문해석

① 당신이 한 인간으로서 당신 자신에 대해 어떻게 생각하는지를 자존감이라고 부른다. ② 높은 자존감을 가진 사람들은 그들이 능력 있고 강하며, 좋은 삶을 누릴 가치가 있다고 생각하는 반면에, 낮은 자존감을 가진 이들은 그들이 자격이 안 되고 가치가 없다고 느낀다. ③ 낮은 자존감은 흔히 어릴 때 발달하여 성인기에 걸쳐 계속되는데, 심한 정서적 고통을 야기한다. ④ 그러므로 어린 나이 때부터 건강하고 긍정적인 자아 의식을 개발하는 것이 중요하다.

⑤ 많은 사람들이 그들의 자존감의 근거를 돈을 얼마나 많이 버는지, 체중이 얼마나 많이 나가는지, 그리고 다른 사람들이 자신을 좋아하고 인정해 주는지와 같은 외적 요소들에 둔다. ⑥ 만약 이러한 외적 요소들 중 한 가지가 변한다면, 그들의 자존감은 크게 흔들릴 수 있다. ⑦ 예를 들어, 당신의 자존감이 다른 누군가가 당신을 사랑한다는 사실에 근거를 둔다면, 그 사람의 사랑이 끝나면 당신은 상처를 받거나 가치 없게 느낄 위험이 있다. ⑧ 마찬가지로, 만약 당신이 다른 사람들에게서 상처를 받았거나 수년간 개인적, 학문적, 또는 직업적 실패로 고통 받았다면, 자존감을 형성하는 것은 쉬운 일이 아니다.

⑨ 자존감을 형성하기 위해서 당신은 당신의 장점과 단점을 정직하게 바라볼 필요가 있다. ⑩ 당신 자신에 대하여 평온한 것, 즉 당신이 누구이며 당신이 다른 사람들에게 무엇을 주어야 하는지에 대해 평온한 것은 높은 자존감을 갖는 데 있어 중요한 부분이다. ⑪ 이러한 내면의 평온은 당신이 당신의 약점을 모르고 있음을 의미하는 것이 아니라, 오히려 당신이 누구인지를 받아들이고 당신의 현재 모습을 진정으로 좋아한다는 것을 뜻한다.

본문파악

이 글은 자존감의 의미와 중요성을 설명한 글이다. 첫째 단락에서는 자존감이 높은 사람과 자존감이 낮은 사람의 특징을 언급하고 있고, 둘째 단락에서는 낮은 자존감이 형성되는 요인을 밝히고 있다. 셋째 단락에서는 자존감 형성을 위해서 필요한 요소에 대해 이야기하고 있다.

문제풀이

1. ③ → 외적인 요소를 중시하면 자존감이 흔들리기 쉽다고 했다. (⑥번 문장 참조)

2. 《해석》 위 글에 따르면, 다음 중 높은 자존감을 갖고 있지 않을 것 같은 사람은 누구인가?
'④ 다른 사람들로부터 칭찬을 기대하는 사람'은 외적 요소에 의존하고 있으므로 자존감이 낮다.
① 다른 사람들에게 의존하지 않는 사람 ② 자신의 결점을 받아들이는 사람
③ 자신의 실패를 극복하는 사람 ⑤ 자기 자신을 믿는 사람

3. ③~④번 문장 참조

4. (A)에는 명사인 pain을 수식하는 형용사 emotional이 적절하고, (B)에는 If절의 주어가 one이므로 3인칭 단수동사인 changes가 적절하다. (C)에는 앞으로 될 당신의 모습이 아니라 '이미 되어 있는 당신의 모습'이 내용상 자연스러우므로 have become이 적절하다.

구문해설

⑩ Being at peace with yourself, [with **who you are** and **what you have to offer others**], is a major part of having high self-esteem.

▷ [ ]는 삽입구로, with yourself에 대한 구체적인 설명이다.
▷ who you are와 what you ... others는 각각 with의 목적어 역할을 하는 의문사절로, 〈의문사+주어+동사〉의 어순을 따른다.

⑪ This inner peace does not mean that you are ignorant of your weaknesses; rather, it means that you accept who you are and genuinely like the person (**that**) you have become.

▷ the person 다음에 생략된 that은 관계대명사로, 관계사절 속 동사(have become)의 주격보어 역할을 한다. 일반적으로 주격보어로 쓰이는 관계대명사는 that을 쓴다.

매슬로우(Maslow)의 자기실현 이론

매슬로우는 인간은 태어나면서부터 기본적인 욕구를 가지고 태어나며 이러한 욕구를 충족하기 위해 행동한다고 보았다. 그는 인간의 기본적 욕구를 다섯 단계로 구분하였다. 이 욕구들은 위계를 이루고 있으므로, 하위의 기본적인 욕구가 충족되어야 상위의 욕구에 관심을 갖고 이를 달성할 수 있다.
1) 생리적 욕구: 인간에게 있어서 가장 기본적이고 강한 욕구로, 음식, 물, 공기, 수면 등 삶을 위한 기초적인 욕구들이 이에 해당한다.
2) 안전에 대한 욕구: 이 욕구는 누구나 잘 정돈되고 조직화되고 예측 가능한 환경에서 생활하고 싶어 하기 때문에 발생한다.
3) 애정과 소속에 대한 욕구: 이 욕구에 의해 동기화된 개인은 타인과 애정 관계를 형성하고 인생의 동반자나 가족, 집단에 소속되고 싶은 갈망을 갖고 있다.
4) 자존감의 욕구: 자존감에 대한 욕구는 자기 존중과 다른 사람으로부터의 존경을 모두 포함한다.
5) 자아실현의 욕구: 자신이 원하는 종류의 사람이 되고, 스스로 성취할 수 있는 모든 것들을 이루려는 욕구이다.

57

SECTION 12. 교육 · 심리 · 언어

의사소통 수단으로서의 인간 언어의 특징

P.144

정답	1. ⑤ 2. ② 3. (존재하지 않았던) 새로운 메시지와 문장을 만든다. 4. ④

본문 필기노트

① An important aspect of language systems is [that they are open]. ② That is, a language is not a finite set of messages [from which the speaker must choose]. ③ Instead, any speaker can use the resources of the language (— its vocabulary and grammatical patterns —) to make up new messages, sentences [that no one has ever said before]. ④ Because a language is an open system, / it can always be used to talk about new things. ⑤ Bees have a remarkable system (of communication), [using a sort of "dance" in the air], [in which the patterns of a bee's flight tell other members (of the hive) about food sources]. ⑥ However, all [bees can communicate about] / is a nectar supply — its direction, distance, and abundance. ⑦ As a consequence, a bee would make a very dull conversationalist, / at least in human terms.

인간 언어의 개방성

⑧ Another aspect of the communicative function of language is [that it can be displaced]. ⑨ That is, we can talk about things [not present] — about rain when the weather is dry, / about taxes even when they are not being collected, / and about a yeti even if no such creature exists. ⑩ The characteristic of displacement means [that human beings can abstract, can lie, and can talk about talk itself]. ⑪ It allows us to use language as a vehicle of memory and of imagination. ⑫ A bee communicates with other bees / about a nectar source / only when it has just found such a source. ⑬ Bees do not celebrate the delights of nectar / by dancing for sheer pleasure. ⑭ Human beings use language for many purposes [quite unconnected with their immediate environment].

인간 언어의 전치성

본문해석

① 언어 체계의 중요한 측면은 그것(들)이 개방되어 있다는 점이다. ② 즉, 언어는 화자가 선택해야 하는 일련의 유한한 메시지가 아니다. ③ 대신, 모든 화자는 어휘 및 문법 양식 등 그 언어의 자원을 사용하여 새로운 메시지, 즉 이전에 그 누구도 말해 본 적 없는 문장을 만들 수 있다. ④ 언어는 개방된 체계이기 때문에, 그것은 새로운 것에 대해 이야기를 하는 데 항상 사용될 수 있다. ⑤ 벌은 공중에서 일종의 '춤'을 사용하는 놀라운 의사소통 체계를 갖고 있는데, 이 춤에서 벌의 비행 형태는 벌집에 있는 다른 벌들에게 먹이 근원지에 대해 알려준다. ⑥ 그러나 벌들이 의사소통하는 것은 모두 벌꿀의 공급, 즉 그것의 방향, 거리, 양 등에 관한 것이다. ⑦ 결과적으로, 벌은 적어도 인간의 기준으로 볼 때 아주 지루한 대화 상대자일 것이다.

⑧ 언어의 의사소통 기능의 또 다른 측면은 그것이 전치될 수 있다는 것이다. ⑨ 즉, 우리는 지금 있지 않은 것들을, 예를 들어 날씨가 건조할 때 비에 대해서, 아직 징수되고 있지도 않는 세금에 대해서, 그리고 그런 생물이 비록 존재하지 않을지라도 설인에 대해서 이야기할 수 있다. ⑩ 전치라는 특징은 인간이 추상화할 수 있고, 거짓말할 수 있으며, 말 자체에 대해 말할 수 있다는 것을 의미한다. ⑪ 그것은 우리가 언어를 기억과 상상의 수단으로 사용하게 해준다. ⑫ 벌은 벌꿀원을 막 발견했을 때에만 그 벌꿀원에 대해 다른 벌들과 의사소통한다. ⑬ 벌들은 벌꿀에 대한 기쁨을 완전한 즐거움으로 춤을 춤으로써 축하하지 않는다. ⑭ 인간은 언어를 그들의 직접적인 상황과 전혀 관련이 없는 여러 가지 목적을 위해 사용한다.

본문파악

이 글은 의사소통 수단으로서의 인간 언어의 특징에 대한 것으로, 인간 언어를 꿀벌의 언어와 비교 · 대조하여 설명하고 있다. 첫째 단락은 제한적인 의사 표현만 하는 벌들과 달리 인간의 언어는 개방적이라는 내용이다. 둘째 단락에서는 인간 언어의 전치 현상에 대해 다루고 있는데, 이는 인간이 꿀벌과는 달리 시공을 초월해 언어 표현을 할 수 있다는 것을 뜻한다.

문제풀이

1. 《해석》 위 글의 제목으로 가장 적절한 것은?
이 글은 의사소통 수단으로서의 인간 언어의 특징 두 가지를 설명하고 있으므로, 제목으로는 '⑤ 인간 언어에 나타나는 독특한 특징들'이 가장 적절하다.
① 인간은 어떻게 설인과 이야기할 수 있는가?
② 인간 언어 대 동물 언어
③ 인간 언어는 어떻게 발달했는가?
④ 왜 인간은 서로 의사소통을 하는가?

2. ②번 문장의 '언어는 일련의 유한한 메시지가 아니다'라는 말과 ④번 문장의 '언어는 항상 새로운 것에 대해 이야기하는 데 사용될 수 있다'가 단서가 된다. 즉, 유한하지 않으면서, 새로운 것을 만들어 낼 수 있음을 나타내주는 말은 '② open'이다.
① 복잡한 ③ 상호적인 ④ 제한된 ⑤ 단순한

3. ③번 문장 참조

4. 《해석》 위 글의 필자는 왜 '벌'에 대해 언급하는가?
필자가 벌을 언급한 것은 동물 언어는 표현이 극히 제한적이나 인간 언어는 무한하다는 것을 보다 더 효과적으로 설명하기 위함으로, 정답은 '④ 인간 언어의 특징을 설명하기 위해서'이다.
① 벌이 훌륭한 의사 전달자라는 것을 보여주기 위해서
② 벌이 새로운 먹이 근원지를 어떻게 발견하는지를 설명하기 위해서
③ 벌이 감정을 전달하는 법을 보여주기 위해서
⑤ 자연에 대한 인간의 우월성을 강조하기 위해서

구문해설

⑥ However, **all** [(that) bees can communicate about] is a nectar supply — its direction, distance, and abundance.

▷ all이 관계사절을 이끌어 주어로 쓰이면 '~한 모든 것은 (…뿐이다)'의 뜻이며, 이때 관계대명사는 보통 생략된다.

⑫ A bee communicates with other bees about a nectar source only when it **has just found** such a source.

▷ has just found는 현재완료의 완료 용법으로 '막 발견했다'의 의미이다.

언어의 일반적 특성

우리말을 포함한 세계의 모든 언어는 언어로서의 일반적인 특성을 지니고 있다.
첫째, 언어의 창조성을 들 수 있다. 언어는 인간만이 가지고 있는 고유의 의사소통 수단이다. 인간을 제외한 동물들의 경우, 무한한 의사 전달과 표현이 불가능하고, 정보의 복합적인 표현도 불가능하며, 제한된 몇 가지 의사 전달 내용만이 가능할 뿐이다. 그러나 인간은 다른 사람이 들어보지도 써보지도 않은 문장을 만들어 낼 수도 있고, 그것을 듣고 이해할 수도 있다. 또한, 상황에 맞는 새로운 단어를 만들어 내고, 여러 가지 다양한 표현으로 긴 문장을 만들어 낼 수도 있다.
둘째, 언어의 이원성(duality)이 있다. 언어는 소리와 의미로 이루어져 있다. 소리 체계와 의미 체계가 독립적으로 분리되어 있는 것이다. 따라서 비슷한 소리로도 전혀 다른 의미를 나타낼 수 있으며, 반대로 다른 소리로 동일한 의미를 나타내는 것도 가능하다.
셋째, 언어는 임의적이며 관습적이다. 임의적이라 함은 언어의 형식과 내용의 관계가 필연적이 아니라는 것을 의미하고, 관습적이라는 것은 언어가 사회적 약속에 의해 맺어져 있다는 것을 뜻한다. 만약 언어가 임의적이거나 관습적이지 않다면 언어는 변하지도 않고 동음어나 동의어가 생겨날 수도 없다. 단, 의성어와 의태어에 있어서는 언어에서 소리와 의미가 필연적으로 여겨지기도 한다.
넷째, 언어는 분석적이고 체계적이며 구조적이다. 언어는 소리의 최소 단위인 음소, 의미의 최소 단위인 형태소로 분석될 수 있고, 단어의 배열과 결합으로 이루어진 문장 속에는 규칙과 방법이 들어 있으므로 체계적이며 구조적이라고 할 수 있다.
마지막으로, 언어는 문화적 전달을 가능케 한다. 인간은 무한한 언어 능력을 지니고 있으므로, 후천적 학습을 통해 모국어 외에 다른 언어를 습득할 수 있다. 언어를 통해 자신의 문화와 다른 문화를 배우고 익힘으로써 지식, 예술, 도덕, 풍습 등 많은 사회적 요소들을 다음 세대로 전승하는 것이다.

58

SECTION 12. 교육 · 심리 · 언어

조지 오웰의 「1984」 중에서

P.146

정답	1. ④ 2. ② 3. 좋음과 나쁨에 대한 모든 개념을 여섯 개의 단어로 충분히 표현할 수 있는 것

본문 필기노트

① 'It's a beautiful thing, the destruction of words. ② Of course / the great wastage is in the verbs and adjectives, / but there are hundreds of nouns [that can be got rid of as well]. ③ It isn't only the synonyms ; there are also the antonyms. ④ After all, what justification is there for a word [which is simply the opposite of some other word]? ⑤ A word contains its opposite in itself. ⑥ Take "good," for instance. ⑦ If you have a word like "good," / what need is there for a word like "bad"? ⑧ Ungood will do just as well — better, / because it's an exact opposite, which the other is not. ⑨ Or again, if you want a stronger version of "good," / what sense is there in having a whole string of vague useless words / like "excellent" and "splendid" and all the rest of them? ⑩ "Plusgood" covers the meaning, / or "doubleplusgood" / if you want something stronger still. ⑪ Of course we use those forms already. ⑫ But in the final version of Newspeak / there'll be nothing else. ⑬ In the end / the whole notion of goodness and badness / will be covered by only six words — in reality, / only one word. ⑭ Don't you see the beauty of that, Winston? ⑮ It was B.B.'s idea originally, of course,' he added as an afterthought.

(It = the destruction of words / is: V / that: 주격 관 · 대 / as well: 마찬가지로 / ; : but / not only A (but) also B: A뿐만 아니라 B도 역시 / which: 주격 관 · 대 / in itself: 그 자체에 / do: 충분하다 / (it is) better / well: (as "bad") / it's: =ungood / the other: =bad / in: in v-ing: ~하는 데 있어 / a string of: 일련의 ~ / still: 훨씬(비교급 강조) / as: ~로서)

본문해석

① '말을 없앤다는 건 멋있는 일이야. ② 물론 많은 낭비가 동사와 형용사에 있지만, 마찬가지로 제거될 수 있는 명사도 수백 개가 있지. ③ 동의어 뿐만이 아니라 반의어도 있어. ④ 결국 단순히 다른 말의 반의어일 뿐인 단어에 대해 무슨 변명이 있겠는가? ⑤ 단어는 그 자체에 반의어를 포함하고 있네. ⑥ '좋다(good)'를 예로 들어 보세. ⑦ '좋다(good)' 같은 말이 있으면, 구태여 '나쁘다(bad)'와 같은 말이 무슨 필요가 있겠나? ⑧ '안 좋다(ungood)'로 아주 충분해, 아니, 더 나아. 왜냐하면 그게 정확한 반의어고, '나쁘다'는 아니니까. ⑨ 아니면 또 '좋다'의 더 강한 형태를 원한다면, '훌륭하다(excellent)'느니 '멋있다(splendid)'느니 그 나머지 모든 것들과 같은 일련의 모호하고 쓸모없는 모든 단어들이 있다는 게 무슨 의미가 있을까? ⑩ '더 좋다(plusgood)'라는 말이 그 의미를 포함하고, 훨씬 더 강한 말이 필요하면 '더욱더 좋다(doubleplusgood)'로 하면 되지. ⑪ 물론 우리는 이미 그러한 형태들을 사용하고 있네. ⑫ 하지만 신어사전의 최종판에는 그 외엔 아무 것도 없을 걸세. ⑬ 결국 좋음과 나쁨에 대한 모든 개념은 단 여섯 단어들로 처리될 것이네. 실제로는 단 한 단어지만 말일세. ⑭ 자네는 그것의 아름다움을 보지 못하나, 윈스턴? ⑮ 물론 그것이 원래는 빅브라더(수령님)의 생각이었다네.'라며 그는 추가로 덧붙였다.

본문파악 이 글은 조지 오웰의 소설 「1984」의 일부분으로 언어(여기서는 영어)를 단순화시키는 것의 편리함과 경제성에 대해 단어 'good'을 예로 들어 설명하고 있다.

문제풀이

1. 《해석》 위 글의 화자는 주로 무엇에 대해 말하고 있는가?
이 글에서 화자는 다양한 어휘의 필요성에 대한 의문을 제기하고 있으므로, 글의 주제로는 '④ 언어의 단순화'가 적절하다.
① 새 단어를 만드는 방법 ② 반의어의 정확한 사용
③ 언어의 다양성 ⑤ 말하기에 있어 정확성의 중요성

2. ⑤번 문장에서 '한 단어는 그 자체에 반의어를 지니고 있다'고 했으므로, 빈칸 (A)에는 good을 이용한 반의어 Ungood이 와야 한다. excellent나 splendid의 의미를 갖는 plusgood은 good보다 의미가 '더 강한' 것이므로, 빈칸 (B)에는 stronger가 적절하다.

3. ⑬번 문장 참조

구문해설

⑧ Ungood will **do just as well** (as "bad") — (it is) better, because it's an exact opposite, **which** the other is not.

▷ 이때의 do는 '하다'라는 뜻의 타동사가 아니라 '충분하다'라는 뜻의 자동사이다.
▷ just as well: '아주 똑같이 (좋게)'의 의미로 뒤에 as "bad"가 생략되어 있는 것이며, just는 as well을 강조한다.
▷ which는 바로 앞에 나온 구 an exact opposite을 선행사로 하는 계속적 용법의 관계대명사로, which 이하를 'but the other is not an exact opposite'이라고 바꾸어 쓸 수 있다.

⑩ "Plusgood" covers the meaning, or "doubleplusgood" if you want **something** [**stronger still**].

▷ 비교급을 강조하는 부사 still은 '훨씬'의 뜻으로 보통은 비교급 앞에 위치하나, 여기서는 stronger와 something의 관계(-thing으로 끝나는 명사는 형용사가 명사 뒤에서 수식)가 우선이기 때문에 stronger 뒤에 왔다.

소설 「화씨 451」

「화씨 451」은 레이 브래드버리(Ray Bradbury)의 공상 과학 소설로 영화화되기도 했다. 조지 오웰의 「1984」가 계층에 따른 정보 독점을 다루고 있다면, 「화씨 451」은 소수 지배층만이 비밀리에 책을 읽고 있다는 점에서 정보 독점을 다룬 작품의 예이다.
「화씨 451」은 책에 대한 탄압이 주된 줄거리이다. 주인공 몬테그의 직업은 방화수이다. 그는 책을 읽거나 소장하는 불순분자들을 찾아내 체포하고 그들의 책을 불태우는 일을 한다. 책은 사람들의 마음을 복잡하게 만들어 사회불안을 조성하기 때문이다. 그런데 어느 날 하루 종일 텔레비전에만 빠져 있는 아내 밀드레드와 달리 책을 읽는 클라리세를 알게 되고 그녀의 집에 초대받게 된다. 클라리세의 집에는 책이 가득했고 그녀의 할머니는 책에 중독이 되어 있었다. 어느 날 몬테그의 차가 출동해 간 곳은 클라리세의 집이었고, 순식간에 여자의 집은 불타게 된다. 끝까지 책을 고수하려던 할머니가 책과 함께 불에 타죽게 되고, 결국 자신의 직업에 회의를 느낀 몬테그는 클라리세와 함께 자유세계를 찾아 탈출한다는 내용이다.

59

SECTION 13. 시사 이슈

디지털 치매(digital dementia)

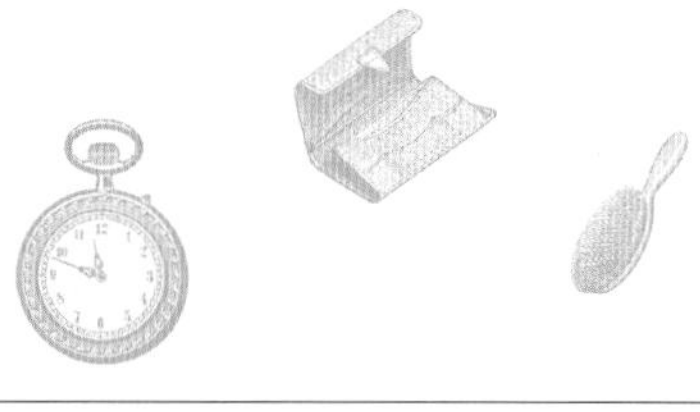

P.150

정답 | 1. ④ 2. ⑤ 3. 손상된 인지 능력, 우울증과 같은 부정적인 정서 상태 4. optimistic

본문 필기노트

① Recent studies have found [that people [who have grown up in the digital age] differ significantly from the older generation in their ability [to recall basic information without assistance from an electronic device]]. ② Researchers believe [that because it is easier [to search for information], the skill of memorization has begun to atrophy due to a lack of regular practice].

(that 이하는 목적어 / 주격 관 · 대 / differ from: ~와 다르다 / 기억하는(형용사적 용법) / ~로부터 / that 이하는 목적어 / 가주어 / to 이하는 진주어 / ~때문에)

디지털 기기에의 지나친 의존 결과로 나타나는 기억력 쇠퇴 현상

③ Some neuroscientists argue [that excessive interaction with digital technology has resulted in impairment [resembling that of a person [suffering from head trauma or a psychiatric disorder]]]. ④ This deficit in cognitive abilities, such as short-term memory and concentration, [caused by the overuse of technology] is known as digital dementia. ⑤ Constant access to digital devices fosters an imbalance in the brain, / with linear and information-searching skills being strengthened / while intuitive thinking and emotional capabilities / deteriorate. ⑥ This results in not only impaired cognitive skills but also negative emotional conditions such as depression.

(that 이하는 목적어 / 현재완료(결과) / =impairment / ~으로 고통받다 / be known as: ~로 알려지다 / ~로의 접근 / with+O+분사: O가 ~한 채로 / ~하는 반면 / not only A but also B: A뿐만 아니라 B도 역시)

디지털 치매의 정의 및 그것이 두뇌에 미치는 영향

⑦ The good news is, / however, / [that experts tentatively speculate [that digital dementia can be reversed, based on the fact [that this happens in some forms of dementia / when the source of the problem is removed]]]. ⑧ The effects of digital dementia, therefore, may not be inevitable / if users are willing to take measures [to actively promote brain health].

(that 이하는 보어 / 동격의 that / that 이하는 목적어 / ~에 근거하여 / = / be willing to-v: 기꺼이 ~하다 / 촉진하기 위해(부사적 용법))

디지털 치매의 회복 가능성에 대한 전망

본문해석

① 최근의 연구는 디지털 시대에 자라난 사람들이 전자 기기의 도움 없이 기초적인 정보를 기억해 내는 능력이 나이 든 세대와 크게 다르다는 사실을 발견했다. ② 연구원들은 정보를 찾기가 더 쉽기 때문에 주기적인 연습의 부족으로 기억 능력이 감퇴되기 시작했다고 생각한다.

③ 어떤 신경과학자들은 디지털 기술과의 지나친 상호작용이 머리 외상 또는 정신 질환을 앓는 사람의 것과 비슷한 장애를 낳았다고 주장한다. ④ 기술의 남용으로 인해 발생하는 단기 기억력과 집중력과 같은 인지 능력의 이러한 결핍은 디지털 치매라고 알려져 있다. ⑤ 디지털 기기에 대한 지속적인 접근이 두뇌의 불균형을 촉진하여, 일차원적인 기술과 정보 검색 기술은 강화되는 한편 사고력과 정서 능력은 악화된다. ⑥ 이것은 손상된 인지 능력뿐만 아니라 우울증과 같은 부정적인 정서 상태를 초래한다.

⑦ 그러나 좋은 소식은, 몇몇 치매 유형에서 문제의 원인이 제거되었을 때 이것(원상태로의 복귀)이 발생했다는 사실에 근거하여 디지털 치매가 회복될 수 있다고 전문가들이 조심스럽게 추측한다는 것이다. ⑧ 따라서 사용자들이 적극적으로 두뇌 건강을 촉진하기 위해 조치를 취하고자 한다면 디지털 치매의 결과는 불가피한 것이 아닐지도 모른다.

본문파악

이 글은 디지털 기기에 지나치게 의존하는 데서 발생하는 디지털 치매에 대한 글이다. 첫째 단락에서는 디지털 시대에 사는 사람들의 기억력 감퇴 현상과 그 원인을 설명하고 있다. 둘째 단락에서는 디지털 치매의 정의를 제시하고 그것이 두뇌에 미치는 영향을 자세히 설명하고 있다. 셋째 단락에서는 디지털 치매의 회복 가능성을 언급하고 있다.

문제풀이

1. 《해석》 위 글의 목적은 무엇인가?
   본문 둘째 단락에서 디지털 치매의 발생 경위와 결과를 상세히 설명하고 있으므로 글의 목적으로는 '④ 무엇이 디지털 치매를 일으키는지를 설명하고 두뇌에 미치는 영향을 약술하기 위해'가 가장 적절하다.
   ① 어린 시절 두뇌 발달의 과정을 설명하기 위해
   ② 디지털 치매의 새로운 치료법을 소개하기 위해
   ③ 디지털 기기 사용의 긍정적인 효과와 부정적인 효과를 비교하기 위해
   ⑤ 정부에게 디지털 치매를 예방하는 정책을 도입하라고 촉구하기 위해

2. (A)에는 문맥상 전자 기기의 '도움'없이는 정보를 기억해내는 능력이 떨어진다는 것이 자연스러우므로, assistance가 적절하다. (B)에는 디지털 기기와의 '지나친' 접촉이 인지 능력의 결핍을 낳는다는 맥락이므로, excessive가 알맞다. (C)에는 앞의 while을 통해 앞에 나온 내용과는 반대되는 내용이 들어가야 함을 알 수 있으므로 '악화되다'의 의미인 deteriorate가 오는 것이 적절하다.
   cf. assistant (조수) / insufficient (부족한) / improve (개선하다)

3. ⑥번 문장 참조

4. 《해석》 위 글의 필자는 디지털 치매의 치료 가능성에 대해 낙관적인 태도를 취한다.
   ⑧번 문장에서 적극적인 노력만 있다면 디지털 치매는 회복될 수 있다고 언급하였으므로, 빈칸에는 'optimistic(낙관적인)'이 적절하다.

구문해설

③ Some neuroscientists argue [that excessive interaction with digital technology has resulted in impairment **resembling that** of a person **suffering** from head trauma or a psychiatric disorder].

▷ 첫 번째 [ ]는 argue의 목적어로 쓰인 명사절이다.
▷ resembling와 suffering은 각각 impairment와 a person을 수식하는 현재분사구이다.
▷ that은 앞에 나온 명사를 대신하는 지시대명사로, 여기서는 impairment를 대신한다.

⑦ The good news (S) is (V), however, [**that** experts tentatively speculate [**that** digital dementia can be reversed based on the fact [**that** this happens in some forms of dementia when the source of the problem is removed]]].

▷ 첫 번째 that 이하는 be동사의 보어로 쓰인 명사절로 '~이라는 것'의 의미이다.
▷ 두 번째 that 이하는 speculate의 목적어로 쓰인 명사절이다.
▷ 세 번째 that 이하는 the fact의 내용을 설명하는 동격의 that절이다.

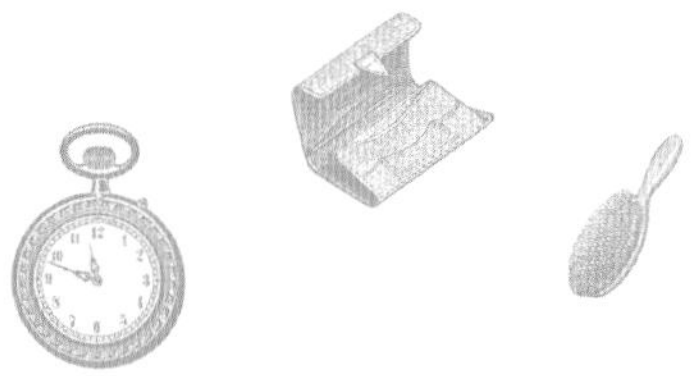

60 SECTION 13. 시사 이슈
이민자에 대한 시각 차이

P.152

정답 | 1. ⑤ 2. 저숙련 이주 노동자들이 언어, 전통, 종교 면에서 더 이질적인 인상을 주는 경향이 있어 이러한 차이가 보통 사회적, 문화적 위협으로 받아들여지기 때문이다. 3. ③

본문 필기노트

① Across the world, / social and political conflicts are frequently instigated / by
전 세계에
discord (over immigration and the public policies / [formulated in the interest of
~을 위하여
regulating it]). ② While the issues [related to immigration] are often regionally
~하는 한편
specific, there are also underlying patterns [that can be observed on a global scale
주격 관 · 대
and used [to facilitate the legislation of effective immigration reform]].
용이하게 하기 위해(부사적 용법)

전 세계적으로 발생하는 이민에 대한 갈등

③ The economic benefits of immigration are often touted / by advocates of open
~의
immigration policies, / as an influx of new workers and consumers /can boost
~이기 때문에(접속사)
local economic growth / and raise tax revenues. ④ What's more, immigrant
더구나, 게다가
workers — especially those of the low-skilled variety — have been shown to
=immigrant workers
largely complement the existing labor force rather than compete with it. ⑤ In
A rather than B: B라기보다는 오히려 A =the existing labor force
America, for example, [where the percentage of working-age adults without a
관계부사 S′ ~없이
high school education / has plummeted from more than 80% in 1950 to about
V′ from A to B: A에서 B로
10% currently], there are simply more low-skill positions available / than potential
employees (willing to accept them). ⑥ These advantages of immigration, however,
do little to quell anti-immigrant sentiments, as these sentiments tend to possess
~이기 때문에(접속사) tend to-v: ~하는 경향이 있다
social rather than economic roots. ⑦ Social science research has shown [(that)
~라기보다는 오히려 that 이하는 목적어
despite the dire need for low-skilled workers, these types of immigrants are met with
(who are)
greater resistance from the native population than those [possessing professional
~로부터 =immigrants
skills, such as physicians and technicians]]. ⑧ This may be because low-skilled
A such as B: B와 같은 A
migrants are likely to present a more alien image in terms of language, traditions
be likely to-v: ~할 가능성이 있다 ~면에서
and religion ; such differences are commonly perceived as a social and cultural
부연설명 ~로서
threat.

이민에 대한 찬반 입장

본문해석

① 전 세계적으로 사회적 · 정치적 갈등이 이민과 그것을 규제하기 위해 만들어진 공공 정책에 대한 불화에 의해 주로 유발된다. ② 이민과 관련한 문제들은 보통 지역적으로 특수한 한편, 세계적인 규모로 관찰될 수 있으며 효과적인 이민 개혁의 입법을 용이하게 하는 데 사용될 수 있는 근본적인 패턴 또한 존재한다.

③ 이민의 경제적 이익은 흔히 개방적인 이민 정책의 옹호자들에 의해 내세워지는데, 새로운 근로자와 소비자의 유입이 현지의 경제 성장을 북돋고 조세 수입을 끌어올릴 수 있기 때문이다. ④ 게다가, 이주 노동자들, 특히 숙련도가 낮은 부류의 노동자들은 기존의 노동력과 경쟁하기보다는 대체로 그것을 보완한다는 것이 증명된 바 있다. ⑤ 예를 들어, 고등학교 교육을 받지 않은 취업 연령 성인의 비율이 1950년의 80% 이상에서 현재 약 10%로 급감한 미국에서는, 구할 수 있는 저숙련 일자리가 기꺼이 그것을 받아들이려 하는 잠재적 고용인보다 훨씬 더 많다. ⑥ 그러나, 이러한 이민의 이점은 반이민 정서를 진정시키는 데는 거의 기여하지 못하는데, 이 정서는 경제적 근거보다는 사회적 근거를 지니는 경향이 있기 때문이다. ⑦ 사회과학 연구는 저숙련 근로자에 대한 심각한 필요성에도 불구하고, 이런 부류의 이민자들은 의사나 기술자와 같이 전문 기술을 보유한 사람들보다 현지인으로부터 더 큰 저항을 받는다는 것을 보여준다. ⑧ 이것은 저숙련 이주자들이 언어, 전통과 종교 면에서 더 이질적인 인상을 줄 가능성이 높기 때문일지도 모른다. 그런 차이는 흔히 사회적, 문화적 위협으로 인식되기 때문이다.

본문파악

이 글은 이민으로 인한 사회적, 정치적 갈등을 설명하는 글이다. 첫째 단락은 전 세계적으로 이민으로 인해 발생되는 갈등을 소개하는 도입부이다. 둘째 단락 전반부에서는 이민자 유입으로 인한 경제적인 이점을 언급하고 있지만, 후반부에서는 그들이 사회로부터 받는 정서적 저항에 대해 언급하며 우려를 표하고 있다.

문제풀이

1. 빈칸 뒤에 나오는 미국의 사례를 통해 저숙련 이주 노동자가 노동력이 부족한 일자리에 유용할 것임을 알 수 있으므로, 빈칸에는 '⑤ 기존의 노동력과 경쟁하기보다는 대체로 그것을 보완한다'는 내용이 들어가는 것이 적절하다.
   ① 새로운 근무 환경에 빠르게 적응한다
   ② 새로운 사회적, 문화적 체제에 쉽게 순응한다
   ③ 현지의 저숙련 근로자들보다 일반적으로 더 교육받았다
   ④ 현지의 저숙련 근로자들과 비교했을 때 더 유능하다

2. ⑧번 문장 참조

3. (A)에는 the public policies를 뒤에서 수식하는 분사구를 이끌며, the public policies와 의미상 수동 관계에 있는 과거분사 formulated가 적절하다. (B)에는 뒤에 완전한 절이 나오므로, America를 선행사로 하는 관계부사 where가 와야 한다. (C)에는 문맥상 앞에 나온 immigrants를 대신하는 복수형 지시대명사 those가 오는 것이 알맞다.

구문해설

② While the issues [**related** to immigration] are often regionally specific, there are also underlying patterns [**that can be observed** on a global scale and **used** to facilitate the legislation of effective immigration reform].

▷ 첫 번째 [ ]는 the issues를 수식하는 과거분사구이다.
▷ 두 번째 [ ]는 underlying patterns를 선행사로 하는 주격 관계대명사절이다.
▷ 동사 can be observed와 used가 접속사 and에 의해 병렬연결되어 있다.

⑦ Social science research has shown [that, despite the dire need for low-skilled workers, these types of immigrants are met with greater resistance from the native population than those [**possessing** professional skills, such as physicians and technicians]].

▷ [ ]는 has shown의 목적어 역할을 하는 명사절이다.
▷ possessing 이하는 those를 수식하는 현재분사구이다.

61

SECTION 13. 시사 이슈

공유 경제(sharing economy)

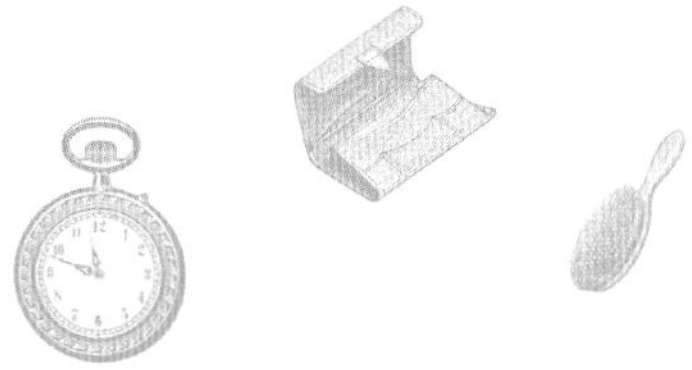

P.154

정답	1. ④ 2. natural resources, environmental issues, innovative technology 3. ⑤ 4. (1) T (2) F (3) T

본문 필기노트

① [Renting a room from an overseas host with Airbnb] or [having someone else handle your grocery shopping with TaskRabbit] — these are just two examples of the developing sharing economy, [which has swelled (to) a staggering $26 billion globally and encompasses a diverse array (of economic transactions)]. ② Sharing economy participants buy, rent, and sell unused or unwanted items collaboratively.

동명사구 / have+O+동사원형: O에게 ~을 시키다 / which의 선행사 / 주격 관 · 대(계속적 용법) / ~까지

공유 경제의 개념

③ Sharing has been an integral component of human survival [going back to hunter-gatherer societies and cooperative agriculture], but the modern-day obsession with private ownership in capitalist economies has resulted in excessive consumption and a surplus (of) personal belongings. ④ However, in light of dwindling natural resources and a greater understanding of environmental issues, consumer behavior is shifting back / toward more sustainable methods of consumption. ⑤ Another contributing factor / is the emergence of innovative technology, / [which has streamlined and simplified sharing-based transactions]. ⑥ The sharing economy allows consumers to reinvent the market by conducting transactions with each other directly. ⑦ This approach (to) buying and selling, in contrast to the traditional market, has an impact on the culture itself, [moving from an individualistic society to a more collective perspective].

현재완료(계속) / S / 현재완료(결과) / ~의 / ~에 비추어, ~을 고려하여 / which의 선행사 / 주격 관 · 대(계속적 용법) / allow+O+to-v: O가 ~하는 것을 허락하다 / by v-ing: ~함으로써 / ~에 대한 / in contrast to: ~와 대조되는 / have an impact on: ~에 영향을 주다 / 부대상황의 분사구문 / from A to B: A에서 B로

공유 경제 대두의 배경과 그 영향

⑧ (As) the number of participants in peer-to-peer transactions continues to grow, the success (of the sharing economy) will rely more heavily on its central principle the establishment of trust between strangers. ⑨ [Inherent within all activities of nature], trust is the key to enabling these transactions to occur.

~함에 따라(접속사) / 계속해서 ~하다 / rely on: ~에 의지[의존]하다 / = / (Being) 부대상황의 분사구문 / a key to+(동)명사: ~의 열쇠(비결) / enable+O+to-v: O가 ~할 수 있게 하다

공유 경제의 핵심 원칙

본문해석

① 에어비앤비로 해외의 주인에게서 방을 빌리거나 태스크래빗으로 다른 사람에게 식품 구입을 시키는 것, 이것은 발전하고 있는 공유 경제의 두 가지 예에 지나지 않으며, 전 세계적으로 무려 260억 달러 규모로 불어나며 다양한 경제 거래를 아우른다. ② 공유 경제 참여자들은 사용하지 않거나 불필요한 물품을 공동으로 구매하고, 대여하고, 판매한다.

③ 공유는 사냥-채집 사회와 협동 농업까지 거슬러 올라가는 인간 생존의 필수 요소이지만, 자본주의 경제에서의 사유(私有)에 대한 오늘날의 집착은 과도한 소비와 개인 소유물의 과잉을 낳았다. ④ 그러나, 감소하는 천연자원과 환경 문제에 대한 더 깊은 이해에 비추어, 소비자 행동은 다시 보다 지속 가능한 소비 방법을 향해 변화하고 있다. ⑤ 또 하나의 기여 요인은 혁신 기술의 출현으로, 그것은 공유 기반 거래를 능률화하고 간소화했다. ⑥ 공유 경제는 소비자들이 서로 직접 거래를 수행함으로써 시장을 개혁할 수 있게 해 준다. ⑦ 구매와 판매에 대한 이러한 접근은, 전통적인 시장과는 대조적으로, 문화 자체에 영향을 미쳐서 개인주의적인 사회에서 보다 집단적인 관점으로 이행하도록 한다.

⑧ 소비자간 직접 거래의 참여자 수가 계속 늘어남에 따라, 공유 경제의 성공은 그 중심 원칙, 즉 타인 간의 신뢰 구축에 더욱 많이 의존하게 될 것이다. ⑨ 공유의 본질을 띤 모든 활동에 내재한 신뢰는 이러한 거래가 일어날 수 있게 하는 열쇠다.

본문파악

이 글은 소비자 간에 서로 물건과 서비스를 대여 및 사고파는 경제 활동인 공유 경제에 관한 글이다. 첫째 단락에서는 숙박 공유 서비스인 에어비앤비와 단기 아르바이트 제공 서비스인 태스크래빗을 예로 들며 공유 경제의 개념을 설명하고 있다. 둘째 단락에서는 공유 경제가 발전하게 된 배경과 그에 따른 문화적 영향을 언급하고 있다. 셋째 단락에서는 공유 경제의 중심 원칙인 신뢰 구축의 중요성을 강조하며 글을 마무리하고 있다.

문제풀이

1. 《해석》 위 글의 주제는 무엇인가?
본론인 두 번째 단락에서 공유 경제 대두의 배경과 그 영향에 대해 이야기하고 있으므로, ④가 글의 주제로 가장 적절하다.
① 공동 소비의 다양한 유형들
② 공동 소비를 지원하는 단체들
③ 공유 경제와 관련한 비판과 논란
④ 공유 경제의 발달과 문화적 영향
⑤ 공유 경제 이후 새로운 형태의 경제의 등장

2. 《해석》 필자에 따르면, 공유 경제의 등장에 영향을 미친 몇몇 요인이 있다. 첫째로, 소비자 행동은 줄어드는 천연자원과 환경 문제 때문에 지속 가능한 소비 수단에 보다 초점을 맞추기에 이르렀다. 둘째로, 혁신 기술의 개발이 그것의 절차를 용이하게 함으로써 공유 경제를 가속했다. (각 단어는 본문에서)
④번, ⑤번 문장 참조

3. (A) 사유에 대한 집착이 과도한 소비와 개인 소유물의 과잉을 야기했다는 ③번 문장을 통해 공유 경제 이전에는 '개인주의적인 사회(individualistic society)'였음을 알 수 있다.
(B) 공유 경제는 물품을 공동으로 구매하고 대여하고 판매하므로, 문화적 관점이 '보다 집단적인 관점(more collective perspective)'으로 이행되었음을 알 수 있다.

4. 《해석》 다음 진술에 대해 T(참) 또는 F(거짓)로 표시하시오.
(1) 공유 경제는 전 세계적으로 규모가 증가했다. (①번 문장 참조)
(2) 사유에 대한 집착이 공유 경제가 발달하는 데 이바지했다. → ③번 문장에 따르면 사유는 과도한 소비와 개인 소유물의 과잉을 낳았다.
(3) 신뢰는 공유 경제의 성공에 핵심 요소이다. (⑧번, ⑨번 문장 참조)

구문해설

⑦ This approach to [buying and selling], in contrast to the traditional market, **has an impact on** the culture itself, [moving from an individualistic society to a more collective perspective].

▷ 첫 번째 [ ]는 전치사 to의 목적어로 쓰인 동명사구이다.
▷ have an impact on: '~에 영향을 주다'
▷ 두 번째 [ ]는 부대상황을 나타내는 분사구문이다.

⑧ As **the number of** participants in peer-to-peer transactions **continues** to grow, the success of the sharing economy will rely more heavily on **its central principle — the establishment of trust between strangers**.

▷ the number of는 '~의 수'라는 뜻으로, 동사는 단수에 일치시키므로 단수동사 continues가 왔다.
▷ its central principle과 the establishment of trust between strangers는 서로 동격이다.

62 SECTION 13. 시사 이슈
도의적 공정성 운동

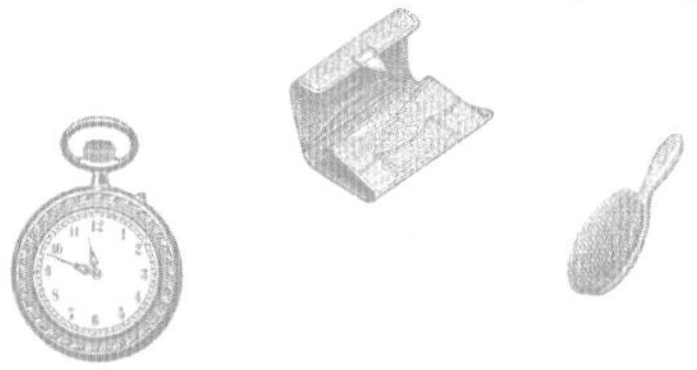

P.156

정답

1. ⑤ 2. 80~90년대의 운동은 편파적 발언에 제약을 거는 한편으로 소수집단의 의견이나 관점이 문학이나 역사에서 더 잘 나타나도록 하는 반면, 오늘날의 운동은 대학생의 개인적인 정서적 안녕을 위한 운동이다. 3. (1) microaggression (2) trigger warning 4. ④

본문 필기노트

① American universities and colleges / have become a breeding ground / for a new form of political correctness. ② This movement is barely recognizable from its predecessor of the 1980s and '90s, whose dual aim was to place restrictions on hate speech while paving the way for minority voices and perspectives to be better represented in the presentation of literature and history.

whose의 선행사 / 소유격 관 · 대(계속적 용법) / 제한을 두는 것(명사적 용법) / ~하는 한편 / 의미상의 주어 / 더 잘 표현되어지도록(부사적 용법)

새로운 형태의 도의적 공정성 운동의 출현

③ The recurrence of politically correct speech in its present-day form focuses on the emotional welfare of the individual, [operating on the assumption [that the fragile psyche (of university students) must be shielded from offense, thereby [preventing psychological damage]]. ④ This predominantly student-driven movement has precipitated a shift in interpersonal communication, and the previously obscure terms "microaggression" and "trigger warning" have come to the forefront of modern language. ⑤ A microaggression is an action or speech act [that is classified as a form of violence despite a seeming lack of hostile or discriminatory intent]. ⑥ A trigger warning is a statement [given to an audience] signaling [that the following content potentially unsettling material]. ⑦ University professors are increasingly expected to issue such warnings so that students [who have experienced trauma in the related area] may opt to avoid exposure to the work altogether, thus [forestalling the evocation of unpleasant memories or feelings].

~의 / focus on: ~에 초점을 맞추다 / 동격의 that / ~의 / 부대상황의 분사구문 / = / S' / V' / 결과의 분사구문 / = / 현재완료(결과) / 주격 관 · 대 / ~로서 / ~에도 불구하고 / that 이하는 목적어 / be expected to-v: ~하기로 예상되다, 기대되다 / so that ~ may ...: ~가 …할 수 있도록 / 주격 관 · 대 / ~에의 노출 / 결과의 분사구문

현재의 도의적 공정성 운동의 목적과 그 예시

⑧ Those [who obstruct the campaign to erase uncomfortable ideas from university life, whether intentional or not], face harsh accusations of insensitivity, ignorance, hostility, and more. ⑨ This culture of fierce protectiveness may be tightening the stranglehold on intellectual diversity and freedom of expression.

주격 관 · 대 / 지우기 위한(형용사적 용법) / whether A or B: A든지 B든지 간에

도의적 공정성 운동에 대한 비판적 견해

본문해석

① 미국의 대학과 전문대학은 도의적 공정성을 육성하는 새로운 형태의 장이 되었다. ② 이 운동은 1980년대와 90년대의 선례와는 거의 분간할 수 없는데, 그것의 두 가지 목표는 편파적 발언에 제약을 거는 한편 소수의 의견과 관점이 문학과 역사의 표현에서 더 잘 나타날 수 있도록 여건을 조성하는 것이었다.

③ 오늘날의 형태로 다시 나타난 도의적으로 공정한 발언은 개인의 정서적 안녕에 초점을 맞춰 대학생들의 연약한 정신을 공격으로부터 보호하여 심리적 피해를 예방해야 한다는 전제를 바탕으로 작동한다. ④ 대체로 학생이 주도하는 이 운동은 대인간 의사소통의 변화를 촉발했고, 예전에는 잘 알려지지 않았던 '미묘한 차별'과 '촉발 경고'라는 용어들이 현대 언어의 중심으로 등장했다. ⑤ 미묘한 차별은 겉보기에는 적대적이거나 차별적인 의도가 없는데도 일종의 폭력으로 분류되는 행동 또는 발언이다. ⑥ 촉발 경고는 이어지는 내용이 잠재적으로 꺼림칙한 소재를 포함할지도 모른다고 청중에게 주어지는 공고문이다. ⑦ 대학교수들은 관련된 영역에서 트라우마를 경험한 적 있는 학생들이 그 작품에 대한 노출을 아예 피하기로 선택하여 불쾌한 기억 또는 감정의 환기를 미리 방지할 수 있도록 그러한 경고를 하도록 점점 더 기대되고 있다.

⑧ 의도적으로든 아니든, 대학 생활에서 불편한 생각을 지워 버리기 위한 그 캠페인을 방해하는 사람들은 무감각하고 무지하고 적대적이라는 가혹한 비난에 직면한다. ⑨ 이 맹렬한 보호 문화는 지적 다양성과 표현의 자유를 옥죄고 있는지도 모른다.

본문파악

이 글은 미국 대학가에서 학생들의 정서적 안녕을 위해 일어나고 있는 운동에 관한 글이다. 첫째 단락에서는 과거 소수 집단의 권리 신장을 위한 도의적 공정성 운동에 대해 설명하고 있다. 둘째 단락에서는 현재 대학 내 도의적 공정성 운동은 대학생들의 정서를 보호하기 위한 것이며, '미묘한 차별'과 '촉발 경고'라는 용어가 새롭게 떠오르고 있음을 예시를 들어 설명하고 있다. 마지막 셋째 단락에서는 이러한 새로운 도의적 공정성 운동이 한편으로는 지적 다양성이나 표현의 자유를 옥죄고 있는지도 모른다고 경계하고 있다.

문제풀이

1. 《해석》 위 글의 제목으로 가장 적절한 것은?

미묘한 차별로부터 대학생 개인의 연약한 정신을 보호하기 위한 현대의 도의적 공정성 운동에 대한 글이므로 '⑤ 학생들을 의도하지 않은 차별로부터 보호하기 위한 운동'이 글의 제목으로 가장 적절하다.

① 도의적으로 공정한 발언이 실제로 효과적인가?
② 대학 강의실에서 학습을 유발하는 단어들
③ 언어 치료: 새로운 형태의 심리 치료
④ 언어 공격 대상자들이 정신적 트라우마에 시달리다

2. ②~③번 문장 참조

3. 《해석》 다음 상황을 읽고, 괄호 안에서 알맞은 단어에 동그라미 치시오.

(1)은 ⑤번 문장을 통해, (2)는 ⑥번 문장을 통해 알 수 있다.

(1) 백인이 아닌 학생들에게 어디 출신이냐고 묻는 것은 (미묘한 차별 / 촉발 경고)인데, 미국인으로서의 그들의 지위가 불법이라는 뜻을 암시하기 때문이다.
(2) 한 교수가 가정 폭력을 묘사하는 책에 대한 강의를 하기 전에 그러한 폭력에 희생당한 적이 있는 학생들이 수업을 피할 수 있도록 (미묘한 차별 / 촉발 경고)를 했다.

4. 캠페인을 방해하는 사람들은 그 의도와는 상관없이 무지하고 적대적이라는 비난을 받는다고 하였으므로, 빈칸에는 이 맹렬한 보호 문화가 '④ 지적 다양성과 표현의 자유'를 옥죄고 있는지도 모른다는 내용이 들어가는 것이 알맞다.

① 인종 간 조화와 사회적 화합
② 전통적인 고정관념과 비방의 사용
③ 집단 괴롭힘 행동과 교실 내 위협
⑤ 알맞은 학습과 동등한 기회의 교육

구문해설

⑦ University professors are increasingly expected to issue such warnings **so that** students [**who** have experienced trauma in the related area] **may** opt to avoid exposure to the work altogether, thus **forestalling** the evocation of unpleasant memories or feelings.

▷ so that ~ may ...: '~가 …할 수 있도록'
▷ [ ]는 선행사 students를 수식하는 주격 관계대명사절이다.
▷ forestalling 이하는 결과를 나타내는 분사구문이다.

Word Test

SECTION 01. Art · Literature

정답

1. ③ **2.** (1) obey (2) obscurity (3) crucial (4) imposing **3.** (1) inspiration (2) sensitive (3) masterpiece (4) imitate **4.** subject

해석

1. ① 건축가: 건물을 설계하는 직업을 가진 사람
② 초상화: 어떤 사람의 그림이나 사진
③ 배출구: 사람들을 불안하게 하는 강한 충격의 느낌
④ 접근하다: 어떤 사람이나 사물 쪽으로 또는 가까이 이동하다
⑤ 정의: 단어나 구의 의미를 설명하는 표현

2. (1) 법을 따르지 않으면 큰 액수의 벌금을 물어야 할 수도 있다.
(2) 작가들은 작품에서 모호함을 이용하여 독자들을 괴롭혀서는 안 된다.
(3) 에드워드는 일요일에 팀이 3대 2로 승리하는 데 중요한 역할을 했다.
(4) 이 새로운 세금은 고용인들에게 부당한 부담을 부과하고 있다.

4. • 오늘의 토론 주제는 환경이 될 것이다.
• 내가 가장 좋아하는 과목은 세계사이다.
• "메리가 공을 던졌다."라는 문장에서 '메리'는 주어이다.

SECTION 02. Science

정답

1. (1) ⓑ (2) ⓐ (3) ⓓ (4) ⓒ **2.** (1) ⑤ (2) ③ (3) ① (4) ③ **3.** adopt **4.** (1) ⑤ (2) ③ (3) ④ (4) ②

해석

1. (1) 충돌 ⓐ 직접적으로 언급되지 않고 제안되거나 이해된
(2) 함축적인 ⓑ 두 물체나 사람이 서로 부딪치는 사건
(3) 가설 ⓒ 명확한 계획이나 양식 없이 발생하거나 선택된
(4) 임의의 ⓓ 어떤 것을 설명하려고 시도하지만 아직 사실로 증명되지 않은 생각

2. (1) 많은 속담이 겸손한 태도는 항상 성공으로 이끈다고 말한다.
① 오만한 ② 증명할 수 있는 ③ 신중한 ④ 비판적인 ⑤ 겸손한
(2) 그는 린다의 강력한 지지자 중의 한 사람이다.
① 경쟁자 ② 비평가 ③ 지지자 ④ 반대자 ⑤ 상대
(3) 그들의 요구가 충족되어, 직원들은 파업을 중단하기로 결정했다.
① 멈추다 ② 파괴하다 ③ 표준화하다 ④ 알아보다 ⑤ 주장하다
(4) 양 측이 협상하려고 노력하지 않았기 때문에 그 논쟁은 불가피했다.
① 용인된 ② 의지할 수 없는 ③ 불가피한 ④ 불필요한 ⑤ 미심쩍은

4. (1) 인권 운동가들은 우리 모두가 빈곤이 없는 사회에서 살기를 상상한다.
① 능가하다 ② 예방하다 ③ 설득하다 ④ 반박하다 ⑤ 상상하다
(2) 목격자의 말은 서로 모순되어 그 사실은 여전히 불분명하다.
① 찬성하다 ② 확인하다 ③ 모순되다 ④ 지지하다 ⑤ 해석하다
(3) 과학자들은 암의 치료책을 찾는 데 있어서 비약적인 발전을 희망하고 있다.
① 피해 ② 영향 ③ 증거 ④ 비약적인 발전 ⑤ 반대
(4) 우리는 날씨에 상관없이 경주를 계속할 것이다.
① 앞으로 ② 상관없이 ③ 전체의 ④ ~에도 불구하고 ⑤ 독립된

SECTION 03. Society · Culture

정답

1. (1) ② (2) ⑤ **2.** (1) coercion (2) exceptional (3) collective (4) intuition **3.** (1) ③ (2) ④ (3) ⑤ **4.** practice

해석

1. (1) 일단 그 군대가 전복되면 합법적인 정부는 되돌아올 수 있다.
① 도덕적으로 훌륭한 ② 법에 의해 허용된 ③ 매우 강력한
④ 변하지 않는 ⑤ 어떤 것에 의해 조정받지 않는

(2) 그 회사는 직원들을 위해 진보적인 보육 정책을 시작했다.
① 어떤 것을 추천하는 ② 논리적으로 말하는 ③ 하도록 장려받는
④ 변화를 꺼리는 ⑤ 새로운 방법을 지지하는

2. (1) 대부분의 학생들은 강요를 받으며 공부하기를 원하지 않는다.
(2) 이것은 예외적인 경우인데 나는 전에 그런 것을 한 번도 본 적이 없다.
(3) 그 팀은 이전 프로젝트의 실패에 대해 집단적인 책임이 있다고 인정했다.
(4) 나는 내가 어떻게 알았는지를 설명할 수 없다 — 내 직관이 사고가 있었다는 것을 말해준다.

3. (1) 그 영화의 줄거리는 너무 복잡해서 나는 따라갈 수가 없었다.
① 유기적인 ② 모호한 ③ 복잡한 ④ 습관적인 ⑤ 함축적인

(2) 그들은 그들이 필요하다고 생각하는 어떤 행동이든 취하라고 들었다.
① 제외했다 ② 조사했다 ③ 잘못 이해했다 ④ 숙고했다 ⑤ 강조했다

(3) 나는 이것처럼 감정이 전혀 없는 편지를 읽어 본 적이 없다.
① 알고 있는 ② 널리 퍼진 ③ 반대의 ④ 부당한 ⑤ ~이 없는

SECTION 04. Information Technology

정답

1. (1) T (2) F (3) T (4) F **2.** (1) ③ (2) ⑤ (3) ② **3.** (1) representing (2) uphold (3) simultaneously (4) considerable **4.** implication

해석

1. (1) 세련은 다른 것들보다 더 고급의 성질이다.
(2) 자극은 보통 동시에 지어진 많은 집과 빌딩이 있는 지역이다.
(3) 성취는 많은 노력 후에 얻게 되는 성공적인 것이다.
(4) 비용은 연습을 통해 얻는 특정 분야의 특별한 기술이나 지식이다.

2. (1) 경찰은 정상회담 동안 군중의 행동을 감시할 것이다.
① 거부하다 ② 금지하다 ③ 주시하다 ④ 방해하다 ⑤ 돕다

(2) 회의를 기록하는 것은 사람들이 그들의 의견을 표현하는 것을 방해할 수 있다.
① 안심시키다 ② 격려하다 ③ 설득하다 ④ 강조하다 ⑤ 방해하다

(3) 향후 암과 같은 질병의 근절은 가능한 영역이다.
① 건설 ② 영역 ③ 공간 ④ 용량 ⑤ 입자

3. (1) 교사를 대표하는 노동조합 대표들이 오늘 정부 당국자들을 만났다.
(2) 판사는 그들이 선고를 내릴 때마다 헌법의 가치를 지지해야 한다.
(3) 레오나르도 다 빈치는 동시에 한 손으로 그림을 그리고, 다른 손으로는 글을 쓸 수 있었다.
(4) 최근의 과학 발전 덕분에 군대는 상당한 군사적 진보를 이루었다.

Word Test

SECTION 05. Philosophy

정답

1. (1) ⓓ (2) ⓒ (3) ⓑ (4) ⓐ **2.** (1) overlooked (2) substance (3) superstition (4) correspond
3. (1) attempt (2) superior (3) provide (4) principle **4.** yield

해석

1. (1) 유명한 ⓐ 무언가에 대해 알려는 욕구
(2) 중력 ⓑ 영원히 존재하거나 계속되는
(3) 영원한 ⓒ 사물을 지면으로 떨어지게 하는 힘
(4) 호기심 ⓓ 특별한 자질 때문에 잘 알려지거나 유명한

2. (1) 사고는 안전 점검이 간과될 때 발생한다.
(2) 물질의 녹는 점이 또한 어는 점이다.
(3) 미신에 따르면 만일 당신이 사다리 아래를 걷는다면 그것이 당신에게 불운을 가져다 줄 것이다.
(4) 그날 밤 무슨 일이 있었는지에 관한 그의 이야기가 목격자의 진술과 일치하지 않았다.

SECTION 06. Media

정답

1. (1) T (2) F (3) T (4) T **2.** (1) psychological (2) extensive (3) prediction (4) demand
3. (1) option (2) appeal (3) stereotype (4) distributing **4.** regard

해석

1. (1) 광고판은 광고를 하기 위한 커다란 간판이다.
(2) 중재자는 책, 영화, 음악 등에 대하여 의견을 제시하는 직업을 가진 사람이다.
(3) 통념은 사람들이나 사물이 어떠한지에 대해 사람들이 갖고 있는 고정된 관념이다.
(4) 청중은 같은 것을 보거나 읽거나 듣는 사람들의 집단이다.

2. (1) 해리의 문제는 육체적인 것이기보다는 심리적인 것이다.
(2) 화재는 그 섬의 숲들에 광범위한 피해를 끼쳤다.
(3) 아무도 세상이 11월 12일에 끝날 거라는 그녀의 예언을 믿지 않았다.
(4) 수요를 맞추기 위해 2021년까지 18,400채의 새 집이 필요하게 될 것이다.

SECTION 07. History

정답

1. (1) ③ (2) ⑤ **2.** applied, apply, Apply **3.** (1) ④ (2) ② (3) ③ (4) ⑤
4. (1) objective (2) particular (3) basis

해석

1. (1) 대통령은 세금을 감축하는 계획에 대해서 여전히 아무 말도 안 했다.
① 들을 수 없는 ② 찬성하지 않는 ③ 말하기를 꺼리는 ④ 볼 수 없는 ⑤ 동의를 나타내는

(2) 그녀가 아기 때 부모님이 돌아가셔서 그녀는 숙모에 의해 키워졌다.
① 높이 들어올리다 ② 돈을 모으다 ③ 어떤 것을 언급하다 ④ 누군가를 구하다 ⑤ 사람을 보살피다

3. (1) 우리는 균형 잡히고 편견에 치우치지 않는 서비스를 제공할 작정이다.
① 불공평한 ② 형편없는 ③ 편안한 ④ 공정한 ⑤ 합리적인

(2) 나는 남동생의 결혼식에서 연설을 해야만 했다.
① 지지하다 ② (연설을) 하다 ③ 결론을 내리다 ④ 받아들이다 ⑤ 망치다

(3) 그녀는 종교적인 이유 때문에 의료 치료받기를 거부했다.
① 분배하다 ② 분석하다 ③ 겪다 ④ 암시하다 ⑤ 추정하다

(4) 도움을 바라는 가정 폭력의 아동 피해자들의 수에 엄청난 증가가 있었다.
① 실행할 수 없는 ② 지배적인 ③ 사실에 기반을 둔 ④ 호환이 되는 ⑤ 엄청난

SECTION 08. Environment · Ecology · Medicine

정답

1. ③ **2.** (1) deep (2) mental (3) has (4) influenced (5) inhabitants (6) illness **3.** raise
4. (1) ④ (2) ② (3) ④ (4) ③

해석

1. ① 채식주의자: 육류나 생선을 먹지 않는 사람
② 통근하다: 출근하기 위해 어느 정도의 거리를 정기적으로 여행하다
③ 생존: 어떤 것이 성취되는 것을 어렵게 만드는 것
④ 멸종: 동물이나 식물이 더 이상 존재하지 않는 상황
⑤ 면역의: 몸속에 있는 특정 물질로 인해 특정 질병으로부터 보호되는

2. (1) 그들은 얕은 강에서 수영을 했다.
(2) 그는 신체장애를 가지고 있는 아이이다.
(3) 케이트는 드문 지적 능력을 가진 여자이다.
(4) 이혼이 그녀의 삶의 모든 면에 영향을 끼쳤다.
(5) 그 지역 거주자들은 주차 공간이 부족한 것에 화가 났다.
(6) 그 병의 첫 번째 증상은 고열이다.

4. (1) 새 전구는 전기를 덜 소비한다.
① 향상시키다 ② 제출하다; 항복하다 ③ 제거하다 ④ 소모하다 ⑤ 회복시키다

(2) 그 파이프는 액체를 담는 역할을 한다.
① 구조하다 ② 담고 있다 ③ 포함하다 ④ 예방하다; 방해하다 ⑤ 멈추게 하다

(3) 청소년에게 술을 판매하는 것은 법으로 금지되어 있다.
① 개정된 ② 진보한 ③ 번성한 ④ 금지된 ⑤ 강화된

(4) 조사에 참가한 사람들 중 19%가 아직 누구를 뽑을 건지 결정 못했다고 한다.
① 암시되는 ② 생산된 ③ 조사된 ④ 강조된 ⑤ 설치된

SECTION 09. Economics · Business

정답

1. ③ **2.** (1) motivation (2) initiated (3) fluctuates (4) commodities **3.** (1) comparative (2) private
(3) property (4) agricultural **4.** premium

해석

1. ① 위험 (요소): 위기나 위험의 근원
② 외부의: 바깥쪽 또는 표면 위에 있는
③ 제외하다: 누군가에게 무엇을 하라고 설득하다
④ 전략: 목적 달성에 사용되기 위해 계획된 방법
⑤ 전통적인: 오랜 기간 동안 일반적인 것으로 여겨지는

2. (1) 그녀의 이번 학기 저조한 성적은 동기 결여의 결과이다.
(2) 연구원들은 증강현실에 관한 첫 번째 실험을 착수했다.
(3) 호수의 수위는 그 전 해의 겨울 눈 양에 따라 매년 변동한다.
(4) 옥수수와 감자는 신대륙으로부터 유럽으로 가져온 첫 농산물이었다.

4. • 어떤 사람들은 공연의 가장 좋은 좌석을 구하기 위해 초과액을 지불할 것이다.
• 나는 건강 보험을 위한 보험료를 자동 이체를 통해 지불한다.
• 그 자동차 회사는 올해 초 첫 고급의 세단을 출시할 것이다.

Word Test

SECTION 10. Ethics

정답

1. (1) ⓑ (2) ⓒ (3) ⓓ (4) ⓐ **2.** (1) addicted (2) derived (3) emphasize (4) constitute
3. (1) ② (2) ④ (3) ③ (4) ② **4.** object

해석

1. (1) 지지자 ⓐ 원하는 것을 얻다
(2) 속이다 ⓑ 어떤 특별한 신념이나 계획을 지지하는 사람
(3) 내과의사 ⓒ 어떤 사람으로 하여금 사실이 아닌 것을 믿게 만들다
(4) 획득하다[얻다] ⓓ 일반적인 기술을 가진 의사

2. (1) 요즘에는 인터넷 검색에 중독된 아이들이 많다.
(2) 영어 단어 'olive'는 라틴어 'oliva'에서 유래했다.
(3) 작품에서 한 단어를 강조하기 위해 당신은 이탤릭체를 쓸 수 있다.
(4) 여러 사람이나 사물이 어떤 것을 구성한다면, 그(것)들은 함께 그것을 형성하는 부분이다.

3. (1) 상황이 매우 심각하고 더 악화되고 있는 것처럼 보인다.
① 긍정적인 ② 심각한 ③ 사소한 ④ 고무하는 ⑤ 완벽한
(2) 그녀는 늘 그가 일하는 방식을 비난한다.
① 칭찬하다 ② 무시하다 ③ 능가하다 ④ 비판하다 ⑤ 반대하다
(3) 그는 인구 과잉 도시의 문제점에 관한 기사를 읽었다.
① 비난하는 ② 포함하는 ③ ~에 관한 ④ 제안하는 ⑤ ~을 제외하고
(4) 부모는 그들의 자식들을 교육시킬 법적인 의무가 있다.
① 조치; 척도 ② 의무 ③ 교리; 원칙 ④ 형벌; 벌금 ⑤ 논쟁

SECTION 11. Politics

정답

1. (1) individual (2) unanimity (3) circumstance (4) disparity **2.** (1) Public (2) preference (3) focal (4) rectify
3. (1) ② (2) ④ (3) ④ **4.** issue

해석

1. (1) 사회로부터 개별적으로 여겨지는 사람: 개인
(2) 모든 집단 구성원들 간의 완전한 의견 일치: 만장일치
(3) 상황, 활동, 사건에 영향을 주는 조건들: 환경
(4) 둘 혹은 그 이상의 것 사이의 차이점, 특히 불공평한 것: 차이

3. (1) 내가 처한 상황의 어려움을 당신이 어떻게 이해할 수 있겠어요?
① 무시하다 ② 이해하다 ③ 극복하다 ④ 경감하다 ⑤ 예방하다
(2) 저것은 그것을 하는 적절한 방법이 아니다.
① 미묘한 ② 틀린 ③ 쾌적한 ④ 적절한 ⑤ 특정한
(3) 그 회사는 적당한 가격의 인터넷 공급자이다. 게다가 공유 소프트웨어를 자유롭게 이용 가능하게 해준다.
① 즉 ② 그러나 ③ 그렇지 않으면 ④ 게다가 ⑤ 따라서

SECTION 12. *Education · Psychology · Language*

정답 **1.** (1) ② (2) ⑤ **2.** (1) finite (2) occupation (3) literally (4) version **3.** (1) covers (2) opposite (3) suffering (4) vague **4.** term

해석 **1.** (1) 타고난 기질이나 능력은 당신이 학습한 것이 아니라, 갖고 태어난 것이다.
① (수준 · 질이) 괜찮은 ② 타고난 ③ 획득한 ④ 잠재적인 ⑤ 개인적인

(2) 상처입기 쉬운 사람은 신체적으로나 정신적으로 약하거나 상처받기가 쉽다.
① 성실한 ② 유능한 ③ 긍정적인 ④ 무지한 ⑤ 상처받기 쉬운

3. (1) 운동은 광대한 범위의 활동들을 포괄하는 단어이다.
(2) 그 자동차는 반대 방향에서 오는 트럭과 충돌했다.
(3) 그는 이 년 동안 알츠하이머 병을 앓아왔다.
(4) 법의 어떤 측면들은 다소 모호하고 불명확하다.

SECTION 13. *Current Issues*

정답 **1.** (1) fragile (2) innovative (3) influx (4) cognitive **2.** (1) ② (2) ⑤ (3) ① **3.** (1) alien (2) transaction (3) dwindling **4.** (1) ⑤ (2) ③ (3) ②

해석 **1.** (1) 쉽게 부서지거나, 망가지거나, 손상을 입는: 부서지기 쉬운
(2) 새로운 생각이나 시스템을 도입하는: 혁신적인
(3) 상당히 많은 사람들의 도착: 유입
(4) 이해나 사고와 같은 의식적인 정신 활동과 관련한: 인식의

2. (1) 경찰은 시위 행진에서 시위자들을 차단했다.
① 촉진했다 ② 막았다 ③ 모였다 ④ 촉진했다 ⑤ 정의했다

(2) 그 재능 있는 가수는 태어날 때부터 시력 장애를 가졌다.
① 주제, 사안 ② 치매 ③ 수술 ④ 처분; 배치 ⑤ 장애

(3) 그 익명의 기부자는 그 고아원에 엄청난 액수의 돈을 기부했다.
① 놀라운, 대단한 ② 일상적인 ③ 기여하는 ④ 가능하게 하는 ⑤ 전체의

4. (1) 놀랍게도, 이 인기 도서는 무명의 철학자에 의해 쓰였다.
① 예상되는 ② 원치 않는 ③ 효과적인 ④ 이용할 수 있는 ⑤ 무명의

(2) 그는 열렬한 동물 인권의 지지자이기 때문에 존은 동물 학대를 혐오한다.
① 판사 ② 의사 ③ 지지자 ④ 지휘자 ⑤ 저항

(3) 티나는 청결에 대한 강박관념이 있어서, 매시간 손을 씻는다.
① 영향 ② 강박 ③ 혐의, 비난 ④ 떠올림, 환기 ⑤ 설립

MEMO

능률 고급 영문독해

능률 최고의 영어교육 전문 회사가 만든

고급 수능을 뛰어넘는 최고 수준의

영문독해 엄선된 인문·사회과학·자연과학·시사 지문

지금까지 이런 교재는 없었다!

- 정치·경제·사회·문화·역사·철학·과학·시사에 이르는 다양한 분야의 깊이 있는 지문으로 비판적 사고력과 논리력 향상
- 수능 만점과 수시 논술·구술 면접 대비를 원하는 학생들을 위한 유일한 선택
- 첨삭 지도식 지문해설로 고난이도 구문과 어휘를 스스로 완전학습